AMERICAN BLOCKBUSTER

SIGN, STORAGE, TRANSMISSION

A series edited by Jonathan Sterne and Lisa Gitelman

AMERICAN BLOCKBUSTER

MOVIES, TECHNOLOGY, AND WONDER

CHARLES R. ACLAND

DUKE UNIVERSITY PRESS · *Durham and London* · 2020

© 2020 DUKE UNIVERSITY PRESS
All rights reserved

Designed by Matthew Tauch
Typeset in Whitman and Helvetica LT Standard by Westchester Publishing Services

Library of Congress Cataloging-in-Publication Data
Names: Acland, Charles R., [date] author.
Title: American blockbuster : movies, technology, and wonder / Charles R. Acland.
Other titles: Sign, storage, transmission.
Description: Durham : Duke University Press, 2020. | Series: Sign, storage, transmission | Includes bibliographical references and index.
Identifiers: LCCN 2019054728 (print)
LCCN 2019054729 (ebook)
ISBN 9781478008576 (hardcover)
ISBN 9781478009504 (paperback)
ISBN 9781478012160 (ebook)
Subjects: LCSH: Cameron, James, 1954– | Blockbusters (Motion pictures)—United States—History and criticism. | Motion picture industry—United States—History—20th century. | Mass media and culture—United States.
Classification: LCC PN1995.9.B598 A25 2020 (print) | LCC PN1995.9.B598 (ebook) | DDC 384/.80973—dc23
LC record available at https://lccn.loc.gov/2019054728
LC ebook record available at https://lccn.loc.gov/2019054729

Cover art: Photo by Rattanachai Singtrangarn / Alamy Stock Photo.

FOR AVA, STELLA, AND HAIDEE

A technological rationale is the rationale of domination itself. It is the coercive nature of society alienated from itself. Automobiles, bombs, and movies keep the whole thing together.
—**MAX HORKHEIMER AND THEODOR ADORNO,**
Dialectic of Enlightenment, 1944/1947

The budget is the aesthetic.
—**JAMES SCHAMUS,** 1991

(CONTENTS)

Acknowledgments ix

PART I THE SPECTACLE INDUSTRY

ONE. Blockbuster Ballyhoo 3
TWO. Industrial Regimes of Entertainment 35

PART II THE RISE OF THE BLOCKBUSTER

THREE. Delivering Blockbusters 87
FOUR. The Business of Big 124
FIVE. Hollywood's Return 160
SIX. Cosmopolitan Artlessness 191

PART III THE TECHNOLOGICAL SUBLIME OF ENTERTAINMENT EVERYWHERE

SEVEN. The End of James Cameron's Quiet Years 233

EIGHT. The Technological Heart of Movie Culture 266

EPILOGUE. Exhausted Entertainment 297

Notes 305
Filmography 337
Bibliography 347
Index 373

(ACKNOWLEDGMENTS)

This book is the product of my boundless affection for movie culture. It equally emerges from an intellectual conviction that popular culture is foundational to the formation and understanding of our world, its pleasures and disappointments, its hopes and horrors, its privileges and struggles. Affective attraction and critical distance are not opposing forces; they create an interlocking dynamic, a productive tension. After all, the goal of cultural critique is not to resolve contradiction but to identify forces at play, investigate them, demonstrate the consequences they have for the way we live, and help point the way toward a more equalitarian existence.

Over the years, many teachers, colleagues, friends, and students have shaped my thinking on these matters. One towers over everyone: Haidee Wasson. With her unsurpassed critical facility that she keenly applied through countless conversations about this book, I know that what appears here has been improved immeasurably, and I thank her for that.

Among the many dear friends who have expanded my outlook on the topics addressed here, most powerfully influential were Keir Keightley and Peter van Wyck. Both, in their own ways, helped me with their elevated levels of scholarly and civic conviction, boosted even further by their distinctive wit. Jennifer Holt's remarkable intellect and spirit inspired me to sharpen and improve my arguments. I offer infinite gratitude to all three. At Concordia University, I ran ideas by scholars and received so much in return, most significantly from Krista Lynes, Jeremy Stolow, Fenwick McKelvey, William J. Buxton, Sandra Gabriele, Matt Soar, Kay Dickinson, Marc Steinberg, Joshua Neves, Masha Salazkina, Luca Caminati, Catherine Russell, Joanne Sloane, Darren Wershler, and Louis Pelletier. In Montreal other cherished interlocutors are Will Straw, Joseph Rosen, Jonathan Weiss, Darin Barney, Carrie Rentschler, Matthew C. Hunter, Jenny Burman, and Jonathan Sterne. Farther from my hometown, but just as important, are Greg Waller, Barbara Klinger, Julie Turnock, Rick Prelinger, John Caldwell, Lisa Parks, Vanessa Schwartz, Tom Kemper, Alison Trope, J. D. Connor, Jacob Smith, Erkki Huhtamo, Larry Grossberg, John Erni, Dana Polan, Fred Turner, Bill Hannigan, Carrie Hannigan, Andrew deWaard, Peter Lester, Brian Fauteux, Hannah Spaulding, Blaine Allen, Mike Zryd, Tess Takahashi, Lee Grieveson, Paul Grainge, Michael Cowan, Patrick Vonderau, Petr Szczepanik, Lucie Česálková, Yvonne Zimmermann, Malte Hagener, and Vinzenz Hediger. The book leapt ahead during my year as a Distinguished Visiting Scholar in the Department of Film and Media Studies at the University of California, Santa Barbara, where friends and colleagues provided generous counsel, among whom were Greg Siegel, Ross Melnick, Michael Curtin, Bhaskar Sarkar, Bishnupriya Ghosh, Janet Walker, Peter Bloom, and Charles Wolfe.

I am thankful for the excellent research assistance I received over the years from Zoë Constantinides, Charlotte Orzel, Smriti Bansal, Rob Hunt, Julio Valdes, Quinn Valencourt, and Ashley McAskill. The editorial and production team was outstanding, as usual, and I thank Courtney Berger, Sandra Korn, Liz Smith, Matt Tauch, and Kim Miller.

Opportunities to rehearse the arguments included conference presentations at the Society for Cinema and Media Studies (Boston and New Orleans), ARTHEMIS/Permanent Seminar on the History of Film Studies (Montreal), the Canadian Communication Association (Kitchener-Waterloo), the 3D FLIC Conference on Stereoscopy (Toronto), and the "What Is Film?" Symposium (Portland). Invited talks allowed me to refine the ideas further, most memorably at the University of California, Santa Barbara; Northwestern University; Carleton University; McMaster University; and Indiana University (for the James Naremore Lecture).

Chapter 7 is a modified version of "The End of James Cameron's Quiet Years," in *International Encyclopedia of Media Studies*, volume 6, *Media Studies Futures*, edited by Kelly Gates (London: Blackwell, 2013), 269–295. "Senses of Success and the Rise of the Blockbuster," *Film History* 25, nos. 1/2 (2013): 11–18, has been broken up and rewritten to appear in chapter 1 and chapter 4.

Early versions of parts of chapter 7 and chapter 8 appeared as "You Haven't Seen *Avatar* Yet," *FlowTV* 13, no. 8 (2011), www.flowtv.org, and "*Avatar* as Technological Tentpole," *FlowTV* 11, no. 5 (2010), www.flowtv.org.

American Blockbuster was made possible by the Concordia University Research Chair in Communication Studies fund and a Social Science and Humanities Research Council of Canada Insight Grant.

PART I THE SPECTACLE INDUSTRY

(CHAPTER ONE)

BLOCKBUSTER BALLYHOO

Y ou've just walked out of a multiplex movie theater having seen a Hollywood blockbuster movie. This being the early twenty-first century, you've likely witnessed a motion picture packed with visually dynamic scenes, saturated with color and sound. You may have been thrilled or dizzied by sprawling, swirling, and soaring images, the product of actual or simulated camerawork. And the appearance of action that ignores the laws of physics may have been inventive. Or annoying. Or both. You may have been underwhelmed by the newest multichannel sound system, which promised pinpoint locations for sounds but mostly delivered volume. You may have been impressed by the novel situations and visual effects, and you may have enjoyed spending time with a cherished performer or been introduced to new talent. The settings, situations, and characters may have been familiar, part of a generationally expansive franchise and part of a seemingly complete rendering of a fictional world. Attending may have had more to do with a sense of duty and obligation to see the entirety of a franchise than actual desire for another installment in that story world. Or the movie might have been a stand-alone production, exploring what blockbuster aesthetics offer a nonfranchise tale. Whatever sensations you have at the closing credits— the exhausting, endless credits that scroll through countless corporations, personnel, and legal waivers—you may leave with a feeling of wonderment about the film's drama or boredom with the monotonously familiar narrative clichés. Skillful emotional tugs may stick with you for a time, as do the abrasive projections of brutality and destruction. Blockbusters, as we have come to know them, engage, distract, and transport us, often in visceral ways that shake our senses and clot our ears. And you have surely paid what you imagine is the uppermost price point for such a sensory privilege. After all, neither wonder nor boredom comes cheaply.

Blockbuster films are as connected to the summer months as school vacations and mosquito bites. We hear the heavy-footed march of their approach, with calculated advance promotional peeks at the final product serving as processional trumpets heralding a new arrival. In ordinary conversation we expect people to recognize the titles of the day, the new entries into our popular image world, many of which are part of massive franchises and comprise elaborate story worlds that provide direct and immediate connections between films: "Lord of the Rings," "Star Wars," "Star Trek," "Indiana Jones," "Die Hard," "Mission Impossible," "Harry Potter," "Avatar," "Matrix," "Transformers," "X-Men," "Pirates of the Caribbean," "Terminator," "Toy Story," "The Fast and the Furious," "Hunger Games," "Marvel Cinematic Universe," "Batman," "Superman," and the grandfather of them all, "James Bond." When the opportunity arises, we may feel personally compelled to see one, coerced by family and friends to see another, and powerfully determined to avoid others. And though blockbusters do not make up a genre per se, we expect such films to share characteristics with and to display generic links to action, science fiction, disaster, fantasy, or family animation movies. This is the case even for the more baroque generic hybrids, where a "Western" blockbuster can have significant science fiction and action elements, drowning out many connections to precursors from the American Western (for example, *Cowboys and Aliens* [2011], *The Wild Wild West* [1999], and *The Lone Ranger* [2013]).

Or, at least, the claims just itemized about blockbusters in the preceding two paragraphs capture contemporary common sense about popular entertainment. We refer to a movie as a "blockbuster" and assume that others will understand what we mean—which is what I've just done—and that the movie will be loud, bright, dynamic, and familiar. Exceptions abound. There are comedy blockbusters, where we find more complete control by and showcasing of women producers, writers, and performers than in the action-oriented franchises. There are auteurist blockbusters that have tried to develop an interrogative style with the heavy industrial machinery of blockbuster production. These ostensible auteurist entries propose a paradoxical personal-impersonal cinema. Christopher Nolan's name may have popped into your head, or maybe Robert Zemeckis, James Cameron, and Steven Spielberg. The further we move from our contemporary franchise-driven entertainment culture, the more we bump into alternative models of big-budget filmmaking, ranging from prestige middlebrow works to the slow-paced historical action films of the past, like *Lawrence of Arabia* (1962) and *The Guns of Navarone* (1961).

More than any other single quality, blockbusters promise to be entertaining. This simple truism needs to be embraced as a foundational mandate. Where entertainment has conventionally given critics license to ignore and dismiss work, I stand in an opposing camp that recognizes the supposed inconsequentiality of popular culture as one arena in which the contours of our world form and its meanings are expressed. "To be entertaining" is not a natural and timeless state of being. It encompasses sensibilities about the pleasant, the enjoyable, the relaxing, and the inventive. To be sure, entertainment simplifies, clarifies, appeases, and comforts. It provides a safety valve, letting off critical pressures to allow society to return to a stable and predictable state, and paving over unsettling truths. But we can also see moments of disruption and struggle in entertainment, and can use popular works to detect anxieties and uncertainties about the world we share. Richard Dyer's classic argument about the ideology of entertainment alerted us to the wish-fulfilling utopian appeals of escapist films. Spectacle, in particular, according to Dyer, provides evidence of abundance, energy, intensity, transparency, and community, all of which can be lacking in everyday life. The feeling that results presents possibilities of "something better."[1] In this way, entertainment recognizes certain lived needs and contradictions, even as it shuts down acknowledgment of others.

The fact that "blockbuster" immediately conjures an image of a particular kind of movie, with an associated aesthetic, marks it as popular entertainment, deserving critical attention. Blockbusters are in-your-face. For all the pleasure offered, they can be like the rude houseguest who arrives without invitation and lingers a bit too long. Notices appear in all media, synchronized to circulate with a calculated eye on when and where audiences might take the time to spend some money on the work being promoted. They occupy our senses and set the agenda for the precious few hours of our leisure time. Blockbuster movies are counted on to be valuable additions to a screening schedule, a broadcast schedule, or a streaming service. They are highly visible and hence raise the visibility of other services and commodities. Their popularity—their visibility—is a central motivation for this book. Whether they are thought of as good movies or bad ones, they are unavoidably there.

The widespread certainty about what defines a blockbuster is curious given the term's actual definitional slipperiness. "Blockbuster movie" alludes to tonnage, to outsize production budgets, unusually elaborate promotional campaigns, and significant box-office results. Only one of those attributes is required for the term to apply, so one hears of low-budget blockbuster hits and high-budget blockbusters that are box-office flops. Notoriously demonstrating the latter is Eddie Murphy's ill-fated vehicle *The Adventures of Pluto Nash* (2002), which remains one of the biggest money losers of all time with a $4.4 million domestic return on a $100 million blockbuster investment. Conversely, *Paranormal Activity* (2009) may be one of the biggest blockbuster moneymakers of all time, with domestic box-office revenue of $108 million for a movie that reportedly cost initially just $15,000, and whose success spawned a franchise of similar small-scale horror entries.[2]

The bigger the blockbuster, the more it connects with other sources of revenue and the more it is implicated in the circulation of other commodities. This is the case whether the movie is a part of a franchise or not. Risk diversification is a factor here; if the domestic box office for a movie is disappointing, it still has a chance at international, television, video game, or merchandising success, or it could be a launching pad for a more successful film to come later. Blockbusters are not just single films. They are elaborate orchestrations of commodities and investments. Eileen Meehan has shown that the varying corporate structures of "the Big Six"—Disney, Sony, Comcast, National Amusements, News Corporation, whose Twenty-First Century Fox is now part of Disney's holdings, and Time Warner, now called Warner Media and merged with AT&T—reveal nonsynchronous relations among entertainment sectors, hence differing approaches to industrial strategy.[3] But they do make up what Thomas Schatz calls "Conglomerate Hollywood," in which films are only one facet of a wide, cross-media, interindustry plan.[4] In industry terms, blockbusters are described as "tentpoles," meaning they are the centerpiece for the coming season, under which less capitalized works will be sheltered. In effect, blockbuster success provides cover for other works to be produced and distributed. Importantly, the motion picture tentpole extends to other media and commodities, such that a blockbuster is as much a T-shirt, poster, television content, magazine article, video game tie-in, and advertising opportunity as it is a movie.

Popular audiences and critics share the term "blockbuster" with industry agents. Trade publications are replete with discussions about films that are more than hits or financial successes; they are events, cultural and economic bellwethers, and signals of the health of the entertainment industry. The term is part industry insider lingo, part outsider lingo for what industry lingo might be, and also reflects a general-audience idea about a big film of the moment. The importance of this multisectoral aspect is that usage references ideas about the economy of entertainment; it alludes to the market-driven machinations that produced and circulated the movie as much as the movie itself. Constance Balides showed us how the economic world inside *Jurassic Park* (1993) mirrored the merchandising outside the film, and J. D. Connor has elaborated on the allegories of capitalism in Hollywood entertainments.[5] As these and other scholars have taught us, popular cultural forms are more than cultural commodities governed by market forces and investment decisions. They circulate ideas and sentiments, arguments and thrills, including ideas about capitalism itself. Fredric Jameson made a comparable claim, describing "mass culture not as empty distraction or 'mere' false consciousness, but rather as a transformational work on social and political anxieties and fantasies which must then have some effective presence in the mass cultural text in order subsequently to be 'managed' or repressed."[6] Just as Roland Marchand wrote of advertising as the social realism of capitalism, blockbusters are likewise social realist products of a capitalist culture that is imagistic, affective, and international.[7] Put another way, "blockbuster" performs that "transformational work on social and political anxieties and fantasies," capturing and shaping an encounter between industry and culture; it is part of our language about movies and capitalism.

Whatever the definition, whether used with a priority connection to budget, promotion, or revenue, "blockbuster" represents a deliberate and calculated industrial strategy, one that has been central to the operations of Hollywood for many decades. Schatz correctly pinpoints *Jaws* (1975) as a key work that solidified the "hit-driven" focus of "Conglomerate Hollywood." There were key precursors two decades earlier. Schatz has outlined the forces following World War II that produced Hollywood's new and lasting concentration on big productions and promotions, along with a regularization of the "event movie." He noted that Hollywood's reliance on prestige productions really took hold and became standard practice in 1955, following a postwar period of uncertainty and upheaval largely driven by the studios' requirement to get out of the exhibition business and by competition from television for moving-image audiences. Though the full impact was not settled until the 1970s, Schatz showed that budgets and expectations of revenue continued to rise, more marketing took place on a film-by-film basis, and Hollywood began to look further afield, to independent producers and international locations, for ways to finance, coproduce, and shoot bigger and riskier projects through the 1950s.[8] As Schatz elaborated, the mid-1970s may not have seen the first blockbusters, but they were "a new breed of blockbusters," with an aesthetic and financial plan attuned to developing ancillary markets of home video and premium cable as well as franchises.[9]

Building on this history, *American Blockbuster* explores the origins, impact, and dynamics of the blockbuster movie, this highly visible and highly capitalized cultural form. It studies the turn to a "hit-driven" focus for the American film industry from the beginning of the 1950s and elaborates how this turn was a major reorientation for the entertainment business as well as for popular expectations about culture. *American Blockbuster* traces the blockbuster's rise to a lasting position of dominance in popular culture. More than a movie, a blockbuster is a set of ideas about spectacle, culture, and economy. For this reason, I refer to a "blockbuster strategy" as the rationale that embraces the big-budget cross-media production at the expense of other industrial and artistic approaches. Most influential among the naturalized ideas about a blockbuster strategy is a core presumption about technology and its centrality in entertainment. As will be explored, the emergence of the blockbuster, and the settlement of an associated industrial strategy, accelerated the prominence of technological innovation in both the entertainment business and modern American life. In the end, the rise of the blockbuster went hand in hand with the emergence of our contemporary technological society.

Schatz referred to "the blockbuster syndrome" and "blockbuster mentality," capturing the complete attention that big films received from producers, to the exclusion of other types of films, and showing that this focus drove the rekindling of Hollywood after the industrial restructuring demanded by the Paramount Decree of 1948.[10] That turning point for the American film business forced the Hollywood studios to retreat from their control of movie theaters. Relinquishing this market power opened up competition for screens, thus making the bidding for films by exhibitors more transparent and advantageous to owners of movie houses who had no studio connections. At the time, though, moviegoing took a massive hit from television, and exhibitors as well as the film industry as a whole entered the 1950s in a state of crisis about future prospects.

So, Schatz described a "syndrome" and "mentality" about big films that emerged in response to the crisis. Jon Lewis, for his part, referred to the "blockbuster mindset," seeing the mental blinders that drove Hollywood to similar decisions about the financial attractiveness of large-scale productions for decades.[11] The psychological obsession implied by these terms— "mindset," "syndrome," "mentality"—is appropriate to what each author, and others who follow suit, hope to capture, namely, the single-minded focus on the big film as a path to financial health for the industry, sometimes followed even when it defied reason. But with "blockbuster strategy," I wish to signal that there *was* a cultural and economic logic that drove the conventionalization of the "big" in film entertainment, and that that logic by and large remains intact and dominant today. Accordingly, this book charts the backstory to our current era of "Conglomerate Hollywood" and examines how blockbuster movies have become especially important to a broader economy of new media.[12]

The technological specificity of "big" Hollywood movies has been considered by some scholars. Steve Neale and Sheldon Hall have elaborated on the importance of state-of-the-art cinematic technologies in the development of the Hollywood epic production of the 1950s, most visibly the varied widescreen and large-gauge formats, many of which did not last long but nonetheless served the purpose of pushing the distinctive technological features of the films to which they were attached.[13] Geoff King has smartly responded to the claim that special effects set pieces arrest narrative momentum, and in so doing he commented on the function of spectacle. He took note that the first era of blockbuster production in the 1950s presented long, languishing attention to vistas, showcasing the new widescreen theatrical experience. The result was an encouragement of contemplation, one that melded well with the construction of a sensibility of bourgeois prestige in the exhibition venue and the "quality" film. King argued that in recent decades the aesthetic of television commercials and music videos, including saturated colors, quick-pace editing, and disregard of spatial continuity, became a conventional expectation of blockbusters. The style seemed to prohibit the contemplation encouraged in David Lean's and Cecil B. DeMille's approaches to epic films. Despite this shift in style, King detected a strong continuation of the classical narrative structure, though it had been adjusted to provide room for extravagant effects sequences that, in effect, made technology the story.[14]

Peter Krämer provided a critical illustration, writing about one of the most prevalent descriptions of contemporary blockbuster narrative: the rollercoaster ride. He did this through a study of *Contact* (1997), directed by the generally ill-considered Robert Zemeckis, who is in fact one of the more advanced and consistent Hollywood filmmakers, with deep investment over several decades in producing films designed to explore technological wonder. Krämer suggested that *Contact*'s explicit rollercoaster set pieces visualize the spiritual uplift that rests at the heart of the blockbuster, an emotional journey through a technological apparatus that promises to lead to another plane of serenity.[15]

The movie ride produces more than the thrill of sublime dizziness. Yvonne Tasker has effectively demonstrated that the technological architecture of the Hollywood action movie has equally produced gendered figures. The conventions of excess, and the representational modes that privilege spectacular experience, have most particularly made a spectacle of the male body and masculinity. Tasker pointed out the complicated pleasures of these exaggerated masculine bodily displays and performances while showing the dimensions of class and race that result. She remarked on "the complex ways in which popular cinema affirms gendered identities at the same time as it mobilises identification and desires which undermine the stability of such categories."[16] The politics of blockbuster affect, in other words, only amplify with the increasing focus on sensation.

King pointed out that one can see the shift away from contemplation toward technological flash in minor ways within franchises. Each new installment promises a faster, more action-packed experience than that offered by the previous one. Tom Shone described this as the "inflationary drive of blockbuster thrills."[17] It is especially the case with special effects, where, according to King, "the main *point* of the blockbuster sequel . . . might be to provide the opportunity to display the latest advances in special-effects capabilities."[18] Even the most relentless of contemporary action editing will pause for a brief contemplative rest, if only to better launch into the next visual and aural onslaught, so a historical split between contemplation and flash is not so cut-and-dried. But King's observation is useful as an indication of a general tendency that matches contemporary aesthetic expectations: blockbusters confront audiences with accelerated editing, amped-up sound, and obsessively considered visual effects. In each of these directions, they showcase technological features.

Michael Allen, charting innovations spanning from synchronized sound to digital effects, showed how blockbusters highlight new cinematic technology.[19] In many respects, the most elaborate and circumscribed special effects sequences function as display cases for cutting-edge innovations. Blockbusters court this status, and blockbuster production can entail an anxious exploration of novel forms of technological wonder, forms that are supposed to surpass previous efforts and contemporary competitors. Though this tendency can be seen with physical effects and stunts, it has been amplified with digital effects. As Michele Pierson observed, "audiences do make demands on special effects that they don't make on other types of computer-generated images, and this has put the producers of this imagery in the position of having to find new ways of soliciting audiences' attention once the aesthetic novelty of a particular technique has worn off."[20]

Other authors have highlighted the promise of the sublime rooted in the large-scale technological wonder of the blockbuster. Scott Bukatman understood that "what is evoked by special effects sequences is often a hallucinatory excess as narrative yields to kinetic spectatorial experience."[21] He saw this as producing kaleidoscopic perception, composed of "equal parts delirium, kinesis, and immersion."[22] The most elaborate of special effects sequences illustrate Bukatman's point best, representing a will to break free of the limits of physical constraint, and with that the limits of rationality, in favor of pure, dizzying, sensation. His broad claim was that this focus was "the narrative process of technological accommodation."[23] Kristen Whissel has read similar textual dimensions of impossible physics as a desire to break free of historical constraint. Whether the seemingly endless expanses of creatures and people squeezed into the frame by digital effects, or the soaring verticality of gravity defiance, Whissel saw an allegorical "radical break" from hierarchies of power. The digital multitudes of battles in "Lord of the Rings" and the verticality found in *Titanic* (1997) just before the ship sinks visualize rupture from the past. Here, the fantastical physics of digital effects are a commentary on historical disruption.[24]

Sean Cubitt expanded arguments typified by Bukatman and Whissel, seeing technological excesses as ways to siphon off representational freedom from actual historical circumstances. In describing the sumptuous aesthetic of what he called "neobaroque cinema," Cubitt focused on the creeping perpetual motion of the Steadicam camera and digital effects that transformed spatial organization into an indeterminate geography, one that could be infinitely expanded and removed from the world. With neobaroque, as he saw it, spectators identify with fictions that are sealed off from historical context and consequence, instead invested in world building. In the end, Cubitt wrote, "Digital technologies promise to elevate fantasy worlds above the troublesome everyday world."[25] He continued to see a demolition of what might have been a social realist impulse in popular cinema, claiming, "The digital corresponds so closely to the emergent loss of an ideological structure to social meaning because it no longer pretends to represent the world."[26] He wrote, "Each closed diegetic world is replete, condensed, full as an egg, solid as a billiard ball."[27]

The impact of this technological focus expands beyond filmic construction and special effects. Blockbusters have played a special role in advancing cross-media relations since the 1950s and have eased the introduction of new technologies, whether for cinematic, consumer electronic, medical, military, or educational use.[28] Pierson reminded us that early computer animation developed to feed software for special effects but also industrial and military applications.[29] J. P. Telotte's study of Disney's relationship to technological development similarly showed us the ideological high-wire act they conducted between the world of tomorrow and the world of yesterday, in the process embracing new technological processes in film, television, and other entertainment media. He wrote that theme parks "are not fantasy worlds but great technological wonders."[30] Blockbusters do comparable cultural work. Many current blockbusters feature computer-generated imagery, can be connected with new generations of video game systems, and might be central to promotional material selling new formats (Blu-ray, 3-D home technologies, virtual reality gear). Whether overtly or by virtue of their form, featured properties or franchise entries are strategically promoted to advance new platforms, hardware, and media systems, and as such they act as *technological tentpoles*.

Avatar (2009) was unusually highly developed in this respect, with 3-D filming processes, 3-D exhibition, digital exhibition, and 3-D home entertainment banking on its success. Consider *Avatar*'s newspaper advertising, which promised the routine geographic reach of a wide-release blockbuster ("everywhere") but also format choice ("every*way*") between 2-D, digital 3-D, and IMAX 3-D presentations, each with distinct appeal and pricing (figure 1.1). Panasonic later used *Avatar* in an international cross-promotion deal to sell its own new HD 3-D Home Theater system, with mobile units offering point-of-purchase illustrations while the film was still in theaters.[31] This deal was extended with the first 3-D home version of the film, released in December 2010—available only on Blu-ray and compatible only with Panasonic's Viera set for a little over a year (figure 1.2).[32] This exclusivity ran until February 2012. *Avatar*'s promotion demonstrated a heightened *platform consciousness*. In essence, the campaign sold media format and film at once.[33] As intensified as these multiplatform features of our popular film industry have become, the roots are found in the

FIGURE 1.1 *Avatar* newspaper advertisement, 2010

initial settlement of the meanings of "blockbuster," as a type of film and as an industrial strategy, seventy years ago, with a comparable investment in technological advancement.

Accordingly, this book is about technological innovation in relation to entertainment industries. Technological innovation has been inseparable from the history and vitality of the American film industry. But today, as Thomas Elsaesser described them, blockbusters are prototypes for the future of cinema.[34] More than this, blockbusters are, and have been, prototypes for ideas and commodities associated with the future of technology and culture. Blockbusters, directly or indirectly acting as technological tentpoles, are complex cultural machines designed to normalize the ideologies of our technological era.

A full history of spectacular entertainment would stretch back several millennia and would encompass theatrical and athletic performance of various kinds, some cruel and some amazing, as with Roman circuses and the modern

FIGURE 1.2 Panasonic advertisement for Viera 3-D television cross-promoting *Avatar*, 2010

Olympics. The global pop star, the worldwide best-selling book series, and the international television franchise all offer illustrations of hit-driven and geographically flexible cultural commodities. So there are precedents and companions to the brilliant visibility of the blockbuster movie. Some features, though, mark the blockbuster movie as distinctive. Not only does it enjoy a dominant presence in so many locations, often in a highly compressed time frame, but its seasonal release schedule makes its appearance predictable and regularized. Blockbusters are slates of popular works presented globally as such. They are the new foliage of each season of commercial entertainment. Moreover, blockbuster movies are among the most fully realized *American* cultural products of our time. Virtually every national cinema culture has its version of a blockbuster. But at the top end, where a handful of films each year are the most popular and lucrative films across international markets, those movies are overwhelmingly American.

Here's the thing, the troubling element that shakes the global triumphalism of the blockbuster: there is a widespread consensus about how bad they are. There are multitudes of fans for various franchises, and the enthusiasm for beloved characters and compelling dramatic or comedic moments lifts any popular work beyond its immediate economic function. The power of popular works lies precisely in their ability to wend their way into people's lives, and there to provide emotional, intellectual, and communal sustenance. But the very idea of the blockbuster, its industrial provenance and commercial intentions, draws out suspicion and resides as inconsequential: "It's only a blockbuster." For all the fandom, blockbuster efforts are habitually vilified by audiences and critics alike, sometimes even before their release or viewing. The American blockbuster movie, for all its popularity, is one of the most agreed-upon vacuums of cultural value. Cultural critic Alexander Huls wrote about the major films of 2013:

> Blockbusters have never been a particular source of maturity or sophistication. That's been mostly by design, given that they've always traded in trying to capture something of our inner child's fantasy and awe. It's why we're often prone to framing the success and failure of big-budget spectacles in those terms: "*Pacific Rim* was great and made me feel like a kid again" vs. "*Transformers* was awful and only a kid would like it." But thanks to a growing emphasis on mass-destruction in recent years, blockbusters have started to feel like they're not so much facilitating child-like states as they are regressing into them.[35]

Many will no doubt agree with Huls's appraisal of the films he discussed. But notable are several qualities that are presumed to be understood about blockbusters: immaturity, lack of sophistication, spectacle, fantasy, and awe. The argument hinges on the claim that blockbusters have "always traded" in childishness.

There is plenty of critical excuse-making that suggests their sorry state comes from their formulas, their "brewed-in-a-lab" veneer, and their targeting of teenagers. For every cherished film—*Star Wars* (1977), *E.T.* (1982), *Titanic*, *Lord of the Rings: The Fellowship of the Ring* (2001), *Harry Potter and the Sorcerer's Stone* (2001), *Wonder Woman* (2017), *Black Panther* (2018), and what have you—and for all the elaborate displays of enthusiastic fandom, even the most committed devotee of popular filmed entertainment will still speak disparagingly of the all-too-plentiful crass and vapid blockbusters. They—even the youngest of teenagers—will quickly revert to a lament about the industrially manufactured soullessness of the general category of the blockbuster.

A beautiful, irresistible example of blind presumptions about blockbusters is Slavoj Žižek's essay on *Avatar*, published in the *New Statesman* a few months after the film's release, as it was just crossing into record-breaking box-office territory. His essay made some observations about compulsory heterosexuality in Hollywood films, drawing illustrations from *Reds* (1981) and *Titanic*, pointing out that grand historical events were there to provide a backdrop for romantic couplings. The ideological consequence, he reasoned, is that potentially revolutionary ideas are neutralized, however progressive the narrative may appear to be. Žižek identified this especially in tales that emphasize contact with a class or ethnic Other, whose role is really to bestow characterological development on the protagonist and their love life. This, Žižek wrote, is what *Avatar* does. The film embraces indigenous culture and provides a surface-level critique of imperialism, only to twist its priorities toward the romantic couple of the aboriginal princess and the disabled marine.

In this short essay, Žižek highlighted some standard narrative tropes of popular American film, which are useful to revisit. The essay, though, has some clunkers. He wrote that Hollywood habitually adds sex scenes that don't appear in original source material, when, actually, Hollywood's skittishness about sex is one of its defining characteristics. While Žižek's argument rested on an observation that Hollywood film gives prominence to the stabilizing force of romantic couples, he contradicted this core claim by suggesting, following commentary from Alain Badiou, that "the very notion of falling in love, of a passionate attachment to a sexual partner, is considered obsolete and dangerous."[36] And the details about *Avatar* were slim, imprecise, and not nearly as exact as the descriptions of scenes from *Titanic* and *Reds*. But the vague treatment of *Avatar* can be easily explained: he had not seen the movie.

Pause to consider that for a moment. At that particular moment, *Avatar* was the most viewed and hotly debated motion picture on the planet. And yet Lacanian popular cultural critic Žižek did not consider it necessary to see the film when embarking on an essay about it. To be fair, he has claimed not to have seen half the films he has written about and that, for a Lacanian, the idea—which in his case means his imagined sense of the work and not its actuality—is enough to go on.[37] Pride in such blatantly irresponsible scholarly behavior is no doubt part of his self-constructed persona as a bad-boy critic. But the level of generality with which he wrote about *Avatar* makes it evident he was writing without having examined the film carefully. As an opera lover and a critic who has written about the political potential of opera, it is doubtful that Žižek would advocate writing about one based only on a synopsis, or that he would encourage a student of Lacanian theory to avoid reading Jacques Lacan. His scholarship has encouraged us to take the symbolic realm of popular film seriously; to double-back, saying you don't have to take works seriously in order to take them seriously, is astonishing. It exposes a deep presumption about the obviousness of popular film, its simplicity and predictability. A counter-example is the work of Katie Ellis, who provided a dead-on reading of *Avatar* that shows the unstable progressive heart of its representation of disability, easily upturning the surface claims of Žižek.[38] Ellis's smart argument took care and paid attention to the actual movie, meaning, you know, she saw it.

Žižek is not alone in his presumptions about the obviousness of popular film. Themes of commercial artlessness, and the valiant efforts of brave auteurs to battle the system, populate Hollywood historiography. Virtually every period has its seductive narratives that reproduce the admiration of mavericks outside the studios and cunning nonconformists within. Particularly emblematic of this tone are the tales of the New Hollywood of the 1970s. Peter Biskind popularized the rendition in which Hollywood, moribund under the weight of its own ambitions, was saved by a new generation of artists who investigated, and consequently revived, familiar genres, doing so with film language that owed as much to the French New Wave as it did classical Hollywood style. These filmmakers, among them Francis Ford Coppola, Hal Ashby, Elaine May, Robert Altman, and Peter Bogdanovich, in short order produced some of the most original and popular Hollywood motion pictures ever, only to be struck down by the commercial and artistic barriers erected as the industry again reorganized itself to focus on blockbusters post-*Jaws*. Challenges to that new orthodoxy came in the 1990s with the surprising successes of the Sundance Film Festival and independent producer and distributor Miramax. Part of Miramax's story, in Biskind's version and elsewhere, was of the terrorizing rampages and general intimidation of one of its founders, Harvey Weinstein.[39] This story is being rewritten with accusations of persistent sexual harassment and assault, which eventually led to Weinstein's conviction.

Janet Maslin had earlier voiced a version of Biskind's assessment about the New Hollywood and its demise, marking June 1975 as the turning point, when Robert Altman's *Nashville* (1975) and *Jaws* each appeared on the cover of different national magazines. This was the end of the artistic high of the New Hollywood, represented by the former film, and the beginning of the era of the blockbuster. She wrote, "When *Jaws* made it possible for every would-be viewer in America to be targeted for a unilateral marketing blitz, it created irrevocable change. Films would now be held to a different and increasingly exacting standard, one that accepted across-the-board popularity as the ultimate sign of merit. A stellar new generation of film makers would do their best to translate personal concerns into broad, crowd-pleasing terms, and would often do so with great success. But the golden age was over. The time of the blockbuster had begun."[40] Maslin extended the binary claim about artistic quality and commercial success, adding recognizable comments about "across-the-board popularity" and "broad, crowd-pleasing terms" with regard to the films of the blockbuster era post-1975. She, as many critics do, also gave the impression that this kind of film had not ruled Hollywood before this moment: "The time of the blockbuster had begun."

On the one hand, Biskind's and Maslin's stories are exciting and illuminating accounts. On the other hand, they are partial, downplaying how "Hollywood" the New Hollywood was, with considerable overlap with the stars and filmmakers of the earlier studio era. The flow between old and new, from set dressers to scriptwriters to actors to marketing teams, was substantial and constant. Far from being obscure artistic statements, many of those pre-1975 personal films were exceptionally popular with broad audiences and were by most measures blockbusters in their own right. Some even set new "exacting standards" for box-office success, especially *American Graffiti* (1973), *The Godfather* (1972), and the sequel *The Godfather: Part II* (1974). Conversely, the quintessential blockbusters of the 1970s were considerably indebted to the new film language that had come to be associated with those New Hollywood mavericks. *Jaws*, *Star Wars*, and *Close Encounters of the Third Kind* (1977) include overlapping dialogue, improvisational acting styles, photorealist flourishes like lens flares, rich saturated colors, and a misty atmospheric look. Julie Turnock developed this assessment in her research on Hollywood's increasing reliance on "expanded blockbusters" in the mid-1970s. She wrote, "While most critics perceive the special effects-driven blockbuster as the opposite of the auteurist-driven 'personal' film, instead I see these films, especially *Star Wars* and *Close Encounters*, as extensions of this ethos."[41] The familiar story of *Jaws* putting the brakes on the artistry of a new generation of Hollywood filmmakers is apocryphal at best but is perhaps closer to a critical fantasy that reflects recognizable middlebrow cultural hierarchies (*Nashville* over *Jaws*, personal films over blockbusters).

In the narratives of Hollywood economics deposing Hollywood artistry, Francis Ford Coppola often gets a pass, perhaps because he did not benefit as stupendously as George Lucas and Steven Spielberg. As Pierre Bourdieu wrote, in bourgeois art sensibilities, we take "failure as a sign of election and success as a sign of compromise."[42] But let us remember that "The Godfather" was one of the most expansive and lucrative franchises to emerge from the 1970s. And what are *Apocalypse Now* (1979) and *One from the Heart* (1981) if not big-budget extravaganzas that rest on advanced cinematic technology for physical and photographic effects?

The entwining of what we commonsensically understand as "Hollywood" with contrasting and more artful film cultures is the subject of Sherry B. Ortner's *Not Hollywood: Independent Film at the Twilight of the American Dream*.[43] In it, she shows how the rise of the American "independent" film in the 1990s was the consequence of many factors, including new production/distribution units like Miramax operating outside the major studios, the majors' own efforts to capitalize on the independent film wave and establish their own indie wings (like Sony Pictures Classics and Fox Searchlight), and more venues to integrate outsiders, such as festivals and film schools. Ortner describes a generational shift in the United States, showing that the experience of economic precarity produced filmmakers and audiences who sought to understand conditions beyond what had been prevalent in the dominant cinema. Key to her study is a reigning idea of Hollywood. So powerful was this idea, as much as Hollywood's actual economic might, that it was able to assimilate its own alternative even as "Hollywood" served as the touchstone against which that independent film movement of the 1990s emerged in the first place. No film form better typified what Hollywood means than the blockbuster, and the immediate response, the one that sparked indie film energy, was disgust.[44]

The art/commerce divide, paired as it is with the personal film/impersonal blockbuster duo, rules our hierarchical organization of value for popular film. And yet, as with all categories of cultural value, these binaries provide notable exceptions, like the possibility of a "blockbuster auteur."[45] Christopher Nolan, Sam Raimi, the Wachowskis, and Peter Jackson illustrate what blockbuster auteurs might look like; Steven Spielberg, George Lucas, and, further back, David Lean have figured as such as well. But the very fact that a blockbuster requires the modifier "auteur" to count as good reveals the sense that the two are not easily appended to one another. The blockbuster—or, more precisely, the idea of the American blockbuster movie—travels as an agreed-upon extreme manifestation of industrial culture; it exudes artlessness unless otherwise designated. As Julian Stringer has described it, there is always a suspicion on the part of audiences that with the newest, most extravagant blockbuster, one has the "impulse to recoil in the face of vulgar exhibitionism."[46]

Following Bourdieu, collective social action builds our cultural hierarchies, doing so by establishing mechanisms through which cultural value can be identified and agreed upon. The supposedly clear-eyed recognition of art in fact requires a range of interventions, though those interventions must be hidden or thought of as transparent. He wrote, "The constitution of the aesthetic gaze as a 'pure' gaze . . . is linked to the *institution* of the work of art as an object of contemplation, with the creation of private and then public galleries and museums, and the parallel development of a corps of professionals appointed to conserve the work of art, both materially and symbolically."[47] The more obvious interventions, especially those of the market, place the work further from the realm of art. Accordingly, one might say that the field of cultural production occupied by the contemporary blockbuster is that of what Bourdieu called *heteronomous* culture, the field of large-scale production beholden to the laws of the market, as opposed to the more artfully inclined, and commercially sublimated, field of restricted *autonomous* production, which is where the auteur film, with its evocation of personal style and supposed disregard for market potential, conventionally resides. We all know which one holds the most cultural value. And the clarity and obviousness of that divide is precisely what Bourdieu marks as the cultural power to build and reproduce differential taste formations and class hierarchies.

★ ★ ★ ★

How did the term "blockbuster," this point of intersection of ideas about commerce and entertainment, find a stable and lasting place in contemporary vernacular? How did the normative meanings about blockbusters come to be situated so securely at the heart of how we understand popular motion pictures? A blockbuster strategy has defined the American film industry for decades and indeed has proven flexible enough to persist even after earth-shifting industrial upheavals in the business of entertainment. Technological change has upturned standard practices of production, promotion, and distribution, most powerfully represented by the adoption of digital formats in every facet of the media industries. Significant corporate restructuring, including mergers and acquisitions involving businesses outside the entertainment industry and new sources of capital coming from international entities, means Hollywood is now entwined with industries far afield from narrow definitions of the film, television, and music businesses. Still, blockbusters and their appended assumptions about business and entertainment remain central.

The longevity of "blockbuster" and its wide circulation are not without precedent in the entertainment world. A number of terms that move between industrial and popular contexts similarly provide a basic lexicon for addressing and comprehending film culture, including genre designations, star personas, film cycles and franchises, and production entities and locations. Yet there is surprisingly little documentation on how the blockbuster strategy emerged and rose to the position it currently enjoys. The derivation of "blockbuster" has been left largely to rumor and supposition. As Stringer put it, "because 'event movies' seem always to be *there*, in the public eye, we have thought about them less than we should."[48] The presumptions of crassness, our familiarity with the titles and the attention the films seem to crave, make us more likely to take them for granted and conclude that we already know all we need, or care, to know about them. It is time, finally, to get down to sorting out the history of this idea that came to be so tightly woven into our understanding of popular entertainment.

Some tell the apocryphal tale that "blockbuster" migrated from the live-theater trade, where a play that has audiences lining up around the block is a blockbuster, claiming that the movie business appropriated the same reference for box-office lineups as its measure of success. Extensive research in trade and general readership publications reveals that no corroborating evidence supporting that story exists. In another bit of historical misdirection, one still encounters erroneous claims that *Jaws* was the first blockbuster movie.[49] This claim, too, is apocryphal and historically myopic. Even a critic as historically aware as Tom Shone still began his book *Blockbuster: How Hollywood Learned to Stop Worrying and Love the Summer* with the story of the summer release of Spielberg's shark opera. *Jaws* is an essential work, no question, and it is best understood as yet another watershed moment in Hollywood's reliance on big box-office hits and as a catalyst for a new phase of popular usage of the term "blockbuster." But the term did not originate with Spielberg's surprise hit (which was actually the third surprise smash of his career).

So uncertain is the status of the concept of the blockbuster that specialized film dictionaries and glossaries do not consistently include an entry for it. For example, such different reference books as Frank Eugene Beaver's *Dictionary of Film Terms: The Aesthetic Companion to Film Art*, Susan Hayward's *Cinema Studies: The Key Concepts*, and Ephraim Katz and Ronald Dean Nolen's *The Film Encyclopedia: The Complete Guide to Film and the Film Industry* do not include entries for "blockbuster."[50] Steve Blandford, Barry Keith Grant, and Jim Hillier's *The Film Studies Dictionary* includes one, succinctly contrasting the use of the term in the 1950s, referring to a particular kind of epic and big-budget film often released through road-showing, with the post-1970s use that referenced virtually any financial success and was more associated with saturation releasing, which is a superior definition.[51] The absence of the term in those other resources is perplexing. After all, we are not talking about a localized microscopic film phenomenon. We are talking about the most watched, discussed, and economically productive movies in motion picture history.

Some works have charted the rise of the blockbuster era of the 1950s, countering the ahistorical accreditation of *Jaws* as the first, and have investigated the aesthetics and significance of the most spectacular films of various eras.[52] For instance, Sheldon Hall and Steve Neale's history *Epics, Spectacles, and Blockbusters: A Hollywood History* made the essential observation that what we now call blockbusters—big-budget spectaculars and big-grossing films—had variants from the beginning of Hollywood cinema. Their historiographic approach took the lavish production as central to Hollywood history, and they found this to be a point of continuity across periods. And John Sanders made an attempt to solidify the blockbuster as a genre of Hollywood film and in the process anachronistically applied the term to films he considered exemplary, for example, *Intolerance* (1916), *Gone with the Wind* (1939), and *Bambi* (1942).[53] He included these films as they, respectively, were "big and spectacular, with dramatic narrative sweep," had a "grand story and visuals . . . indelibly etched into the collective cinema memory," and were financially successful.[54] Though he, like many scholars and fans, specifically dated the current phase of blockbusters to the mid-1970s, he also wrote that "the blockbuster has always been a mainstay of Hollywood cinema."[55]

In other words, our understanding of blockbuster films has assumed that the term can be used to reference big-budget and successful films from any era. But what do we find if we consider the actual historical specificity of the term, its emergence and circulation, rather than transporting our current usage backward? To date there has been only the thinnest of treatments of how we came to settle on this specific term. Steve Neale noted, "Originally coined to describe a large-scale bomb in World War II, the term was taken up and used by Hollywood from the early 1950s on to refer on the one hand to large-scale productions and on the other to large-scale box-office hits."[56] There is no elaboration on these origins. Here is another typical rendering from Marco Cucco: "The word 'blockbuster' has a military origin and was used to indicate the large-scale bombs used during the Second World War. Later, during the 1950s, the word came into use in the cinematographic field."[57] In both, the breezy, self-propelled movement from bomb to movie has no intervening stage. Filling in the details of this migration is not Neale's nor Cucco's purpose, but it is striking that a detailed account of this prominent and lasting term is not available elsewhere either.

A noteworthy exception is Sheldon Hall's "Pass the Ammunition: A Short Etymology of 'Blockbuster.'" This research resonates productively with the work I present in these pages. Hall comments on the origins of the term, considering additionally the parallel developments of other terms like "block" and "block-booking," a practice in which distributors required exhibitors to rent packages of films rather than bid on each one individually. He correctly identifies the World War II provenance of "blockbuster" and traces other military associations promoted by Hollywood. As will be elaborated in subsequent chapters, Hall connects the more regularized usage of the term in the American film business with changes in postwar exhibition practices and post–Paramount Decree relations between exhibitors and distributors.[58]

Many accounts associate the origin of the blockbuster with the cycle of biblical epics of the 1950s. For example, the headline for *Variety*'s November 1951 review of *Quo Vadis* (1951) called the film "a boxoffice blockbuster" (figure 1.4).[59] Hall and Neale referred to this as the moment after which "the term quickly passed into trade and public vocabulary to become all but ubiquitous by the mid-1950s."[60] *Quo Vadis* certainly displays the production extravagances associated with blockbusters. Based on a popular bestseller from the late nineteenth century, which had been adapted for the screen at least three times

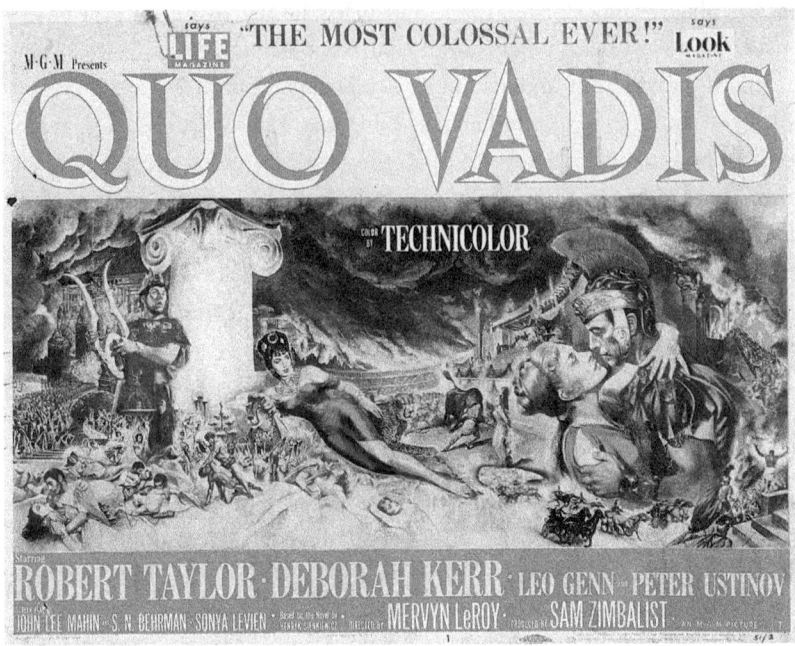

FIGURE 1.3 *Quo Vadis* lobby card, "the most colossal ever," 1951

before, it is nearly three hours long and boasts spectacular sets and dramatic events, especially a staging of the burning of Rome. With 200 speaking parts, 30,000 extras, and 120 lions, the film would be unimaginably—prohibitively— expensive to produce today. At the time, the gargantuan production expenses paid off. *Quo Vadis* was in theaters for almost two years and was released again in 1964. In 2005, adjusted to contemporary U.S. dollars, it was still in the top one hundred domestic box-office hits.[61]

Notably, the *Variety* review of *Quo Vadis* that described the film as a blockbuster also referenced the "now-cliched 'super-colossal' term" and "super-spectacle" to characterize the unusual expansiveness of *Quo Vadis*.[62] Both of those terms had been used by Hollywood to drum up interest in especially big-budget films for years. Productions might be called "super-westerns" or "super-musicals" to distinguish big-budget genre offerings from more modestly produced fare. For a film like *Quo Vadis*, "epic" and "spectacle" were primary qualities, hence "super-colossal" and "super-spectacle."

The ascendancy of "blockbuster," however, was already in process by the time that leading trade publication's review appeared. One week earlier in the

Quo Vadis
(COLOR)

A boxoffice blockbuster.

Metro release of Sam Zimbalist production. Stars Robert Taylor, Deborah Kerr, Leo Genn, Peter Ustinov. Directed by Mervyn LeRoy. Screenplay, John Lee Mahin, S. N. Behrman, Sonya Levien, based on Henryk Sienkiewicz's novel; music, Miklos Rozsa; cameras (Technicolor), Robert Surtees, William V. Skall; editor, Ralph E. Winters; lyrics and historical adviser, Hugh Gray; dances, Marta Obolensky, Auriel Millos; special effects, Thomas Howard, A. Arnold Gillespie, Donald Jahraus; costumes, Herschel McCoy. World premiered at Astor, N. Y. (twice-daily reserved) and Capitol, N. Y. (continuous), Nov. 8, '51. Running time, 171 MINS.

Marcus Vinicius	Robert Taylor
Lygia	Deborah Kerr
Petronius	Leo Genn
Nero	Peter Ustinov
Poppaea	Patricia Laffan
Peter	Finlay Currie
Paul	Abraham Sofaer
Eunice	Marina Berti
Ursus	Buddy Baer
Plautius	Felix Aylmer
Pomponia	Nora Swinburne
Tigellinus	Ralph Truman
Nerva	Norman Wooland
Nazarius	Peter Miles
Terpnos	Geoffrey Dunn
Seneca	Nicholas Hansen
Phaon	D. A. Clarke-Smith
Acte	Rosalie Crutchley
Chilo	John Ruddock
Croton	Arthur Walge
Miriam	Elspeth March
Rufia	Strelsa Brown
Lucan	Alfredo Varelli
Flavius	Roberto Ottaviano
Anaxander	William Tubbs
Galba	Pietro Tordi

"Quo Vadis" is a b.o. blockbuster. No two ways about its economic horizons. It's right up there with "Birth of a Nation" and "Gone With the Wind" for boxoffice performance.

It has size, scope, splash and

FIGURE 1.4 *Variety* review for *Quo Vadis*, detail, "a boxoffice blockbuster," 1951

same publication, Dore Schary, soon to be Metro-Goldwyn-Mayer's (MGM) production head and one of *Quo Vadis*'s producers, drew a notable distinction between blockbusters, which were in color, expensive, and more plentiful than ever, and "orthodox" pictures.[63] Less than two months later, for *Variety*'s forty-sixth-anniversary issue, producer Hal Wallis and director Stanley Kramer both wrote articles critical of the "so-called blockbuster."[64] The vice president of Republic Pictures, James R. Grainger, voiced an early argument against an exclusive focus on the big-budget film, also referring to it as "a so-called blockbuster." Elucidating reasoning that would gain steam through the 1950s, he argued that what was important to producers and to exhibitors was "a steady flow of product to keep their screens occupied, and [that] every picture can't be a 'blockbuster.'"[65] Other guest columnists in the anniversary issue discussed big-budget films but used older terms like "colossal" and "super-colossal" pictures.[66] But "blockbuster" was already recognizable enough for one contributor, director George Sidney, to use it anachronistically, reminiscing that when he first arrived in Hollywood in 1934, "Dick Arlen was killing them in such blockbusters as *Come On Marines* and *Let 'Em Have It*."[67] Action packed as these films were, they do not fit contemporary ideas about blockbusters and were modest genre films. But these references to something called a blockbuster, by prominent industry insiders, reveal that prior to our accepted narrative about "the Hollywood blockbuster"—beginning with the religious epics of the 1950s or even later with *Jaws* in the 1970s—some earlier currency had already been established.

"Blockbuster" did indeed originate in World War II as a way that newspaper reporters described the new four-thousand-pound bombs dropped by Allied Forces on enemy cities, and chapter 3 explores this in detail. Beyond the catchy ring of the term's alliteration, it is surprising that a colloquialism for an instrument of destruction came to be a lasting designation for an expensive and lucrative cultural commodity, whether for stage, screen, print, or broadcast markets. Investigating this terminological migration is one objective of this book. These pages open up the history of the settlement and dispersion of "blockbuster" by providing instances of its early cultural usage. I approach this topic with the analytic stance that the settlement of a term of this kind, which becomes a common way to reference popular works, involves more than the appearance of a new word. Along with the term go assumptions about and organizing principles of entertainment culture. Examining the emergence of a term is also a way to evince dominant priorities in culture and society.

The next chapter, "Industrial Regimes of Entertainment," continues part I, "The Spectacle Industry," by surveying the place of blockbuster franchises in the contemporary popular entertainment industry, showing how they are a product of a calculated effort to find economic advantage through globalized culture, cross-media integration, and technological innovation. The four chapters in part II, "The Rise of the Blockbuster," develop a chronological historical examination of the 1940s and 1950s to show how we arrived at our current situation. Chapter 3, "Delivering Blockbusters," documents the first uses of the term "blockbuster." The World War II origins, most strikingly, demonstrate how early usage was bound up with ideas about the public display of new technology. Chapter 4, "The Business of Big," traces the migration of the term, and its appended connotations, to the film industry, where big movies and spectacular exhibition formats came to be understood as key to the future economic viability of Hollywood, from the late 1940s to the early 1950s. Chapter 5, "Hollywood's Return," recounts the competition among industry insiders as they vied to bank on the rising interest in blockbuster entertainment through the first years of the 1950s. Chapter 6, focusing on the later years of the 1950s, captures the moment in which the term stabilizes as a recognizable type of film for the general moviegoing public. That chapter, "Cosmopolitan Artlessness," presents how the blockbuster circulated simultaneously as the peak of cinematic achievement and as a symptom of everything that was wrong with Hollywood, its capitalist underbelly, and its investment in technological grandeur at the expense of tasteful film art. The chapter ends with a discussion of the deflation of the expectations for the blockbuster strategy in the late 1960s, only for it to return ever more mightily in the 1970s. Since then, it has dug in and remained a dominant part of the motion picture industry.

In the service of providing a fuller account of the longevity of the blockbuster strategy, part III, "The Technological Sublime of Entertainment Everywhere," moves away from the chronological narrative and returns to the second chapter's claims about the blockbuster in contemporary popular entertainment. Chapter 7, "The End of James Cameron's Quiet Years," is a detailed case study of perhaps the most influential film in recent history, *Avatar*. In it, the core approaches to technology, media integration, and popular franchise environments that had been in formation for decades reach absolute realization. Chapter 8, "The Technological Heart of Movie Culture," addresses the place of popular film in a wider culture that highly values technological devices and infrastructure. The chapter explores the variety of technological aspects that shape film culture, including DVD supplementary material and the contemporary theatrical experience. Closing the book is an epilogue, "Exhausted Entertainment," which speculates on the impact of a blockbuster entertainment culture that celebrates technology as it does.

At one level, the chronological portion of this book in part II is a version of one of the most maligned and risky forms of historical research—the origin story. All it takes is some ephemera from Tuesday, after I insist it all starts on Wednesday, to ruin the argument. Obviously, I want to be more delicate than that and wish to tell a story of the conditions that helped launch a taken-for-granted set of meanings that converge around the term "blockbuster." To do this, I take cues from work on film noir, especially James Naremore's *More Than Night: Film Noir in Its Contexts*, which explores the historical development and mobility of that term to illuminate how "noir" describes so many different film styles and uses and yet is still understood as relatively coherent.[68] Stringer framed his edited collection on blockbusters with this approach, making the evocative observation that if "night" is the structuring term for film noir, the relevant term for blockbusters is "size."[69]

In considering how a set of ideas is talked about and explained by industrial participants, critics, and audiences, and how these conceptual arrays come to rest at a particular terminological location, we see that "blockbuster" displayed a high degree of indeterminacy in its early years in the 1940s. When we focus on how "blockbuster" circulated, a greater range of noncanonical films, objectives, and ideas about popular movies come into view, revealing an intricate effort on the part of industry agents, critics, and general audiences to make sense of the popular cultural environment and economy. In short, blockbusters are not only big-budget and high-grossing productions. The term is also shorthand for ideas about cultural value, economic success, and innovation, ideas that are acted on and that form the basis for future investment, artistic, and consumption decisions.

Media historian Lisa Gitelman astutely recommended that we see media as "socially embedded sites for the ongoing negotiation of meaning" and as "a vast clutter of normative rules and default conditions that develop around and help define new media practices and technologies."[70] This approach allowed Gitelman to show that media are not so unified with clear boundaries between them. Instead, she pointed us to the overlapping characteristics and practices associated with media and technology from which culture emerges and is organized. She promised to approach media topics in a manner that "keeps things muddy" and encouraged media critics to do so as well.[71] Her important point is that our media and cultural worlds emerge from deep historical contexts that structure, order, and prioritize people and practices, rather than from stable sets of singularly determining media qualities and features. Moreover, media technologies are not isolated agents of change, with set "affordances," but are themselves products of their time and place. To illuminate these functions, we can reverse-engineer their operations to gain access to culturally privileged ideas.

Extending this approach, I suggest that we treat cultural forms, and the discourses about cultural forms, as similarly produced through normative rules, default conditions, and negotiated meanings. In this respect, the various active languages about film give us access to what we agree the rules, norms, and contested features of popular entertainment culture are. "Blockbuster," so imbricated with our everyday language about popular cinematic practice, is one such active term, functioning as a mechanism through which the entertainment culture and industry has circulated and been understood for years. This book shows that as the term "blockbuster" settled in as a long-standing feature of industrial and popular film language, so too did a set of ideas about success, taste, economy, entertainment, and technology.

The various trade articles in the aforementioned 1952 anniversary issue of *Variety* illustrate in miniature the methodological approach to be followed in this study. A keyword search did not give me these appearances of "blockbuster," nor would a search of that kind offer the contextual and discursive commentary that I have just presented. Reading—targeted, focused, and purposeful, but still reading—is the primary activity I engaged in during the course of the research presented here. And I do mean reading, actual reading, not machine reading, which, after all, as Johanna Drucker explained, is not reading at all but mechanical recognition.[72] Some algorithmic assistance was provided, and searching digitized databases of articles of all kinds helped me assemble a basic collection of materials. Other digital tools that provide portraits of a large number of sources have some usefulness, albeit quite limited. Google Ngram Viewer can provide broad date parameters, but that's about it. There, search terms are sought among millions of books, so it offers some advantages of scale. But the items searched are not curated, they are untended, and they are not organized for specific subject areas; it sweeps wildly over one publication format. Ngram Viewer might help confirm dates for the appearance of terms and their peak usage in books. But beyond that, few other conclusions can be drawn. As with any sky-high view, there is no illumination of discourses in operation, which is equally true of some of the other digital humanities tools, like the distortions of topic modeling and the codification of data into surrealist graphic representations. Colorful renderings of data as Rorschach tests that we read with wild interpretive freedom, just like those psychological tests, tell us more about the thinking of the interpreter than about the world the image is supposed to represent.

The Arclight search app (projectarclight.org) improves on Ngram Viewer and comparable shotgun search mechanisms. Teams at Concordia University and the University of Wisconsin–Madison, led by Eric Hoyt and me, collaborated on this tool. The Arclight app provides portraits of the metadata for material in the Media History Digital Library (MHDL). For this reason, the results are more directly relevant to scholars and students of film and media than those of other, more general search mechanisms. Valuing simplicity and clarity of visual design, it allows a user to grasp quickly the overall historical appearance of keywords and can limit searches to specific publications and years available in the MHDL. Because an omnibus graphic of results has only so much value to historians, the Arclight app was built to allow the user to jump directly into the digitized material that constitutes the search results.[73] In a test of the scholarly potential of the app, Fenwick McKelvey and I conducted a study of film trade publication terms to see the degree of crossover in usage between business lingo and fan magazines. Concentrating on the 1930s, years that have relatively complete collections for select trade and fan publications in the MHDL, we found little evidence of crossover except for the term "contract." This suggested to us that today's sharing of business language is historically specific and that "contract" might be an important initial point of understanding about the film industry on the part of popular audiences.[74]

Used to identify what is to be found where and when within a specialized corpus, the Arclight app is valuable. And I have seen, and been told anecdotes of, its pedagogical advantage where students can see the rise and fall of media topics and be encouraged to explore further. This is the key point. The results one receives provide the starting point for historical parameters and investigation. The hard work of assembling material, locating additional sources not covered in the digital corpus, figuring out the contextual matters, and beginning to construct an argument that will illuminate and bring understanding still has to take place after the Arclight app or any other such tool returns results for your search terms. And this can only be done by reading.

Searching digital databases provides advantages that allow a researcher to increase reading speed. One can search for terms and topics in order to triangulate a set of dates, locations, and publications within which closer reading will be advantageous. Digital databases, though, also amplify the expectation of coverage, drawing a wider field of evidence onto the lap of the researcher. You can cover more ground quicker in that first level of identifying relevant material, but you are now obligated to cover more ground. There are multiple hazards here, most significantly that all appearances can be mistaken as equivalent when, in fact, they are not. Some results will have appeared before a wider audience, and some will have appeared in venues of greater or lesser prestige and impact. Moreover, at a certain point, the kind of popular historical material this book rests on begins to turn up repetitions and redundancies; one can then safely conclude that key resonances and patterns of appearance and usage have been identified. A comprehensive accounting of all occurrences provides no additional insight; there is a diminishing value in one more global search. Certainly, there remains a risk that the next search will uncover the one detail that upsets the pattern, but with each instance included, the risk and influence of that potential anomaly decreases, becoming a comfortable uncertainty that all scholars must live with.

Thus, search mechanisms are best thought of as an initial layer of findings. They offer some possible general tendencies, and, most valuably, they offer date ranges within which closer examination and hunting might take place. The glitches of optical-character-recognition (OCR) software are significant enough that one must expect glaring gaps and misidentifications in digital searches. In the end, one must rely on a slow and time-honored method of historical examination: reading. You have to read—everything that you possibly can, as carefully as you can. And you must do so in context, reading related and unrelated parallel material. And then, with the hints and clues offered about key events, people, institutions, texts, venues, and so on, you must begin more targeted archival work, digging through hard-copy and digital documents.

It may seem strange to make a case for reading as method. This is obvious to many, I'm sure. Yet in recent years the turn toward an embrace of machine reading has encouraged an impression that the larger the corpus, the faster the scanning of that corpus, and the less direct human interpretive intervention with the corpus, the better the research. So prevalent, and for some accepted, are these claims that we need more statements to the contrary, ones that point out the limits and the end point of such algorithmically tainted research, namely, humanities without humans.

My previous book, *Swift Viewing: The Popular Life of Subliminal Influence*, was the product of years of consultation and article accumulation as directed by such resources as the *Reader's Guide to Periodical Literature*.[75] Only after the work was in manuscript form were various historical periodical databases readily available, and robust enough, for digital search mechanisms, which then played a supplementary role, helping me verify my coverage right at the end of the project. But the work still required, and today would still require, years of reading and hunting, most of which came from hunches and suppositions rather than the clear and direct insertion of a keyword into a magical rectangular box.

This current work, initiated with feet more surely rooted in the era of digital databases, has benefited from the online resources that have been bulked up. And more archives have taken up an idea of access and begun to offer more of their materials to people in digitized forms. The online documents provided by the Margaret Herrick Library, Educational Resources Information Center (ERIC), the Library of Congress, and others have been important to the research presented in these pages.

And yet I can't say that with these digital resources this research progressed any more rapidly, nor that the results are more comprehensive and better armed against counterclaims. Once those initial layers of digital materials had been processed and considered, the more obscure work had to be sought. I probably spent as much time with microfilm as with the ProQuest Historical Newspapers database. I probably traveled to as many archives and specialized holding institutions as I have for my previous books. Popular culture is not consistently included in archives, official corporate documentation, or libraries of media productions. It includes a vast set of publicity, advertisements, and various ephemera, much of which is rarely systematically held on to for future consultation, let alone lovingly curated for digital formatting. Seeking such documentation becomes a major task, one that invariably leads us away from the digital realm back to the material culture of museums, archives, and junk shops.

Part of this methodological approach arises from the conceptual backbone of this book. "Blockbuster" is a term, but more centrally it is a "nodal point," a meeting place for ideas and understandings about popular entertainment and industry. It works to fix an array of ideas about business, capital, and popular culture. And it can only be studied in context, and grasped as part of a living and dynamic cultural environment, an approach to cultural analysis outlined best by Raymond Williams.[76] The appearance of the term is at best symptomatic of something else to explain. It is, in a sense, a "command metaphor," broadcasting its meaning to wide audiences, and with it a general understanding of popular entertainment. Motivating this conceptual approach is the fact that "blockbuster," as much as it locates the very idea of these large-scale films, is an impediment to our thinking and appears to confirm our worst fears about commodity culture without nuance, without contradiction, automatically shutting down analytic advantage.

As will be elaborated, the ascendancy of the term was part of the rise and stabilization of a hit-driven approach to the movie business. This "blockbuster strategy" increased the investment in, and hence the risk of, any single film, increased the amount of marketing required, and decreased the number of films in the American film business. As risk and investment grew, more media, technologies, and consumer products were brought on board to both sell and ride along with the fortunes of the primary blockbuster work. Decades later, the blockbuster film itself became less and less of an economic and cultural focus, and more of an engine for the development of a brand, a franchise, or a product line. Sure enough, even in the first years, when the blockbuster strategy was taking shape in the 1950s, there was considerable pushback, notably from exhibitors, some of whom felt that a steady stream of reliably performing films was preferable to riskier and less predictable hits, and from critics, who eventually saw the blockbuster as lacking in the personalized artistic merit that could be found in smaller productions. The exhibitors' complaint had an impact, and distributors contradictorily promised an ongoing supply of extraordinary hits, films that would keep elevating the expectations for audience interest and financial success. This book documents the stabilization of the blockbuster strategy, first by taking account of the initial popular usage of the term "blockbuster," then by exploring its adoption by the movie business, and finally by presenting the underlying claims and assumptions about entertainment and cultural value that it helped to organize, ideas that continue to inflect our popular media universe today.

From our vantage point, the blockbuster's stable and powerful presence gives it the appearance of timelessness. "Blockbuster" carries with it an implied understanding of budgets, financial expectations, cultural success, affective impact, and audience appreciation. It radiates influence over how we see popular entertainment and how corporate decisions are made to build and profit from that cultural milieu. It has the effect of flattening history and transforming the conditions of our cultural universe into a static realm. But this vernacular about film culture was built by a number of forces, including the orchestrated traffic between corporate agents, cultural and industrial commentators, and moviegoing audiences. As Bourdieu directed, "the sociology of art and literature has to take as its object not only the material production but also the symbolic production of the work, i.e. the production of the value of the work or . . . of belief in the value of the work."[77] Or, in the case of the blockbuster, what is produced is ultimately a belief in its limited cultural value.

We turn now to a portrait of the economic edifice of new media technology in which the blockbuster, especially in its franchise incarnation, plays a leading role and has helped to stabilize and expand an industrial regime of entertainment.

(CHAPTER TWO)

INDUSTRIAL REGIMES OF ENTERTAINMENT

Film extravaganzas have thrilled audiences since the earliest flickers of the medium. The surprising verisimilitude before our eyes, and the illusion of something so present in front of us but not there at all, has kept audiences attentive and alert to the next astonishing visual wonder. Over the years, the increasing complexity in film construction, in editing and lighting, supplemented ambitions in set design, costuming, and the mise-en-scène. Consequently, a baroque tendency toward ornamentation, vast scenes, and spectacular set pieces is part of the history of moving-image entertainment. The semblance of reality, and its plasticity, may have been a point of departure for motion pictures, but so was awe-inspiring impossibility.

Movie magic, of course, necessitated extreme lengths, processes, and labor to mount those wondrous and impossible scenes that typify popular entertainment. No type of film represented this baroque tendency more than the big-budget epic film with its unmatched ability to fabricate spectacle. Big-budget extravaganzas enchanted us. *Ben-Hur* (1925) from MGM was one such effort, with its thousands upon thousands of extras. No less a personage than the Italian Marxist Antonio Gramsci took note of the scale of human participation in such epics, seeing it as symptomatic of an industrial and American form of objectification. He wrote that as many as thirty thousand Italian women sent photos for an epic's casting call. Capturing the adornment of the mise-en-scène their legions represented, as in such epic movies, and the gendered dehumanization involved, Gramsci described the state of women in contemporary capitalism as that of "luxury mammals."[1]

This chapter investigates the economic and cultural forces that have taken this history of filmed extravagances and transformed the big-budget Hollywood movie into the globalized financial engine that it is today. There is an aspirational dimension to the blockbuster concept: though some are purpose-built blockbusters, every film might just become one. At one level, "blockbuster" is a form of vernacular speech for popular audiences and industry agents; it harbors both an industrial strategy and a way for audiences to talk about the outcomes of industrial strategy. But, as this chapter elaborates, blockbusters are familiar as a mode of spectacular entertainment, geared toward the display of economic, technological, and aesthetic excesses. I argue that the blockbuster concept is an idea about entertainment and success, and that films described as such operate specifically as technological tentpoles, instrumental to the development of our integrated media economy and the valorization of technological wonder.

The term "blockbuster" references production budgets, success, and industrial strategy, and has done so for decades. It is not select jargon for experts and insiders. It circulates widely, from the corridors of media corporations to the quotidian conversations of moviegoers worldwide. Indeed, the term is an influential American export, with many international contexts using the English word "blockbuster" rather than some local coinage to describe such films. Countries and regions have their own standards and metrics for popular success, such that you have what might be nationally, regionally, or linguistically bound blockbusters. But few moving-image works glide across international boundaries as easily and as regularly as the American franchise film, and this fact gives it a special status in popular culture and a high degree of visibility for global popular audiences.[2]

Miriam Hansen described the long history of American popular film and its international appeal. With their tradition-breaking humor and narrative speed, she saw a strain of both ideological reinforcement and disruption to cultural hierarchies as well as to norms of community, class, ethnicity, and gender. The circulation of movies across geographic and social divides meant they produced a "vernacular modernism," meaning an accessible and immediate "range of cultural and artistic practices that register, respond to, and reflect upon processes of modernization and the experience of modernity."[3]

Hansen gave special credit to Hollywood for producing a "global vernacular." She argued "that the hegemonic mechanisms by which Hollywood succeeded in amalgamating a diversity of competing traditions, discourses, and interests on the *domestic* level may have accounted for at least some of the generalized appeal and robustness of Hollywood products *abroad*. . . . In other words, by forging a mass market out of an ethnically and culturally heterogeneous society (if often at the expense of racialized others), American classical cinema had developed an idiom, or idioms, that travelled more easily than national-popular rivals."[4] Hansen was especially insistent that the engines of capitalism were not the only feature being reproduced by popular American film. In her reasoning, she could be writing about the blockbuster, but here she commented on the key importance of the appeal of popular cinema as bound up with the dreams and possibilities offered by mass consumption: "We have to understand the material, sensory conditions under which American mass culture . . . was received and could have functioned as a powerful matrix for modernity's liberatory impulses—its moments of abundance, play, and radical possibility, its glimpses of collectivity and gender equality."[5]

The American film industry had, and has, structural advantages that boosted that international influence. The U.S. domestic market, which in the conventional industrial measures includes Canada, makes up over 35 percent of worldwide theatrical revenue. The multiple exhibition windows of television, streaming, subscriptions, and DVD services mean theatrical releases provide but a minority stake in the overall revenue generation of a film. Nonetheless, on theatrical terms alone, the United States has continued to be the most lucrative moviegoing market for decades, though others, notably India, show greater rates of moviegoing. China's box office has been rapidly gaining on the United States and is currently the second-largest theatrical market, but the statistics from China can be unreliable and rife with political interference and, at times, outright corruption, making predictions about future economic performance an act of wishful thinking. For the moment, at least, the United States' status as the richest film market gives American-based film enterprises a unique economic advantage, a power that helps keep Hollywood in its dominant position as the most influential and global of entertainment hubs.[6] If you make it there, you are on your way to making it everywhere.

Beyond American borders, the top ten countries together make up about 75 percent of all the world's theatrical receipts, which amounts to an extraordinarily high degree of concentration of moviegoing revenue. By implication, evocations of "the global film business," however ambitiously distributors may target the entire planet, in actuality attend most carefully to the tastes and tendencies of moviegoers in a handful of national markets. On the ground, distributors primarily focus promotional, lobbying, and trade-pact efforts on but a fraction of countries and languages. Attention to both foreign and domestic audiences, however selective, does translate into careful calculations to produce a filmed commodity appropriate for a degree of internationalism, if you will, the production of *limited cosmopolitan ease*. This limited ease surfaces in movies as smatterings of multilingualism, a Cook's tour of international settings and shoots, both prominent and incidental use of international talent, reworkings of genre conventions from diverse cinema traditions, and just enough ideological indeterminacy to welcome local interpretive gestures. Probably the most American aspect of this limited cosmopolitan ease might just be the U.S. industry's border-hopping quest for talent, ideas, and capital, making "Hollywood" a material and imagined intersection for international personnel, styles, and money.

Blockbusters are complicated agglomerations of products, texts, merchandising, advertising, and career vehicles, all of which count on the success of these relatively few visible international big works. Thomas Elsaesser evocatively proposed that film, and the film industry, is ambiguously both a production and an experience, a commodity and a service, and that it operates as part of a macrolevel capitalist system and as part of a microlevel set of pleasures. For him, the blockbuster is an exemplary artifact that holds these elements together, satisfying financial and libidinal demands in equal measure.[7] Because blockbusters are clusters of commodities and services, their life span stretches and overlaps with the product life cycle and cultural experience of multiple formats and materials, including the mutating form of the film itself as it makes its way from theatrical release to DVD/Blu-ray, streamed, and broadcast content. The library value of a work and its characters is an especially challenging thing to predict. The elements of the work can have an alternate life span as leverage for other products, whether official merchandise or referential shorthand for creators: the screen grab from *Avatar* (2009) posted to a website on environmental causes, the clip of *Hello Dolly!* (1969) that plays in WALL-E (2008), and the posters for *Rogue One: A Star Wars Story* (2016) that were prominent during the 2017 Women's March, repurposed to signal feminist rebellion.

The life cycle, circulation, and multiplatform release paths of contemporary film complicate assessing their economic worth. Other factors exist beyond the horse race of box-office revenue, which remains a key popular measure of success despite its diminished status in the overall financial value of a film property. The trade publication *Deadline* provides an annual forensic analysis, using publicly available sources, that documents some of the elements involved in a blockbuster's profit performance for distributors. Where standard measures of domestic box-office gross would rank the 2016 top-five films as *Rogue One: A Star Wars Story, Finding Dory, Captain America: Civil War, The Secret Life of Pets*, and *The Jungle Book*, *Deadline*'s research produces a different ranking, one that includes television, home video, and various costs, with *The Secret Life of Pets* at the top, followed by *Deadpool, Rogue One, Finding Dory*, then *Zootopia* (see table 2.1).[8]

The multisector commercial engine we recognize today was being acknowledged as innovated following the success of *Jaws*. In 1981 economist David A. Garvin wrote about the enthusiasm for blockbusters across the media industries. He defined them according to the revenue they generate, pegging a movie blockbuster as one that brings the distributor $50 million in theatrical rentals, which would mean about $80–$90 million at the box office. Garvin wanted to understand how blockbusters seemed to dominate all media markets simultaneously. He suggested that the twentieth century saw a gradual erosion of the differences between media, at least from the point of view of the consumer, such that audiences choose among all media options rather than discrete categories of movies, books, radio, and so on. Additionally, distributive scope grew, so average audience size increased for any single work. To cater to these massified audiences, producers relied on identifiable stories and talent, which encouraged even closer ties across media as both source material for movie narratives and future revenue. As he summarized it, "vast increases in market size, the growing importance of subsidiary income, and increased intermedia competition have all enhanced the appeal of [blockbusters]."[9] Garvin indicated that the costs of production have risen faster than the prices charged for media, meaning the break-even point kept pushing upward, necessitating greater audience numbers. One consequence, he pointed out, was that blockbusters became a conservative strategy, especially when they relied on pretested stories and talent, while middle-range works became that much riskier to pursue. Noting the potentially disruptive arrival of new media, which were cable television and laser discs at the time he was writing, Garvin saw only ongoing incentives for the domination of the blockbuster strategy across the media industries. The rise of the blockbuster, which Garvin does not date with any precision, entailed many other factors than the ones he outlined. Still, his analysis shows us how even in the early

TABLE 2.1 *Deadline's* Most Valuable Blockbuster Tournament, 2016 (currency in millions USD)

	The Secret Life of Pets	**Deadpool**	**Rogue One: A Star Wars Story**	**Finding Dory**	**Zootopia**
Rank	1	2	3	4	5
Domestic box office	$363.4	$363.1	$531.4	$486.3	$341.3
Foreign box office	$448.8	$420.0	$453.8	$503.9	$446.9
China box office	$58.3	–	$70.00	$38.0	$235.6
Global box office	$870.5	$783.1	$1,055.2	$1,028.2	$1,023.8
Domestic theatrical/nontheatrical rental	$184.0	$181.5	$287.0	$243.1	$170.6
Foreign theatrical rental	$179.0	$168.0	$182.0	$201.5	$178.7
China theatrical rental	$14.5	–	$17.5	$9.5	$59.0
Worldwide home entertainment	$164.4	$159.3	$182.0	$191.8	$156.0
Domestic TV	$76.0	$66.0	$92.5	$83.5	$73.5
Foreign TV	$73.7	$72.7	$74.5	$75.0	$73.6
Foreign contribution	–	–	–	–	–
Total revenues	$691.6	$647.0	$835.5	$804.4	$711.4
Net production cost	$75.0	$58.0	$200.0	$200.0	$150.0
Worldwide prints and ads	$140.0	$120.0	$160.0	$165.0	$159.0
Domestic prints and ads	–	–	–	–	–
Worldwide video costs	$49.0	$48.0	$58.7	$57.0	$47.0
Participations	$15.0	$65.0	$35.0	$25.0	$10.0
Residuals and off-the-tops	$25.2	$23.9	$28.2	$26.8	$25.0
Interest and overhead	$12.8	$9.9	$34.0	$34.0	$25.5
Total costs	$317.00	$324.8	$515.9	$507.8	$416.5
Studio net profit	$374.6	$322.2	$319.6	$296.6	$294.9
Cash on cash return (revenue/cost)	2.18	1.99	1.62	1.58	1.71

SOURCE: Mike Fleming Jr., "How 'The Secret Life of Pets' Beat 'Deadpool' and 'Rogue One'—the Data behind the Dollars," *Deadline*, April 4, 2017, deadline.com.

1980s the blockbuster strategy was accepted as dominant across the media industries, how its novelty was a topic for economic debate, and how intermedia links were thought to be contemporary innovations.

As Garvin's research implies, at the production end of the process, rather than designating revenue-generating performance, the "blockbuster strategy" describes the corporate rationale that substantial financial investment in a film, with various appended and trailing commodities, will result in substantial financial success, assuming one is able to appeal sufficiently to mass audiences. This pull toward the familiar resulted in a representational marginalization of many populations, such that casting of women and people of color in central roles was presumed to risk the loss of broad audience appeal. With fewer mid-budget works to offset those gaps, which might respond to diverse interests and situations, a formidable absence of difference powered dominant movie culture. Timidity about what might compel general audience engagement left us with blockbuster conventions mostly built upon the compulsory heterosexuality of white male protagonists. The blockbuster strategy and its representational logic has time and again proven to be unreliable, and at times outright disastrous. But no matter. The inflated expectations of profit pay off just enough to keep the dream of the universally appealing entertainment alive.

Garvin was addressing the industry from the late 1970s, and his work handily describes that of the 1980s and 1990s. In recent years, though, an assessment concluded that the time of the blockbuster had passed and that the influence of big shared media culture was waning. Blockbuster Video, which launched in 1985 and filed for bankruptcy protection in 2010, bracketed a phase of entertainment history that featured VHS and DVD rental as cultural and economic pillars for the movie business. The demise of the biggest American video rental enterprise, a retail outlet built on high-volume new mainstream titles and now owned by DISH satellite network, seemed to signal the close of the blockbuster era as much as a technological shift away from physical audiovisual content toward online streaming services.

Digital commerce was thought to have unseated the centrality of the blockbuster and replaced it with microniches. The statistical "long tail," meaning the minority cultures promised to be served by web-based circulation, would be profitable and would cater to a more expansive range of tastes.[10] Malcolm Gladwell captured the enthusiasm for the long tail in his *New Yorker* article "The Science of the Sleeper: How the Information Age Could Blow Away the Blockbuster."[11] Primarily writing about the book trade, Gladwell declared that there are two types of success: purpose-built blockbusters and unexpected word-of-mouth sleepers. This is a split, as Gladwell saw it, between known and unknown entities; consumers, with limited time and money for entertainment, will head toward the familiar. These claims are too pat to be correct. Not all cultural entities that are designed to be successful are blockbusters, and sleepers can be strategically orchestrated as such and are not always so surprising. Moreover, many sleepers include recognizable elements, say an actor or genre, and consumers will shy away from a work that seems too derivative and too familiar, regardless of its production provenance. Gladwell reasoned that the targeted searching and recommendations of the internet will advantage sleepers, aided by algorithmic processes of "collaborative filtering." He ventured to describe it as antiblockbuster. One of his main examples was a movie recommendation site, MovieLens, that relies on the voluntary labor of members rating films. If you like action films with Arnold Schwarzenegger, the site will, surprise, recommend more. No question, there have been many examples to support iterations of this algorithmic recommendation process, of which Netflix is an obvious example, though the actual long-term profitability of such enterprises remains to be seen; also, since the publication of Gladwell's article, both ends of the production-budget spectrum, high and low, have begun to use the same online paths to audiences.

Not infrequently, short-term dips rattle corporate expectations that their profits should always expand. Doomsday commentary predictably follows. The poor box-office performance of some blockbusters during the summer of 2014 led to considerable questioning of the assumptions about big-budget moviemaking, as did 2016. Perhaps the big movie had seen its day, and we would be left with the relatively limited, but convenient, offerings of streaming services like Netflix. In fact, the filtering machine of Netflix is no one's idea of a source of sleeper hits; their algorithms strategically bring back the most general genre categories, new releases, and their own productions. At best, what Gladwell and others have documented are the contemporary modes for promotion and commentary rather than a technological distinction between big, impersonal blockbusters and smaller, idiosyncratic hits. Most obviously, twenty years after critics like Gladwell foresaw the twilight of the blockbuster, the exact opposite has come to pass, and expectations for the epic largeness of production, marketing, and revenue have only spiraled upward. Following the "poor" box-office performance of 2014, the blazing success of *Star Wars: Episode VII—The Force Awakens* (2015) prompted enthusiastic trade and popular commentary about the resilience of the blockbuster idea and of moviegoing specifically. The film, launching the third "Star Wars" trilogy, followed Disney's purchase of Lucasfilm and the franchise, and it was given the full blockbuster treatment in terms of production, promotion, and distribution. But the box office struck surprisingly high levels, beyond even ambitious industry expectations. When all was said and done, it sailed past the record-setting grosses for *Avatar* and affirmed yet again Hollywood's commitment to the blockbuster strategy. So much for the expectations that digital culture and the long tail would "blow away the blockbuster."

Anita Elberse supported this affirmation in her book *Blockbusters: Hit-Making, Risk-Taking, and the Big Business of Entertainment*. It arrived in 2013 to fend off questions about the profitability of the big, and it was welcomed with unusual fanfare, including a rare published excerpt and a column by Peter Bart in *Variety*.[12] Elberse's book confirmed the continued centrality and effectiveness of blockbuster strategies. She made several missteps, however, beginning on the first page, where she claimed that tentpole films are "those thought to have the broadest appeal."[13] It is possible that this is the case, but tentpole films are primarily designated as such because they carry the weight of considerable investment and are integrated with other works and commodities. Studios and financiers look for bankable prospects with big returns, which includes broad audience appeal. This may have to do with the clarity of the specific audience segment as much as its breadth, but it's not always the broadest that makes the most sense. Otherwise, we'd only ever see family films become tentpoles, and not PG-13 films, or even the occasional R-rated, which we do.

Elberse repeated the historically myopic mind-set of studio heads, for instance, Alan Horn of Warner, who said that the tentpole idea really began in 1999; prior to that year it had not been "'really pursued as a strategy.'"[14] So egregious is this claim that it is possibly a typo, and the starting date may have been intended as 1989, the year of Warner's *Batman* launch. Still, this is several decades off the mark. Trying to describe star power in blockbusters, Elberse wrote, "MGM made a stunning move by offering Tom Cruise a part of a movie *studio* rather than a part of a movie—an ownership stake in MGM's United Artists."[15] This line doesn't account for the context for this unusual deal. Viacom, Paramount's parent company, had just ended a decade-and-a-half-long relationship with Cruise's company Cruise/Wagner Productions, in part because of how expensive Cruise had become. This move was symptomatic of an industry-wide reconsideration of the box-office value of A-list stars. Worth knowing, too, is that United Artists then had a ten-year record of mostly midrange-budget films and middling box-office results, which is better understood as a counter-blockbuster effort. This studio-head position was not a reward for Cruise's box-office performance. Elberse's focus on the importance of star power for blockbusters does not explain the actual performance of many with actors who had fledgling careers at best but who were not yet stars, including *Titanic* (1997), *Star Wars: Episode IV—A New Hope* (1977), *E.T.* (1982), and "Harry Potter," to name just a few.

Elberse concluded that the blockbuster movie is an essential facet of Hollywood production and that it embraces risk and innovation but promises considerably more in terms of financial rewards. She even suggested that alternate strategies are risk adverse.[16] This claim, of course, pushes aside the clunkers and bombs, and fails to recognize that a blockbuster is often the safest bet for a producer or investor, especially if it is a known property and an installment in an already successful franchise. Riskiest would be a tentpole film that tried to launch a franchise written and created originally for the screen, such as *Avatar*, but these are comparatively rare. Otherwise, many blockbusters are designed to be conservative vehicles for the generation of investor wealth.

Understand, though, that Elberse's book is not a scholarly work of media criticism but a business aide to decision-making. With that in mind, note that she hit on a fundamental, and at the time of publication counterintuitive, argument that the reigning ideas about micromarkets, hypertargeted advertising, and democratization of consumer choice were misleading. If anything, she rightly redirected us to the fact that many of the supposedly new elements of digital media are quite old imports from legacy media, for example, the reinvigoration of the idea of channels, taken from broadcast media into streaming platforms. And Elberse equally demonstrated that the disruption and clutter of new-media circulation will only make big and identifiable works that much more valuable. She wrote, "In this rapidly evolving marketplace, blockbusters and superstars gain in relevance—and blockbuster strategies thrive."[17] Gady Epstein, writing in the *Economist*, affirmed that the long tail, with its dream of democratic microniches, has not flourished in digital culture. On the contrary, a handful of companies dominate the majority of online traffic, only a tiny percentage of available popular songs are streamed and profitable, and a small number of films account for large portions of annual box-office revenue. He speculated that in light of so many entertainment options, the easy choice is to head toward the familiar, toward the shared, toward the work one thinks everyone else is also picking. Algorithms were supposed to guide us to unknown pockets of taste; instead, they direct us to safe bets. With this evidence, Epstein reasoned in agreement with Elberse, a blockbuster effect is reinforced.[18]

We are repeatedly instructed that theatrical film is dead, or will be shortly, and that the future of media is social, participatory, and user-generated and does not follow the predetermined paths of mass media. This is the context to which Elberse's work and Epstein's article respond. My approach here similarly challenges the inordinate attention that has been devoted to social media and other digital aspirants as disruptive, because this attention masks the many media operations and consequences that construct our communicative, political, and cultural environment. A fundamental misapprehension is that blockbuster movies are separate from that digital realm. On the contrary, not only do they thrive in our contemporary media universe, but blockbusters have played a crucial role in building and organizing our culture of perpetual technological change.

Blockbusters are the dark suns of media culture, with a density of financial investment and a textual richness that pull innumerable other works and practices into their orbit. The gravitational weight they exert is both coordinated, representing a high level of commodity integration, and random, inspiring public responses and practices that might be unrecognizable to the original producers, owners, and investors.

One would have to be excused if one felt that the media mix of contemporary life had reached a point of saturation. The sheer plenitude of images and sounds, textual demands and promotional appeals, and endlessly competitive bids for our attention has formed a kind of media blockade that is difficult to navigate around or to avoid. For this reason, commentators for years—decades, really—have fussed about the endless "mess media" that constitutes our habitat, a mess that has swamped our lives with distractions and drowned our senses in the constant drone of textual flow. This plenitude of sensory taxation troubles access to essential and vital materials, and it is the font from which assessments of information overload have sprung. The most recent statistical embrace that we call "big data" is less an innovation of algorithmic order than a promise that all the random and stored textual crumbs might actually, finally, be legible and not just a toxic dump of informational tailings. That's the promise, though the correspondence between the vast caches of data and actuality remains hypothetical and mysterious. With big data, we are still at the stage of reading tea leaves, albeit reading them by the truckload rather than the teacup.

So, one also has to excuse the pundits of excess, because, after all, our messy media mix does seem more than a little bit, well, excessive. With so many possibilities of text and utterance, surely nothing remains unsaid, unseen, unheard, and unrealized in media form. Jean Baudrillard's comments on the obscenity of a media world that represented everything and left nothing to the imagination are a celebrated rendition of this position. He wrote of "the obscenity of the visible, of the all-too-visible, of the more-visible-than-the-visible. It is the obscenity of what no longer has any secret, of what dissolves completely in information and communication."[19] That view felt correct in the 1980s and captured an experience of an encroaching media culture that we recognized. Of course, this is but one of many versions of the information overload argument, which coalesced in the late 1950s and circulated to give a historical impression that load capacity has been met in our infrastructural and sensorial apparatuses.[20] It is some surprise, then, that load capacity—cable and wireless speeds, storage, processing power, and so on—has been able to keep pace, so far at least, and that the information overload of yesterday now looks like a dull drought of textual scarcity.

Others understand the most extreme, impulsive, and fantastical images and utterances made available and accessible via the web as now conventional and ordinary. Reading a string of hateful commentary added to a YouTube posting, or scanning through the endless viscera of a Twitter hashtag, you know something has changed. We confront, are made to confront, the textual fact of what might have previously resided in the realm of idle speculation ("I wonder if anyone has a photo of *x*? Chances are . . . never mind, here it is").

That having been said, the infinite possibilities of expression and language mean we have yet to hit the bottom of the representational well. Quite the contrary. Just as there is a plenitude of utterances to see and hear online, there is and always will be a limitless reserve of the unsaid. Consider how supremely absurd the idea of expressive totality, toward which concepts of overload bend, is. It leaves us with statements like, for every film made, there is an incalculable number of unmade works. As long as human society exists, there will be additional contributions to the said. To turn to a more concrete version of the abundance argument, for every film available—in release, in theaters, on television, on a streaming service, and so on—there are so many others that are inaccessible for a variety of reasons ranging from economics to fragility. For every work in print, there are others you cannot buy or see even if you wanted to. For every blisteringly predictable political commentary, there are views and arguments that are hidden or marginal. This is to say, while our media age gives us the impression of expressive totality, conventionality and scarcity rule representation, just as they always did.

One rendition of the obscene-plenitude assessment of contemporary media exists in the work of Slavoj Žižek. He makes this clear in his cheeky embrace of the persona of the pervert, indiscriminately oriented toward the consumption of more. For all the inspired criticism about the contradictory desires that propel contemporary capitalism, he holds on to a model of excessive and extreme forms of popular expression, especially in the age of the internet. You get the feeling that he imagines that Georges Bataille and Larry Flynt are über-cultural producers who control what moves online and see their job as confronting people with manifestations of secret desires, ones people don't even know they have until they see the image, which then haunts them and can never again be unseen. Often, popular forms lurk behind Žižek's more politically engaged theorization, some of which he uses to structure assertions by drawing on themes and applying them to conceptual conundrums, and others he uses to sound an alarm. His book *Trouble in Paradise* used the Ernst Lubitsch comedy of the same name from 1932 as a framing device about class and desire but dips into a fearful response to the viral video "Gangnam Style," which he described as a "sign of the collapse of civilization." That music video "mobilizes people into a collective trance" and produces "obscene *jouissance* in all its stupidity."[21] Most serious scholarship on popular culture has moved away from such dismissive terms drawn from Gustave Le Bon's nineteenth-century ideas about the irrationality of crowds. But Žižek keeps returning to popular examples, and movies in particular, no doubt because, in his understanding, they are so easy to interpret for grand historical impact.

In actuality, our internet is far more regulated and constrained, not the perverted fantastic universe imagined by some. It consists of forms, bureaucratic necessities, and basic local information. It is as much a work obligation or a social one, demanding the dull entry of information, as it is an endless carnival of libidinal excess and manifestos for murderers. Computers, tablets, and smartphones are maps, thermometers, clocks, traffic reports, phone books, catalogues, vacation planners, bank statements, utility bills, movie and concert listings, children's math games, fashion magazines, trashy novels, and on and on. For every hour spent building social media connections, viewing outrageous images, or inflaming a reasoned political debate with scattered outbursts, countless more hours are spent on the more mundane tasks related to earning pay, tending to friends and family, and keeping households running smoothly. It's *there*, in that mundane bureaucratic realm, that we find the ideological core of contemporary capitalism. We are not, it seems, the online libertines we might think, or wish, we are.

Žižek knows this. Clearly he is aware of the high degree of predictability and repression in the media world, where, rather than an excess of everything possible being blurted at once, we are more typically confronting the familiar and limited range of our imaginations. Nonetheless, the impression of the obscene of contemporary media drives one of his most often cited assessments, that we live in an age of declining symbolic efficiency. This is an updating of the poststructuralist, postmodernist view of the fundamental artificiality of our times, an artificiality that has produced a crisis of meaning. Baudrillard's work in the 1970s and 1980s is one such example. Signs no longer point to reality outside their own signifying functions. Signs can only point to other signs. The historical catalyst of this situation "back in the day" was the media overload represented by broadcast television. That seems so quaint now, and cyberculture is the new evidence for this artificiality, this circularity, this endless pursuit of a significatory difference we can believe in.

Jodi Dean helps us understand Žižek on this point. She does so in the service of her generative concept "communicative capitalism," which sees new capitalist mechanisms and a new capitalist subject emerging from the circulation of information and entertainment. The way our media networks construct platforms on which we encounter, participate with, and understand one another, and the way capital builds and regulates itself through these media, has left us in need of new analytic and political models. A central feature of this communicative capitalism is the decline of symbolic efficiency. She describes this as the reduced mobility of meaning, that is, a reduced communicative capability going from one point or person to another. She sees blogs as a primary contemporary example, writing, "Sometimes it's difficult to tell when a blog or a post is ironic and when it's sincere, when it's funny or when it's serious."[22] It is easy to recognize the ambiguity of address and intention Dean describes, though this is not an operation uniquely associated with blogs, and years of reader-oriented scholarship have provided us ample evidence of interpretive variability across representational formats. But Dean proposes a different symbolic regime that is associated with newer media forms and with cyberculture.

Dean elaborates the reasons for a decline in symbolic efficiency, describing three "threats." First, there is the "loss of the binding power or performative efficacy of words," which presupposes an advance invitation to insincerity that people simply cannot resist.[23] She assumes playfulness, or an inability to discern seriousness about something written or said. For Dean, this is driven by new digital media, but it has been a conundrum since writing first spatialized speech thousands of years ago. Second, symbolic efficiency is threatened by "the dissolution affecting identity and desire," wherein Dean sees digital forms as offering so many realizations of fantasies that what used to be subterranean motors of desire now have a surface textual appearance.[24] She understands that the prospects of these realizations are so tempting as to be impossible to deny, such that "instant gratification fills in the lack of constitutive desire . . . fantasies that are completely realized cease to be fantasies."[25] While intuitively right, this angle misses the regenerative capacities of libidinal drives and fantasies; realization is never finally and forever complete. Third is "a threat to meaning," in which the distance between the utterance and its significance has been reduced, leaving no room for interpretation or "the possibility of feeling convinced, of the sense that an answer can be or is 'right' rather than just another opinion."[26] Stephen Colbert captured this with his running joke about "truthiness." This line of argumentation reiterates a founding claim of postmodernism, namely, that we have entered an era in which the master narrative of Truth is in crisis. This predates the internet and has no specific link to the rise of blogs. These three threats, which Dean abbreviates as the loss of performativity, desire, and meaning, together make for a psychically and socially unstable communicative environment. Not only do people find it difficult to express what they mean, they also can't be understood as meaning what they say. People don't say too little, but say too much, with each utterance meaning proportionally less even though more of our libidinal life sees textual daylight. And she does not hedge her bets on these claims, writing, "This decline in symbolic efficiency is a fundamental feature of communicative capitalism."[27]

The contradictions in these claims make them difficult suppositions to build on. After all, they have been said of other media at different times. In this idea of digital culture, there is both too little communicative precision and too much. And yet what Dean and Žižek are wrestling with are core questions about the steely resilience and adaptability of capitalism, and most perplexingly our apparent drive to embrace it. Clearly, the rewards of capitalism—or at least the dreams about them—are legion, and they satisfy to a sufficient degree material and libidinal needs, regardless of the actual disparities and exploitations that transpire. My commentary here targets only Dean's and Žižek's readings of digital culture, which are conventionalized critiques and reproduce clichés about the internet and the popular. What critics like Dean and Žižek largely see as the most salient and consequential aspects of the internet are its inauthenticity, its disruption of seriousness, its subversion of expertise, its extreme and detrimental publicness, its insincerity, its immediacy, and its appeal to desire. As leading poststructuralist critics, they express no direct statement of nostalgia for a Habermasian form of a rational and sober public. But their criticism implies a public realm of discourse, serious and logical, with expert opinion given its full due, that has been disastrously interfered with by cyberculture's irresistible and irrepressible expressive plenitude.

As media scholars, we must walk our understanding of digital culture back from the fantastical in order to grasp a few fundamentals. The fact that social relations are mediated doesn't make them inauthentic. There are plenty of hierarchies of expertise and seriousness online. People surfing the web habitually discover blocked access, privacy walls, and gaps in availability of material. People experience sincerity, frustration, and deadened desire everywhere, online and off. One example contradicts all the expressive excess, significatory ambiguities, and libidinal freedom that some critics pore over: ever file your taxes online?

Blogs are an important form, and many display the qualities described by Dean, but the operations and conventions she identifies did not originate with blogs, online discussion platforms, or the internet, and they do not transfer to all other realms of the digital world, nor even to all blogs. For instance, blogs can be extensions of legitimate authority. She is rightfully, and forcefully, skeptical about the democratic possibilities of cyberculture, arguing that those who see revolutionary potential in increased social media participation are missing the actual contribution to and fortification of existing structures of communicative capitalism. Yet, she is perhaps naive about the ethical political action of random attacks and disruption by hackers, neglecting how they too can act in the service of state and capitalist interests. She imagines a vanguard—an elite who will lead us to a necessary historical severance with the current conditions of capitalism and who somehow in this age of symbolic inefficiency can still find meaning and truth—without sufficient concern for the totalitarian potential of such models. Indeed, in *The Communist Horizon*, Dean wishes to rehabilitate communist equalitarianism, doing so by separating it from Stalinism, which dominates the American understanding of the concept.[28] This would be a fine project, were it not for the fact that she can't confront Stalin's genocides except in the most cursory fashion. As a result, she can't tell us how claims about a disruptive revolutionary vanguard will avoid authoritarian directions. She is not alone in this. Žižek has portrayed himself as a "friendly Stalinist." Claiming to advocate for radical visions that would destroy society, in the hope something better will replace it, he follows his own logic to such nonsense assertions as that the Nazis were not violent enough during World War II, and then offers weak defenses that make sense only if you believe Nazism was a progressive movement that made some mistakes in the party's democratic pursuit.[29] These could be dismissed as additions to his long career of statements made for the purpose of provocation. But it's not charming. In a world supposedly without symbolic efficiency, where truth and ethics are a minefield of contingencies, an expectation that social progress might be provided by isolated and autonomous factions who elect themselves into positions of decision-making power without any recourse to constituency, or by grand violent movements murdering millions, is sheer horrific fantasy.

For my current purposes, I want to concentrate my commentary on the image of the chaotic, symbolic free-for-all that undergirds the claim of symbolic inefficiency. I'm not addressing only Dean and Žižek here, who each have contributed unparalleled insight into the relation between desire and a receding democratic project, despite the significant political limitations I have just mentioned. What they offer are really a rendition of the information overload thesis, the idea that new media have delivered us to a Tower of Babel where plenitude has made language and expression meaningless, and where there is always a humorous, sexy, or grotesque bauble to distract us from our actual conditions of exploitation. But here is the catch, the contradiction: our media environment has entered a moment of industrial change, and old infrastructures are creaking under the weight of new technologies. Every new business model—social media, streaming, over-the-top boxes and consoles, wireless and on-demand services—brings with it a host of entrepreneurial initiatives, enterprises that dream of being the most visible and unavoidable entity to provide that new service. Regulatory regimes are made arcane, and ambitious users invent ways to circumvent laws. But the most important feature, the takeaway, is that *not much actually changes*. Communicative capitalism bends back in on itself and supplies the lifeblood of profit capitalism in general needs to survive.

Our media are not really the province of libidinal promiscuity that sits so vividly in the minds of some critics. We need to take account of the ratcheting down as much as the unhinging of desires. The internet is massively regulated and limiting: subscriptions, purchases necessary for services, content moderation and scrubbing, forms that allow only certain kinds of entries, tags that limit the items returned by searches, content and recommendations that appear based on automated processes, and, of course, our computer-as-viewing-device, which shows us what's available, not what's possible. And, as comedian John Mulaney observed about internet use, "you spend most of your day telling a robot that you're not a robot. Think about that for two minutes and tell me that you don't want to walk into the ocean."[30] As José van Dijck documents, online we do not find a wild realm of communication; instead, with "the interconnection of platforms, a new infrastructure emerged: *an ecosystem of connective media*."[31] The Netflix model is currently a centerpiece for an idea about access and plenitude in moving-image culture, yet its catalogue of about six thousand "viewables"—which is Netflix's own measure, one that includes each individual episode of a television show, regardless of length—is well below what one could expect at a midsized video rental store a couple of decades ago. As of 2019, Classic Video, a small single-location rental operation in Kingston, Ontario, Canada, since the 1980s, still had more than fifty thousand titles available. This is only to say that many have mistaken the immediacy of certain kinds of availability as plenitude when, in fact, some of the services on offer are more restrictive than other analog means had been.

In light of this, and with full acknowledgment that digital culture *does* provide a stage for some wild forms of expression, sharing, and connection among people near and far, we need to aim our critical sensibilities at the coordinated and regulated sphere of media culture, the sphere in which we find a highly structured arena of cultural commodities. The more officious bureaucratic functions of communicative life—all those formulaic and phatic dimensions of expression—make up a substantial part of media discourse. It is here that the blockbuster operates, serving a special function.

Blockbusters are a counterexample, a counterweight, to the argument about the decline of symbolic efficiency. They are about certainty in audience, as well as investor, expectation, a mode of branded entertainment experience. They are about simplicity of characterization, thin shades of narrative growth and depth, and rudimentary story elements, ones that can be flexibly adopted by various audiences. There is rarely a contradictory, or alienating, moment for a viewer. David Bordwell has written that the contemporary Hollywood film truly carries forward the lessons and conventions of classical Hollywood form, contrary to claims about postmodern narrative structures. He argued that the blockbuster era from the mid-1970s onward has been associated with a shift in storytelling strategies toward more fractured, ride-driven, at times incoherent form. But this so-called postclassical or high-concept Hollywood film, Bordwell wrote, is really not so different from earlier styles, and there is more narrative coherence, and careful structuring, than if one only pays attention to the special-effects set pieces. In fact, he contended that the focus on the contemporary blockbuster has come at the expense of the quite diverse films and genres Hollywood still produces.[32] Agreed, and accordingly we should see that blockbusters are one stratum—one circuit—of film culture, partly defined by their economic expectations, their high level of investment, and their visibility. And their calculated construction and relations to other media products give them a greater, not lesser, degree of symbolic coherence.

My position runs counter to scholarship that emphasizes the confusion contemporary blockbusters can create for some audience members. For some, the louder assaults of action films might seem uninviting and potential sources of sensory injury. But the rapid, spatially confused editing is conventional and holds an appeal for fans, and it links with the pleasures of dizziness. Scott Bukatman has elaborated on this aspect as *kaleidoscopic perception* "comprised of equal parts delirium, kinesis, and immersion."[33] Moreover, the major franchised blockbusters orchestrate their stories and presentations to be as legible as humanly possible, with laser beam clarity, across geographic and cultural divides, and recognizable to eight-year-olds as well as octogenarians (though the latter are usually happily sacrificed in the name of grooming a younger generation for future franchise entries). Blockbusters are remarkable for how mechanically effective they have been in constructing an impression of cultural universality, with the result of making some forms of difference invisible. They offer illustrations of a tightly bound province of hyperefficient signification. Instead of a decline of symbolic efficiency, blockbusters telegraph symbolic brutalism, obviousness, and rock-solid unambiguity.

Degrees of interpretive freedom are not the same as communicative ambiguity, nor is connotative variation. Debates about meaning and intention are not communicative ambiguity. Symbolic value can be about significatory openness. The fact that *Avatar* is both an American ideological vehicle and a deep critique of American imperialism is a testament to its symbolic efficiency, and not a symptom of a lost register of ideological stability. This hyperefficiency may be a major part of the appeal of the form. In the context of a sense of symbolic inefficiency and diminished stability for political subjects, blockbusters provide reparation.

Even as democratic and civic potential is lost in the snowstorm of specks of speech, there is still ideological predictability and coherence. One ideological register is the way our cultural forms lift high the impression of timeless individual sovereignty. Our popular cultural environment also activates a communal ideological formation. We easily identify works that are shared widely and that operate as points of contact among people. The culture in common, in common for a multitude of people, prompts wild uses and interpretations. And yet some features of cultural works are beyond debate, fixed elements that precisely make them common. At the very least, symbolic efficiency is found in the ability to signal "in-commonness," that is, a work's own status as popular.

So it is with blockbuster movies, those works that by definition communicate something about their own popularity, whether achieved or aspirational. The shared and common dimension of blockbusters is not limited to a single film, for, as outlined earlier, blockbuster movies are not simply movies but an integrated and coordinated circuit of media production, distribution, and consumption. They travel with a series of related texts and commodities, and they become a parade of shared coordinated expressions. And although blockbuster movies, by convention, are oriented toward a theatrical release, they gesture toward their eventual movement through successive media forms.

For this reason, blockbusters are technological tentpoles, their "in-commonness" deeply invested in new platforms and technologies, which they help to normalize and advance. Some franchises are direct in this operation, for example, the "James Bond," "Batman," "Marvel Cinematic Universe," and "Bourne" films, which feature contemporary technological devices and integrate both fantastical and naturalistic representations of computer media into the diegetic story world. Even without this thematic attention, essentially all contemporary blockbuster franchises also appear as cross-media commodities, beginning with theatrical exhibition but then becoming hotel and airplane media content, followed by release via Blu-ray and DVD, streaming, cable, and television. They are soundtracks, novels, cars, watches, booze, and other spin-off and integrated products. They generate online clips, interviews, press coverage, and topics of commentary. These cross-media and cross-product shifts normalize the life cycle of media products but also, more pointedly, normalize the infrastructural paths—the theater chain, the internet service, the retail outlet—required for this cultural commodity life cycle. Blockbusters fortify what Van Dijck called the "ideology of making online sociality *salable*."[34]

What some authors have described as the ideological incoherence of Hollywood films transpires at the level of theme and story and is better thought of as ideological slipperiness. One can easily identify the strategic slipperiness of American blockbusters, such that they invite interpretations and pleasures that slide the work toward whatever political pole happens to be advantageous to winning a widely dispersed audience. Ideological stability and predictability, though, remain, but it is at the level of form, format, and apparatus. There, a blockbuster consistently becomes an advertisement for the economic and technological system that brought it into being, that coordinated the related works, and that delivered it to your eyes and ears. Blockbusters are the dark suns of symbolic efficiency, selling the capitalist operations that produce such blasting and deafening spectacles.

Vistas, populated with costumed multitudes and semidomesticated animals, dominated the big films in the 1950s. In them, we find spectacle in the unusual and elaborate events that unfold, like a chariot race or the burning of Rome. But we also find it in the sheer volume of dressed characters, extras, and sets. Kristen Whissel described today's "digital multitude," in which computer-generated imagery crams filmic space with tiny dots of animated crowds, until spectacular scenes of rushing and undulating populations, armies, and alien hoards seem impossibly vast.[35] Such sequences point the viewer to the hidden work of the digital artist and software, composing, coloring, and animating every granule of screen space that appears, and the work of the contemporary blockbuster includes the coordination of multitudes of nondigital subcontracted pixel pushers. In contrast, the multitudes of *Quo Vadis* (1951) and *The Ten Commandments* (1956) direct us to the actuality of the humanity captured, the flesh and blood of extras, costumed and styled for the scene, dwarfed by sets and fellow *figurants*, to be cruelly reduced to a split-second appearance in a long shot, a blip of a historical document. Yet the sum of that multitude of extras produces the blockbuster. The crowd-management skills involved—arranging the action of hundreds of extras, feeding them, cutting their checks—cannot but impress the viewer. Every vast portrait of distant times and peoples conveys awe at the resources—labor and capital—and logistics necessary to produce such a re-creation.[36] For all the joy and pleasure, a hint of sadness surfaces. These worlds, so cleverly, if not always convincingly, re-created, are temporary, destined to be fleeting. The extraordinary efforts to mount the spectacle of warships colliding, armies clashing, and ancient games unfolding—the talent and skill involved, the organizational and financial pull exercised—are rapidly consigned to dust, replaced by other building and production needs. *An epic is partly a filmed record of waste*, and the bigger the epic, the larger and more egregious the waste.[37]

The filmed record captures more than the extras and sets of an earlier era. Set construction may offer a physical space for action to unfold, but the composite images, mattes, and rear- or front-screen projections are equally foundational elements of the world assembled. The hint of waste, and the glance toward the material requirements for filmic construction (skill, resource, time, capital, technique, etc.), extends to all facets of the moving-image presentation. Such a broad claim, one may say, can apply to all art and artifice. No doubt, but the blockbuster production is distinctive if only for the fact that sheer size is one of its primary defining characteristics. It is always, to some degree, about its making, about its largeness, about its own material presence as a product of unusually elaborate plans and unusually abundant resources. The blockbuster movie works by reminding us about its own mammoth production.

Is it any wonder, then, that the past four decades have seen production budgets cross over from being circulated in trade venues to becoming popular entertainment news items? Specifically, the escalating numbers are easily the most uniform measures of what we call a blockbuster, authorizing its status as a resource gobbler. Fascination with epic films encompasses fascination with size, with the gigantic, and hence with the elements that make up that giganticism. The scale of production, and the circulation of stories about that scale, is a most conventional facet. One of the first stages of blockbuster production, a sure sign of blockbuster strategy in action, is talk about the size of the production. The raw integer of budget totals points to the finished movie, and the finished movie points back to the raw financial investment. They are not equivalent, but the idea of seeing the money on the screen is at once an ordinary way to talk about audience pleasure and a way to fulfill big-budget promise. I imagine that never in the history of the American blockbuster has a producer said, "Let's make sure our investment is not apparent on the screen," however concealed from the untrained eye an effect or technique may be. It simply runs counter to the workings of the blockbuster. The money makes the movie, but it also *makes* the movie; it guarantees a special experience associated with the big and the loud.

With so much written about the original *Star Wars* (now called *Star Wars: Episode IV—A New Hope*), and its deserved place as a milestone in the emergence of a new phase of hit-driven Hollywood, grasping just how exceptional it was is a difficult task today. Other films had merchandise, but nothing like *Star Wars*, where many products were released and available all at once, and for which marketing plans assured a high level of awareness of those products and the film itself. The talk was about the film and its merchandise *and* about the very fact of the film's merchandising and interest in it. Here in the mid-1970s was a new way to encounter and come to know a movie. I have clear recollections of discussing the film's budget, months before its opening day. An $11 million figure still comes to mind. I am not saying it was accurate, only that my first awareness of the film title was accompanied by awareness of a price tag for the production. This was virtually unheard of, though the contemporary remake of *King Kong* (1976) also participated in this mode of budgetary promotion. For the blockbusters of the past, the production budgets circulated, but not with such a strong promotional association for the moviegoing public. And, most mind-boggling, $11 million was not such a strange figure. It was no record-breaking investment—for example, the *King Kong* remake's budget was $24 million—and was, in many respects, a relatively modest sum for the kind of film *Star Wars* was. Yet the figure stuck and, with it, the idea that titles and dollars have something to do with one another. Utterly unaware of Hollywood production processes, and with no basis of comparison, I had conversations with friends about how on Earth anyone would spend such sums on a movie. It wasn't a sign of quality, we teenagers knew that much (we were thirteen years old that summer), but we had a feeling that this investment had to be on-screen somewhere, likely in the special effects, and on that basis alone interest in seeing the film arose. Remember, the film had no stars; George Lucas was a bit of a name, after *American Graffiti* (1973), but he was hardly big enough to ensure audience turnout. Alec Guinness and Peter Cushing were not teenage draws, and science fiction had become the province of dark social commentary (*The Planet of the Apes* [1968], *2001: A Space Odyssey* [1968], *Silent Running* [1972], *Soylent Green* [1973], *Logan's Run* [1976]), not crowd-pleasing entertainment. The film's bigness, its production finances, its narrative scale, and its commercial buoyancy were the star attractions. The title planted the seed of this immensity; it was not called "Rocket Battle" but the galaxy-spanning, plural, *Star Wars*. The movie sold bigness with bigness.

In the 1980s, the blockbuster settled into a definitional realm that included post-factum designations based on financial success, most particularly box-office revenue. The actual distance between box-office revenue and profit can be considerable, the latter of which is far more important to investors and far more difficult to measure with any degree of precision. Profitability is a feature of distribution deals, exhibition arrangements, production and promotion budgets, the longevity of the work, and its relationship with other products and texts. Knowing the details of only one of these provides a partial view of market performance. Still, the intense manufactured fascination with box-office winners is yet another way to engage with blockbuster giganticism. Attention to box-office revenue shows an enduring interest in popular film, even as audiences grasp the shrinking power of theatrical exhibition and understand that theatrical runs for blockbusters, in many ways, are advertisements for their franchise properties and for their appearance on television or via DVD, streaming, or premium cable outlets, to be watched a few months later. Promotional material incorporates claims derived from box-office performance, and movies temporarily nab bragging rights as "America's Number 1 Movie" or "Number 1 Comedy Last Weekend." No audience member thrills at the bundles being raked in by investors (unless, I suppose, you are, work for, or are related to one of those investors). They thrill at the abstract concept of so many people seeing a particular movie. Grasping the giganticism of the audiences, their "massness," and the movie's success (again, its ability to appeal to a vast population, rather than its actual financial triumph) becomes part of the meaning of the work, and that meaning runs through the work and subsequent engagements with it.

Blockbusters, as cultural commodities for mass consumption, must reference the financial features and reaches of the motion picture business. Numbers are a significant part of what blockbusters are about, and this facet permanently links these movies to balance sheets and accounting practices. Numbers have a shifting connotative function and are not absolutes. The respectable million-dollar budget of the 1940s translates into only an extremely low-budget independent effort today. The historical meaning of *Jaws* (1975) was its breaking through the $100 million revenue mark, setting a new standard for box-office grosses. Today films regularly surpass that tally, and $1 billion has become the cherished success that the biggest productions target.

Whatever the metric, Jon Lewis has gone so far as to refer to this as Hollywood's "fetishization of financial data."[38] Blockbusters are entities of investment and revenue generation, and they are infused with the expectations that they will not simply be profitable but will be hits. Blockbusters work by attracting purveyors of capital just as any other investment opportunity might do, whether lumber or wind power. Plans for films are poked and prodded for their plumpness. They are sorted by recognizable and reassuring signs of future success, of future hit status, which means familiar ingredients advantage a package. Talent with a track record, stories and characters that are already popular, are major assets and are worth a premium precisely owing to their past success and their familiarity to audiences. The demands for revenue-generating performance are considerable. The general guideline is that a work has to make two and a half times the negative cost, meaning the expense to get the film completed and into the can (today, onto the data-storage unit), which does not include expenses related to distribution, promotion, prints, and so on.[39] For all the human affection and appreciation generated, celebrity culture functions to guarantee the flow of capital to new projects. Movie stars are, after all, walking, talking testimonies to previous hits, evidence of track records. A retrospective bias, a conservative pressure, on decision-making partly explains why iconoclastic producers stand out so much and why some stars seem to never go away.

In the 2000s, large private-equity firms saw motion pictures as a particularly advantageous investment target, one that offered quick and high returns. Producers find the arrangements attractive because outside entities cover the cost of increasingly expensive blockbusters and accept some of the risk. Though these partnerships were not exclusive and lasting, venture capital firm Dune Entertainment financed Twentieth Century Fox films, Relativity Media invested in Sony and Universal projects, and Merrill Lynch dealt with United Artists.[40] While the global financial meltdown at the end of 2008 made access to financing temporarily more difficult, by the middle of 2009, equity firms large and small agreed that motion pictures were a fairly safe investment bet. These investors, providing hundreds of millions of dollars, have been known to want more recognition of their services than that of a bank loan officer. Production credit can be extracted. There is no better example of this than Steven Mnuchin, former head of Dune Entertainment, and then Relativity Media, whose affection for the glamor of Hollywood is such that his name began to appear as executive producer on such films as *Sully* (2016), *Suicide*

Squad (2016), and *Mad Max: Fury Road* (2015) following a deal with Warner in 2013. He even had a rather wooden wordless cameo as a Merrill Lynch executive in *Rules Don't Apply* (2016), on which he is also credited as a producer. Even after his appointment and confirmation as President Donald Trump's secretary of the treasury, films he had financed, and received credit as executive producer for, continued to be released through 2017. Hollywood glamor, though, is a bonus. The centrality of capital is truly what determines the terms of success, and return on investment is a bottom-line statement of the status of the work. One question and one question only matters: is the ink red or black?

Talk of blockbusters, then, is a form of discussion about cultural works in which their status as commodities and investment vehicles always hovers nearby. They are artifacts that have been fully financialized. In the buzz of the blockbuster hums the expectation of accumulated capital; they exist only insomuch as they are able to generate that hum. There is no such thing as an amateur blockbuster, a do-it-yourself blockbuster, or an outsider or folk blockbuster. Even the "cult blockbuster" pushes the boundaries of the term and really refers to a sleeper hit or a film promoted with the trappings of niche fandom. These are oxymoronic terms. A blockbuster, by its very nature, exists in relation to forces of industrial production. Here we locate their special association with bigness. When it comes to capital accumulation, there is no ceiling on expectations or ambitions. While Hollywood accountants keep financing a mysterious secret, we do know that at the top end budgets of $100 to $200 million are fairly common. Audiences have become blasé about such figures, and the sharpness of their significance has dulled. But these numbers are stratospheric. There are few, if any, points of comparison in the world of film, entertainment, and art. The production budget for a single American blockbuster franchise entry dwarfs the budgets found in other national motion picture industries, with few exceptions. Are there any cultural products that have budgets as big, that have as many resources and financial advantages, as these do, and that also harbor inflated ideas about how much business they are destined to generate? Big-budget Broadway productions averaged around $10 million for musicals and under $3 million for other genres in 2012.[41] These figures explain why the doomed musical *Spider-Man—Turn Off the Dark* (2011) was so anomalous with its eye-popping $75 million production budget; its budget was more like that of a movie blockbuster than a Broadway blockbuster.

Tables 2.2 and 2.3 present the top box-office films for the domestic and international markets for each year from 2010 to 2016. The titles are sure

TABLE 2.2 Top Box-Office Films, 2010–2016, Domestic

Year	Title	Studio	Domestic box office for year (millions USD)	Foreign box office for year (millions USD)	Lifetime global box office, as of publication (millions USD)	Overseas top 100 ranking	Estimated production budget (millions USD)
2016	Finding Dory	Disney	$486	$533	$1,030*	4	$175 to $200
2015	Jurassic World	Universal	$652	$945	$1,670	2	$250
2014	Guardians of the Galaxy	Disney	$333	$441	$774	11	$196
2013	Iron Man 3	Disney	$409	$806	$1,215	1	$200
2012	The Avengers	Disney	$623	$891	$1,514	1	$220
2011	Harry Potter and the Deathly Hallows: Part 2	Warner Brothers	$381	$964*	$1,345*	1	$250 (includes Deathly Hallows: Part 1)
2010	Avatar (2009)	Fox	$477	$1,953*	$2,852*	1	$237**

SOURCES: See table 2.3.
*Source number is imprecise.
**Especially contentious.

TABLE 2.3 Top Box-Office Films, 2010–2016, International

Year	Title	Studio	Domestic box office (millions USD)	Foreign box office (millions USD)	Lifetime global box office (millions USD)	Domestic top 250 ranking	Estimated production budget (millions USD)
2016	Captain America: Civil War	Disney	$408	$707	$1,150*	3	$250
2015	Furious 7	Universal	$353	$1,079	$1,515	5	$250
2014	Transformers: Age of Extinction	Paramount	$245	$845	$1,091	5	$210
2013	Iron Man 3	Disney	$409	$806	$1,215	1	$200
2012	The Avengers	Disney	$623	$891	$1,514	1	$220
2011	Harry Potter and the Deathly Hallows: Part 2	Warner Brothers	$381	$964*	$1,345*	1	$250 (includes Deathly Hallows: Part 1)
2010	Avatar (2009)	Fox	$477	$1,953*	$2,852*	1	$237**

SOURCES FOR TABLES 2.2 AND 2.3:

2010: "'Top Worldwide Grossers 2010," *Variety*, January 17–23, 2011, 8; "Domestic Top 250 of 2010," *Variety*, January 10–16, 2011, 12–13; Josh Dickey, "'Avatar's' True Cost and Consequences," *TheWrap*, March 17, 2010, www.thewrap.com.

2011: "Top Worldwide Grossers 2011," *Variety*, January 16–22, 2012, 11; "Domestic Top 250 of 2011," *Variety*, January 9–15, 2012, 22–23; Daniel Frankel, "Get Ready for the Biggest 'Potter' Opening Yet," *TheWrap*, November 17, 2010, www.thewrap.com.

2012: "Domestic Top 250 of 2012," *Variety*, January 7–13, 2013, 10–11; "Top International Grossers 2012," *Variety*, January 14–27, 2013, 10; Anthony Breznican, "'The Avengers': Your First Look at the Dream Team!," *Entertainment Weekly*, September 30, 2011.

2013: "Top 250 of 2013;" *Variety*, January 6, 2014, 38–39; "Int'l Top 100 of 2013," *Variety*, January 15, 2014, 42; Mike Fleming Jr., "2013 Most Valuable Blockbuster Championship Game—#1 'Iron Man 3' vs. #3 'Despicable Me 2,'" *Deadline*, March 27, 2014, deadline.com.

2014: "Top 250 of 2014," *Variety*, January 6, 2015, 30–31; "Overseas Top 100 of 2014," *Variety*, January 14, 2015, 40; Mike Fleming Jr., "No. 5 'Guardians of the Galaxy'—2014 Most Valuable Blockbuster Movie Tournament," *Deadline*, March 13, 2015, deadline.com; Mike Fleming Jr., "No. 1 'Transformers: Age of Extinction' Is 2014's Most Valuable Blockbuster," *Deadline*, March 13, 2015, deadline.com.

2015: "Top 250 of 2015;" *Variety*, January 13, 2016, 42–43; Brent Lang, "Overseas Top 100 of 2015," *Variety*, January 19, 2016, 28; Mike Fleming Jr., "No. 3 'Jurassic World'—2015 Most Valuable Movie Blockbuster Tournament," *Deadline*, March 28, 2016, deadline.com; Mike Fleming Jr., "No. 5 'Furious 7'—2015 Most Valuable Movie Blockbuster Tournament," *Deadline*, March 23, 2016, deadline.com.

2016: "China Hiccup Drives down Global B.O.," *Variety*, January 24, 2017, 19–21; Dave McNary, "'Finding Dory' Swimming for Record $140 Million Opening," *Variety*, June 18, 2016, www.variety.com; Mike Fleming Jr., "No. 8 'Captain America: Civil War' Box Office Profits—2016 Most Valuable Movie Blockbuster Tournament," *Deadline*, March 28, 2017, deadline.com.

*Source number is imprecise.

**Especially contentious.

to ring a bell: *Avatar*, *Furious 7* (2015), *Jurassic World* (2015), and so on. The budgets for these blockbusters hover around $200 million, though these numbers are contentious, especially for *Avatar*, whose budget some have estimated as being over double that. But the return on this is staggering, with $1 billion an accepted benchmark for the global box-office gross. Their international receipts exceed domestic receipts in every instance, though the U.S. domestic market remains robust and, as mentioned above, easily the single most lucrative moviegoing territory in the world. Table 2.4 offers some international points of comparison for budgets. In the United States, the Motion Picture Association of America (MPAA) members' film budgets for 2006 have increased to an average of $65.8 million per film, with non-MPAA members hitting $30.3 million. The closest average budget is found in the United Kingdom, with $13.6 million, followed by $6.6 million in France. Table 2.5 provides more extensive comparison with other countries for 2006, 2007, and 2008. The list is not comprehensive (for instance, there was no information available for Russia), and as the sources differ from those used in table 2.4, numbers for 2006 also differ. Still, the figures offer some indication of the different film economies that are in operation, showing how out of step the U.S. is. Taking the 2008 data, the $26.0 million average budget per film has Germany as the closest comparator at $11.9 million. Most countries, though, reside far below this, even those with major production centers: $5.7 million for Japan, $2.7 million for South Korea, $1.5 million for Mexico, $1.5 million for Hong Kong, $1.3 million for China, $1.3 million for Egypt, and $0.2 million for India.

A related feature of blockbusters is distributive scale. Blockbusters travel; they are border hoppers, and they are designed to move. Media formats, geographic boundaries, demographic categories, time zones—blockbusters leap over such designations. They are not truly everywhere; they stumble over barriers just as any cultural work does, and there is considerable friction that limits the access to and availability of their wonders. But they are "everywhere," built on an idea of their own ubiquity, as their promotion and trailers habitually promise. The global domination intimated by the everywhere of blockbusters is a product of decades of lobbying and trade pacts. And it is not only the moving-image commodities that move. Business arrangements exploit the mobility of investment capital, making many big American movies landing pads for international finance. Moreover, production flexibility has produced jurisdictional competition in what it means to build a film-friendly environment for the spending of these funds. In short, enfolded into the meaning of blockbusters is a concept of their fluidity, their atmospheric

TABLE 2.4 Average Production Budgets of Feature Films, 1990–2006 (in millions USD)

Year	U.S. (MPAA members)	U.S. (MPAA subsidiaries and affiliates)	United Kingdom	France	Italy	Australia
1990	$26.8	not available	$6.5	$3.9	$2.4	<$6.5
1991	$26.1	not available	$7.3	$4.2	$2.9	<$7.3
1992	$28.9	not available	$7.0	$4.9	$2.4	<$7.0
1993	$29.9	not available	$5.0	$4.0	$2.5	<$5.0
1994	$34.3	not available	$8.3	$4.7	$2.7	<$8.3
1995	$36.4	not available	$8.1	$5.6	$1.9	<$8.1
1996	$39.8	not available	$8.9	$4.8	$1.8	<$8.9
1997	$53.4	not available	$5.4	$5.4	$1.7	<$6.2
1998	$52.7	not available	$6.8	$4.8	$2.2	<$6.8
1999	$51.5	not available	$7.0	$4.2	$2.0	not available
2000	$54.8	not available	$7.0	$4.3	$2.1	not available
2001	$47.7	$31.5	$6.2	$3.9	$2.5	not available
2002	$47.8	$34.0	$9.0	$4.2	$3.1	not available
2003	$66.3	$46.9	$17.0	$5.2	$3.8	not available
2004	$65.7	$29.0	$13.3	$6.6	$5.2	not available
2005	$63.6	$23.5	$13.3	$6.2	$4.9	not available
2006	$65.8	$30.3	$13.6	$6.6	not available	not available

SOURCES: André Lange, ed., *Focus 1998: World Film Market Trends*, European Audiovisual Observatory (Paris: Marché du film/Festival de Cannes, 1998), www.obs.coe.int; André Lange, ed., *Focus 1999: World Film Market Trends*, European Audiovisual Observatory (Paris: Marché du film/Festival de Cannes, Paris, 1999), www.obs.coe.int; André Lange, ed., *Focus 2000: World Film Market Trends*, European Audiovisual Observatory (Paris: Marché du film/Festival de Cannes, 2000), www.obs.coe.int; André Lange and Susan Newman, eds., *Focus 2001: World Film Market Trends*, European Audiovisual Observatory (Paris: Marché du film/Festival de Cannes, 2001), www.obs.coe.int; André Lange and Susan Newman-Baudais, eds., *Focus 2002: World Film Market Trends*, European Audiovisual Observatory (Paris: Marché du film/Festival de Cannes, 2002), www.obs.coe.int; André Lange and Susan Newman-Baudais, eds., *Focus 2003: World Film Market Trends*, European Audiovisual Observatory (Paris: Marché du Film/Festival de Cannes, 2003), www.obs.coe.int; Susan Newman-Baudais, eds., *Focus 2004: World Film Market Trends*, European Audiovisual Observatory (Paris: Marché du film/Festival de Cannes, 2004), www.obs.coe.int; Susan Newman-Baudais, eds., *Focus 2005: World Film Market Trends*, European Audiovisual Observatory (Paris: Marché du film/Festival de Cannes, 2005), www.obs.coe.int; Susan Newman-Baudais, eds., *Focus 2006: World Film Market Trends*, European Audiovisual Observatory (Paris: Marché du film/Festival de Cannes, 2006), www.obs.coe.int; Susan Newman-Baudais, eds., *Focus 2007: World Film Market Trends*, European Audiovisual Observatory (Paris: Marché du film/Festival de Cannes, 2007), www.obs.coe.int.

TABLE 2.5 Average Budget per Film, 2006–2008 (in millions USD)

	2006	2007	2008
USA	$30.7	$31.0	$26.0
New Zealand	$9.1	$14.7	$11.8
UK	$11.6	$12.8	$9.7
Germany	$8.5	$9.0	$11.9
France	$7.1	$7.2	$9.3
Ireland	$4.8	$5.4	$4.3
Japan	$5.1	$5.0	$5.7
Canada	$7.7	$8.7	$9.7
Netherlands	$3.5	$3.8	$3.3
Denmark	$2.9	$3.0	$3.6
South Korea	$4.2	$4.2	$2.7
Italy	$2.8	$3.5	$3.2
Switzerland	$3.3	$2.7	n/a
Belgium	$3.9	$4.2	$8.8
Spain	$4.0	$3.5	$4.0
Sweden	$2.0	$2.5	$3.5
Malaysia	$0.4	$0.4	$0.4
Australia	$3.2	$7.6	$4.2
Norway	$2.6	$2.4	$3.4
Austria	$2.7	$2.6	$2.4
Mexico	$1.5	$1.5	$1.5
Thailand	$0.9	$1.0	$1.1
Finland	$1.4	$1.5	$1.7
Hong Kong	$5.3	$6.3	$1.5
Iceland	$2.2	$2.4	$2.0
South Africa	$2.3	$2.3	$1.9
Brazil	$1.4	$1.5	$1.7
Slovakia	$1.3	$1.3	n/a
Czech Republic	$1.5	$1.5	$2.6

	2006	2007	2008
Luxembourg	$2.2	n/a	$2.2
Egypt	$1.1	$1.0	$1.3
Lithuania	$0.9	$1.1	$0.3
Israel	$0.7	$1.0	$0.9
Slovenia	$1.2	$1.4	$1.4
Poland	$1.5	$1.7	$2.0
Singapore	$0.5	$1.8	$2.0
China	$1.0	$1.1	$1.3
Taiwan	$0.7	$0.7	$0.7
Turkey	$1.8	$2.0	n/a
Portugal	$1.8	$1.6	$1.8
Greece	$0.8	$0.8	$0.9
Hungary	$0.7	$0.9	$1.3
Romania	$0.8	$1.0	$1.2
Chile	$0.6	$0.6	$0.2
Estonia	$0.7	$0.8	$1.9
Argentina	$0.9	$0.9	$1.0
Latvia	$0.4	$1.5	$1.4
Indonesia	$0.3	$0.2	$0.2
Venezuela	$0.3	$0.3	$0.4
Philipines	$0.3	$0.4	$0.3
Bulgaria	$1.0	$1.0	$1.4
Bangladesh	$0.1	n/a	n/a
India	$0.1	$0.2	$0.2
Colombia	$0.2	$0.2	$0.2
Vietnam	$0.2	$0.2	$0.3
Croatia	n/a	n/a	$0.3

SOURCES: "Film Production and Distribution: Steady Growth Continues in World Feature Film Output," *Screen Digest*, July 2007, 205; "Global Film Production/Distribution: US Makes Fewer Feature Films as World Total Sets New Record," *Screen Digest*, July 2008, 205; "Global Film Production Falls: Key Territories Hold Firm but World Production Levels Drop," *Screen Digest*, July 2009, 205.

presence. They fill up the air of popular culture, and they do so in every conceivable corner of the globe. Let me be clear, only the rarest of films actually does this, but the design and publicity of blockbusters aspire to these reaches. And even the annual success stories, which may not top any historical records for audiences or profits, still represent a level of commonality that few new works in any form ever come close to showing so rapidly.

In this respect, a vector of the global popular can be seen in the life of the blockbuster film, a cultural entity that moves, with limited cosmopolitan ease, through more media pathways to more geopolitical localities than most other works. As such, it plays in diverse contexts and situations. Audience encounters with these popular works transpire over a condensed time period. Generally, popularity of a work can increase over time, and we can point to certain classics—say Shakespeare, Victor Hugo, Tom Jobim—whose lasting presence has moved them into the ranks of shared global culture. Blockbusters, though, owing to their promotional and distribution machinery, can achieve vast commonality with exceptional speed. The virtually simultaneous launches of wide releases in metropolitan centers across the globe has been common for the past three decades; this simultaneity has been supplemented by the similar release and circulation plans of other exhibition windows, including on-demand and streaming services. These distribution plans keep revenue flowing for an extended period of time across media. In contrast, in the 1950s, blockbusters provided theatrical returns on investment over several years, a pace that upset conventional accounting practices, which were accustomed to having costs covered within fiscal years. Today blockbusters recoup investment costs rapidly and then continue to earn, most lucratively if they are part of a franchise. In this way blockbusters inhabit and express both transnationalism and contemporaneity. Blockbusters are an internationally shared *now* that encompasses globally dispersed audiences and anxious investors.

Blockbusters' narratives, settings, and talent reflect this internationalism. American blockbusters are home to actors and creative personnel from across the globe. They can be filmed and made in any number of active production centers worldwide. A German director, a French star, a Chinese star, a Japanese source novel, a Bollywood dance sequence, a Polish cinematographer, Brazilian and Australian financing, a U.K. visual effects outfit, and sequences shot in Dubai, Toronto, and Rome: such combinations constitute the high end of American film, organized with consideration for budget, skill, reputation, and market access. The appearance of heroic Chinese plot points (*Gravity*, 2013), characters (*The Martian*, 2015), and stars (Donnie Yen in *Rogue*

One: A Star Wars Story) is no random creative development. Each film was looking to win one of the few restricted spots for international film releases in Chinese theaters, tightly controlled as access to that market is.

The art of the blockbuster film package includes the strategic visibility and hierarchization of international participation, the result of which is the cosmopolitan film, a concept best elaborated by Vanessa R. Schwartz. Through a detailed examination of *Around the World in 80 Days* (1956), Schwartz, pinpointing shifts in Hollywood and French film culture in the 1950s, demonstrated that the new global film commodity was not simply and singularly American but a self-aware cultural entity that bespoke the transitional dreams of a liberal world order. She wrote, "The cosmopolitan film represents both a mode of production and a film's self-conscious relation to its own status as somehow reaching beyond nations and national identity in search of a global consciousness and cosmopolitanism."[42] Not only is the American blockbuster a global work, designed to develop paths to exploitable entertainment markets worldwide; it is self-conscious of this operation, and it transparently assembles the most visible and legible features of its internationalism. There is a veneer, a hard shell, of globalism in the postcard exposition shots of cities, in showcase shooting locations, in characters and actors identifiable for their ethnic and national particularities. The cosmopolitanism of the blockbuster is an easy-to-read surface manifestation of the work and its own energetic circulation.

The cosmopolitan nature of the blockbuster strata of American film is part of what appeals to international investment. As Schwartz noted, the flow of film funding varies and can move from the United States to major productions abroad as well as from abroad into American productions. In contrast to the "runaway" productions in the 1950s, in many cases to accommodate limits on transference of foreign currencies back to the United States, today there is a regularized process. Despite the protestations to the contrary, the very concept of the runaway production no longer makes sense, given the normalized level of internationalization of finance, production, and audience for American film. One can identify a backdrop of geopolitical links smoothing the way, most recently with China emerging as a key partner.[43] China Film Group and Columbia Pictures coproduced *The Karate Kid* (2010), recasting the tale of intergenerational friendship with an American boy transplanted to China, featuring rising American star Jaden Smith and established Hong Kong icon Jackie Chan. Director Harald Zwart is Dutch, shooting mostly in Beijing. The American blockbuster is not less American for these characteristics. It is more surely defined by its articulation of internationalism, one that cynically accepts cooperation within an antidemocratic regime with an abysmal human rights record in order to tell an underdog story that requires respect for one's elders, bridges to new cultures, and, of course, exciting scenes of gory violence presented as righteous. Authoritarian regimes everywhere take note: Hollywood will work with you if you pay and have a growing economy.

So what compares to the production and marketing expenses of the modern American blockbuster? No art form has regularized budgets at this elevated level. Art markets move in this territory, and the art of the deal has saturated even the finest of fine arts. But at the production end, movies stand alone, or, more precisely, the behemoth entities called blockbusters do. Market value is a function of time. As fickle as art markets can be, they can require the passage of time for value to accrue. By way of contrast, return for blockbusters is designed to be rapid and immediate, and also to gather steam in order to leverage future productions. In terms of speed, movie investments are closer to the real estate flipper than to the patient investor who hangs on to their holdings for years or the art collector who waits for an artist to stop producing and die.

The closest comparator to blockbusters may be bridges and buildings. The architectural comparison is apt. Blockbusters operate analogously to the signature, branded office towers that shape the uppermost outline of major cities, emblazoned with corporate markings and stylistic distinctions. Blockbusters similarly constitute the skyline of the moving-image entertainment vista and are intended to last, to be a part of the popular cultural scene for years. They loom over a city's array of popular distractions and set the tone for popular pleasures. Just as signature head-office skyscrapers blast their corporate affiliation, flying the flag of their ownership with names and signage, blockbusters' presence also marks that vista with the corporate brand of the distributing studio; it is not just James Cameron's *Avatar* or Michael Bay's *Transformers* (2007) but Twentieth Century Fox's *Avatar* and DreamWorks SKG/Paramount Pictures' *Transformers*. In the shadow of each towering feature, one might stumble on smaller-scale architectural gems down below—the independent, art house, "quality," or international films treasured by critics and middlebrow audiences. The moving-image skyline composed by blockbusters represents an *international style of architecture for popular film*.

Blockbusters pop up in the cities of the world and are differently at home in every one, regardless of continental or cultural context. They are designed to signify placelessness and everywhereness as they equally announce their status as new, contemporary, and cosmopolitan works. Every year, the same blockbuster titles appear across the lists of the most popular films in different countries. Among the more localized hits, those that have traveled shorter distances to become nationally or regionally popular, we find attempts to imagine blockbusters along the lines developed and advanced by the American industry. On this point, Julian Stringer saw this as "the revelation that filmmakers, critics, and audiences the world over are actively reconstructing the blockbuster as a generic category."[44] He went on to wonder whether, given the populations of countries like China and India, perhaps their most successful films were not always blockbusters. But in proposing this, Stringer loses sight of the factors that make the American blockbuster historically distinctive, spectacular, and able to move across so many national borders.

In a UNESCO report on its survey of the state of feature film worldwide, I charted the relative mobility of film across countries.[45] Paying close attention to the annual top-ten films in each reporting country, mostly measured by attendance, though some countries used box-office revenue, we find but a handful of titles repeated across these lists. For 2009, 168 different titles appear at least once on the top-ten lists gathered from the 115 countries participating in the survey. Only *eleven* films appeared on ten or more of those lists, making them the most internationally visible films of the year. Notably, the film *2012* appeared on forty-seven top-ten lists, *Avatar* on forty-five, *Harry Potter and the Half-Blood Prince* on fifty, *Ice Age: Dawn of the Dinosaurs* on fifty-three, and *The Twilight Saga: New Moon* on forty-three. Weighting this tabulation, to account for a film's placement in the top-ten lists for the year (assigning 1 to a tenth-ranked title and 10 to the first-ranked title), provides us with an even clearer indication of the high level of concentration around a select number of films. Sticking with 2009, we find there are eight high-scoring films worldwide, listed here in order: *Ice Age: Dawn of the Dinosaurs*, *Harry Potter and the Half-Blood Prince*, *2012*, *Avatar*, *The Twilight Saga: New Moon*, *Up*, *Angels and Demons*, and *Transformers: Revenge of the Fallen*. After these films, the weighted scores plummet, and we see the number of titles expand greatly. This result was replicated for the comparison years of 2007 and 2008 (see tables 2.6–2.8).

These measures, presented side by side in figure 2.1, by no means capture the fullness of audiovisual entertainment. They are about theatrical releases and attendance. And though the UNESCO cultural statistics outfit combs the surveys for anomalous reporting and data, it is not always clear

TABLE 2.6 Global Top-Twenty Feature Films, 2007

Rank	Title	Origin	Type	Language	Weighted score	Sequel or franchise (film or TV)
1	Pirates of the Caribbean: At World's End	USA	Fiction—action/adventure	English	374	Yes
2	Harry Potter and the Order of the Phoenix	UK/USA	Fiction—action/adventure	English	333	Yes
3	Shrek the Third	USA	Animation—family	English	290	Yes
4	Spider-Man 3	USA	Fiction—action/adventure	English	239	Yes
5	Ratatouille	USA	Animation—family	English	197	No
6	The Simpsons Movie	USA	Animation—family	English	166	Yes
7	Transformers	USA	Fiction—action/adventure	English	131	Yes
8	Mr. Bean's Holiday	UK/FRA/DEU/USA	Fiction—comedy	English	98	Yes
9	300	USA	Fiction—action/adventure	English	83	No
10	Night at the Museum	USA	Fiction—family	English	50	Yes
11	Live Free or Die Hard	USA/UK	Fiction—action/adventure	English	43	Yes
12	Rush Hour 3	USA	Fiction—action/adventure	English	28	Yes
13	The Bourne Ultimatum	USA/UK/DEU	Fiction—action/adventure	English	26	Yes
14	Ocean's Thirteen	USA	Fiction—drama	English	21	Yes
15	Taxi 4	FRA	Fiction—action/adventure	French	20	Yes
16	Fantastic 4: Rise of the Silver Surfer	USA/DEU/UK	Fiction—action/adventure	English	18	Yes
17	The Irony of Fate 2 (Ironiya sudby. Prodolzhenie)	RUS	Fiction—comedy	Russian	17	Yes

Rank	Title	Origin	Type	Language	Weighted score	Sequel or franchise (film or TV)
18	Empties (Vratné lahve)	CZE/UK	Fiction—comedy	Czech	16	No
19	I Am Legend	USA	Fiction—action/adventure	English	14	No
20	I Served the King of England (Obsluhoval jsem anglického krále)	CZE/SVK	Fiction—comedy	Czech (some German)	13	No

SOURCE: See table 2.8.

NOTE: On weighted score, see table 2.8.

TABLE 2.7 Global Top-Twenty Feature Films, 2008

Rank	Title	Origin	Type	Language	Weighted score	Sequel or franchise (film or TV)
1	Kung Fu Panda	USA	Animation—family	English	254	Yes
2	Madagascar: Escape 2 Africa	USA	Animation—family	English	237	Yes
3	Mamma Mia!	USA/UK/DEU	Fiction—musical	English	237	No
4	Quantum of Solace	UK/USA	Fiction—action/adventure	English	233	Yes
5	The Dark Knight	USA/UK	Fiction—action/adventure	English	228	Yes
6	Indiana Jones and the Kingdom of the Crystal Skull	USA	Fiction—action/adventure	English	223	Yes
7	Hancock	USA	Fiction—action/adventure	English	121	No
8	Sex and the City	USA	Fiction—comedy	English	113	Yes
9	WALL-E	USA	Animation—family	English	112	No

(continued)

TABLE 2.7 (continued)

Rank	Title	Origin	Type	Language	Weighted score	Sequel or franchise (film or TV)
10	The Mummy: Tomb of the Dragon Emperor	USA/DEU	Fiction—action/adventure	English	101	Yes
11	Iron Man	USA	Fiction—action/adventure	English	66	Yes
12	Asterix at the Olympic Games (Astérix aux jeux olympiques)	FRA/DEU/ESP/ITA	Fiction—family	French	61	Yes
13	The Chronicles of Narnia: Prince Caspian	USA/NZL	Fiction—action/adventure	English	45	Yes
14	Journey to the Center of the Earth	USA	Fiction—action/adventure	English	42	Yes
15	Welcome to the Sticks (Bienvenue chez les Ch'tis)	FRA	Fiction—comedy	French	38	No
16	The Irony of Fate 2 (Ironiya sudby. Prodolzhenie)	RUS	Fiction—comedy	Russian	31	Yes
17	Wanted	USA/DEU/RUS	Fiction—action/adventure	English	27	No
18	I Am Legend	USA	Fiction—action/adventure	English	26	No
19	Admiral	RUS	Fiction—drama	Russian	24	No
20	Bathory	CZE/SVK/GBR/HUN	Fiction—drama	Czech/English/Slovak	20	No

SOURCE: See table 2.8.

NOTE: On weighted score, see table 2.8.

TABLE 2.8 Global Top-Twenty Feature Films, 2009

Rank	Title	Origin	Type	Language	Weighted score	Sequel or franchise (film or TV)
1	Ice Age: Dawn of the Dinosaurs	USA	Animation—family	English	450	Yes
2	Harry Potter and the Half-Blood Prince	UK/USA	Fiction—action/adventure	English	334	Yes
3	2012	USA	Fiction—action/adventure	English (some Tibetan, Mandarin)	304	No
4	Avatar	USA/UK	Fiction—action/adventure	English	302	Yes
5	The Twilight Saga: New Moon	USA	Fiction—drama	English	197	Yes
6	Up	USA	Animation—family	English	188	No
7	Angels and Demons	USA	Fiction—action/adventure	English (some Italian)	173	Yes
8	Transformers: Revenge of the Fallen	USA	Fiction—action/adventure	English	154	Yes
9	Slumdog Millionaire	UK	Fiction—drama	English (some Hindi)	64	No
10	The Hangover	USA/DEU	Fiction—comedy	English	57	Yes
11	Fast and Furious	USA	Fiction—action/adventure	English	43	Yes
12	Inglourious Basterds	USA/DEU	Fiction—action/adventure	English	36	No
13	The Proposal	USA	Fiction—comedy	English	32	No
14	Terminator Salvation	USA	Fiction—action/adventure	English	31	Yes
15	Bolt	USA	Animation—family	English	28	No

(continued)

TABLE 2.8 (continued)

Rank	Title	Origin	Type	Language	Weighted score	Sequel or franchise (film or TV)
16	The Girl with the Dragon Tattoo	SWE/DNK/DEU	Fiction—drama	Swedish	28	Yes
17	The Girl Who Played with Fire	SWE/DNK/DEU	Fiction—drama	Swedish	24	Yes
18	Michael Jackson's This Is It	USA	Documentary	English	23	No
19	Night at the Museum: Battle of the Smithsonian	USA	Fiction—family	English	23	Yes
20	Madagascar: Escape 2 Africa	USA	Animation—family	English	18	Yes

SOURCE FOR TABLES 2.6–2.8: Charles R. Acland, *From International Blockbusters to National Hits: Analysis of the 2010 UIS Survey of Feature Films* (Montreal: UNESCO Institute of Statistics, 2012), www.uis.unesco.org.

NOTE: Weighting accounts for a film's placement in annual top-ten lists for each country, assigning 1 to a tenth-ranked title and 10 to the first-ranked title. A higher weighted score represents a stronger presence on more top-ten lists for the year.

how comparable measures are across countries. But the data do show that while there are many popular films, most of which play with significant success within one or two countries but not in others, a small cadre of films play unusually well in many countries. These films are on a particular circuit; looking at the titles, we see that they overwhelmingly originate in the United States, though they are occasionally coproduced with the United Kingdom, English-language, and franchise entities. This is one representation of the American blockbuster circuit.

These films register the internationalist style of popular film. As varied as it may be and as far-flung its dispersion, this circuit announces another core idea—American cultural and economic values. These films present consistently as American: individualism as the primary narrative force, immodesty as self-empowerment, white as the predominant skin color, violence as necessary to community survival, consumerism as the natural social and economic system, liberalism as progressive and noncontroversial, skepticism of state and corporate institutions as a civic duty, racism and human rights

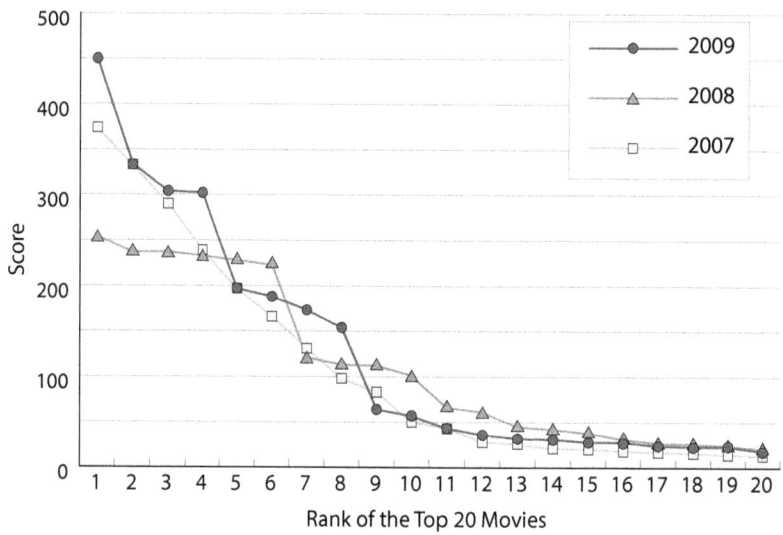

FIGURE 2.1 Scores of the top twenty feature films in 2007, 2008, and 2009
SOURCE: Charles R. Acland, *From International Blockbusters to National Hits: Analysis of the 2010 UIS Survey of Feature Films* (Montreal: UNESCO Institute of Statistics, 2012), www.uis.unesco.org.

atrocities as historical blights that friendship can mend, gender roles as open and varied, gender performance as a narrow binary range, romantic attraction as essentially heterosexual, and technology as an immediately available and magical solution. There are plenty of counterexamples, and further precision, that could deepen this list of ideological strains of American popular film. And, to that end, the specific figure of the American smart aleck, a prominent masculine trope that captures many of these elements and helps to humanize the technological environment, is discussed in detail in chapter 8. But these aspects most assuredly reverberate through the most popular movies in one way or another, and are repeated incessantly to the point that they have become broad narrative and thematic conventions.

The drumbeat of their predictability should not keep us from hearing the progressive heart that exists here, however faint it sounds. We find a foundational equalitarianism and a fortified agency, such that a dreamed-of better world for all is possible and just around the corner. The tone deafness to history and to the limits of individual action and privilege stifles whatever utopian impulse may lurk, but one can easily see how inspiring, appealing, and even radical many of these dimensions might be to audiences in restrictive social and cultural settings. In short, American blockbusters build degrees of freedom into their ideological armature, though always within a deeply embedded valorization of some individuals over others, and always via the commodity and technological form of the movie, its mode of production, and its mode of circulation.

These thematic elements, most of which land on an American ideal of individual power and effectiveness, are visually dispersed via the globe-trotting settings of blockbusters. Many American films are shot and set abroad, and we see films built as strategic tours of international scenery. Schwartz identified this in *Around the World in 80 Days*, and in many ways this approach to cosmopolitanism remains one of the templates for the contemporary blockbuster. Examples of elaborate globe-trotting with regard to shooting locations, especially featured in location-specific stunt sequences, can be seen in *Mission: Impossible—Ghost Protocol* (2011, filmed in India, the United Arab Emirates, Hungary, the Czech Republic, Canada, Russia, and California), *Skyfall* (2012, filmed in Turkey, Japan, China, Scotland, and England), and *Furious 7* (2015, filmed in California, Georgia, Colorado, Canada, United Arab Emirates, and Azerbaijan). Each features a vertigo-inducing action set piece in a gleaming office tower in the Arab or Asian worlds. Identifiable monuments become the stages for dramatic fights and stunts, as with Dubai's Burj Khalifa, considered the world's tallest skyscraper, in *Mission: Impossible—Ghost Protocol*. Scenes shot in the United Arab Emirates and images of that particular signature skyscraper were supplemented with computer-generated imagery, and interiors were filmed elsewhere in Dubai. In the same film, a sequence set in Mumbai, India, includes shooting on location there but also street and interior scenes set in Mumbai but shot in Vancouver. In other words, the internationalism of production does not necessarily match the internationalism of a film's settings, but both contribute to the impression of the cosmopolitan ease of the contemporary blockbuster.

Mission: Impossible—Rogue Nation (2015) provides a telling illustration. This film is part of a Hollywood courtship of Chinese funding and audiences. A Paramount release, its production entities include the California-based Skydance and Bad Robot along with the China Movie Channel and Chinese internet giant Alibaba Pictures. The shooting locations included Morocco, Austria, England, and Malaysia. The film, though, boasts action in the additional settings of Belarus, the United States, Cuba, and France. This difference invites confusion between where shooting has taken place and where action

FIGURE 2.2 Tom Cruise and cosmopolitan stunt, *Mission: Impossible—Ghost Protocol*, 2011

is set; the internationalism of the production and that of the diegesis do not match. Marking the distinctiveness of locations are shots of landmark buildings: the Eiffel Tower in Paris; the U.S. Capitol and Washington Monument in Washington, DC; the Menara KL Tower in Kuala Lumpur; Tower Bridge and Big Ben in London; the Vienna State Opera in Vienna; and the Hassan II Mosque in Casablanca. The transitions from one location to another are seamless. The opening sequence, involving an airplane taking off in Minsk, but actually shot in England, is crosscut with characters located in Kuala Lumpur. The image is one of simultaneous participation across time zones and geopolitical boundaries. At one point, playing on the magic of international movement, we are led to believe Ethan (Tom Cruise) is in Havana while on the run, pursued and observed in real time by CIA personnel in Langley, Virginia, but he is revealed to really be hiding in Paris. In this instance, three different locations connect, though the CIA's global surveillance operation is thwarted. Only the film spectator has the total view, though momentarily misled, compressing all three locations into a single sequence. The movements of characters and the story from England to Austria to Morocco and back to England are instantaneous, with no travel time nor arrangements depicted. Early in the film, Ethan defies death hanging onto the exterior of a plane during takeoff in

Belarus and moments later walks up out of an underground station in London. The result is an impression of frictionless flow across these locations. Difficulty and drama arise only when he has to enter or exit particular buildings, not when crossing international borders or time zones.

Blockbusters may celebrate their international inflections in setting and talent, and they may be products of a network of cross-jurisdictional financial incentives. Watching them is an audiovisual illustration of these internationalist forces in which blockbusters figure as a distinctly global iteration of an American economic and cultural engine. Further, they agglomerate capital such that many interests have a great deal riding on just a few cultural commodities. They are object lessons of the end point of a capitalist equation. But unlike the relatively lasting impression architecture makes on a cityscape, blockbusters vary each season, week by week, and with each slate of releases. The ebb and flow of films as they are released to theaters produces an in-process vista of the popular image world, with the franchise as the lasting entity that bridges this changing scene. The current cinema—namely, those newly released titles in theaters—becomes an ephemeral, never-to-be-exactly-repeated palette of cultural offerings at multiplexes near you, a slate that then migrates to an extended life in other media.[46] This provisional slate of offerings is a snapshot of the global American popular scene.

The sheer monetary value of blockbuster films makes them especially prized entities for the potential economic injection they represent. On the production side of the equation, for cities, states, provinces, and countries, winning a blockbuster shoot or postproduction work and having substantial sums spent locally in a relatively short time frame, along with the multiplier effect of the secondary economic activity such productions generate, means that blockbusters quite literally build roads, bridges, schools, and other infrastructure. For example, a study of the economic impact of *Iron Man 3* (2013), filmed in Wilmington, North Carolina, found that $180 million was spent in the state, creating work for over two thousand people. It resulted in nearly nine dollars of economic output for every dollar of tax credit received.[47] The employment generated—mostly short-term contract work—supplemented the tax dollars collected during the usual operations of business. Of course, this is a fickle economy, at the mercy of unpredictable winds like currency valuation and local policy battles, along with all the other forces that try to cheapen labor and advantage investors. Additionally, financially favorable jurisdictions have become lightning rods for fiscally conservative politicians with their neoliberal economic agendas, who see film-friendly policies as corporate welfare, picking winners and not allowing the free market to make decisions about local economies.

From time to time, industry reports seek to support these neoliberal economic views. For example, the University of Southern California's Michael Thom released research in 2016 that showed limited benefit from tax credits for film and television production.[48] The MPAA vigorously challenged Thom's basic claims, correctly pointing out that he used broad definitions of entertainment jobs, including ones that had no relationship to the incentives in question, hence diluting their impact.[49] Nonetheless, despite ample solid evidence of the economic advantages of media production incentives, Thom's report was symptomatic of a wide swing against these measures, which resulted in some states, including Michigan and North Carolina, withdrawing them and sending productions elsewhere. The mobility of contemporary production processes means that when one financially favorable location disappears, movement to another venue is almost always an option. In this way blockbusters typify our phase of advanced capitalism and emblematize a top-heavy form of post-Fordist flexible production, able to leapfrog from one location to another at a moment's notice with relatively little consideration of the impact such movement has on people's lives.

Put differently, a blockbuster, encapsulating contemporary ideas about big-budget entertainment, is a movie and an industrial strategy perfectly in tune with other contemporary investment finance vehicles. The mobile construction site and the fluctuating skyline of blockbuster movies would not be notable or distinctive were it not for their size and prominence. They are globally visible, appearing in a scheduled fashion, and popular awareness of them transcends many limitations of distance and difference.

This display value, the audiovisual and economic lesson they broadcast, is part of the design of the blockbuster. Movies can really only be blockbusters insomuch as they are talked about as such, promoted as such. For this reason, Stringer described blockbusters as "the most public kind of popular cinema, and a key part of the genre's attractions has always been its ability to flaunt its assets and speak in a loud voice—in short, to create audience awareness." He elaborated that "the promise of ever-increasing levels of audio-visual intemperance lies at the heart of the commercial film industry's ability to rejuvenate itself."[50] Assertions about tonnage—star wattage, financial heft, grueling shooting schedules, distant locations, and so on—thus become sites of competition between industry participants and overarching arguments for the amassing of resources. Each blockbuster is a shrill statement saying, "Look what an obscene amount of talent and money produces! Your thrills are a product of an organization of financial mechanisms and skill sets. Consider these factors as you enjoy the next two hours and ten minutes!" Is it any wonder that we have seen volume and running time of such films tick upward? Richard Maltby has called this the "commercial aesthetic" of contemporary film, in which the budget in some way must be apparent on-screen.[51] He quoted producer James Schamus on this point, who bluntly stated, "The budget is the aesthetic."[52] In the final analysis "show me the money" is an internationalist stylistic command.

Technological wonders are essential to the blockbuster's internationalist commercial aesthetic, to their status as resource magnets, and to their function as powerful organizers of meaning and commodities. Technological wonder energizes audiences in a variety of forms. Scientific and industrial innovation has enjoyed significant attention in world's fairs, exhibitions, and museums owing to its display value for over a century and a half. Those venues celebrated the might of transportation, energy, and manufacturing as a national and corporate accomplishment, equally demonstrating core values of modernity and the essential contributions of technological progress. Technological tricks also found their way into popular entertainment. And in popular movies, tricks and wonders elicited delightful laughs and surprises, a welcome and tame version of what otherwise might be remote processes disconnected from life.

There has been a dark side. For all the comforts afforded by the application of new scientific knowledge, the devastating consequences of the unchecked pursuit of progress have left us with expansively inhumane rationality that serves technology rather than human society. Lewis Mumford, perhaps our most sustained critical voice on the illogic of technocratic society, documented the historical and evolutionary limitations of the last turn of human development toward "the vanity of modern 'Technological Man,' that ghost clad in iron."[53] Exterminations, famines, and general planetary suffering have been the indisputable legacy of the "machine-minded technologists," whose capitalist drive will always put things and processes over creatures and environments.[54] One function Mumford identified as part of our machine-mindedness is "technological exhibitionism," the modification of scientific knowledge for the purposes of display. The pyramids of ancient Egypt and the U.S. space program were parallel examples of technological exhibitionism for Mumford; both were impressive examples of the height of scientific and organizational achievement, and both were superfluous to the most pressing needs of their contexts. He specifically worried about the trivialization this represented, writing, "While many admirable inventions have sprung from children's playthings (the telephone, the motion picture, the helicopter), current technological exhibitionism reverses the creative process by turning elaborate and costly technical innovations into trivial toys."[55] There is another angle; the exhibitionism spectacularizes processes and innovations that would otherwise be difficult to grasp, let alone take pleasure in. The ability to produce a pleasing impression, a shock of surprise, and a sense of wonderment is a step toward making technology safe and desirable. The public marriage between science and education, between industry and entertainment, pushes a hierarchy of value that elevates machine-mindedness. Technological exhibitionism sells the ideology of progress, which has been deformed as an ideology of capitalist expansion and dehumanization.

Many venues contribute to normalizing and valorizing machine-mindedness: the science center, the technologically invested classroom, the corporate pavilion at a world exposition, and the production of gadget-wise populations of consumers. But motion pictures have made a special contribution to this project. As an entertainment that burst forth as a practical industrial application, movies have carried the wonderment of the modern world with them. Ross Melnick made a related point when he showed how by the 1920s leading American exhibitors understood their business as one that involved film alongside a number of other converging media and entertainments. In this way the lavish movie palaces of that era were as much palaces of modern media technology as they were film venues.[56] The blockbuster film, then, was no newcomer to the scene. But in the 1950s, the entire American film and entertainment industry would be reoriented around the big, expensive, technologically enhanced production. Technological exhibitionism worked as tiny, local nudges that kept people directed toward the promises of a technological future. And today the blockbuster still operates as a popular representational practice appropriate to our cultural priorities of cosmopolitan ease and technological exhibitionism.

The blockbuster movie is the most successful, and most identifiably American, cinematic form, exported with many of its ideals about spectacle, wonderment, cosmopolitanism, and resource inflation intact. Its display value references its investment in popular pleasure and financial agglomeration, announcing the very logic that produced it. To identify the forces that led to our current situation, I now return to the earliest instances in which the term "blockbuster" appeared. The next four chapters trace the term's migration into the media industries, its circulation to popular audiences, and its formulation as a shorthand idea about commerce and entertainment. Of the concepts it carries about popular pleasure and investment, one resurfaces time and again: technological progress. The blockbuster as a technological tentpole embodies an industrial strategy for an integrated media economy, characterized by technological wonder, new media relations, and cosmopolitanism. And this valuation of the big and the loud has been part of the history of the term "blockbuster" ever since it first began to circulate during World War II as an innovative Allied military ordnance deployed to defeat Adolf Hitler.

PART II THE RISE OF THE BLOCKBUSTER

(CHAPTER THREE)

DELIVERING BLOCKBUSTERS

I n the spring of 1943, the first blockbuster arrived in New York City. It did not arrive in a Broadway theater, a movie palace, or Radio City Music Hall, but in Rockefeller Plaza. There, the Office of War Information (OWI) launched an outdoor exhibit called *The Nature of the Enemy*. Situated between the British Empire building and La Maison Française, the exhibit, designed by OWI deputy director Leo Rosten and produced by Rockefeller Center's director of display, Robert Carson, *The Nature of the Enemy* depicted the loss of freedom that would follow a fascist victory in World War II. Large-scale photographic prints presented black-and-white imagery of Axis devastation, featuring the ruins of Pearl Harbor as well as those of Chinese and European cities (figures 3.1 and 3.2). These huge panels of photojournalism emphasized the faces of terrorized citizens, with destroyed communities as their backdrop: a broken rickshaw behind a crying, maybe screaming, elderly Chinese woman; hands covering anguished faces; civilians walking away from a bombed cityscape carrying a few meager possessions.

Accompanying the large-scale photographs, six dramatic tableaux shocked audiences with book burning, denigration of religious symbols, and child warriors sporting gas masks and guns along with shorts and knee-high socks. One reconstructed a concentration camp, though the full horror of the Holocaust was still hidden from the American public and did not figure in this representation. Hitler appeared in the "Abolition of Justice" tableau as a presiding judge, the court bench emblazoned with the Nazi eagle and swastika; "Slavery" presented Americans being forced to build bombs at gunpoint. The displays were on raised platforms that one newspaper described as "coffin-black" and included printed quotations from Hitler.[1] Running the length of the depictions, a few stories high along an adjacent building, a banner read, "The Enemy Plans This for You." Special guests spoke as part of the exhibit. Journalist John B. Powell, maimed in a Japanese prison, provided firsthand testimony of his inhumane treatment. Eve Curie, National Book Award winner for her biography of her mother, Marie Curie, spoke as well. To complete the multisensory experience, *The Nature of the Enemy* incorporated a soundtrack compiled from captured German films and played through loudspeakers. As attendees walked among the displays, they heard speeches from the *Führer* and shouts of "Heil Hitler!"[2]

The Nature of the Enemy opened on May 16, 1943, with 2,500 visitors, though some reported a smaller crowd of 1,000. This number grew throughout the run of the display, which closed a few weeks later on the democratically symbolic date of Independence Day.[3] Gordon Parks, Roger Smith, and Arthur S. Siegel received the assignment to produce a photographic record of the exhibit. The images confirm the crowds and show a continuous tone between the imaginary future of America under fascism and the large-scale photographs of Axis bombing. Monumental photography was on display in full splendor, the unusually large blowups towering over spectators, melding actual documentary evidence and imagined horrors to come. The displays helped prepare audiences for a long and painful war. They also primed them to buy the war bonds being sold at one end of the concourse.[4]

And the booth selling war bonds included a new weapon: a "blockbuster" bomb. People could inspect it up close and were invited to sign it following a bond purchase, with promises that it would then be delivered to Berlin.[5] "Sign the Block-Buster Headed for Hitler" read the notice over the display (figures 3.3 and 3.4). The back of the booth read, "Buy a Bond and Bomb Berlin." Guarantees that this was more than a bond-drive ruse were necessary. A letter from Lieutenant General Brehon B. Somervell, commander of the Army Service Forces, posted in full view beside the bomb, assured bond-buying Americans that "this bomb will be dropped on Berlin."[6] The booth was right next to a gigantic image of the bombing of Pearl Harbor, reminding people of the surprise attack that had brought the United States into the war

FIGURE 3.1 *The Nature of the Enemy* exhibit, 1943. Photo by Arthur S. Siegel

FIGURE 3.2 *The Nature of the Enemy* concourse, 1943. Photo by Gordon Parks

FIGURE 3.3 *The Nature of the Enemy* war bond booth, 1943. Photo by Arthur S. Siegel

FIGURE 3.4 *The Nature of the Enemy* blockbuster bomb at war bond booth, 1943. Photo by Arthur S. Siegel

FIGURE 3.5 *Desperate Journey* press book, detail of "lobby bomb," 1942

in the first place. The patriotic tactic of weapon display was not unique. The press kit for *Desperate Journey* (1942) recommended that movie theater owners exploit the film by having a thousand-pound bombshell in the lobby for buyers of war bonds to sign (figure 3.5).[7] In Canada there were similar public blockbuster-signing campaigns to sell war bonds, with promises to have the Royal Canadian Air Force drop the autographed bomb on Germany.[8] In the United States, state fairs had blockbusters on display, alongside other munitions, which in Louisiana was used to drive home the fact that peanut farming contributed to the food supply and provided essential lubrication for weapons and machinery.[9] In 1944, at the Southeastern World's Fair in Atlanta, the "March to Victory" theme was enhanced by the presence of a blockbuster and a rocket launcher, both weapons of the future.[10] Invest in one nation, cheer the obliteration of another.

Overlapping with *The Nature of the Enemy* was an exhibition of Norman Rockwell's paintings of the four freedoms—freedom of speech, freedom of worship, freedom from want, and freedom from fear—in the International Building of Rockefeller Center. The exhibit's cosponsors were the U.S. Department of Treasury, the *Saturday Evening Post*, and the Fifth Avenue Association, neatly linking government, journalism, and commerce, the kind of intersector coordination wartime emergencies produce. In an advertisement encouraging the purchase of war bonds, IBM promoted Rockwell's exhibit and directed people to the OWI's nearby *The Nature of the Enemy*, thus adding the corporate technology sector to these aligned American institutions.[11] As part of its multimedia mobilization campaign, the OWI's pamphlet "The Four Freedoms" used a similar technique. It presented photographic depictions of the freedoms with contrasting images on facing pages. Newspaper production represented "Freedom of Speech," and on the opposite page, book burning represented "Suppression of Speech."[12] To extend the theme across Rockefeller Center, the "Four Freedoms" were draped in chains for the duration of *The Nature of the Enemy*.[13] Highlighting the dramatic contrast between democratic freedom and totalitarian enslavement was thought to be an effective tool for education and mobilization.

The binary choice between freedom and slavery dramatized with brutal clarity the virtuousness of the armed conflict that was underway. The need for mass mobilization, for putting millions on notice and in step toward a common military end, required such rhetorical definitiveness. The shock provided by monumental photography of fascistic inhumanity blunted any hesitations that might surface about the goal of this mass mobilization. The war was good enough to justify the means employed, so the reasoning went, and the work of the OWI went a long way to demonstrating this.

Midtown New York had already hosted other site-specific propaganda efforts. Most memorable was the *Road to Victory* exhibit, a collaboration between poet Carl Sandberg and photographer Edward Steichen, at the Museum of Modern Art (MOMA). Subtitled "A Procession of Photographs of the Nation at War," the exhibition featured images of Americans, military and civilian, at work for the war effort. Running from May to October 1942 on the remodeled and open-concept second floor at MOMA on Fifty-Third Street, *Road to Victory* consisted of giant photography, "mural-size enlargements," as the press release stated, "one of which measures 10 feet × 40 feet, and most of which are not less than 3 feet × 4 feet."[14]

Monumental photography had representational advantages for these exhibits. The unusual size seized attention and invited audiences to look at the details of the scenes displayed before them. The scale made their depictions more insistent and urgent. They were the visual equivalent of shouting at the viewer, an image in bold and all caps. Installations of these large-scale images gave dimensionality to otherwise-flat depictions. One walked through and around them, in this way exploring the sequence of images and their themes with one's entire body. And, crucially for the propagandistic agenda of these explorations of national mobilization and totalitarianism, the photographs were decidedly, deliberately, documentary. As superscaled as they were, their realist aesthetic gave them a journalistic value, rather like news from the front lines. These were monumental reports of the world in flames and the people of the nation preparing heroically to meet the horrors of modern warfare together.[15]

The opening crowds at *The Nature of the Enemy* were no accident. The launch coincided with the second "I Am an American Day" of the war, in which people reaffirmed their loyalty to the republic. Declarations from new citizens were especially encouraged and featured. Events took place across the country, and Central Park—a few blocks north of Rockefeller Plaza—had a reported million people gather to participate, certainly an exaggerated number.[16] Only a few days earlier was the public premiere of Frank Capra's *Prelude to War* (1942), one of the most powerful motion picture propaganda works the OWI would produce. By May 1943 the film had already been seen by an estimated six million American military personnel but had not yet been made available to the general public. This first run, before the film opened to the rest of the country at the end of the month, was at the Strand Theater in nearby Times Square, just west of Rockefeller Plaza.

These informational and propagandistic activities were part of the wide-ranging programs of the OWI, and they provided an interpretation of the global historical context, one that was spectacularly direct in its stark depiction of the forces of good and evil. The special added attraction of a blockbuster bomb, though, opens up a historical line for the present purposes. Here, at one capital of the American entertainment business, was an early opportunity to see the newest and most advanced Allied weapon. The ordnance was fresh and lethal, and here it was for audiences to marvel at its size. Mobilized to impress were Hollywood names, famous artists, notable intellectuals, stirring photographic displays . . . and a bomb, all ingredients to provoke emotions and convince people of the rightness of the national emergency. Exhibits presented the urgency of the world situation, and the inhumanity of the enemy, but at some point a path to victory would appear. Allied know-how ensured that fascism would be vanquished. The presence of that nine-foot-high bomb, that towering brute, was evidence of a future victory. The goal of the exhibit *The Nature of the Enemy*, as with many propaganda efforts, was to develop an agreed-upon negative assessment of the nation's foes and then offer a way to do something. The immediate function was to sell war bonds, but loftier goals were boosting morale and promoting coordinated mobilization for the war effort. The new weapon had been completely unknown only a few months earlier. And here it was, in Rockefeller Plaza, a strange destructive beast, a product of military engineering and industrial innovation. A blockbuster.

At the end of 1945, after the war, linguist James Bender included "block-buster" in a list of a couple dozen words introduced or popularized during

World War II that would likely last and find a permanent place in the English language: "blackout," "commando," "convoy," "ersatz," "walkie-talkie," "jeep," and "genocide." At that time, "blockbuster" referred exclusively to a "large, highly effective bomb."[17] Our current usage was still far from being realized. And yet this popular military term—for what is today an eighty-year-old weapon—came to be an ordinary part of our cultural universe. How did a term for a bomb get included in both the popular and the business lexicon as a word for a hybrid industrial entertainment genre? How did an instrument of destruction come to designate an expensive and profitable cultural artifact? There is something vaguely unsettling about the lineage. It would be glib to say that the persistence of "blockbuster" is simply a symptom of the subterranean militarization of our entertainment consciousness. Instead, I ask, what laid the foundation for this persistence, and what traces of the World War II usage remain? What follows is an account of the conditions that coincided with the initial migration from one location to another, from an association with military technology and weaponry to a cultural entity and entertainment-business strategy.

In the first instance, this was no ordinary explosive. Quite the contrary, there had never been a bomb like this. These were the "largest size bombs," with "incomparably greater destructive power" than anyone had ever seen before, including the enemy.[18] The British Royal Air Force (RAF) in 1940 made the first four-thousand-pound high-capacity bomb. "High-capacity" referenced the bomb's destructive power, given its weight. Two years later, the RAF produced eight-thousand-pound bombs, sometimes called "super block-busters."[19] Continuing the inflation of weight and its association with greater destructive power, through 1943 and 1944 British bomb development moved bomb weights to twelve thousand pounds, then twenty-two thousand pounds, each iteration becoming the biggest explosive ever manufactured and deployed. These were called "factory busters" or "earthquake bombs" rather than "blockbusters."[20] Despite their impressive girth, and the attention these gargantuan weapons attracted, the RAF used comparatively few of them. They were simply too heavy to handle and deploy, working better as publicity for military innovation. In contrast, tens of thousands of the four-thousand-pound blockbusters rained down on German cities, as well as hundreds of thousands of medium-capacity and high-capacity bombs weighing from five hundred to eight thousand pounds.[21]

The military term for the four-thousand-pound ordnance was a "cookie." The Germans called them "boilers," because they looked like part of a heating system. But "blockbuster" stuck as the most broadly circulated name, initially written with a hyphen. In 1944 U.S. linguists recorded the term "blockbuster" as originating with the British press in 1942, saying it described the bomb's ability to destroy entire buildings, as in "a block of flats." U.S. newspapers immediately picked up the appellation but mistook the British specificity, believing it referred to the ability to flatten city blocks.[22] In July 1942, in the first official announcement from the RAF about the scope of these bombs' use, Raymond Daniell wrote in the *New York Times* of an attack that dropped fifty of these two-ton bombs on Duisburg. Not yet using the term that would soon become familiar to civilians, Daniell described this "most destructive weapon yet devised" as having "enough concentrated destruction to level a whole city block." Size, newness, power, and unique availability to the Allies distinguished this advanced weaponry, all connotations that would be associated with "blockbusters." One other connotation—effectiveness—sealed the status of these bombs as strategically advantageous. On this count, Daniell wrote simply, "the damage they had done was terrific."[23]

That same week, "RAF 'Block Busters' Blast Hamburg" put the weapon and nomenclature in the headlines in American newspapers.[24] John Collingwood Reade introduced Canadian readers to the term in early August 1942, reporting that Allied Liberators and Flying Fortresses had longer-range capabilities and could carry blockbusters as far as Kiev, Odessa, and Constanța.[25] Prominent early use came from American war correspondent Joe Alex Morris, stationed in London to report on the Allied war effort.[26] He may have been fed the moniker by the RAF, but without a doubt his plentiful articles in U.S. papers ensured the American public became familiar with the ordnance by the end of 1942.

"Block-buster" had an early appearance in the *New York Times*' regular column "Twenty News Questions," which quizzed readers on their knowledge of recent events, in August 1942. This appearance signaled novelty and notability. The question asked for the best definition from the following: "a) a gun designed to destroy block houses; b) a weapon like the Molotov cocktail for use against tanks; c) an aerial bomb; d) crusher used in laying out airfields."[27] Soon, coverage about this weapon expanded, and general readers became so familiar with it that this question would have been far too easy for a trivia quiz.

From the fall of 1942 through the rest of the war, blockbusters were a major reference point for describing the Allied strategy to the American and British public. In September 1942 *Life* published a pictorial feature about the Allied bombing campaign on the occasion of the first appearance of a new large British Lancaster bomber in North America, which landed in Canada. The "heavy bomber" was a key tactical advantage for the RAF; it was best designed to carry the heavy new blockbusters to their targets in Europe.[28]

Americans devoted considerable resources to building planes with as long a range and as much payload capability as those of the RAF. Only British planes could carry blockbusters on bombing runs during the first years of the war. Upon entry into the war, the United States expanded its fleet and weaponry and, like the British, also aimed to go beyond the blockbuster to the "super-block-buster."[29] By 1943 the OWI featured the U.S. Liberator, the heavy bomber designed to carry blockbusters to their targets, in its glossy magazine *Victory*, a wartime publication released in several languages for international audiences.[30] Public engagement with the war involved programs describing the number of readied military personnel, the number of vehicles and weapons stockpiled, the efficiency of industrial production of military equipment, and the speedy advancement of technology. The OWI was specifically charged to do this, producing films, pamphlets, and magazines. The exhibit *The Nature of the Enemy* was one of their more elaborate site-specific efforts. Their inventory of materials and arguments boosted morale and provided concrete evidence that the enemy could be beaten. Touting weapons and military personnel made national industrial might visible and understandable; blockbuster use in the air war was part of this effort to sell this just war. In other words, the blockbuster began its life as a creature of publicity as well as a weapon; it was new and contemporary, and it circulated as a manifestation of World War II and no other armed conflict. Importantly, it belonged to the Allied forces alone.

When first introduced, the blockbuster was the highest-capacity explosive ever developed and deployed. As such, it was material evidence of the technological and industrial prowess of the forces that had produced that mammoth power. This shining example of progress celebrated the might and modernity of the British and American war machine. Many began to use the term to apply to virtually any large bomb used during World War II. But the original blockbuster was the product of a specific design innovation. Other large bombs had been encased in very heavy metal, and the bigger the ordnance, the heavier the casing. This meant that transportation was difficult and costly, and upon impact the explosion would be dampened by the bomb's own thick shell, though the metal casing would break into small pieces and fly through the air to rip apart buildings and flesh. Blockbusters, in contrast, consisted of as thin a metal casing as possible for a multiton ordnance in order to maximize the destructive force of the explosion itself. The blockbuster was about bigness and brutishness, but it was the ratio of explosive power to total weight that was novel, its "high-capacity."

Buildings, not humans, were supposed to be the target. This claim rested at the ethical heart of the entire air war. The bulk of the justifications produced by the RAF declared that facilities that aided the enemy war effort were the primary focus for this weapon. The damage done to civilian life, and the deaths directly and indirectly caused by the air campaign, were known to the Allied command structure, though they were hidden from the public. The operations of the air war promoted the humane and efficient nature of the Allied air strategy, contrary to all evidence received of the devastation to civilians.

Besides the thin metal casing, there was nothing especially thoughtful in the design of the "cookie," and even with the lighter casing, the sheer weight created a number of other operational problems. Few planes could carry something that heavy, and special tracks had to move the bombs to the planes and then, when the planes were over the targets, to the bomb-bay doors. It was about as inelegant as a bomb could get. There was little accounting for aerodynamics, making them terribly inaccurate. The blast radius was so vast that planes had to drop them from great heights to avoid being caught in the explosion, which only compounded the inaccuracy. Besides the physical dimensions of the bomb, other aspects of Allied bombing strategy put the lie to the much-heralded bloodless surgical attack on infrastructure that this marvel of modern weaponry was supposed to allow.

The Allied air strategy did not spring from British and American tacticians alone but had been formed from the changes to modern war that had been amassing since the turn of the twentieth century. The transfer of warfare from land and sea to the air had been in process since the mid-nineteenth century, when hot-air balloons offered a surveillance advantage. World War I introduced experimental efforts in air warfare, with relatively small-scale attacks and bombings coming from biplanes and dirigibles, and with high-altitude bombing of military installations and cities. Peter Sloterdijk observed that the early use of airplanes for combat coincided with biological warfare using poisonous gases. As he commented, the Great War included a general idea about an air war, in which the front moved to the air that surrounded you, and with this came new ethical standards.[31] British bombing of colonial

Iraq in the 1920s, and Japanese bombing of China and German bombing of Spain in the mid-1930s, set the stage for a more complete use of aerial bombing of civilian populations.[32] The German saturation bombings during the Spanish Civil War marked a turn toward intensive and sustained bombing, ignoring the inability to protect civilian populations during such actions. But World War II saw the realization of, and reliance on, strategic bombing as central to wartime strategy. So full was the embrace and perfection of the air war by the Allied Forces that Lewis Mumford identified it as a key illustration of the operation of the "megamachine," a technological orientation of civilization that ultimately hinged on antihumanist assumptions. Mumford wrote specifically of the "extermination bombing" campaigns of the British and American forces, describing them as "an unconditional moral surrender to Hitler."[33]

In response to Nazi bombing of the United Kingdom in 1940 and 1941, Winston Churchill and his military strategists, in particular Arthur Harris, head of the RAF's Bomber Command, devised the most complete realization of industrial warfare yet. In place of a horizontal ground war against military personnel in which territory was defended and recovered as one moved through enemy-controlled areas, they extended the front vertically, up into the air. They targeted the facilities that fed the war machine, including weapons factories, transportation hubs, and fuel refineries. They extended the front to those whose job it was to run those facilities, such as factory workers, railway employees, and oil refiners. This target extension moved on to those who provided support to those workers, which meant basically everyone. In this way, too, the urban industrial nature of this brand of warfare stretched into the countryside, where fresh drinking water and agricultural crops became military targets. Ostensibly, there was no civilian population in this mad calculus. The euphemistic language claimed that the air strategy involved "precision bombing."[34] But a popular version circulated during the war: "terror bombing."[35]

Many Hollywood films about bomber crews through the 1940s and 1950s depicted the air campaign, offering heroic, if utterly erroneous, reassurance about the humane conduct it represented. In actuality, several factors militated against this. Bombing sights had a limited degree of accuracy, despite recent advancements; environmental factors like clouds and smoke interfered with visibility; and there was a human impulse to release payloads quickly in order to return home faster, which produced something called the "creep-back effect," with bombs tending to hit areas shy of the actual targets.[36] In

1942 John Steinbeck wrote *Bombs Away: The Story of a Bomber Team*, a portrait of the training and camaraderie of a U.S. Air Force bomber crew. With little about the actual cargo, Steinbeck documented the various techniques and technologies that crew members had to master, all in the service of accurate targeting.[37] Training for the new bombsights figured in *Bombardier* (1943), with the actual name—the Norden bombsight—never used, in order to maintain secrecy. Instead, it is referred to as the "golden goose," which also appears in the lyrics for the film's "Song of the Bombardier." The golden eggs, presumably, are the bombs. The imagistic version, though, from that movie to the postwar classic *Twelve O'Clock High* (1949), maintains a sense of the courageous legacy of pilots and crew, however fraught their experience may have been. *Fighter Squadron* (1948), following American pilots based in England and flying raids over Germany, is so jaunty that a good portion of the film is light comedy, especially during the air-combat sequences in which the American pilots make offhanded comments during bombings—"A man could get his tail burned," "Hey fellas, a gas station; fill 'er up," "By the rockets' red glare," "Have one on me," "Don't report for work tomorrow"— intercut with actual combat footage in color. The impression is that these pilots are supremely brave and competent, if smart-alecky, as every bomb and machine-gun strafing hits its mark. And every target is presented as obviously military. *The Dam Busters* (1955), depicting the precision of bouncing bombs destroying a German dam (the inspiration for the Death Star attack at the climax of *Star Wars: Episode IV—A New Hope*, 1977), doesn't go on to show the roughly 1,300 civilians, including Ukrainian forced laborers, who drowned downstream as a result.[38]

Efforts to strike only military facilities pale when compared to the overall bombing strategy, which identified densely populated areas as desirable targets. Allied plans and their related public relation materials referred to "marshalling yards," but this meant cities.[39] These were the conditions of pure and total war, a war waged from a distance, from above, from aircraft. As Jörg Friedrich wrote in his chronicle of the Allied bombing of Germany, *The Fire: The Bombing of Germany, 1940–1945*, "The bombing . . . eliminated all previous inhibitions against killing. The honor of the warrior, which once demanded that the defenseless be protected rather than massacred, was fading away."[40] Of the many horrifying features of World War II, one of the most lasting was the perfection of the mass civilian target as acceptable in warfare. There was no such thing as microtargeting from the air—that comes with drones decades later, where similar language of "precision" and "accuracy" obscures civilian casualties.[41] That an unimaginable approach to war, pursued with the confidence provided by technological superiority, was moved to the status of reasonableness haunted the rest of the century. War from the air had existed in a limited fashion before World War II, and the inhumane treatment of civilians during times of war has a deep and sickening history. But nothing compares with the novel scale of civilian targeting and the complete disregard for the distinction between the spheres of military and civilian life that were normalized during that 1940s. The American decision to use atomic weapons on Hiroshima and Nagasaki had, in a sense, already been made in the German bombing of Britain and then the British and U.S. bombing of Germany. On this point, historian John Dower commented that "the moral as well as strategic Rubicon was crossed before the birth of the nuclear age. Deliberately killing non-combatants is hardly new to war, but in World War II it became part and parcel of a new age of 'total war' and ostensibly sophisticated 'psychological warfare.' Modern war breeds its own cultures, and incinerating civilians is one of them."[42]

A significant observation was made by Churchill, Harris, and their staff. Postbombing fires were much more devastating than the high-capacity bombs themselves. Therefore, through careful calculations of physics and materials, Bomber Command pursued the development of a new weapon: the deliberate igniting of fire from the air. More precisely, they designed and implemented an elemental form of warfare: the firestorm. Descriptions of these conflagrations hardly circulated in any elaborate form through the war, and even afterward. As W. G. Sebald elegantly proposed in his book *On the Natural History of Destruction*, the extreme conditions for the firestorm were so beyond comprehension that those who lived through the bombings of German cities demonstrated a systematic inability to describe it. Sebald wrote that the firestorms were "obliterated from the retrospective understanding of those affected."[43] In these storms, flames reached two kilometers into the sky. The fires sucked away so much oxygen that many didn't burn to death but suffocated. The physics of air being drawn into such enormous fires created hurricane-force winds that literally pulled more fuel into the flames, human and otherwise. The heat was so intense that metal and glass melted. These were astonishing and desired results. Once they had successfully created it, the RAF used the firestorm weapon again and again, beyond all strategic advantage, burning Hamburg, Kassel, Dresden, Berlin, and dozens of other cities. The Americans used this firebombing strategy in Japan, where the predominantly wood construction and absence of firewalls between structures meant that the conflagrations were even more extensive and deadly.

Blockbusters had a very specific role in these firestorm bombing runs from 1942 through 1945. They fell alongside lighter incendiary bombs, which were typically between four and fifteen pounds. Airplanes dropped the two ordnances simultaneously, or as part of the same squadron raid, and the heavier blockbusters hit the ground first. With careful attention to the destructive effectiveness of different combinations of payloads, Bomber Command identified the most devastating as one 4,000-pound high-capacity blockbuster and seventeen bomb containers full of incendiaries plus another container one-third full.[44] In fact, before the firebombing campaign, blockbusters were dropped with parachutes to slow their descent and increase accuracy, though this never really worked. In any case, the drop accuracy of a single cookie was no longer part of the RAF's new strategy. Accuracy didn't matter as much in the firestorm plan. Instead, the blockbusters were to break up the city below, destroy firewalls between buildings, and increase the flammable surface area and oxygen flow, all in the interest of creating the best conditions for flames to ignite, spread, and join up with other fires. The blockbusters created the kindling that was then seeded with the small incendiaries. Bomber Command pored over insurance maps for German cities and took stock of the locations of firewalls and the construction materials used in buildings, selecting the most ignitable locations and targeting them with bombing runs that involved the combination of these two types of explosives. This role was concealed, with focus placed on the supposed accuracy of the blockbusters. For example, in *Bombardier* a bombing raid on Japan is to begin with incendiaries to light up targets for better use of the "golden goose" bombsights in order to "drop those blockbusters on there!," as a pilot yells. This misinformation, inverting the actual steps in the tactical use of incendiaries, had been legitimized by the appearance of General Eugene L. Eubank of the U.S. Air Force at the start of the film.

Industrial warfare made all industries, and all support for the operation of those industries, military targets. All of human society was on the front lines; the front itself was converted into a fluid entity. The firestorms that erupted were a postbombing phenomenon, raging unpredictably for days after an initial raid. Bomber Command was not so deluded as to believe they were not bombing civilians. The justification for the normalization of atrocity began from an initial sense of justice: the Germans were the aggressors and deserved this punishment. British political and military strategists characterized the campaign as "dehousing," targeting the homes of people to deprive them of habitable structures, rather than targeting the inhabitants. But the rationalization moved on to a more calculated goal of neutralizing the enemy population's will to continue fighting, as part of the psychological warfare described by Dower. Bomber Command characterized their air attacks as "morale bombing." People suffered, and buildings were demolished, but an additional objective was to shock the civilian population into a state of hopelessness. American reporting appeared almost gleeful when presenting the extent of the devastation. Citing a Swedish journalist in Berlin, an editorial in the *New York Times* from 1943 reported, "Whole districts in the centre of the city have been wiped out, and the industrial suburbs have been so successfully blasted that only a few feet of brick wall remain of one factory a third of a mile long. But what impressed the observer most was the incapacity of the administrative machinery to deal with the havoc. There is no material to build additional shelters or restore damaged buildings, no hospital space for the raid victims, no personnel to handle the cumulative problems of homelessness and breakdown of civilian services."[45] Unapologetically, the targets included civilians and civilian operations, and the disabling of hospitals and air-raid shelters merited notice as much as the incapacitation of industry.

Oddly, evidence seems to suggest that morale was not exactly deflated as planned.[46] But there was a reverse effect among the Allies and their populations back home: pride soared. The bombings, the reports of hits and buildings destroyed, and the stories of enemies killed were standard parts of war coverage, and they indicated that the war effort was working and that the United Nations, as the Allied forces were called at the time, were racing toward the end of hostilities. Whereas some dispute the effect on enemy morale, the bombings definitely boosted British and American morale and were cultivated, through the selective and censored release of information and images, to do exactly that.

In war reporting, one finds a terrible pride, and even beauty, in the poetic justice being exacted on the German people. Edward R. Murrow, a CBS correspondent, provided an eyewitness account from the vantage of an RAF Lancaster, broadcast on CBS Radio December 3, 1943. Murrow recounted the anticipation experienced by the bomber crew as they waited for their mission orders, which turned out to target Berlin. He offered a portrait of the calm sensations associated with a wartime air base, directly contrasting with the hellish chaos of the actual bombing run. Murrow wrote, "A small station wagon delivered a thermos bottle of coffee, chewing gum, an orange and a bit of chocolate for each man. Up in that part of England the air hums and throbs with the sound of the aircraft motors all day. But for half an hour before take-off, the skies are dead, silent and expectant. A lone hawk hovered over the airfield, absolutely still as he faced into the wind."[47] The sweet everyday pleasures of oranges and chocolate—even sweeter to read about during wartime rationing—are interrupted by the mechanical reminder of the task to come. Our airmen will soon replace that solitary hawk. Murrow has set the stage for ordinary recruits to become righteous heroes.

Once the crew is on their way, the mission took Murrow into antiaircraft fire, which seemed "remote" even when he saw a nearby plane shot out of the sky, and through the smoke of multicolored flares that advance planes had dropped to both misdirect the enemy about where they were to release their bombs and guide the pilots to their actual targets. Murrow said it was like "flying straight for the center of the fireworks."[48] Caught in the searchlights from the ground, the Lancaster dove sideways to avoid the antiaircraft fire that was sure to follow, providing Murrow with a clear view of Berlin below. As the payloads fell, he saw the incendiaries exploding, which looked like "a fistful of white rice thrown on a piece of black velvet," and the blockbusters "bursting like great sun-flowers gone mad."[49] He witnessed a firestorm that this bombing raid had ignited throughout Berlin, describing how "the white fires had turned red. They were beginning to merge and spread, just like butter does on a hot plate."[50]

The food euphemisms—rice and butter—joined a primary one: cookies. In fact, Murrow used only this military term for the large bombs in his report, though newspaper reprints of portions of his report headlined it with "blockbuster."[51] When they released their final blockbuster, Murrow reported that the bomb aimer simply said, "Cookie gone," with the smaller incendiary bombs following shortly afterward.[52] Murrow's report ended with the claim that the bombing run was "a massive blow of retribution."[53] In contrast to the faceless and nameless enemy, Murrow then contemplated two air force personnel, introduced at the start of his report, who did not make it back, as well as two reporters, friends of Murrow, who went missing on that run.[54] But the sense of beauty persisted, even as he acknowledged the horror that had been unleashed. Murrow reported, "Berlin was a kind of orchestrated hell, a terrible symphony of light and flame. It isn't a pleasant kind of warfare—the men doing it speak of it as a job. . . . Men die in the sky while others are roasted alive in their cellars."[55] The aesthetics of destruction connected the sheer wonderment of this extreme infernal vision with a sense of accomplishment in industrial craft. Our technological know-how, our industrial might, and our military courage did this, despite the human cost to the good men of the air force and to the enemy, military and civilian.

We delivered this.

Itself a product of advanced industrial processes and logic, the blockbuster was calibrated to destroy the modern urban environment. The name itself included an architectural reference—a block of buildings—which implied a periodization of modern functionalist architecture. The term harbored the indiscriminate approach to battle plans in which a block of flats could be thought of as a military target. The crass volume of the high-capacity weapon had its sights on the equally crass mass of the contemporary large-scale construction of factories, offices, and dwellings. This was modern weaponry targeting the products of modernity, the infrastructure of civilization. But, of course, the science of air war for which the blockbuster was designed was never exact, and their devastation included medieval cathedrals, ancient libraries, nineteenth-century hospitals, and sixteenth-century universities. Bomber Command was generally impervious to the specificities of heritage. Then again, a sense of imperviousness to time and history is one of the characteristics of industrial warfare.

The fury of war produced a celebration of the work a blockbuster could do. And, despite the diminutive name, "cookies" looked mighty, especially when compared to the puny cruel firebombs. Only with the war's end was the fuller picture of the Allied air war provided by the *United States Strategic Bombing Survey*.[56] Information began to circulate that contradicted the impression of blockbuster power and efficiency and exposed the lie about how humane the air campaign was. For the duration, it was evident to the military authorities that small incendiary bombs wreaked far more havoc on German cities and lives than "the widely publicized 'block-buster'" bombs by a factor of 4.4 times when accounting for weight differentials.[57] Only after the war did the truth of the firestorms begin to circulate, though a complete reckoning with the moral and legal implications of knowingly unleashing such a hellish rain on civilians has never transpired. At war's end, the blockbuster still meant size, power, and modern effectiveness.

Deadly battles on land and sea and in the air, and the bloody decisions made in safe bureaucratic strongholds, constituted the primary theaters of wartime operation. But there was also a battle waged for public opinion, and here publicity and rhetorical strategy orchestrated the engagement and participation of citizens in the war effort. Dower wrote of the special overlapping propagandistic function of "shock and awe" in modern warfare, in which weapons are meant to destroy and to be debilitating to enemy morale and inspiring for allies.[58]

Blockbuster bombs remained familiar to the American public throughout the war. Newsreels shown in theaters alongside Hollywood features sustained this publicity with their coverage of the air war. War footage was available for home viewing, too, and film distributor Castle sold 8 mm and 16 mm versions of *The News Parade of 1943* complete with promises of images in which "Naziland gets block-busters."[59] Such publicity helped present the argument that this advanced weaponry provided unparalleled advantage to the United Nations and would lead to victory. On balance, the brutal air war, so the logic went, would save Allied lives by ending the war faster. A *New York Times* editorial even described bombing as a form of reeducation. "The Bomb as Pedagogue" argued that "a four-ton bomb is a weighty argument" and that "blockbusters are facts whose existence must be acknowledged. For certain purposes they are a wonderful educational device."[60] The rationale for warfare can suspend other humanistic reasoning, and cruel conclusions led to exactly such ideas, where weapons of mass and indiscriminate destruction were forms of educational media and where their deployment prompted the enemy's betterment. Versions of this twisted logic continue to appear in retrospective justification for the use of devastating weapons, epitomized by the dropping of atomic bombs on Japan. Indeed, after World War II, "Bomber" Harris would continue to make claims about the success of the air campaign and the idea of "morale bombing" with reference to the destruction of Hiroshima.[61]

The conduct of this warfare stretched ethical limitations thin, and justifications became perverse and unrecognizably flexible. Friedrich ended his book on the Allied bombing campaign with an illuminating analogy. He pointed out that if a soldier opened fire with a machine gun on civilians in the streets of Berlin or London, there is no question that this would be outside acceptable wartime conduct, and it would be unambiguously a war crime. And yet similarly indiscriminate actions taken from the air had become an acceptable part of military strategy. Friedrich noted the contradiction, writing, "The horizontal fire of a machine gun is illegal; the vertical direction of the bomb munitions, on the other hand, is legal."[62]

Bombers, however, prepared to expand into the horizontal. As a leading champion for air warfare, Alexander P. de Seversky, put it, bombs that skipped along the surface of water toward their targets, as well as aerial torpedoes, changed the directionality of weapons dropped from airplanes. He wrote, "We now bomb vertically with four-ton [sic] blockbusters. Aircraft will be able to hurl such bombs horizontally from ever greater distances."[63] A significant propaganda push for de Seversky's strategic position came from a Walt Disney feature documentary, *Victory through Air Power* (1943), which visualized and supported his theories.

The heroic celebration of the American war effort was typical, and wartime Hollywood marketing included war bond sales, quizzes about wartime activities, and publicity articles written to integrate movie subjects with news items about the war. The British film *One of Our Aircraft Is Missing* (1942), an Alexander Korda production originally released in the United Kingdom at the end of June, arrived in the United States with the full promotional push for its October release through United Artists. The press kit included information about the British bombing campaign and the deliberate fictionalizing of the interior of bombers, so that no military secrets would be revealed. Details about warplanes were part of the campaign. United Artists offered sets of "Aircraft Spotters Cards" that instructed in the identification of aircraft, and a glossary informed about terms, or, as the press book put it, invited users to "Cash In on Aviation 'Lingo'!" Available to exhibitors were cardboard models of airplanes and a poster collage of news headlines about the bombing of Europe for display in the lobby. By the time of the film's U.S. release in the fall of 1942, blockbuster bombs had recently become a part of news reporting. Capitalizing on this topicality, the posters made reference to this new weapon and to the RAF campaign. Posters, lobby cards, and newspaper advertisements set the scene as follows: "THE GREATEST AIR SPECTACULAR EVER MADE WITH THE RAF! Ride the skies with the valiant men of the RAF and 1,000 planes loaded with destruction! The deafening roar of the take-off . . . over the channel . . . target sighted . . . heavy ack-ack spraying sudden death. BOMBS AWAY! . . . the crash and thunder and fire of two-ton block-busters on target! Homeward bound . . . flack getting heavier . . ." (figures 3.6 and 3.7). This describes the first moments of the film, which focuses not on the raid but on the survivors of a downed aircraft making their way home behind enemy lines. The copy features air force slang—"ack-ack," "bombs away," and "flack"—and the appearance of "block-buster," though civilian rather than military nomenclature, contributes to the impression of technical specificity in the language. The blockbusters, of course, are "on target," providing casual authorization for the action.[64]

Bombardier by RKO romanticized the supposed accuracy of bombing enemy targets, featuring the new technological means that were to ensure

FIGURE 3.6 *One of Our Aircraft Is Missing* press book, 1942

FIGURE 3.7 *One of Our Aircraft Is Missing* press book, detail, 1942

bombs arrived at their military destinations. Sheldon Hall has pinpointed trade advertisements for this film in May 1943 as the first use of "blockbuster" in publicity for a motion picture, where it appeared as "The block-buster of all action-thrill-service shows!"[65] Though there was at least one earlier use, in the American advertising for *One of Our Aircraft Is Missing,* Hall is right that this is the earliest metaphoric use we currently know of, one that draws a parallel between the impact of the film and that of the two-ton cookie. The description appeared on lobby cards and in newspaper advertisements as "A Block-Buster of Thrill and Action" (figure 3.8).[66] In *Bombardier*'s case, technological might was featured in other ways: displays of weaponry. For instance, at the Palace Theatre showing of *Bombardier* in Chicago, Civilian Defense

FIGURE 3.8 *Bombardier* lobby card, 1943

Air Corps planes flew overhead, and moviegoers saw a lobby exhibit of military equipment, including the newest and most deadly weapon ever created, a blockbuster.[67] This promotional exhibit took place just two months following the *Nature of the Enemy* display in Rockefeller Center.

Other studios contributed to the normalization of mass aerial bombing as a humane and ethical strategy. As part of the ongoing efforts to promote and justify its actions, the War Department, through Paramount Pictures and the OWI, orchestrated a theatrical release for *The Memphis Belle: A Story of a Flying Fortress* (1944), a forty-minute film assembled from U.S. Air Force color footage taken during a bombing raid. Director William Wyler, who would later direct *Ben-Hur* (1959), flew with the crew during the shoot, as did other film personnel. The film's advertising prominently featured photographs and drawings of bombs and boasted that it was "filmed in the flaming sky battlefront over Germany!"[68]

The regime of acceptable atrocity implicated more than military strategists and propagandists. It engulfed the sphere of business and industry. Lockheed used images from Disney's *Victory through Air Power* in its advertising, neatly merging the goals of entertainment businesses, military tacticians, and civilian corporations.[69] Indeed, Roland Marchand wrote, "World War II, thanks not only to the extensive exertions of major corporations but also to the promotional activities of the military forces, was to acquire the character of a public relations war."[70] Inger L. Stole has documented how the OWI and the War Advertising Council coordinated to assist in the rapid and complete mobilization of the United States. Using every channel of communication and information dissemination available, they worked to lobby and guide advertisers to place "A War Message in Every Ad."[71] Establishing an ongoing contribution to the war effort in this way meant aligning government messages with those of corporations. Theodor Adorno observed in *Minima Moralia* that World War II reports on air raids were also reports on companies producing the planes, and "accordingly industry, state and advertising [were] amalgamated."[72] To wit, companies deployed contemporary war imagery to their own promotional advantage, and here the formidable nine-foot-high bomb was a handy point of reference. War bond campaigns referenced blockbusters. They impressed, awed, and promised to vanquish the enemy and to return the world to peace, an American peace. The iconography of the blockbuster was a guarantee of the security of the investment. The Bankers Trust Company implored Americans to "Help Blast the Way to Victory," a chillingly murderous call normalized by war conditions (figure 3.9). Their advertisement included a detailed line drawing of a munitions factory for, as the caption states, "two-ton blockbusters, 9½ foot giants of destruction."[73] With a hint of Lilliputian perspective, the assembly line of bombs dwarfs the faceless factory workers, who climb scaffolds and use pulleys to service the munitions. The scale of the advertisement's image orients the reader to the mechanical power represented by these "giants."

The Bank of New York featured blockbusters in their advertising as a way to link their services with industrial prowess and technological sophistication. They also used this imagery to connect their business with *this* war, to the current historical moment. Their early 1943 advertising copy—notably, only a few months after "blockbuster" begins to appear as a recognizable term for Americans—captures the impression that the bomb and the air campaign are delivering victory, and doing so by devastating the enemy and promising access to the lucrative economy of reconstruction. Matters of military strategy extended beyond winning the war to include winning the peacetime economy to come; the objective encompasses future battles over resources, markets, and finance. Headlined "Block-Busters," the copy begins, "The 4000-pound demolition bomb is the main Allied weapon now used to paralyze war

FIGURE 3.9 Bankers Trust Company advertisement, 1943

production in the Reich. . . . Some of the largest factories in Europe have already fallen into wreckage under these titanic block-busters. In their ruins, the creative power of many old and profitable industries is buried." It takes a very special imagination to target creativity, as we see here. "Creative power" means all forms of innovation that could be harnessed for wartime and eventually peacetime economies. Wartime obliteration of the economic advantage, and the capacity for innovation, of a competitor points the way to riches for others. Lest this seems to imply perpetual military upheaval, the bank's advertisement reassures that wealth will return, saying, "War builds new wealth upon its own devastation. It has aroused a driving demand for new equipment, new methods, new inventions. It has laid the foundations of scores of new peacetime industries. War hastens the normal progress of economic life."[74] I don't think we could find a more complete admission of the true underlying goals of a capitalist war machine. The connection being made exceeds a comforting note that peace would return to say that the mechanisms that have been produced for the war effort will be those that will enrich civilian life after the end of hostilities. The rhetoric is a statement of what Marshall Berman elaborated in *All That Is Solid Melts into Air* as the fundamentally destructive impulse of capitalism.[75] The drive to tear down in order to build up haunts any pronouncements about the expansionism capitalism requires, and, more recently, similarly blunt descriptions of "disruption" and "creative destruction" tell us that the valorization of future relations over existing ones continues to hold sway. In the Bank of New York advertisement, wartime technological and industrial advancement, explicitly designed and deployed to tear down cities and their citizens, and to bury "creative power," emerges as the energy of "the good life." This example captures the deep investments that ran through the publicity of the conflict. The armed conflict was a surface-level engagement. "War hastens the normal progress of economic life." At stake was a conflict for competitive advantage in markets, commodities, and capital while waging war and rallying people to the cause.

Some publicity had even more immediate interests in the air war, notably that for companies counting on defense contracts. Consolidated Vultee Aircraft had a direct stake in the acceptance of the air war; they built planes that participated in bombing campaigns. In six panels of drawings, one newspaper advertisement explained each leg of a bombing run (figure 3.10). In this representation Consolidated Vultee Aircraft counted on the awesome impression of the blockbuster's military accomplishment for the vengeful tone of the advertisement's most prominent tag line. Playing on the then-familiar chilling line, found in news reports, "one of our airplanes is missing," the ad begins with the vengeful slogan, "One of their cities is missing!"[76] The first panel recounts the destruction caused by an Allied bombing run, setting the scene as an on-the-spot news report: "40 minutes ago, there were Nazi factories down there. Now there are no factories. Not even a city. For the last of 1000 Allied bombers has just dropped its block busters." This last line is a reference to the spectacular thousand-bomber raids conducted by the RAF, which involved several nights of consecutive bombing of German cities. Though the more strategically successful raids involved considerably fewer planes, the impression of the thousand-strong force had a parade value, suited to propaganda and the purposes of Consolidated Vultee. The second panel illustrates the resources called on to deploy a thousand planes for a mission over Germany. The next three panels explain the vital role ships, trucks, and trains play in getting materials to where they are needed. The final panel reiterates the theme of coordinated infrastructure and suggests that the benefits will continue when peace arrives. Consolidated Vultee, unsurprisingly, specifically expects that the necessity for military air defense will continue substantially beyond the war's end. As the copy declares, "a permanent postwar Air Force is America's best insurance for a lasting peace." In case the new conditions of advanced warfare are not entirely clear, the ad reiterates the assertion with a bold statement that "no spot on earth is more than 60 hours' flying time from your local airport." This fact validates the reach of the U.S. Air Force, but it also implies that other powers, perhaps enemy powers, have comparable access. A permanent-war footing for defense purposes underlies the argument presented.

Other efforts counted on a more benign presence, making bomb culture humorous and kitsch. A contrast to the actual deadly purpose helped neutralize the destructiveness. Some entrepreneurs seized on the weapon and its popularity as a merchandising opportunity. Available to merchandisers, who could add company names or place-names, was a souvenir box or cigarette holder made of Colorado aspen with Masonite fins in the shape of a blockbuster bomb.[77] The classic Bugs Bunny short *Falling Hare* (1943) opens with Bugs lounging on a large bomb with "blockbuster" written on the side so that audiences could clearly identify the ordnance. He is reading a book, *Victory through Hare Power*, which was a play on de Seversky's bestseller about air warfare that Walt Disney adapted into the aforementioned propaganda film, *Victory through Air Power*.

These illustrations show the way a weapon, a strategy, and connotations about economic and technological progress were organized and presented for public consumption. As individually minor as these notices are, the accumulation of such representational tactics builds a consistent impression of the implications of certain modes of military engagement. The more familiar the blockbuster became, and the more it predictably reappeared in multiple media for various purposes, the more it planted roots as a coherent and stable sign. The blockbuster, from 1942 to 1945, held a primary place in the imagination of devastation and military strength. It synthesized in one device the progress and ingenuity of the Allied war effort, a technological facility that would propel the prosperity that was promised once combat terminated. This weapon, unprecedented for a time in its singular destructive power, provided

FIGURE 3.10 Consolidated Vultee Aircraft advertisement, 1944

a reason for the services directed by mobilization efforts—war bonds, financial matters, and defense contracts—and it served as a tangible product of those efforts. With this weapon, this awe-inspiringly deadly weapon, the war would not last and could not be lost, as the reasoning went. Nor would control of the new world that was sure to emerge following the war be lost. A particularly American vision of democracy, commerce, and peace could be assured a commanding place in the global reconstruction of the coming years. Only after the war did it become public knowledge, though hardly common knowledge, that the blockbuster had not been as effective in leveling German targets as advertised and that it largely played a supporting role to the incendiary bomb. But throughout the war, publicity zeroed in on the impressive metal beast of the blockbuster. Available as corporate and public imagery, *the blockbuster was the opposite of a secret weapon.*

The publicity of the bomb went beyond its availability for advertising and military imagery. At the height of the war in 1943, the U.S. Army and Navy even approved the release of the basic chemical composition of the explosive elements in blockbusters, a combination of ammonia and formaldehyde to make hexamine, which was manufactured by DuPont.[78] This historically powerful weapon was intended to comfort friendly civilians, business investors, and military personnel as much as to terrify enemy forces. The devotion to the concept of the efficacy of gigantic bombs—possible only with the willful deception about their true role, subservient to incendiary bombs—and to the technological innovations that produced them was invested in a future victory in wartime and in economic prosperity. Capturing the idea that blockbusters would be responsible for victory, during the war noted editorial cartoonist Clifford Kennedy Berryman depicted Joseph Goebbels comforting a dejected Hitler who is confronting the error of his claims that "the German Army is invincible—The Reich can never be bombed," represented in a paper he holds (figure 3.11). Goebbels suggests, "Maybe you should have said it louder, Chief," implying that his voice was being drowned out by other events. Behind the two Nazi leaders we see the true reason for Hitler's failing optimism. Three explosions blast news of Allied success, one labeled "Leningrad," one "Libya," and one "Blockbusters."[79]

The blockbuster's central place in the American popular imagination as a path to victory appeared in a New Year's Eve editorial cartoon from 1944, called "The Block Buster?" (figure 3.12).[80] A falling bomb, emblazoned with "1945," descends upon a crumbling stone swastika, thus depicting an alignment between weapon, air war, and the pending finality of the war in the new year. The year and the weapon would see to the busting of the Nazi block. Put

FIGURE 3.11 Clifford Kennedy Berryman cartoon, "Maybe you should have said it louder, Chief," 1943

differently, popular usage associated the blockbuster, for all its immoral purpose as a giant destructive force, with success.

One year after the end of the war in the Pacific, *Daily Variety* commemorated the victory with a front-page cartoon of an atomic mushroom cloud, on top of which nested a proud American eagle. The news item the cartoon referenced was the establishment of the new United Nations, but the image celebrated American might, embellished further with the curiously contradictory caption "First in War, First in Peace."[81] This illustration is not of a blockbuster blast, but it echoes the contemporary way that large bombs and their deployment were understood as signs of victory and success. The peace ahead rested on the devastation delivered to foes via modern technological means.

✶ ✶ ✶ ✶

FIGURE 3.12 *New York Times* editorial cartoon, "The Block Buster?," 1944

With the high visibility resulting from its monumentality, nonmilitary uses of the term "blockbuster" began to appear in 1943. The uniquely impressive size of the bomb was a sound comparator for the largeness of explosive capabilities; soon, other applications used the term to reference scale and impact. Sports reporting launched the appropriations, connecting the term to connotations of masculine power in reference to "the blockbusters of sport—Joe Louis, Ted Williams, Joe DiMaggio, Hank Greenberg."[82] A racehorse called Block Buster was making the rounds the same year.[83] After the war, Jake LaMotta was called the Bronx Blockbuster, and Rocky Marciano was the Brockton Blockbuster.[84]

The migration to cultural texts also began in 1943, primarily in advertising copy or critical assessment. The book trade was an early adopter. A print advertisement for the book *The Air Offensive against Germany* described it as

FIGURE 3.13 *The Air Offensive against Germany* book advertisement, 1943

"a block buster of a book" (figure 3.13). In this instance, the use signaled that the book was, in part, about those bombs and the immediate conflict associated with those bombs, and that its pages were "loaded with facts."[85] The size of the treatment and its comprehensiveness, as well as the topic, warranted the description. Similarly, advertisements for the book *Thirty Seconds over Tokyo*, which told the story of the Doolittle bombing raid on Japan, cited critic Charles Lee of the *Philadelphia Record* commenting that the tale would "stir up your nerves like a block buster," even though those bombs did not play a part in the actual run.[86] Again, this usage fused subject matter and impact. The thematic connection significantly reverberated in some of the earliest film references. For instance, one review described the 1944 film version of *Thirty Seconds over Tokyo* as a blockbuster.[87]

A book about postwar health delivery, *Kaiser Wakes the Doctors*, sold itself as a "medical block-buster."[88] The Carnegie Corporation book series "The Negro in American Life" advertised that it "breaks in on complacency like a blockbuster," described as such owing to its "total fact impact."[89] Critics began to make a connection between film and finance in 1944, with the globe-spanning novel about the war *The Curtain Rises* described as "destined to be a boxoffice blockbuster!"[90] Promotional ballyhoo does not usually match actuality; it never was a film success, or even a film. To seal the status of *The Road to Serfdom*, an anticommunist attack on government planning from the University of Chicago Press, ads said it "exploded like a blockbuster."[91] The cry of sensation echoed as outrage, and a right-wing tilt made many such wartime uses preparatory work for the coming Cold War. Overall, these books were mostly large doorstoppers whose ads promised an impact comparable to the effect of the newly popular and powerful explosive. Put differently, the majority of these early uses in the book trade dovetailed with the Allied war effort.

The earliest film-related appearances of "blockbuster" are surprising from our current perspective, as they did not show a connection to a tale's epic proportions or production. One was a direct comparison between the hail that caused considerable damage to a theater in Millbrook, New York, and Allied bombs: "Blockbuster Hail Stones Cost Theatreman $150 for New Roof."[92] Following appearances of the term in the advertising for *One of Our Aircraft Is Missing* and *Bombardier*, increasingly common was usage like that from December 1943, where critic Theodore Strauss said of Tallulah Bankhead's performance in *Lifeboat* (1943) that she "packs nearly as much explosive energy as a two-ton blockbuster."[93] That same month, the exhibitor trade publication *Boxoffice Magazine* published a review that described *No Time for Love* (1943) as "A comedy blockbuster. Theatre grosses should be blown to ceiling heights," a quote that was included in subsequent print ads, though it was not more prominent than other lines from *New York Mirror* and *Motion Picture Daily*.[94] Here, "blockbuster" strictly referred to comedic success, with metaphoric use of the bombing origin and some connection to financial impact. "Blockbuster" as signaling financial success appeared again, and more directly, in a *Daily Variety* review of *Brazil* (1944) that declared that the film "should prove a blockbuster at the wickets."[95] *Operation Burma* (1945) was a "thrilling blockbuster of a war melodrama" according to the *New York Herald Tribune*, a line that was featured on the *Film Bulletin* movie critic roundup page.[96] When used in these print advertisements and notices, the line was not highlighted above others, giving it a relatively equal status among the other endorsements. Nothing yet referenced lavishness or epic production qualities.

Less predictable and regularized uses appeared. A negative review of *Holiday in Mexico* (1946) was "a blockbuster of wholehearted disapproval," a strange description that again used the large explosive to convey the completeness of the critic's negative view of the film, doing so without reference to either financial results or the expansiveness of the story or production.[97] Distant from our current understanding was East Side Kids' picture *Block Buster* (1944), which, though set during the war, had nothing to do with the bomb and was titled to cash in on topicality.

General-interest and trade publications, like the British theater trade publication *The Stage* and the American *Marquee*, show virtually no theatrical uses of "blockbuster" until the 1950s, contrary to apocryphal tales that the term originated from people lining up around the block for tickets. One exception in August 1943 is a small advertisement describing the variety show *There's a Waar On* [sic] as a "'thousand pound' block buster," seemingly in reference to the scale of the production.[98] Another use appeared in a review of the play *The Innocent Voyage* in the *New York Theatre Critics' Review* in 1943. But here the meaning is consistent with a reference to financial impact and not ticket lines.[99] Frank Gill, in a superlative review of the live-theater Broadway production of *Carmen Jones*, made a direct metaphoric association, writing that producer "Billy Rose has dropped a blockbuster on Broadway."[100]

Most of these uses capitalized on the term's connotation of unusual and expansive impact. A blockbuster is an attention getter, a debate provoker, and a comprehensive treatment. Publicity and critics used the term for works they felt would break through the clutter of other novels and films. Resonance is implied, and a blockbuster would be an agenda setter, a topic of further conversation. We can see that a connection to war themes, or at least explosions, remains, though the connotation of impact occasionally included revenue. We are not yet at a point of consolidation of meaning with respect to popular film for popular audiences.

The blockbuster helped obliterate numerous German cities. And the United States had used it to firebomb Japan. The blockbuster had another purpose. As a creation of publicity, stories of its size and accuracy rallied support for the war. In practice, it was neither accurate nor efficient as a weapon, and it was used to prepare targets for the smaller and more numerous incendiary bombs. But the blockbuster explosive most assuredly worked to "make obsolete" enemies, buildings, and cities. And by the end of the 1940s, it too was becoming obsolete as a military ordnance, not because it was no longer being used in armed conflict—the United States used blockbusters during the Korean War—but because it had been surpassed by the atomic bomb as the most horrifyingly powerful and most technologically advanced weapon in the modern arsenal. As our nuclear winter settled, conventional bombs seemed to lose the ability to terrify in the same way that they had a few years earlier. In 1947 the *Atlantic* predicted, "The next atom bomb . . . will bear about as much resemblance to the Hiroshima bomb as a British blockbuster bore to a hand grenade."[101] They reasoned that such power produced a permanent security crisis and compelled further accelerated technological change in order to race ahead of potential enemy nations by inventing more globally destructive weapons and systems. Scientific and technological progress sprang from a defensive well of national insecurity. After the war the international arms race in fact began in earnest, as did the space and technology race.

Susan Sontag evocatively wrote of "the imagination of disaster," describing science fiction films and their penchant for technological solutions to worldwide disasters.[102] The filmic visions she addressed make comprehendible unimaginable levels of death and destruction. In a way, well-publicized weapons function similarly. The heights of our imagination of disaster were bound up with the blockbuster bomb for a few short years, only to be overtaken by the A-bomb, to be followed by other extremes of possible nuclear conflict. Moving from the blockbuster to atomic weaponry, people were invested in the escalation of destructive potential, not the reduction of it, as one might expect a humane mind to pursue. The cycle of innovation continued, mobilizing the fear of enemy technological advances into a priority to invent and ready more destructive operational means.

The first *New York Times* article about the atomic bombing of Hiroshima, written by Hanson W. Baldwin and published the day after the attack, captured the sense that a new era of catastrophe had been initiated. It is a beautiful and troubling report, evocative in its concern and politically available to bolster the agendas of the Cold Warriors who would rise to rule for the next couple of decades. Baldwin began his report with a sure indication that a new era had begun: "Yesterday man unleashed the atom to destroy man, and another chapter in human history opened, a chapter in which the weird, the strange, the horrible becomes the trite and the obvious. Yesterday we clinched victory in the Pacific, but we sowed the whirlwind."[103] He expressed the new dangers by comparing the A-bomb to other explosive experiences and powers, including the Halifax, Nova Scotia, explosion of a ship carrying a cargo of TNT in 1917, at the time the single most powerful human-made explosion ever witnessed. Baldwin pointedly provided a comparison to the largest blockbusters to offer a sense of the unprecedented magnitude of the newest weapon. Baldwin worried, "Americans have become a synonym for destruction. And now we have been the first to introduce a new weapon of unknowable effects which may bring us victory quickly but which will sow the seeds of hate more widely than ever. We may yet reap the whirlwind." He concluded, "Atomic energy may well lead to a bright new world in which man shares a common brotherhood, or we shall become—beneath the bombs and rockets—a world of troglodytes."[104] And for the rest of his career, Baldwin took this ethical dilemma to fuel his aggressive anticommunism, which manifested in his steady voice for American nuclear superiority and for expanded war efforts abroad.

The devastating upheaval in the imagination of disaster left the earlier weapon as part of a quainter era of destruction. Even just a few months after the attacks on Hiroshima and Nagasaki, an observer of the television industry wrote that low-frequency receivers "may become as obsolete as a blockbuster."[105] Definitional transitions are never automatic, and some earlier meanings drag along and resurface. Although the blockbuster was described as "obsolete" at the end of 1945, in 1947 an advertisement for a radio program said it was "as effective as a blockbuster," drawing on the wartime association with precision and economy.[106] "Effective" yet "obsolete": on the surface they are contradictory descriptions, and yet they summon dominant ways that we talk about technology. We primarily assess value in technological progress as being related to resource efficiency (whether labor or material), to an ability to accomplish a task, and to a lineage of earlier efforts that are superseded by new innovations, making the previous forms things of the past. The integration of presumptions about technological progress into contemporary society has been critically assessed to produce ethics that value technology over humans. In technocratic logic, complex systems are saddled with rational options that enhance their own centrality and leave more humane alternatives outside consideration.[107]

But "obsolete" held fast for a few years. A comment on the government brochure "Atomic Attack: A Manual of Survival" said in 1950, "We have come to regard the old fashioned *block buster* as a conservative, almost gentle form of lethal instrument."[108] Note that: "old fashioned" and "gentle." By 1950, roughly seven years after the term began to circulate in mainstream war reporting, this kind of high-capacity bomb was described as "old fashioned." Nuclear weapons and atomic warfare rested in their status as the most complete rendition of civilization's paradox that the most advanced technological logic was also the most backward. As the incalculable escalation of destructive potential continued to mount, previous generations of weaponry could be talked about as tame by comparison. The aforementioned article in the *Atlantic* claimed that "airmen and scientists already refer to the Hiroshima-Nagasaki missiles as 'old-type bombs.'"[109] In 1947 even A-bombs were beginning their trajectory to their status as formerly state of the art. The blockbuster had been part of the public visual repertoire of World War II, one founded on a valorization of national industrial pride without a specific accounting of the associated blood and suffering. The publicity did not—could not—feature the actuality of the bomb's deployment on a high-density urban population; that was reserved for enemy attacks. By 1950 the term "blockbuster" sealed the ignorance and amnesia that had been there since its first introduction to the public. It was obsolete, yet still resonant and familiar.

"Blockbuster" was an available image of industrial and technological might, founded on the logic that escalation vanquished combatants, hostile or not. At the beginning of the 1950s, it left a residual impression as an idea about success and size. By examining the publicity using the term—the popular circulation and visibility of its technological exhibitionism—we chronicle the mediation of an endgame in military logic for popular consumption, and the migration of aspects of that logic to civilian cultural venues, specifically, the qualities of largeness, comprehensiveness, success, and unchallenged competitive advantage. As the documentation here presented, cultural appropriations of the term appeared earlier than previously recognized, as it was used to describe nonfiction tomes, epic war novels, and war and comedy movies. In the 1940s the term was a sign of contemporaneity; it bespoke the current historical moment. And with the appeal to the state-of-the-art, for a time the blockbuster visualized an investment in the newest forms of technology. As the cultural realm began to take possession of the term, the logic of the spectacular technological display transferred, too.

Incidentally, "to bomb" in the sense of "to fail" does not appear in American slang until the 1960s, by which time "blockbuster" had largely been severed from its military origins.

(CHAPTER FOUR)

THE BUSINESS OF BIG

Two years before the spectacularly successful *Quo Vadis* (1951), the first film reviewed in *Variety* described as a blockbuster, there was Cecil B. DeMille's *Samson and Delilah* (1949). That earlier biblical epic was a key sign that a new Hollywood model was in formation. Throughout the war Hollywood had been curtailing production budgets, but changing outlooks began to set in immediately afterward. Thomas Schatz described *Samson and Delilah* as "not only a throw-back to an earlier era but an augur of things to come."[1] "The first studio-produced, calculated blockbuster effort in years," it was out of step with the films of the moment.[2] Released as it was in the last week of 1949, it was the first film of the 1950s in more ways than one. Schatz quotes *New York Times* film critic Bosley Crowther, who said that the film brought together "the Old Testament and Technicolor for the first time."[3] This pairing of technology and epic would expand throughout the 1950s. Though it arrived at the twilight of the decade, *Samson and Delilah* was the biggest hit of the 1940s both in the United States and abroad, and as such it "rekindled Hollywood's hit-driven mentality while reasserting the currency of the big-budget spectacle, and it heralded a radical redirection of the movie industry in the 1950s."[4]

The very first moments of *Samson and Delilah* announce the film's extravagances, introducing audiences to the expansiveness of the production and instructing them of the technical skill involved. From *Samson and Delilah*'s outset is a promise of the film's epic qualities, especially its cinematographic virtuosity. Below are the opening credits that follow a lengthy overture, the film title, five cards listing the top five lead players (Hedy Lamarr, Victor Mature, George Sanders, Angela Lansbury, and Henry Wilcoxon), and a single card with dozens of other players:

Opening Credit Sequence for *Samson and Delilah* (1949)

Screenplay by Jesse L. Lasky, Jr. and Frederic M. Frank
From Original Treatments by Harold Lamb-Vladimir Jabotinsky
Based upon the history of Samson and Delilah
In the Holy Bible, Judges 13–16

Music by Victor Young

Color by Technicolor
Technicolor Color Director, Natalie Kalmus
Associate, Robert Brower

Director of Photography, George Barnes, ASC
Director of Photographic Effects, Gordon Jennings, ASC
Unit Directors, Arthur Rosson and Ralph Jester

Art Direction, Hans Dreier and Walter Tyler
Process Photography, Farciot Edouart, ASC and Wallace Kelley, ASC
Holy Land Photography, Dewey Wrigley, ASC
Choreographer, Theodore Kosloff
Dialogue Supervision, Frances Dawson and James Vincent
Assistant Director, Edward Salven

Edited by Anne Bauchens
Costumes, Edith Head, Gile Steele, Dorothy Jeakins, Gwen Wakeling, Elois W. Jenssen
Set Decoration, Sam Comer and Ray Moyer
Special Photographic Effects, Paul Lerpae, ASC and Devereux Jennings, ASC

Makeup Supervision, Wally Westmore

Research, Henry Noerdlinger and Gladys Percey

Sound Recording by Harry Lindgren and John Cobe

Western Electric Recording

Produced and Directed by Cecil B. DeMille

A righteous pedigree appears early in this credit sequence. The film has a screenplay, developed from an original treatment, by notable screenwriters Jesse L. Lasky Jr. and Fredric M. Frank, but further citation includes no less authoritative source than the Old Testament, with the precise book and chapters noted, Judges 13–16. Further authority is bestowed with the acknowledgment that this tale is "the history of Samson and Delilah," essentially presenting the movie as a serious lesson. This will ease, no doubt, the acceptance of the parade of scantily clad actors, lascivious women, and sadistic undertones in the depictions that follow. After the music credit, the technological features begin their itemization. Elaboration on the cinematographic process includes corporate credits for "color by Technicolor" and a Technicolor director and associate, then both a director of photography and a director of photographic effects. Additional credits appear for process photography, "Holy Land Photography," and special photographic effects, as well as for unit directors and an assistant director. The exact division of responsibilities among these roles was not standardized. Crediting in this way was a sign of how central photographic processes, including the height of color achievement as well as the ingenuity needed for special photographic effects, were to the mounting of this tale. The final credit before the opening of the story is reserved for the decision-making creative force behind the film, producer and director Cecil B. DeMille. As John Izod has written, even in his earliest films from 1918 onward, DeMille "brought the celebration of unabashed luxury directly to the screen" and skirted sexual mores with skillful ambiguity about the conduct represented.[5] Through the entirety of his career, DeMille had an unsurpassed reputation for this style, whether in his modern melodramas or his historical epics. In other words, he came to *Samson and Delilah* with a track record for exactly this genre of extravagant film and filmmaking.

The opening credits announce other elements of filmic craft. Some are conventional, like makeup, art direction, set decoration, and music. The credit for costumes, though, lists an unusually high number of individuals, five, led by the ubiquitous Edith Head. Where blockbusters of the digital era flaunt their computer-generated imagery, doing so with extended credits for work by various companies on various image elements, here costumes function to effect wonderment. Many scenes are set pieces for the costuming, and the parading of elaborately adorned characters, major and minor, constitutes a visible production extravagance. The fabrics are sparkling, flowing, with elaborate embroidery and inset jewels. The color palette includes mauve, gold, and turquoise, with strong Technicolor blues and reds. Paired with the lush and cluttered decor featured throughout the film, the art direction, set decoration, and costuming dress up the story as a bright showcase not only for the biblical tale but for filmic construction and excess.

The fantastical realization of decor and costume is held aloft by appeals to the authenticity of the historical re-creation, as prompted by a credit that this was not just a biblical tale but "history." Though the film was primarily shot on soundstages in California, some second-unit work included location shooting in the "Holy Land"—the state of Israel was just over a year old when the film was released. Additionally, dialogue supervision and research hold core responsibility for the production's fidelity to historical fact. The actuality of the care for and accuracy of the mise-en-scène is another issue altogether, and, despite any dialogue coaching he must have received, Victor Mature in the male title role only ever sounds like Victor Mature.

Grandiosity continues with the first sequence after the credits. A twirling Earth is seen from outer space, shrouded in smoke, purple light, and a dark blue storm (figure 4.1). The only point of view possible for this shot is that of God. Fog, lightning, talismans of snakes, statues of false gods, and marching Philistines follow in rich saturated yellows, greens, and reds. The narration tells us of the threat of slavery and the enduring battle for freedom. *Samson and Delilah* is more than an entertainment, so the prologue declares; it is a lesson about authoritarianism and rebellion against forces that would oppress people. The connections to the dominant geopolitical struggles of the postwar 1940s are abundant. After the defeat of fascist authoritarianism, the threat of creeping communist authoritarianism made these opening declarations pressingly relevant. A few years later, DeMille would use a similar prologue device, with comparable appeals to the universal struggle between righteousness and evil, in *The Ten Commandments* (1956). That later film, in Paramount's expanded format of VistaVision, employed many personnel from *Samson and Delilah* (including Lasky, Frank, Rossen, Edouart, Salven, Bauchens, Head,

FIGURE 4.1 Prologue, *Samson and Delilah*, 1949

Comer, and Moyer). While thematically echoing the earlier film, the prologue for *The Ten Commandments* consists of DeMille himself emerging from behind a curtain to speak into a microphone as a learned lecturer would do rather than a show business producer. He even announces the running time of the film and reassuringly tells spectators that there will be an intermission.

As the story of *Samson and Delilah* commences, religious freedom immediately becomes the central thread of the movie. We see an old man telling the story of Moses to a small but attentive crowd, including a few children (one of whom is Saul, who, outside of this telling, eventually becomes the first king of the Jews). Philistine soldiers bully the old man; Miriam, who is Samson's intended wife, and Saul intervene, mentioning the might of their hero Samson with admiration. This sequence, with its focus on the importance of retelling Old Testament tales, today functions like a flash-forward to DeMille's greatest film a few years later, his own version of the Moses story. The second scene introduces Samson; we find him holding a lamb in his arms and affectionately bantering with his mother (figure 4.2). The scene looks very much like an image from religious calendar art. Samson's gentle disposition and inclination away from violence, contrasting with the

FIGURE 4.2 Samson, mother, and lamb, *Samson and Delilah*, 1949

soldiers and the needs of his compatriots in the previous scene, couldn't be more clearly articulated.

A destabilizing element surfaces. All the riches and colors, especially in fabrics and decor, provide concrete visual evidence of the epic production. As characters gather to lounge, feast, and fan themselves, each shot displays the elaborate costuming, jewelry, and gluttony. Dancing fighters armed with giant feathers entertain the guests. The depictions primarily associate these extravagances with the Philistines, not the humble, poor, and oppressed people who become inspired by Samson. Interestingly, words like "Jew," "Hebrew," and "Israel" are not uttered throughout the film; they were no doubt too destabilizing to this essentially Christianized version. This had changed by the time DeMille made *The Ten Commandments*, which includes credits for consultation with Jewish community representatives. The material luxuries are sought after by key women in the story, especially the vengeful Delilah, whose love for Samson becomes his undoing, as well as that of the young Semadar. The film presents a dangerous feminine lust for love and things, while at the same time providing a showcase for a spectacular depiction of the objects of those drives. In a pivotal seduction scene, the tools of

FIGURE 4.3 Samson, Delilah, and luxurious costuming, *Samson and Delilah*, 1949

Delilah's seductive skills are not only her beauty and lust but a lush garden, a cool oasis pool at midnight, and extravagant draping fabrics. When we cut from the shirtless brawn of Samson swimming and frolicking with Delilah to him clothed in a sparkling blue, red, and gold robe, we know she has led him away from his people (figure 4.3).

The association between lavish ornamentation and both Philistines and women is dramatically driven home in the final sequence of Samson destroying the temple, which is a complex construction of animation, mattes, composites, and large-scale movable sets (figures 4.4–4.6). The sequence opens with a long take of a busy street scene, but as the camera moves to reveal more of the bustling crowd, and turns 180 degrees, it pulls back to show spinning dancers in the distance, and then tilts up to present the entire multilevel temple, with its towering statues. Samson is chained and held up for public ridicule, while a crowd laughs and enjoys a festival of drinking, dancing, and comical short-stature gladiators tormenting Samson. The sequence closes the cautionary tale and elevates the sacrifices made in the name of freedom

FIGURE 4.4 Samson's final torment, *Samson and Delilah*, 1949

FIGURE 4.5 Philistine audience, *Samson and Delilah*, 1949

from oppression. But it is equally a portrait of cruel entertainment. There are many shots of the bloodthirsty audience, laughing at Samson's torments, which are part of a festive public event. Through it all, Saul and Miriam, figures of virtue, plead for mercy. The pleasures of the blockbuster, its excesses and sensationalism, are those of the godless in DeMille's version, and not of the righteous. Just as this film is itself an extravagant artifact, assembled for a mass audience's amusement, spectators are closer in conduct to the Philistine witnesses to Samson's public torture, though Samson is our focus for heroic identification. In the final moments, Delilah sees the error of her ways, helps the blind Samson to the pillars he will use to pull down the temple, and dies with her beloved whom she had betrayed. Only Miriam and Saul walk away to continue the battle against oppression.

The blockbuster strategy had not yet settled in the way that it soon would. But in *Samson and Delilah* some of the key characteristics are already evident. As Peter Lev's discussion of *The Ten Commandments* shows, DeMille used many of these same elements again, including the biblical setting to provide a platform for licentious depictions, the displacement of contemporary political matters onto situations that are at a safe historical distance, and the attention to costume, location photography, and setting to enhance fantasy, extravagance, and authenticity.[6] In *Samson and Delilah* the material display of filmic production, in this case represented best by the costumes and sets, is a feature throughout the movie. Drawing attention to the technological complexity and corporate involvement prompts an encounter with the advanced production skills required to mount the epic, here including the convoluted credits for cinematography; the labels for Technicolor and Western Electric Recording; and the entertainment promise offered by DeMille, the popular auteur of the spectacular, as well as the studio brand of MGM. And yet there is the contradictory thematic flip in the tale itself: the purveyors of popular spectacle, the audiences who take pleasure in it, and the lavish adornment more generally are all associated with the cruel Philistines and beautiful conniving women, the "luxury mammals" of which Antonio Gramsci wrote.[7] The humble, poor, and righteous keep their moral eyes on simpler pleasures. *Samson and Delilah* leaves no doubt that grandiose entertainments are the crass productions of oppressors made for the amusement of godless fools.

Samson and Delilah had all the production, financial, thematic, and aesthetic elements needed to put it in concert with the blockbusters to come. But it was presented in the standard 4:3 Academy ratio; Hollywood's widescreen experiments were still a few years away. Though we can see a block-

FIGURE 4.6 Spectacle of destruction, *Samson and Delilah*, 1949

buster strategy forming with this film from late in 1949, the idea and the term had not yet settled, and it was not described as such. *Samson and Delilah* may have been worlds away from where the entertainment business is today, but the film was advance notice that the colorful spectacular technologized event might just be the future of moviegoing.

In war, business, and art, largeness is a quality that batters enemies, overwhelms the competition, and impresses audiences. To be big—to pursue the big—expands human potential, rising above standard and expected capabilities and dimensions. The big is aspirational, and it can separate out pretenders. Some are "of the big" and "produce the big," while others stand in awe, are envious, or are subject to some forceful presence. In speaking in this way, the associations with masculine prowess, and anxiousness, are unambiguous; the big has been a brand of phallic command.

The pursuit of ever more colossal structures, sounds, facilities, and spectacles marks an embrace of the ideology of progress. Largeness is the product of pushes to make power and progress material and visible. Speed is similar in this respect. It is a corollary of the big, and it advances the light, small, and miniature instead of the heavy, large, and gigantic. But both the fast and the big allow us to experience power. Indeed, the embrace of speed and spectacle is an aestheticization of power, one that brings us closer to the "fascinating Fascism" of which Susan Sontag wrote. In her essay that critiqued the casual rehabilitation and de-Nazification of Leni Riefenstahl, Sontag described the precepts of fascist aesthetics, namely, its obsession with control and dehumanization. She wrote, "Fascist art glorifies surrender; it exalts mindlessness: it glamorizes death." It celebrates physical perfection and monumentality and in this way makes strength and power beautiful and erotic.[8] When confronted with the immensity of art, we may be unsettled by the productive forces that brought the fast and big into existence, we may be unconvinced of the promises of progress, and we may worry about the implications of resource depletion hidden behind gargantuan displays, but certainly we remain impressed and maybe a little turned on.

The mindless pursuit of innovation and technological change for its own sake has been skewered for the false claims it has rested on. Leo Marx has asked whether or not "technological progress" is even possible, responding that, yes, it can be but only if social progress is placed first and foremost as a guiding principle, rather than technocratic and capitalistic needs.[9] His book *The Machine in the Garden: Technology and the Pastoral Ideal in America* was a groundbreaking study of the tension between technological transformation and pastoral sensibilities in American life and literature.[10] However genuine the American affection for the wild frontier, the idolization of the built environment supersedes all, especially when there is an economic incentive nearby. Financial motives may provide bottom-line reasoning, but deeper, more affective pushes have been part of the culture of technological idols. David Nye expanded the concept of the technological sublime in American life to show how it "permitted both the imagination of an ineffable surplus of emotion and its containment"; importantly, it responded to both nature and culture and did not propose an opposition between the two.[11] Here, though, feminist analysis has revealed that features of this technological sublime work to prop up masculine domination and patriarchy at the root of the ideology of progress.[12] The ability to put this triumph of progress on display, or what Lewis Mumford called "technological exhibitionism," has played a significant role in the reproduction of such hierarchies, providing immediate and tangible demonstrations of the wonder and magic of applied science.[13]

While a number of characteristics can produce a sense of the sublime, gigantic manifestations are powerful statements of the ideology of progress.

Giganticism is an inevitable feature of a competitive social and economic system. And to be sure, it is not the only orientation possible in capitalist culture. Haidee Wasson has comprehensively documented the proliferation of 16 mm film projection, showing that there was another dominant cinema apparatus that powerfully shaped American life in the mid-twentieth century. The multitude of portable cinema technologies, materials, and texts stood in stark contrast to the growing theatrical screen, with a different set of practices, expectations, and economies.[14] Big and small moving image venues worked relationally as part of an overarching technologized cultural circuit. In whatever realm we find it, largeness never just references a self-contained measure of size. It always implies "bigger than." To recognize something as gigantic, one has to make a quick comparative glance at the typical and the expected. As Susan Stewart reasons, the gigantic stretches to encompass landscape and nature. The scale is such that it surrounds us, and our view of it is thus always partial. We can never see all of it. Stewart writes of "the miniature as contained, the gigantic as container."[15] Primarily focused on giants—that is, large-scale humanoids—she understands that they contrast the private intimacy of the miniature, which is designed for ownership. Giants and the gigantic appear oriented toward display instead and hence link with public spectacle. But there is continuity, for as with the miniature, the freak, and the grotesque, a sense of the normal resides in any measure of the unusually big. In the original 1960s television spy spoof *Get Smart*, a frequent line of Maxwell Smart's was to describe an impossibly big thing as "the second largest," as in "That's the second largest magnet I've ever seen." The joke rests on the fact that the eyes of the spectator see the largest magnet *they've* ever seen, and then the spectator is told that it is actually smaller than some other magnet, leaving the imagination to conjure that unseen behemoth.

When a wrathful Aslan destroys Narnia in *The Last Battle*, the final book of C. S. Lewis's "The Chronicles of Narnia" series, he summons Father Time, a sleeping giant who awakens to smash the remainder of the world. His size is indeterminable. He appears to stand over mountain ranges and to stretch up through the sky. He reaches out with arms thousands of miles long to squeeze the sun and put out its flame. Giants populate Narnia and have appeared throughout the books, but Father Time in this novel is something of a different order. He is essentially as gigantic as a being can get, so much so that he is closer to a personified idea than a large creature of some sort, just one notch below a deity. Father Time is not God, but he is large enough to be everywhere at once and to be able to tower outside any physical limitations. He is a liminal entity, an example of an imaginative threshold between the gigantic and the full engulfing of everything. He borders on dispersal into omnipresence, which replaces a measure of size with totality. The vanishing point of the gigantic is "everywhere."

This everywhere was taken up by Hollywood in the 1950s: the screen everywhere you looked, the film everywhere there were theaters, the themes and stories everywhere relevant. The major examples of screen giganticism introduced in the 1950s were the formats Cinerama, CinemaScope, VistaVision, and Todd-AO, but the most lasting contribution was the reshaping of the aspect ratio, in which the squarish Academy ratio passed in favor of the horizontal rectangle of widescreen.[16] Ariel Rogers has observed that promotional address was particularly important to the formation of the sensory appeals of these technological spectacles. She showed the interrelationship among the representation of bodies, film aesthetics, acting styles, and discourses of cinematic experience associated with the new theatrical environment that these experiments constructed. And she drew connections between the widescreen movies of the 1950s and the digital cinema of the 2000s, clarifying the historical continuity of ideas about audiovisual immersion and participation.[17] I extend this line of argumentation to show that from a crisis in the film business came the settlement on a specifically theatrical mode of cinematic experience, one that prioritized giganticism or, more specifically, technological exhibitionism.

The scale of post–World War II screen giganticism stemmed from the size of the domestic television set. Tough competition from the convenient and free domestic moving-image medium meant that moviegoing was dramatically less frequent, and the film industry had to articulate anew its aesthetic and experiential advantages. National broadcast standards limited television content to themes and presentations that were appropriate for family viewing. Accordingly, producers and exhibitors explored more adult fare for theatrical releases, eventually rattling the strictures of the Motion Picture Production Code, which had put serious limitations on the representational repertoire of Hollywood features. Technology provided other advantages for film. Television's lack of color at the time made the color process in movies a powerful selling point, and more Technicolor films circulated. And live television confined the style and image quality, where film's higher budgets could feature a more extravagant mise-en-scène. The generally higher production values allowed Hollywood to promote its wares as vested with greater aesthetic range and distinction than the black-and-white and low-visual-fidelity television image.

The very idea of going out for an evening on the town, a deliberate departure from domestic environs, was deployed as an attribute that made cinemagoing appealing. In 1951 exhibitors mounted a campaign to promote moviegoing, blending upcoming high-profile films from various studios with a general plea for the multigenerational nature of the activity. "Let's go! It's Movietime, U.S.A. . . ." was a newspaper ad campaign that included a cartoon image of stereotypical Americans—old and young, male and female, rich and middle class, coupled and alone, but presumably all white—streaming into a theater (figure 4.7). Publicity stills from generically disparate current films accompanied the campaign, designed to present a thematic variety that was not available on television, given the few broadcasting channels in operation. Ostensibly part of a "Golden Jubilee of the Motion Picture Theatre," though the connection to a specific historical exhibition milestone in 1901 was not declared explicitly, the campaign invited potential spectators to "Go to a Movie Theatre TODAY!" which connected to the fairly recent past when moviegoing was a relatively quotidian pursuit. A few years later, this would have been "Go to a Movie Theatre THIS WEEKEND!" Today, "Go to a Movie Theatre THIS SEASON" would be appropriate. At a moment prior to the experiments with Cinerama, CinemaScope, and other widescreen processes, the campaign still highlighted that moviegoing involved going to see what was playing "on the giant screen of your favorite motion picture theatre!"[18] The Academy-ratio image and the neighborhood theater would soon lack distinction as large-format screens began to be introduced and adopted as a new standard within a decade. A few years later, the Golden Jubilee was being described as a "fiasco," with some theater owners pledging to support "quality" as well as "'gimmick' pix or blockbusters," rather than the practice of moviegoing generally.[19] Of course, the considerable drop in audience numbers at the movies was hardly a product of a poorly executed publicity campaign. In 1948 average weekly attendance at U.S. movie theaters was still at 90 million. Four years later, in 1952, weekly attendance was 51.4 million, and by 1956 it was 46.5 million. Even more dramatic, the 1956 figure included 34.8 million attending regular theaters with the remaining 11.7 million going to the drive-in.[20]

The postwar tumult was not unique, and economic winds had regularly shifted how Hollywood conducted its business. Two decades earlier, to deal

FIGURE 4.7 "Let's go! It's Movietime, U.S.A. ...." campaign, 1951

with dire economic conditions during the Great Depression, exhibitors had reduced ticket prices and adopted the double-feature format, which offered a roughly three-hour program that included two feature-length movies. The secondary feature on the bill, essentially the less expensive one to rent, became what we now recognize as the B movie. These films tended to be made by the smaller Poverty Row outfits, like Monogram and Republic, though the major studios set up their own units to produce low-budget films for this format, too.[21] Even with the expansion into this market, World War II had seen a precipitous decline in the number of films released by the eight major studios—Warner, Twentieth Century Fox, RKO, MGM, Universal, Columbia, Paramount, and United Artists—from 388 films in 1939, to 243 in 1940, and then 252 in 1946.[22]

Industrial tides turned against Hollywood with the Paramount Decree in 1948, which required major studios to divest their holdings in exhibition venues. Though the studios' divorcement from theater ownership unfolded over the next decade, Izod noted many consequences that rapidly took effect. Without revenue flowing from their own theaters, major distributors began to charge exhibitors more for film rentals. To do this, they had to provide more obvious guaranteed film successes, and these films had to be sold to exhibitors, as distributors could no longer rely on steady and easy access to screens for their profits. Exhibitors became a key target for studio publicity, increasing the importance of trade advertisement campaigns and press books that provided ready-made images, prose, and ideas on how the exhibitors in turn could sell a film to moviegoers. This shift in practice killed the double bill, and, as Izod wrote, "put pressure on production units to turn out 'sure things' rather than 'prestige items.' Experimentation was taboo."[23] This may have been the dominant impression. Nonetheless, experimentation did take place, although it focused less on stylistics or thematic matters and more on production and exhibition formats and technology. Decreases in output continued, with the five major studios that were most directly affected by divorcement releasing only 116 films in 1956 combined.[24]

Not everyone foresaw the downturn, even after the Paramount Decree mandated industry restructuring. In fact, there was considerable foot-dragging on implementing the required divorcement. And with many independent exhibitors still complaining about unfair practices into the 1950s, a U.S. Senate subcommittee of the Select Committee on Small Business held a hearing on the topic, eventually recommending, among other things, more oversight of the antitrust decisions that had already been made.[25] And the impact of the Paramount Decree itself was in question. At the time, economist Simon

Whitney concluded that exhibitors believed it had created a product shortage in the early 1950s, raised rental rates for certain films, and created more work by mandating bidding on individual films rather than block-booked packages.[26]

Sector upheaval and uncertainty was the order of the day, and this was a new experience for many working in the film business at the time. Movies had been generally understood as immune to the ups and downs of economic fortune. During recessions, movies were an affordable break from everyday strife. In times of affluence, movies benefited as an accessible petty luxury. Leo A. Handel's important survey of research on American moviegoers, *Hollywood Looks at Its Audience: A Report of Film Audience Research*, published in 1950, is indicative of these impressions. Handel wrote of the industry's bright outlook, given expectations for a strong economy and an expansion of consumer power. He cited a survey of consumer trends that saw rising consumer spending, especially for recreation for the next decade, which pointed to "the growth potential of motion pictures." Optimistically, Handel summarized:

> Films, as the largest single economic factor in recreation and entertainment, can be expected to absorb nearly a fifth of all money spent on recreation. An increased future attendance may also be seen in another development which, however, would need further investigation. Many of today's older persons could not acquire the movie habit while they were young because they had no chance to see pictures then. This holds especially true for the foreign-born population. . . . Other factors which may result in higher future attendance frequencies [include] the increasing proportion of urban population, the shorter work week leaving more time for recreation, and a comparatively new appearance in the motion picture market, the 16mm film which will try to bring pictures to small isolated communities which could not maintain regular theaters. Also drive-in theaters are creating additional audiences.[27]

As represented here, a range of factors—habitual moviegoing, immigration, urban populations, more leisure time, growing alternatives to movie theaters like 16 mm and drive-ins—all supported the view that the road ahead was a prosperous one for Hollywood. Even an evident imminent threat was not reported as such. Handel wrote, "Television is beginning to make itself felt in the field of entertainment. This medium, however, is too new to permit a prediction of how it will affect the motion picture attendance of tomorrow."[28]

The writing was soon on the wall and television was generally understood as a major competitor for audiences. Other factors that kept people from the movie houses, as Whitney noted, included the rising popularity of night baseball and suburban gardening, and the inflated cost of going out related to parking and babysitters.[29] Moviegoing was no longer taken for granted as immune to the economy nor as a timeless practice. Action had to be taken to rebuild not just the structure of the industry but the very practice of moviegoing.

The advantages of big films with big promotional plans seemed more significant and irresistible than ever before. Big-budget filmmaking would distinguish film from television, draw audiences away from their living rooms to witness unprecedented motion picture splendor. The brute economics of this solution, which included financial support for grand film projects and investment in new production and exhibition facilities, were not easily won. The various campaigns to rally Americans back to moviegoing, such as "Movietime, U.S.A.," called out to potential investors and captains of capital, made skittish by reports of the deterioration of the movie business, as much as they spoke to the average moviegoer. Exhibitors, too, required special consideration, and big films promised to appeal to those who were opting to nestle in front of the television set. Theater operators have always cried out for a steady flow of films, obviously preferring hits to duds. By 1954 they specifically called for distinctive and spectacular products. So ingrained had this plea become that by the end of that year, exhibitors were complaining that they had to wait for the big Christmas releases, having to settle for second-rate products through the fall.[30] Why not bring Christmas earlier?

The pursuit of cinematic grandeur resulted in upscaled moviegoing, technological novelties, and "seriousness" in motion pictures. The special place of the prestige film in a general releasing pattern was one way Hollywood could confront the rise of television. The prestige film captured a brand of middlebrow cultural import, which might have to do with an idea of timeless stories—for example, *Samson and Delilah*—and adaptations of identifiable literary works. A particular manifestation of the prestige film was "roadshow" releasing. Versions of roadshowing had been used for high-profile films for decades, but in the 1950s it became a regularized strategy. A roadshow is a form of exhibition and distribution that tried to imitate the trappings of bourgeois live theater. A roadshow release would typically offer limited runs, in luxurious theaters; limited screenings per day, with longer film running times; extra material like programs; and a soundtrack that included orchestral overtures to open the film and to accompany intermissions. This special treatment, which also came with higher ticket prices and reserved seating, contrasted with the then still dominant practice of continuous showings appropriate to habitual moviegoing. The increasingly selective American moviegoer needed the enticement of the "event movie," the performance of prestige in theatrical surroundings, and was willing to spend more for the privilege. Roadshowing was a much-discussed distribution tactic in the mid-1950s, though only sixteen features from 1956 through 1959 (inclusively) were truly released in this way. In the 1960s this tactic was so prevalent that twelve films received such treatment in 1968 alone.[31]

With the filmic extravagances of the roadshow, movies offered themselves as entertainments for educated and discerning moviegoers, and they catered to less frequent attendees willing and able to pay an inflated ticket price. These were adult and sophisticated presentations, framed as cinematic, historic, or artistic events. Attending a screening lent prestige to the audience members and catered to cosmopolitan sensibilities. Works roamed to locations worldwide and drew inspiration from already popular middlebrow theatrical productions. Worldliness was a dominant theme, and the trappings of prestige deliberately sought to give the impression of an elevated cultural work. The trailers for *Ben-Hur* (1959) illustrate this tendency. After the film's historic sweep of the Academy Awards in early 1960, the promotional trailers focused on the industry accolades. But before the film's release, the trailers constructed a sense of the high cultural pedigree of the source novel, introducing it as one of the great, almost-sacred works of world literature. One trailer concentrates on *Ben-Hur*'s reverential treatment of its religious subject matter. It does so by presenting what appears to be a tour of a museum gallery that displays Renaissance religious paintings. The slow-moving camera, the contemplative pauses at the paintings, and the gilded frames communicate the cultural importance and seriousness of the treatment. Even a velvet rope, a sign of both luxury and constraint, keeps viewers from coming too close to the precious paintings on display. The film, *Ben-Hur*, becomes an extension of this elevated cultural world, not an American cultural work but a work that is classic in its representational glory and global in its thematic concern. Reigning senses of the adult and the global built distinctiveness for this visible and highly capitalized wing of the Hollywood business. Though the roadshow spectacles were not advertised as blockbusters in the first part of the 1950s, producers and critics talked about them as such with growing regularity and consistency, and often in terms similar to the reverential seriousness represented by *Ben-Hur*'s trailer at the end of the decade.[32]

Roadshows also put technological processes and presentational innovations in the foreground. Technological display in the 1950s came in many forms, but the most universally discussed were the new widescreen formats. Nowhere were giganticism and motion pictures better represented than in the turn to widescreen technologies and projects, which included Paramount's VistaVision, Twentieth Century Fox's CinemaScope, Todd-AO, and, most unusual, the three-projector curved and immersive image of Cinerama. For a confined period in 1953 and 1954, 3-D films were momentarily sensational. The expense of projection and production made them a tenuous financial prospect, and the quality of the 3-D effect was marginal.[33] That it didn't became standard practice was unsurprising. Nonetheless, the move to experiment with 3-D, and the temporary widespread curiosity it provoked, had aspects in common with other developments: the importance of technological spectacle, the privileging of illusions of immersion in the image, and the production of an image that overwhelms.

The exclusivity and prestige of roadshowing were on full display with the surprising success of independent films like *This Is Cinerama* (1952). This globe-trotting travelogue showcase for Cinerama is generally credited with sparking interest in widescreen processes. And entrepreneur Michael Todd helped develop the wide-angle bug-eye-lensed Todd-AO widescreen format, first used in *Oklahoma!* (1955) and then in *Around the World in 80 Days* (1956), as a one-camera/one-projector approximation of Cinerama. These widescreen processes often incorporated narratives of progress that saw the new format as an advancement over more primitive forms of art and verisimilitude. Such tales, which might be described in a roadshow printed program or in a filmed prologue, invited audiences to marvel at the wonder of light and sound that loomed large and loud in the auditorium. In fact, *Quo Vadis*, a hit through 1952, rather than being the first movie blockbuster named as such, should actually be acknowledged as one of the last such extravagant productions not to embrace the technological wonderment of widescreen processes, being instead presented in the standard Academy aspect ratio.

Spiritual immensity drove the first era of the blockbuster. The religious epic was a fixture of Hollywood spectacle from the early days of feature film, with huge sets, large numbers of extras depicting the entirety of humanity, and a cinematic style that privileged long shots to present the fullness of the realization. The postwar iteration gathered up comparable elements, though using Technicolor and other color processes, and crammed the screen with lavish sets, matte shots, and multitudes of costumed figures.

The religious subject matter lent itself to pious representational modes, with aesthetic inspiration liberally drawn from the iconography of European religious artwork. The realist conventions of the religious epic held tight to the composition of the tableaux, the large-format painting, and the panorama. Not everyone cheered this version of filmic wonder. Manny Farber wrote upon the release of the first widescreen biblical epic, *The Robe* (1953), "This is the age of elephantine, humorless films that show little if any artistic endeavor."[34] This film was the very first CinemaScope release, using Twentieth Century Fox's dramatically elongated widescreen format; on this, Farber commented further, "The screen is exploited here chiefly for spectacular mural-type photographs in which every detail is clearly defined: the movement of the camera lens is usually a slow sideways one, giving you the impression of looking at the world through a slot-in-the-wall."[35] The technologically enhanced spectacles of biblical vistas did not lift the static treatment of the subject, leaving Farber to conclude that they reminded him "of nothing so much as the worst examples of calendar art."[36] In fact, so muddied was 1953 with gimmicks like 3-D and widescreen that Farber summarized the state of film as follows: "Wherever you look today, you find the movie artist subordinating himself in order to glorify a mechanical process."[37]

Roland Barthes's brief ruminations on widescreen are equally revealing. Where Farber saw subordination to the mechanical, Barthes wondered about a new relationship between image and spectator, perhaps even "a new dialectic between human and horizon, between human and objects," one characterized by interdependence.[38] Barthes thought, counterintuitively, that widescreen, rather than making viewers subservient to the image, lifted the spectator onto an equal plane with the enlarged image. A visual field opened up and brightened, inviting viewers into the image's expansiveness. The spectator becomes, in Barthes's words, "a god, since I am no longer beneath the image but in front of it, in the middle of it."[39]

As both Farber and Barthes identified, the spectatorial experience of the engulfing image put the technological mode on display as much as the filmed content itself. Theatrical settings are the primary venue for large projections, and, as such, they are the primary home for blockbusters. Even as other sites of film viewing surpass the movie theater in audience numbers and revenue, the first stop for blockbusters, and the setting for which they are initially constructed, is still the movie theater. Blockbusters are an ongoing statement of faith in the time-honored, though embattled, distribution plan in which movies open in movie theaters. This was the case in the 1950s, and it remains the case today. The widescreen innovations of the 1950s made this bid that much more certain. However ponderous *The Robe* may have been, the new screen technology helped draw out enough curious moviegoers for the film to be a hit during a severe attendance drought.

At the behest of Columbia Pictures, the Gallup organization conducted an extensive survey of audience responses and opinions about these new screen technologies in 1953, in many ways truly the first year of the rollout of these experiments.[40] A nationally representative survey asked respondents about 3-D, widescreen, and stereo sound, hoping to determine which was thought to be an improvement over standard formats, which would prompt attendance, and which they would pay more for. The participants had to have seen at least one 3-D or widescreen film and were drawn from cities with at least 100,000 inhabitants, thus limiting the survey to urban moviegoers. Audience Research Inc. contacted 2,500 individuals, of whom 875 became survey participants. The sample was heavily weighted toward those who had experienced 3-D, who accounted for 92 percent of those surveyed, while 18 percent had seen a widescreen film (excluding Cinerama) and only 7 percent had seen Cinerama. In an effort to construct a nationwide sample, participants from across the country were included, though the largest region represented was the "East." There were no indications of class or ethnicity, but the sample was evenly split between men and women.[41] In a sign that the dramatic decrease in attendance was not yet fully in evidence, 52 percent reportedly went to the movies at least once per week, and 48 percent went less frequently, even though 74 percent were already members of a television-owning household.[42]

The finding for 3-D signaled a finite interest in the gimmick. The survey found that people were generally favorable toward the new format, with the highest level of approval among teenagers and those with television sets. Just less than half (47 percent) said they liked 3-D better than regular movies, 36 percent would pay more to see them, and 22 percent reported that 3-D would encourage them to actually go to the movies. But most (53 percent) preferred standard-format films or had no preference, 36 percent reported eyestrain or discomfort with the obligatory 3-D glasses, and, in test cases, 3-D did not improve desire to see the movie. Overall, the survey indicated that 3-D lacked lasting drawing power and predicted that interest would soon wear off.

In contrast, widescreen showed a more favorable response (62 percent), and in test cases a widescreen film generated more interest in seeing the movie than the regular format did. As was the case for 3-D, there was not significant willingness to pay more for widescreen specifically, and the number reporting that having all films in widescreen would prompt more attendance was about the same as for 3-D (22 percent). Still, Audience Research concluded that, over time, widescreen would have more potential as an audience draw than 3-D. More favorable still, 69 percent of those who had experienced a movie in stereo sound liked it better than regular film sound, and 71 percent of the small sample who had seen Cinerama liked the panoramic curved-screen projection better than films in the standard aspect ratio.[43] According to this survey, widescreen, stereo sound, and Cinerama held more promise for the construction of a distinctive motion picture entertainment offering than did 3-D, and they were more likely to contribute substantially to box-office revenue than 3-D once it was no longer novel.

Those who did not attend at least once per week were asked about their relative lack of frequency in moviegoing. The interviewees reported that television satisfied their entertainment needs but also that there were not enough good films worth going out to see. As the report put it, "This seems to be consistent with the industry's experience in recent years that the advent of television has made its greatest inroads in the 'middle grade' pictures and has had the least effect on the 'top grade' pictures."[44] This singular snapshot of the American moviegoer is far from comprehensive, but it does illuminate several factors. The 3-D format was properly understood as providing a limited boost to box-office sales. In contrast, experiments with other formats had prospects as long-term attractions. The very structure of the inquiry, focusing directly on the exploitable potential of new technological features, concluded with a recommendation that the high end of quality films was ground that could not be encroached on by other media of the day, most specifically television. For movie exhibitors, producers, and distributors, an explicit connection was being drawn between prestige and new technology.

Various paratexts, including promotional materials and film prologues, drew audience attention to the special features of the processes, from image size to sound innovations, making new technological trappings a central part of a movie event. The poster for *The Robe* displays the investment in the exhibition format by making the film title and Fox's format equally prominent, describing it as "The Modern Miracle You See Without Glasses!" (figure 4.8). This tagline presents CinemaScope as an immersive technology that improves on the then faddishly popular 3-D. It equally aligns the "miracle" of film technology with the "miracle" of Christ, an example of promotional hubris if there ever was one. In fact, other elements were so far down the list of priorities for publicity that Jean Peters's face appears beside star Richard Burton on the

FIGURE 4.8 *The Robe* poster featuring CinemaScope, 1953

poster, even though she had been replaced by Jean Simmons during production. The film begins with a shot of a red velvet curtain, as though it covers the screen, and the first credit reads, "Twentieth Century Fox presents a CinemaScope Production." The format here is elevated to the level of a production entity. Following the simple credits, the curtain draws back, a motion that emphasizes the horizontal elongation of the screen, to reveal a Roman spectacle in process.

The success of *The Robe* and CinemaScope prompted Twentieth Century Fox to release a sequel the following year. *Demetrius and the Gladiators* (1954) continued the story, with Victor Mature, Michael Rennie, and Jay Robinson reprising their roles as Demetrius, Peter, and Caligula, respectively. The trailer begins with written text that links the wonders of the new format, the epic tale, and Christianity, over scenes of Roman pageantry:

> In Scope! . . .
> In Faith! . . .
> In Drama! . . .

THE BUSINESS OF BIG · 147

> In the Mighty Tradition of "The Robe" . . .
> 20th Century-Fox Proudly Presents
> "Demetrius and the Gladiators"
> In the Miracle of CinemaScope

Following an introduction to the key players, the trailer returns to the epic production:

> And A Spectacular Cast of Thousands!
> Here is the tremendous continuation of "The Robe"
> As CinemaScope fills the screen like it has never been filled before!
> Through CinemaScope Your Eyes Behold . . .
> The Glory . . .
> The Grandeur . . .
> The Pleasure . . .
> The Passion . . .
> The Spectacle . . .
> And the Splendor that was Rome!

Placing emphasis on sensual spectacles, these titles mention *The Robe* four times and CinemaScope five times, three of which replicate the swooping curve of the logo (figure 4.9). The last mention presents CinemaScope and stereophonic sound together, claiming they "Add Breath-Taking New Dimensions . . . New Vistas of Entertainment . . . ," followed by the final mention of *The Robe* and "color by Technicolor." The original film's initial trailer was not as singularly focused on CinemaScope as that for this sequel, but here technological exhibitionism is front and center.

Of the various experiments, CinemaScope became the most standardized of the widescreen formats in industrial practice for a time. Overall, the widescreen aspect ratio, with its elongated, rectangular image designed to cover more of the spectator's field of vision horizontally, settled as a lasting convention in a less expansive form than CinemaScope. As familiar as widescreen may be, having now been taken up in the shape of contemporary television sets even though this often results in distorted images as we stretch them to fit the screen, it originated in a moment of innovation that privileged the spectacle of technology for the theatrical environment. We see from these innovations the idea that technological change can guide entertainment, can make entertainment distinctive, and can be entertainment. Once embraced as an

FIGURE 4.9 *Demetrius and the Gladiators* trailer featuring "the Miracle of Cinema-Scope," 1954

industrial rationale, innovations in cinematic mechanisms became a primary battleground for sector competition. It would not be a secondary, behind-the-scenes arena for technicians and professional guilds. These skilled craftspeople and technical experimenters were the heroes of cinematic magic and, as such, a new front-line force for capital that would guarantee a good return on investment.

During this time of transition, uses of "blockbuster" to convey ideas about event entertainment were more plentiful but were yet to conform to the meanings that would later command our understanding. Through the 1950s, not just movies but theater, television, and sports began to promote flagship productions as "blockbusters." The programming of ABC was a "Friday TV Blockbuster" for 1953.[45] And Danny Thomas's show at the Sands in Las Vegas delivered "a laugh blockbuster" with his "Irish-Catholic priest yarn."[46] Critics picked up on the term, with Saul Bellow's *The Adventures of Augie March*, for example, described in reviews as a "blockbuster of a novel."[47] "Blockbuster" was a brand of popcorn, a children's toy, and a singing group. When General Electric placed an unusually substantial sixteen-page advertisement in *Business Week* and *Fortune* in 1953, marketing commentators described it as a "'blockbuster' insert."[48] A discriminatory real estate practice that had been around throughout the twentieth century came to be called "blockbusting" in the late 1950s. All these illustrations demonstrate a shift in usage, and the fact that a weapon of destruction became the name for a toy and a snack is a statement about connotative mobility.

Following World War II, "blockbuster" began to describe big-budget film productions (notably multistar vehicles) in the trade press. For instance, a *Daily Variety* article from 1948 referenced "Leo's Blockbusters," that is, the MGM lineup of *Command Decision* (1948), *A Date with Judy* (1948), *Julia Misbehaves* (1948), *Sun in the Morning* (1948), *The Bribe* (1949), *Act of Violence* (1948), *Easter Parade* (1948), and *Vespers in Vienna* (1948).[49] A *Daily Variety* article reported the large number of "the 20th-Fox blockbusters," about to be released, along with their unusually high budgets: *The Black Rose* (1950), $3.5 million; *Lydia Bailey* (1952), $3 million; *The Snake Pit* (1948), $2.7 million; and with budgets of $2 million, *Price of Foxes* (1949), *Twelve O'Clock High* (1949), *Down to the Sea in Ships* (1949), and *The Beautiful Blonde from Bashful Bend* (1949).[50] The thematic connection to World War II air force films continued after the release of *Twelve O'Clock High*, described in *Variety*'s grosses roundup as a "Blockbuster at $34,000" at the Fox Theatre in Philadelphia.[51] Similarly, Columbia Pictures producer Sam Katzman's then upcoming, but ultimately unreleased, film *Bomber Command* (1950) was a "Technicolor blockbuster," prefiguring where the term would settle in relation to technological specificity (Technicolor) as opposed to box-office performance alone.[52] However, the settling of the term's meaning was not linear and coherent: columnist Mike Connolly announced Budd Boetticher's *The Number One* (released as *The Magnificent Matador*, 1955) as "another bullfight blockbuster," using the term to denote "action packed."[53]

These examples show that by the 1950s many media and commercial enterprises described featured and successful products as blockbusters, but the term equally referenced low-budget productions. The concept was a promotional mechanism, a way to present the most impactful among alternatives. The term's secure settlement as a type of motion picture and an industrial strategy was not yet complete. While some early uses mesh with our own, this material indicates that these appearances were *not* yet directly or specifically related to epics and roadshow spectaculars. Claiming otherwise relies on a retrospective attentiveness to the most successful and visible films from the period, presuming that big-budget films were identified as blockbusters then as we would identify them now.

Most surprisingly, before the big-budget films and hits of the 1950s used the term in their promotional material, smaller genre films were doing so. Print advertisements for *The Atomic City* (1952) quoted reviewer Jane Corby of the *Brooklyn Eagle*, who wrote, "This is one of those films that come like a bolt from the blue. It's a block-buster. *The Atomic City* belongs in anybody's list of good films to see" (figure 4.10).[54] This notice was distinctive as it appeared at the same time *Quo Vadis* was burning up the box office, a film that did not use the "blockbuster" descriptor in its ads, trade or otherwise. *Quo Vadis* promotion opted to feature an older term for a spectacular film, one that was perhaps more connotatively suitable to the ancient Roman setting of its tale: "colossal." Interestingly, in the promotional materials for *The Atomic City*, "block-buster" only meant that it "belongs in anybody's list of good films." The description did not connote superlative quality or production extravagances. Instead, it was about the surprise of the film's thematic impact, and it drew on a connection to the subject matter of a terrorizing explosive threat.

The only explosions in *The Atomic City*, in fact, are stock footage of blasts at the movie's opening. The rest of the film is a combination of police procedural, noir melodrama, and espionage thriller, in which the child of an atomic scientist working at Los Alamos is kidnapped and held for ransom in exchange for atomic secrets. One memorable sequence includes the enlisting of television cameras, in the midst of a live broadcast of a baseball game, to assist with surveillance of a suspect. The sequence sparks the imagination about the ways that new media might assist domestic defense and public safety, going further to portray easy cooperation and support for warrantless community scrutiny. Given the timeliness of the subject matter, the exploitation potential for this low-budget film was high. But Paramount did not mount a fully coherent campaign, a marketing uncertainty that extended even to the title. During production the film was first titled *Bomb*, then *Los Alamos Story*, and then it was finally released as *The Atomic City*.[55] Paramount made an unusual move and released it in some markets, including Los Angeles, under yet another title, *19 Elevado Street*.[56] Beyond this inconsistency at the most rudimentary promotional stage of naming the film, there was a direct and highly developed attempt to promote the film via the migration of other industrial terminology. As an early, if minor, incorporation of "blockbuster," *The Atomic City* ad campaign notably featured the term "sleeper." So unfamiliar to the general audience was the term "sleeper" that ads included an asterisk leading to the following definition: "Sleeper in show business is known as a surprise smash hit!" (figure 4.11).[57]

FIGURE 4.10 *The Atomic City* press book, with "block-buster" in the *Brooklyn Eagle* quote, 1952

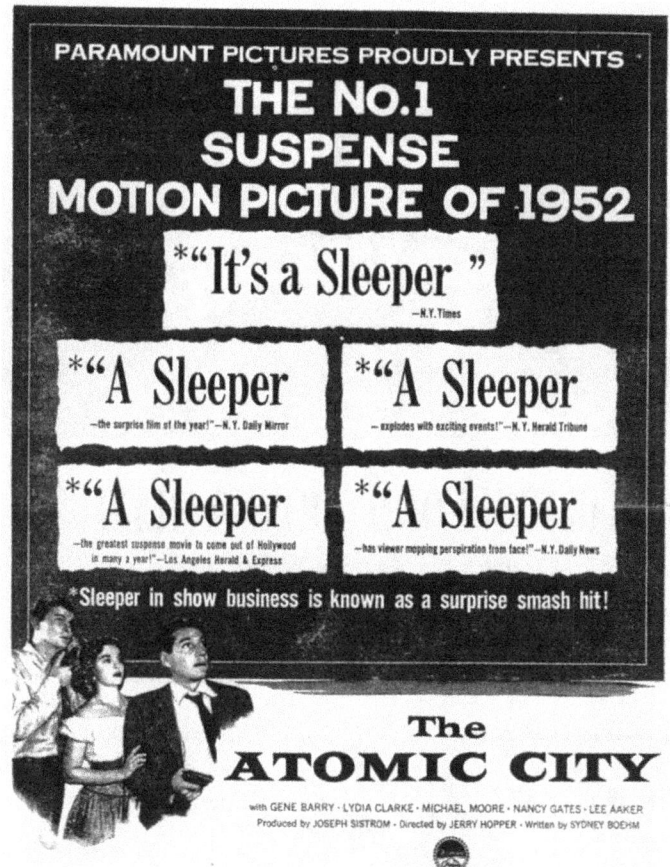

FIGURE 4.11 *The Atomic City* press book, explaining "sleeper," 1952

The term "blockbuster" was not yet fixed to notions of superlative success. Thus, *Boxoffice* described United Artists' two features of 1952, *The African Queen* (1951) and *High Noon*, as their blockbusters because they were among the top ten highest-grossing films of the year. They were hits, to be sure, and they were fast earners, returning their investment easily. But these are successful films rather than record-smashing and cinema-changing efforts.[58] Other studios weighed in as well, though they were not as systematically invested in developing the approach. In 1955 another kidnapping thriller, MGM's *Ransom!* (1956), was described as "a new dramatic blockbuster that crashes into the headlines like 'Blackboard Jungle' and 'Trial'!"[59] Rare for the time,

THE BUSINESS OF BIG · 153

FIGURE 4.12 *Ransom!* press book, describing it as a "dramatic blockbuster," 1955

FIGURE 4.13 *Ransom!* press book, describing it as a "dramatic block-buster," 1955 "dramatic blockbuster" appeared in newspaper advertisements for the film, making this an early example of crossover usage (figures 4.12 and 4.13).[60] An additional sign of this transitional moment is that this marketing campaign was not consistent in the spelling of the term, with some advertisements continuing to use the hyphenated "block-buster" and others the conventional spelling used today, "blockbuster." At the same time, MGM tried the phrase for a rerelease of *Thirty Seconds over Tokyo*.[61]

Studio management of the concept was calculated and usage more frequent, if imprecise. Industry observer Army Archerd commented that Columbia had deliberately held *The Caine Mutiny* (1954) back from release in 1953 as it already had a box-office success and they saw "no sense in having two blockbusters in one year."[62] The idea that the category was a precious resource would shift dramatically, with some studios promising blockbusters to exhibitors on a regular basis. Even so, we can see that certain films could be pegged with high expectations well in advance of their release and designated as hits with, of course, the associated promotional treatment. Columbia acquired *The Caine Mutiny*, produced by Stanley Kramer's independent outfit, as part of a package of eleven other films, in part because Columbia "needed a tremendous boxoffice blockbuster."[63] It was indeed a rousing box-office success, a "big blockbuster."[64]

Kramer had an unusual position during the 1950s as a well-known producer and director, and his career shows us some of the range and adultness that was possible under the auspices of the newly developing blockbuster idea. He worked through his own independent film production company, Stanley Kramer Productions, which had a long-standing distribution deal with Columbia and then later with United Artists. For both, Kramer predictably turned in topical and liberal social-issue films, some of which were big-budget flagship productions for major studios that became both critical and box-office hits. In an era of Cold War self-censorship and ideological chill, Kramer was a political director, a mainstream one known for taking on issues thought to be controversial. What may now seem to be rather blandly melodramatic films that personalize social issues, and navigate complex situations to acceptable dramatic closures, were at the time distinctive prestige treatments. And they were popular. *The Defiant Ones* (1958), *On the Beach* (1959), *Inherit the Wind* (1960), *Judgment at Nuremberg* (1961), and *Guess Who's Coming to Dinner* (1967) all showed what a serious and adult popular film might be. And while his silliest, *It's a Mad, Mad, Mad, Mad World* (1963), had all the dead weight of a star-laden monstrosity, with an expansive production that ground down the lightness of the comedic subject matter, it is still an ambitious blockbuster social satire about greed. In Kramer we can see an early model for the liberal political popular hit-making auteur, including all the possibilities and limitations that come with that form of filmmaking.

Aside from relatively rare and metaphoric uses, and unlike the fast take-up of its use to sell books to a general audience, "blockbuster," for the movie business from 1943 to 1957, was primarily part of trade lingo. Its use responded directly to the industrial upheaval of the period, in which the studios and exhibitors were significantly worried about the place of the film attraction in light of the rise of television. But the general logic of the big—that big investments and big promotion and big technological features returned big profits—was starting to become more formalized. Very soon, the concept of the blockbuster would join that wave of technological exhibitionism for popular audiences.

By the mid-1950s, the first Todd-AO film (*Oklahoma!*), Cinerama films, and *The Ten Commandments* were all being described in the trade press as blockbusters, named as such owing to their production, technological, and box-office extravagances. Todd-AO head Michael Todd had worked for Cinerama, which his own format emulated. The connection to Cinerama was strong enough for exhibitor Charles Skouras to ask that Todd-AO films come with a prologue that included aerial photography akin to the soaring documentary images of *This Is Cinerama*, used to show off the technological apparatus, though the suggestion was not acted upon.[65]

Joe Schoenfeld, in *Daily Variety*, not only recognized *Oklahoma!* as a blockbuster but noted the relationship to technological change. He wrote that the film "presages a new era in the motion picture industry. The Todd-AO process offers audiences the same type of story participation that they get in the legitimate theatre; the six-track sound is the finest and most exciting experience of its type that theatre audiences have yet enjoyed. It makes obsolete all sound systems as now known; it dwarfs all other dimensions other than Cinerama."[66] Upon the film's release, this line of argumentation continued. His later review declared that, like the stage production, this film "is likewise a motion picture blockbuster." Ample reference was made to sound technology, the screen-size innovations of Todd-AO, and especially the budget, which was unusually high for the time, in part because of the research and development expenses. Schoenfeld wrote, "Not counting all the coin that went into developing Mike Todd's Todd-AO system, *Oklahoma* cost around $6,000,000. With the financing of the system, the Magna Corporation [one of the film's production companies] has around $11,000,000 total in this initial film, but it now looks like a small investment in comparison to the likely huge return 'Okla.' will bring."[67] Such attention to the financial contribution of the technological format propelled even further consideration. For instance, when the box-office performance of "a trio of blockbusters" was highlighted, all three were widescreen, big-budget, color spectaculars, and two were directly connected to new cinema technologies: *Cinerama Holiday* (1955) (Cinerama), *Oklahoma!* (Todd-AO), and *Guys and Dolls* (1955).[68] In short, this was the nascent strategy of the *technological tentpole* film, one that entwined popularity and success with the advancement of a media format.

There was, of course, no guarantee that technological innovation would be worth the considerable investment required. When *Oklahoma!* was in preparation, it was uncertain how many theaters would make the investments needed to screen in Todd-AO, so they shot it simultaneously in CinemaScope. In the end, most of the audience saw the CinemaScope version. But by the time Todd was ready to release his next Todd-AO film, *Around the World in 80 Days*, more sites were ready to receive the film in that format. It is difficult to grasp today what an extraordinary hit *Around the World in 80 Days* was. By the end of 1957, the film, still in theaters a year after its release, was the fourth-highest-grossing film of all time, right behind *Gone with the Wind* (1939), *The Ten Commandments*, and *The Robe*. It had amassed $16.2 million and had done so with only 145 engagements.[69] The film continued to play in Todd-AO–equipped locations through the end of 1958, at which point it went into general release in other formats.

Seeing the industry turn toward a new screen shape for motion pictures, Paramount committed to its widescreen process, VistaVision. They released twenty such films in 1955, and planned the same for 1956; that later year's slate represented the entirety of their films for the year. The trim number, all sporting their flagship process, matched up with Paramount's focus on big, distinctive films, most notably *The Ten Commandments* and *War and Peace* (1956).[70] In essence, prestige, middlebrow film topics (biblical epic and literary classic) and treatments (a high production budget and A-list talent) deserved an equally prestigious technological process for filming and projection. The certainty of the category appeared in *Variety*'s review for *War and Peace*, which featured the subheading "A Blockbuster Destined to Be a Perennial

Cinematic Classic." Reiterating clearly that this film was expansive and of high quality, the review began, "*War and Peace* is a real blockbuster. This is not a celluloid entry for once or even twice around. It is a rich contribution to the art form of the picture business in the best tradition. It is an entertainment and educational force and a production powerhouse on size and stature values alone. It is big in the biggest sense of the cinematurgical art and, in this alone, there is a payoff."[71] The hallmarks of an appeal to cultural uplift are all evident in this review, most explicitly in the reference to education and art. But so is the spectacle of bigness, alluded to side by side with this uplift. Similar rhapsodic tunes would be sung for other Hollywood film epics, but this was being echoed most directly by a film already in preproduction, but released only at the end of 1959, *Ben-Hur*.

The path to standardization is a meandering one. Many of the screen innovations were too expensive and substantial for exhibitors to undertake. Cinerama and Todd-AO were, in the end, destined to be marginal and of dwindling interest after a few years in the sun. Even CinemaScope, which required fewer deviations from existing exhibition practice, had issues. Though the adjustments of special screens and projector lenses were relatively minor investments for exhibitors, CinemaScope initially needed stereo sound equipment.[72] This proved too much, and after exhibitor complaints, CinemaScope films were made available in mono. Peter Lev additionally notes that theater owners made an effort to establish their own technical standards in 1952, hoping this would push back on the technological demands of distributors and producers, at a time when the coming of 3-D and theater television, meaning television screenings in movie theaters, were the primary matters at hand, but a cooperative agreement did not progress, leaving technological innovations to the whim of market forces.[73]

The 1955 Venice Film Festival captured some of the changes that were unfolding. There, organizers for the first time equipped festival venues for CinemaScope, VistaVision, and other widescreen projection systems. In addition to accommodating format variations, other technological additions included the installation of new anamorph-stereo sound equipment. As these cutting-edge exhibition features drew the attention of festivalgoers to the future of the cinema environment, other events drew people back to earlier stages of motion picture history. For instance, Iris Barry from MOMA curated a seven-day silent film retrospective that included material that ranged from 1895 actualities through to *The Mark of Zorro* in 1920.[74] In this way the festival featured the future of the varying cinematic apparatus while showcasing the past, revealing that historical consciousness was in part technological.

Despite this prominent appearance on the international stage, some thought that the technological supplements were not enough to carry films overseas. Industry reporter Fred Hift commented, "Hollywood's great big Technicolored, CinemaScoped, star-spangled, escapist musical films which are a staple boxoffice attraction of the home (United States and Canada) market and a good bet for Britain remain a real 'hard sell' for the film fans of the world."[75] The need, then, to sell the cinematic system internationally along with the film was apparent, though Hift noted that the American specificities of the two most prominent musicals at the time—*Oklahoma!* and *Guys and Dolls*—might also explain their limited appeal in other countries.

There may have been some stumbles in the move toward a global American blockbuster film, but this did not slow down the efforts to build it. The coming years would see significant expansion of popular film markets, well beyond national borders. From *Samson and Delilah* to *The Ten Commandments*, a blockbuster strategy was beginning to be locked into place, and with it an eye toward bourgeois audiences beyond the United States. In the end, the production's size and the promotional plans that featured details about the production were important elements of the blockbuster strategy. During the 1950s, when they were still a rarity among the films released, the roadshow films transformed the familiar moviegoing activity into one with the trappings of a more elevated and cultured practice. Roadshowing made going out to a film akin to a theatrical or literary event, and it offered an added educational value. An inspirational tale, or a classic story remounted, provided part of the cultural alibi. The state-of-the-art technological features supplemented the experience, acting as a showcase for the peak possibilities in motion picture arts. Uplift was the promise of this breed of entertainment, and the nature of the uplift included the cultural, the social, and the technological. Accordingly, theaters amplified and made visible the technological components of screen performance and screen environment, and privileged the big. The blockbuster—the event movie—was becoming the most appropriate film form for a multimedia entertainment context. Blockbusters would settle in as Vanessa R. Schwartz's "cosmopolitan film," and middlebrow internationalism circulated widely. With technological exhibitionism defining the biggest film presentations, prestigious films would be cultural *and* technological events.

(CHAPTER FIVE)

HOLLYWOOD'S RETURN

Everyone wanted in on the action. The exclusive end of big-budget filmmaking rested primarily with a few maverick producers, like Michael Todd and Cecil B. DeMille, as well as the highly capitalized major studios, especially Paramount and MGM. But in the wake of the rising prominence of big, attention-getting films, there were many imaginative competitive moves. Because the films were creatures of publicity, describing them as "blockbusters" became an inflationary game, where competitors tried to grab public attention with successively exaggerated claims. Big films were also something to program against and to confront with opposing approaches to movie entertainment. The contraction of the majors, which were making and releasing fewer movies, was an opportunity for the smaller studios Universal, Columbia, and United Artists (UA). All three increased their rentals and began to focus on big-budget A pictures themselves. A growing number of independent production outfits filled the lower-budget end of things; many of them had distribution arrangements with the studios.¹ The studios initially had limited production budgets, but starting in 1954 this austerity began to be reversed, with more color, widescreen, and epic productions.² In all of these directions, the public was growing accustomed to a new set of expectations for moviegoing.

One thing was certain: the overall health of the film business was linked to blockbusters. The previous chapter examined the actions taken in response to industrial upheaval, in particular the investments in distinctive big-budget productions and new cinema technology. And these seemed to be paying off. In 1954–1955, understood as a generally strong year for Los Angeles exhibitors, industry reporter Bill Brogdon explained the upswing as related to an "admissions tax cut, as well as a number of block-buster pictures that enjoyed lush, long runs, and an increase in the number of weeks of first run operation for some of the situations."[3] Leonard Goldenson, the head of ABC-Paramount, the theater and television corporation formed following divorcement, now separate from the film producer-distributor Paramount Pictures, explained the impact of the Paramount Decree in 1956: "The decree placed the balance of power in the hands of the producers. It brought about the product shortage, the multiple runs, the exorbitant film rentals, overextended playing times and competitive bidding."[4] Many of these consequences were equally direct results of the acceptance of the blockbuster strategy.

Nevertheless, these changes could not mask the fact that serious problems lay ahead for the movie business as a whole. For instance, it was understood that costs for the production and distribution of a film did not rise in equal proportion to the budget, and that there were economies of scale with big-budget films. This impression pushed budgets and production ambitions higher and higher. Izod indicated, "The problem with belief in the inherent efficiency of large-scale productions is that it becomes hard to decide what should be the limit of size."[5] So with the blockbuster strategy came an irrational exuberance that encouraged financial riskiness.

Such contradictory pressures of film finance—a contracting market producing encouragement for more liberal investments—created an opening. Working in the shadow of blockbusters was becoming a tactic for parts of the American film industry. Some smaller studios, eager to edge their way onto a field dominated by the larger players, responded with their own version of the blockbuster. In 1954 UA trumpeted a "monthly blockbuster" release strategy.[6] Arthur Krim, head of UA, defined a blockbuster as "a film which will gross $2,000,000 or more in domestic (U.S. and Canada) rentals."[7] The first four films of UA's schedule of blockbusters had a total budget of $8 million, which, interestingly, means there was no significant expectation of unusual profit. The films were expected to do little better than break even. The attention to the entire slate of films, with the special assistance from more high-visibility films, would produce an overall advantage for UA. Krim managed this plan as a response to exhibitor complaints about lack of product, offering a steady flow of releases in which, each month, there would be something in the "blockbuster class."[8]

Other outfits had their own appropriation of the term. American International Pictures (AIP) was especially active, as with its "A Boxoffice Blockbuster" advertisement to proclaim the success of the double-billed *Hot Rod Girl* and *Girls in Prison* in 1956, and 1957's "Double Boxoffice Blockbuster No. 4!" for *Shake, Rattle and Rock!* (1956) and *Runaway Daughters* (1956), in addition to a string of future double bills to come throughout the rest of the year.[9] In 1958 AIP's trade advertisements for *I Was a Teenage Frankenstein* (1958) and *Blood of Dracula* (1957) described them doing "Blockbuster Business."[10] That these films were doing blockbuster business implicitly suggests they were *not* actually blockbuster productions. As president of AIP James H. Nicholson explained it, the big box-office successes were "either blockbusters or the 'gimmicks' shows."[11] The AIP productions were the "gimmicks," and they worked, as Nicholson said, "as a 'necessary bridge to keep the exhibitor going until the next big one.'"[12] Offering a vivid illustration of the popular film landscape of the 1950s, he put it, "'We've been sandwiched between "Giant" and "10 Commandments" and we're following Cinerama in Oklahoma City.'"[13] He saw the detrimental effect the big-budget films were having. Distributors forced exhibitors to accept terms that made it difficult for the blockbuster to pay off for the theater owner, despite all the audience members that were coming through the lobbies. One survey of theaters revealed that film rentals were 31 percent of box office in 1946, then 36 percent in 1953. Distributors, though, were demanding as much as 70 percent for the big films, like *The Robe*.[14] The films themselves were disconnected from American taste, according to Nicholson, who said Hollywood made "'too many films inside its ivory towers.'"[15] Instead, producers should cater to popular tastes, just as AIP did with their low-budget movies, and provide exhibitors with terms on which they could thrive.

As smaller studios and production companies piggybacked on the new industry term "blockbuster" and found a continued place for B films, there was no actual brand confusion. No exhibitor, or audience member, would mistake *Hot Rod Girl* for *Around the World in 80 Days* (1956). The gimmick films remained short, quickly made black-and-white genre offerings. The biggest blockbusters, in contrast, pushed up running times, with some adding musical overtures that meant audiences stared for several minutes at a static screen projection of "Overture" as they took their seats, intermissions that similarly included a musical soundtrack and a static projection of "Intermission," and seemingly interminable credit rolls. They stretched the definitional limits of a feature, reaching lengths that were punishing for viewers. *The Ten*

Commandments (1956) came in at 3 hours and 40 minutes, *Around the World in 80 Days* ran 2 hours and 55 minutes, and *War and Peace* (1956) was nearly three and a half hours long. These lengths produced a time crunch for screenings, limiting the number of performances possible in a day. Exhibitors, who counted on cycling groups of fresh ticket buyers through their doors, did not appreciate the resulting reduction in the turnover of audiences. But some filmmakers saw an angle they could exploit in the outsize running times. Arthur Cohen, who made short films for Universal, proposed, hopefully, that "the blockbuster feature will prove a boon to the abbreviated film making them a natural coupling. . . . The long and short of film lengths offer a more attractive package than the double feature."[16]

Running times were not the only bulked-up aspect of blockbusters. Paramount committed considerable marketing heft to the concept for their 1955 slate of films. They kicked off the year with a trade advertisement promising, "Your Business Will Continue to Thrive in 'Fifty-Five with More Blockbusters from Paramount."[17] Still in January, Paramount broke new ground for expanded publicity with a ten-page spread for *The Bridges at Toko-Ri* (1954) in *Daily Variety* (figure 5.1).[18] This film was a topical, hard-hitting, and uncharacteristically downbeat film about the Korean War, about which there had been exceptionally few films. In bold block letters across the top of two pages, the advertisement described the film as "PARAMOUNT'S FIRST BOXOFFICE BLOCKBUSTER OF 1955," and the tasteful layout featured a large amount of white space with single credits in the center—directed by Mark Robson, screenplay by Valentine Davies. Subsequent pages presented the film's major stars with their image, their name, and their character—Grace Kelly as Nancy Brubaker, Fredric March as Rear Admiral George Tarrant, and so on. Such a lavish advertisement, looking like a program handed to audiences at a roadshow screening, targeted industry agents, specifically exhibitors, with its placement in *Daily Variety*. In their 1955 press packages, Paramount continued this approach, promoting their Bop Hope vehicle *The Seven Little Foys* as an addition "to that long line of Paramount blockbusters."[19] The trade notice for *We're No Angels* (1955) declared it "Another Blockbuster from Paramount . . . in August!"[20] Confirming for exhibitors the steady flow of exceptional material, Paramount used this film to push another product of theirs, VistaVision, including a description of satisfied exhibitors at demonstrations of the wide and high screen format.

Redirecting resources to fewer, albeit bigger, films exacerbated the overall reduced flow of movies. Exhibitors complained vociferously about a shortage

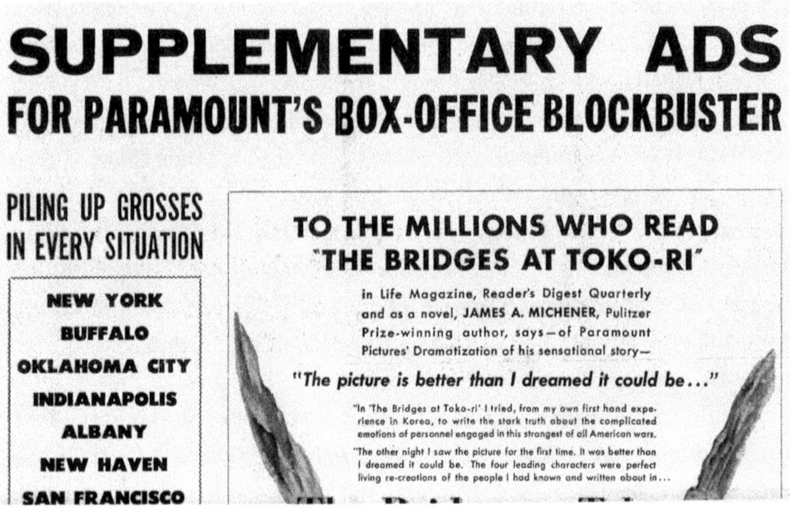

FIGURE 5.1 *The Bridges at Toko-Ri* trade advertisement, press kit, detail, 1955

of films. Some claimed, however, that exhibitors were to blame for the situation, not the studios. The president of Allied Artists, Steve Broidy, publicly lambasted exhibitors for wanting only big-budget films, claiming further that the studios responded. But Broidy pointed out that, "'as we all know, every picture that starts on the planning boards as a "blockbuster" does not always hit its mark. In fact, the entire industry does not turn out more than 15 to 20 "blockbusters" in any year.'"[21] *Variety* later reemphasized this view, declaring that "'shortage' of product is today not a matter of total numbers of pictures, but rather shortage of consistent blockbuster quality."[22]

Among industry insiders, the blockbuster strategy was familiar, and the size of the production and the box-office take determined whether or not a movie was a blockbuster. And even though by the mid-1950s "blockbuster" was becoming conventionalized as a *type* of film, it was still used to reference a range of genres. For example, reporting on persistent exhibition business during the inclement weather of the 1955 winter, *Daily Variety* wrote, "Blockbusters drew heavily, with lines Saturday night at the Music Hall ('Glass Slipper'), Loew's State ('Blackboard Jungle'), and the Astor ('East of Eden')."[23] These three very different films—a Leslie Caron vehicle, a midbudget social issue film, and a glossy prestige melodrama—were all blockbusters owing to their impact and prominence, though not their production qualities. A circularity in the definition tells us that blockbusters are visible and prominent films, and that visible and prominent films are blockbusters. Despite its relatively low-cost, black-and-white production, *Blackboard Jungle* (1955) had a moment of recognition as a blockbuster in part because it was a box-office success and in part because it addressed an explosive social issue, juvenile delinquency.[24] Even *Lady and the Tramp* (1955) and *Not as a Stranger* (1955) had the designation attached.[25]

So familiar was the term that retrospective application was increasingly casual. *Casablanca* (1942), *King's Row* (1942), and *Cheyenne* (1947) were described as "blockbusters" even though they had not been described as such during their initial release.[26] Less extravagant films, without the fantastical colors and locations of the highest-profile films, could share in the blockbuster designation. Entertainment columnist Frank Scully noted this about director Mark Robson, describing his films *The Champion* (1949) and *The Harder They Fall* (1956) as being directed with "block-busting realism."[27]

The currency of the publicity-oriented designation of the blockbuster strategy made alternative approaches that much more distinctive. Smaller films, like *Marty* (1955), ran counter to the emerging logic of the blockbuster production. This film, adapted from a teleplay, showed that a newly forming brand of televisual realism might work in the movie theater. Other such transpositions from teleplay to film followed, again with critical and box-office success, including *Patterns* (1956), *No Time for Sergeants* (1958), and *Days of Wine and Roses* (1962). After *Marty* won the Academy Award for best picture, among other awards, its box office was expected to benefit. This contrasted with expectations for bigger films, as blockbuster winners had substantial promotional plans and didn't need a boost from an Oscar.[28] Blockbusters would certainly receive their share of industry accolades, but constructed as these films were for popularity and with the benefit of the full force of Hollywood marketing efforts, awards did not seem to affect their box office. This claim, oddly, ignored the impact over time, discounting the effect of awards over the longevity of a blockbuster. Nonetheless, films like *Marty*, in contrast, which were not purpose-built long-term revenue generators, were thought to stand a better chance of experiencing a bump with distinctive honors at awards competitions. And, sure enough, modest dramas, typically in black and white, without the flash of new technological features, maintained a strong critical presence through the decade. *On the Waterfront* (1954) had won the Oscar for best picture the year before *Marty*, and a few years later *Ben-Hur* (1959) faced off with the British kitchen-sink drama *Room at the Top* (1959). These smaller films were called "in-betweeners," meaning they were neither lavish blockbusters nor low-end gimmick flicks. Many of the expectations for a tasteful popular American cinema came to rest with these films.

Almost inadvertently, commentary in 1956 named a category of popular film that would not truly be activated for another two decades: the summer blockbuster. Studios shared a plan to release blockbusters during the summer of 1956. *Variety* announced this turn with "Line Up Big Films in the Summer Alleys (with Blockbusters Included)," observing further that summer had not been a key battleground for distributors to that point.[29] That year would be dominated by Paramount's *The Ten Commandments* and UA's *Around the World in 80 Days*, but UA's *Trapeze* (1956) was the "first of the summer's blockbusters to go into release."[30] This notice described the organization of big-name releases and commented on the competition to come, but it voiced most directly the summer blockbuster idea.

Moving from a steady flow of films to the seemingly oxymoronic regularized extraordinary releases raised the importance of coordinating the calendar. Scheduling was made even more essential by the long runs of blockbusters, which tied up screens for extended periods of time and thus reduced the number of bookings a distributor could make. Mapping out weekends, holidays, and seasons, and doing so with an eye to competing distributors' plans, became a key planning operation. In an effort to generate moviegoing interest, Greater Movie Season began in 1954, versions of which had been initiated since the 1920s. This promotion circulated the idea that Labor Day kicked off an intensive movie-release schedule for the fall. Only a few years later, with television networks also picking the fall to launch their new programming, distributors and exhibitors pushed their offerings earlier into the summer. So in 1958 this initiative defined a *summer* movie schedule, confusingly also called the "Greater Movie Season."[31] Two points concerning this initiative: first, what we see are members of an industrial sector cooperating to raise interest in and the profile of the entire business, essentially coming to a tacit agreement about their operations, in this instance with regard to the timing of releases; and, second, this example shows us that a seasonal orientation emerged as an explicit part of ordinary operations.

As is evident in the distributor actions charted here, the blockbuster concept was deliberately and calculatedly used as a relational term to situate films big and small with respect to other films of the moment. In this way it spoke to an overarching industrial strategy, beyond the features of any single film. This was the case regardless of how uniquely expensive, visible, or prestigious a production may have been. And this engulfed smaller films that positioned themselves either as counterpoints or as distinctly impactful in their own right. For all the range of meanings and connotations of "blockbuster," there remained an ever-solidifying center, making some films unambiguously blockbuster entities in terms of their elevated budgets, production expanses, technological advancement, promotional heft, high audience awareness, and box-office success. And then there were the other films that gestured toward one or two of those qualities, baby blockbusters, if you will. In the years preceding 1958, "blockbuster" was only rarely used to advertise a film to the moviegoing public, and even then it was used to describe the impact of the subject matter rather than a type of film, in a quote or small font. In 1957, we begin to see the term referenced in popular sources with greater frequency and consistency. But as a blockbuster strategy became a more stable reference point among industrial agents, it functioned largely through the first seven years of the 1950s as *a way to sell films to exhibitors* and remained a vehicle through which new relationships between distributors and exhibitors could be forged in the era of television and loss of studio control of cinemas.

"Bigness" set the agenda for the relevance and financial viability of Hollywood in the 1950s in a way that had never been seen before. After years of declining audiences and revenues, a glimmer of Technicolor sunshine broke through. This is seen in the hit films of the summer of 1955, of which Gene Arneel wrote that every "major distributor has at least one 'blockbuster' making the rounds," citing Warner's *Mister Roberts* (1955) in CinemaScope, Paramount's *To Catch a Thief* (1955) in VistaVision, and Stanley Kramer's adult melodrama *Not as a Stranger* from UA.[32] Even nontrade publications began to take notice. Fan magazine *Picturegoer* looked ahead to 1956 as "filmdom's best year," with blockbusters and new large-screen formats battling television with "entertainment that could not possibly be cramped into that postcard screen in the parlour."[33] Freeman Lincoln characterized the upswing as nothing less than "the comeback of the movies." Noting industry-wide enthusiasm and cheery economic prospects, Lincoln commented that the increased box-office revenues were not for moviegoing in general but for "particular movies," suggesting that audience selectivity might be "a new order of movie things."[34] The measure of this film-specific boom was that for the thirty years before 1953, fewer than a hundred titles had earned more than $5 million; in the two years since 1953, more than thirty had, including *The Robe* (1953), *How to Marry a Millionaire* (1953), *Mogambo* (1953), *Shane* (1953), and *From Here to Eternity* (1953). The complete reorientation of the film business toward a hit-driven model is evident in the all-time top-grossing films from the period. In 1957, of the top fifty highest-grossing films, forty of them, or 80 percent, had been released in the previous seven years.[35] David O. Selznick's *Gone with the Wind* (1939) remained at the top of the list, though ever bigger blockbuster efforts came ever closer to that supreme success.[36]

To keep its technological wonders in the headlines, Twentieth Century Fox orchestrated a one-year anniversary for CinemaScope on the date of the first release of *The Robe*. The event included additional information about the process through reports on television and in print news, as well as lobby displays in theater houses that had converted to CinemaScope.[37] While the bigger studio films styled themselves as technological as well as cinematic wonders, Lincoln noted the importance of nonstudio enterprises, like Cinerama, which opened up an unforeseen new movie market. Lincoln wrote that the boom in moviegoing was best typified by the surprise success of Cinerama. But he also pointed to other counterintuitive examples, including UA, whose lower overhead costs made it easy for them to produce smaller films, and Universal.[38] A contradictory development appeared: the bigger-budget theatrical spectacles drew more moviegoing attention, yet the industrial upheaval had opened up paths for independent and smaller studios to seize attention and box-office share. Denise Mann documented the rise of the independent production outfits at the time, many of which were talent centered, organized around or owned by star actors or directors, and operated with special relationships with the studios, in particular for distribution. Mann suggested they were responsible for an influx of darker themes and varied styles, seen in their midrange-budget productions. As a result, in these independent productions one can find a blurring of the distinction between what were thought of as art and mainstream films. She showed, moreover, that not only did the decreasing studio power following divorcement create an opportunity for independent outfits, but the studios' response included the development of more lavish film spectaculars in order to create an identifiable studio brand. She wrote, "The evolution of the blockbuster trend, besides responding to reduced box-office returns and competition from television, can be traced to a backlash among studio executives to the growing independence and iconoclasm of the filmmakers, and to efforts to extend Hollywood's global reach by adding to elements that had long been that cinema's calling card—lavish spectacle and production values—with new ones oriented to the global marketplace—international cofinancing arrangements, international stars, and foreign locations."[39] While accurate overall, to this assessment we should add that some of the biggest blockbusters were themselves independent productions, undertaken by a nonstudio entity, though with significant backing by a major distributor that both facilitated raising investment capital while also diversifying studio risk. The thorough restructuring of the flow of production meant that 57 percent of the releases from the main twelve distributors were produced by independents by 1957.[40] Rather than "backlash," there was an emerging organization of relations between independent and studio operations, as well as between different types of film and film investments.

Contrary to the promotional extravagances of the film business, movies and moviegoing did not have a monopoly on glamor and astonishment. While television nestled into people's daily routine, it would be mistaken to assume that broadcasters presented only the drab and ordinary, or that audiences thought of television as a dull and artless medium. Television in the 1950s was the future. It presented the features that continue to be taken as the qualities of advanced media technology: it was immediate, convenient, live, geographically expansive, and democratic. These characteristics were thought to be lacking in the movies, especially with the exclusionary ticket pricing, making them seem backward and cumbersome; in many ways, movies are still haunted by this perceived liability. Whatever critiques eventually emerged about television's conventionality, the new medium found an enthusiastic audience who saw in it forms of community and meaningful augmentation of daily life.[41] Movies, as a special trip requiring more time and money, could not match television on those terms.

Broadcasters mounted their own blockbusters to compete with the extravagances of the theatrical roadshows of big movies. Fighting for similarly spectacular attention, Albert McCleery, executive producer of NBC's *Matinee*, described that show as "tv's first daytime blockbuster" largely owing to the size of the production—four thousand actors, a hundred writers, ten directors, and five one-hour shows weekly.[42] Another case in point was the Sunday-night broadcast on all four major networks of *Light's Diamond Jubilee* on October 24, 1954. David O. Selznick produced the two-hour broadcast celebrating the seventy-fifth anniversary of Thomas Edison's introduction of electric light, and it represented Selznick's first foray into television. With segments directed by Hollywood veterans Norman Taurog, William Wellman, and King Vidor, and appearances by celebrities such as Kim Novak, Dorothy Dandridge, and David Niven, the show was an unusually grand endeavor, one that at least one studio executive characterized as a "blockbuster." Film agents reported that the movie box office did not suffer considerably from this direct spectacular competition at home, and this was taken as an opportunity to proclaim the resilience of moviegoing.[43] Still, the reality was that a coordinated effort like *Light's Diamond Jubilee* demonstrated that television could be just as engaged in event production and programming as film.

In turn, with relations among media in flux, television didn't shy away from confronting film producers on their own terms. Or, rather, television networks participated in forms of film production that would eventually find their way into their broadcasting schedules. When hit films arrived on television screens, the audience response was surprisingly strong, and consistently so.[44] This finding was shocking to some, and it suggested that the value of screen size was more flexible than had been presumed. Encouraged by this observation, CBS Television entered into a deal to coproduce major releases with Louis de Rochemont, which included properties with Orson Welles attached and budgets ranging from $500,000 to $1 million.[45] Keeping track of hits as they appeared across formats, as they moved from stage to screen to television, or through some variation of that flow, emerged as one of the hallmarks of the developing cross-media components of entertainment.

A particularly notable illustration of this was *No Time for Sergeants*, a relatively modest theatrical play that turned into a considerable success and garnered critical accolades. And it was a cross-media sensation, with Mac Hyman's novel (1954) adapted as a live television play by Ira Levin in the winter of 1955, and then expanded by Levin into an adaptation for Broadway by the fall. A smash hit, it ran for about three years. *No Time for Sergeants* was adapted for the screen in 1958 and then appeared as a television series in the 1960s, with all but the last iteration starring Andy Griffith, making him a lasting star for decades to come and giving him a popular character that he riffed on in subsequent roles. The down-home comedy was a charming celebration of average American virtue, where a simple man from the country can excel, at times in spite of himself, in the big bureaucracy of the U.S. Air Force. *New York Herald Tribune* theater critic Walter F. Kerr concluded his review of the Broadway incarnation by describing it as a "blockbuster," meaning a hit, a claim that was torn from the review and featured for years as the main endorsement, placed above the title, in newspaper advertisements.[46] Let me reiterate this: "blockbuster" was the primary description used to advertise the Broadway production *No Time for Sergeants*, beginning shortly after its opening in 1955 and continuing through to the end of its run in 1957. The significance of this is that the newspaper appearance of "blockbuster" as a way to describe and promote this play ran adjacent to the movie advertisement pages, at a time when "blockbuster" had yet to be used in any substantial and sustained way for films outside trade publications. It is possible that this usage is the source of the widely held belief that "blockbuster" was originally a term that pertained to live theater.

During the 1950s, then, we can see that the film industry narrowed in to focus on gargantuan enterprises for their special financial and critical appeal. The blockbuster strategy enveloped other domains of cultural and commercial life, too. The essential element is the way that a dynamic relationship between culture and economics came to be organized by the idea of the big investment and the highly visible work. This relationship circulated and was adapted to fit a variety of media economies. Still, the big, prominent film came to typify this more than anything else, and the blockbuster strategy was about to be pushed out of the trades by the American film business into the realm of popular entertainment for general audiences.

With all its multimedia success, *No Time for Sergeants*—the play, the novel, the teleplay, the film, and the television series—was symptomatic of another problem the entertainment business had in understanding American audiences. It pointed to the limits of the urbanity pursued by most middlebrow technological film spectaculars. Industry observers noted a growing disparity between what would draw urban audiences back to the theater and the interests of rural audiences. The received wisdom, by the end of 1956, was that only big-budget blockbusters and small, quirky adult movies offered audiences entertainment that was not available on television and so would attract the number of moviegoers necessary for continued industry success. Family and action films didn't mesh with this assumption, so they were to be avoided. But this gradually began to be upturned; exhibitors increasingly recognized the tastes of rural movie patrons, where small-town settings and values could attract an audience more than racy adult dramas.[47] As the *Variety* headline declared, "Sticks Now on 'Hick Pix' Kick," a reference to one of their most famous headlines from two decades earlier that contrarily stated "Sticks Nix Hick Pix."[48]

For 1956 blockbusters were the big revenue generators. Yet, Hy Hollinger observed, "What appears to [be] happening, however, is a return to the formula of picture-making that preceded the advent of television. There appears to be developing a school of thinking that the motion picture industry might have been perhaps a little too hasty in dropping its varied program of production."[49] Pushback against the blockbuster strategy, in this instance mainly from exhibitors, challenged the single-mindedness of a few big and expensive films for everyone, to the detriment of providing many small films of varying kinds.

The mysteries of popular taste—which to Hollywood executives meant the uncertainties of box-office revenue—kept industry agents and observers busy dissecting market metrics. The question of what special brand of motion picture entertainment, with what form of promotional strategy, would regularly draw television-friendly audiences out to theaters drove experimentation on the part of the studios. More than anything, predictability was the ultimate and most elusive goal. Studios and exhibitors alike asked, with this strategy and this product, what revenue performance might we expect? For all the risk that capitalists enjoy celebrating, at heart investors crave predictability.

The promise of eliminating the riskiness of cultural commodities drew audience research firms to Hollywood. George Gallup's Audience Research Institute provided surveys of moviegoers' likes and dislikes from the 1930s into the 1950s, and at the time Leo A. Handel wrote of the efforts to know patrons in his book *Hollywood Looks at Its Audience: A Report of Film Audience Research*.[50] A notable effort to advance a "scientific" approach to managing box-office uncertainty was Albert Sindlinger's study of *Giant* (1956). He had worked for Gallup before striking out on his own in the late 1940s. Following lawsuits against audience research firms Nielsen and Hooper, and several attacks on the statistical usefulness of ratings, he developed a subscriber clientele of producers and exhibitors for his in-depth, large-scale surveys of audience behavior. His clients received Sindlinger's claims as authoritative, and they were frequently excerpted for publicity material in trade publications.

In 1957 his market survey firm, Sindlinger and Company, concluded that statistical examinations of specific features could identify precise measurements of success, ones that he claimed were clear enough to be incorporated into the development of production, exhibition, and promotion plans. He proposed "know-about" and "talk-about" as key categories. Much of what he examined concerned how one "prepares" an audience for a big film. His wide-ranging surveys concluded that *Giant* was responsible for stopping the five-year-long downward spiral of moviegoing, in particular by sparking a return of the female audience. Sindlinger claimed that his research for *Giant* was so extensive that it was the most surveyed film in Hollywood history. He tabulated that for this research his survey takers had conducted a thousand personal interviews daily and seven thousand interviews weekly in more than two hundred markets across the United States, thereby surveying in excess of a hundred thousand participants. The questions were not singularly about their awareness of *Giant*, and in fact the actual focus of the study was hidden from the interviewees. These surveys charted general media usage, in which *Giant* was only one possible topic of discussion. And Sindlinger's personnel conducted the surveys before the film's release, comparing their predictions to its performance after release.[51]

Sindlinger's press announcement about this research came approximately three months after the film had been released in theaters, at which point *Giant*'s considerable success had become evident to all. The press announcement was itself an elaborately orchestrated event, involving approximately forty journalists, from trade and general-audience publications, traveling to spend the day at the company's headquarters at Ridley Park, near Philadelphia, with many arriving via a specially organized train from New York.[52] The excitement around the prospect of box-office predictability prompted *Variety* to begin its report on Sindlinger with "If motion picture boxoffice can be scientifically reduced to a formula of 'Giant' size the industry will have taken the first major postwar step forward [in] administering a hype to the theatre wickets crosscountry."[53]

Sindlinger had approximately a thousand theaters as clients, and they could match his prerelease predictions with the hard evidence of actual box-office revenue. In addition to a weekly market report, his company produced what it called the Motion Picture Audience Action Index, which projected attendance based on surveys. *Giant* generated the highest score ever. The extensive work on *Giant*, conducted for Warner, began in April 1956, a full seven months before its release in November. A sizable audience would see the now-dead James Dean for the first time on-screen, more than a year after his fatal car accident. His "know-about" score was high, as a result of this tragedy, but Sindlinger's research also laid to rest Warner's concerns that audiences would not come to a film with a dead star. The other stars, Elizabeth Taylor and Rock Hudson, along with the familiarity of the director, George Stevens, pushed the "know-about" score even higher, but Sindlinger commented that the measures would have been lower for each of those personalities indi-

FIGURE 5.2 Lobby card for *Giant*, reportedly the most surveyed film in Hollywood history, 1956

vidually. This, he claimed, supported the idea that the package, the carefully coordinated relationship among several talents, could improve box-office prospects. His research further suggested that the unusual success of *Giant*, which made back its negative cost in a matter of weeks, would lift the industry generally, pointing specifically to women audience members who saw trailers for coming attractions at screenings of *Giant* and then returned to the theater in subsequent weeks to see other movies.[54] Moreover, the film played well abroad, for instance, in Japan, alongside other blockbusters including *War and Peace*.[55] Most crucially, helping to fortify with empirical evidence the blockbuster strategy that had been in formation, Sindlinger concluded that "more 'Giant'-type pix would bring a flood of 'newcomers' to boxoffices."[56]

Sindlinger's audience research combated market uncertainty about a new media environment, focusing on awareness and preferences. How accurate or reliable his information proved to be is difficult to ascertain. But the approach appealed to producers and exhibitors, in the very least, as a way to justify and support decision-making. And his work gave credence to the blockbuster strategy, especially the orchestrated entertainment package that privileged marquee talent and a hot property, be it a novel or a musical with high existing audience awareness. Sindlinger prided himself on his company's independence from the industry, despite an agreement with Warner Brothers for research on *Giant*. With 225 field staff in 187 U.S. markets interviewing more than a thousand people daily, using various surveys and in-depth interviews, his company offered the basic raw nationwide information about moviegoing audiences that producers, distributors, and exhibitors needed. Moreover, he celebrated the statistical analyses his company could perform.[57] His reports gave detailed comparisons between television and film audience activity, providing some of the truisms about what kind of entertainment would draw folks out of their living rooms. Well into the 1960s, his reports documented and commented on changes in studio power, including the end of the star system. While his operations were not alone in this field, they do stand out for their originality and longevity.

Sindlinger's career offers a fine indication of some of the changes that transpired in American consumer markets as well. Marketing and advertising embraced demography and, with it, more experimental forms of surveying, compiling, and interpreting attitudes, sentiments, and personalities. The impact of psychographics can be seen in consumer campaigns that made emotional appeals, gave voice to personal and social anxieties, and built brands in relation to lifestyles, rather than the functionality of products. The conclusions drawn from the reports on the affective priming of consumers fed the decisions being made at the level of product development, which in the movie business involved the assemblage of an entertainment package with the appropriate talent, property, and budget. Sindlinger and his consumer survey outfits honed the skill of observing and measuring awareness and its relation to purchasing activity in the culture market, namely, for movies. Developing his insights and methods, and applying them to consumer behavior on a national level, Sindlinger is most known today for his consumer-confidence surveys, which have been modified into various indices that continue to take the temperature of the economy and measure its health. The approach advanced by Sindlinger and other consumer-survey enterprises was to propose that evidence of awareness and an affective association could be the fodder for generating purchases and economic involvement. With these measures, producers and exhibitors sold more than tickets. They sold an experience, an event, and a lifestyle, that is, conditions for ongoing participation in a consumer environment.

The rise of demographics and psychographics in market research changed the operations of many industries. In media businesses it promised to provide actionable portraits of cultural consumers. While each category and explanation invariably simplified the complex interests and drives of book readers, television watchers, music listeners, and moviegoers, the advantages of imagining a predictable and demonstrable market tempted industry agents to treat these categories as fact. With so much capital at stake, even more so with the big bet on the blockbuster, additional validation for a production and promotion decision was needed and was reassuring. The more "scientific" models developed since—think here of our current affection for the "truth" of brain imaging, data mining, algorithmic studies of social media and mood, and so on—are only ever "accurate" when someone is making money on the information provided. There is no clear evidence whether we know culture, taste, and people any more fully or not with our digital mechanisms. What we do see is the nervous foundation on which the industry of media entertainment rests today.

The statistical heft of Sindlinger's reports, taken as authoritative support for the blockbuster strategy, helped till the ground for future formations of the media industries. But still the steep risks involved with blockbuster productions left many unconvinced. Strong film packages with high audience awareness and topflight talent—the "know-about" and "talk-about" qualities—cost a lot of money. Numerical evidence could only reassure investors so much. They were still required to put their capital into what amounted to an article of faith. Exhibition-industry commentator Ivan Spear echoed the concerns of many when he expressed skepticism about "super-colossal" productions, writing, "For all their astronomical costs, their intensified ballyhoo and, in most cases, their productional [sic] and entertainment excellence, they nonetheless constituted a piddling percentage of the world's output of motion pictures." Nonetheless, he continued, "many are the opinions—among industryites [sic] and laymen alike—that in such mastodons lies the future fate of the movie trade."[58] The irony of banking the future of the industry on an extinct beast may have been lost on Spear and his readers. This is likely the case because the mastodons he referenced were showing considerable economic life and tended to pay off well for distributors. For example, Warner Brothers reported a 70 percent increase in profit for the fall of 1956 over the fall of 1955, attributing this to their blockbusters, citing *Moby Dick* (1956), *The Bad Seed* (1956), and *Giant*, the last just a week after its release.[59]

More evidence seemed to side with the blockbuster strategy than not. And this had a cumulative effect on the inner workings of investor psychology. While the future of the film industry continued to be uncertain from an investor's point of view, the plumping up of budgets and the willingness of studios to approve and make extravagant attractions signaled confidence in moving-image entertainment. And while fewer pictures were being made, relatively speaking, the calculated risk paid off handsomely when a film struck gold. Wall Street began to see that "just a couple of blockbuster pictures can substantially improve a financial statement and conversely a couple of expensive duds can be murder," though reporting veered toward the enthusiastic with "Blockbusters, Ahoy."[60] Some on Wall Street had high hopes for the industry and were willing to invest copious amounts of money. Twentieth Century Fox increased its releases to twenty-six for the first half of 1957, compared with thirty-two for the entire previous year. Competition with television meant that films had to have "new stories and star value, and added production plusses." The UA releases were set at thirty-six, down from their usual forty-eight, but "with new emphasis on 'bigness.'"[61] Paramount, Warner, and Universal all reported expanding fortunes with both big films and increasingly diversified media operations. Some studios were not yet benefiting from this industry optimism. Allied Artists was losing money and was sticking to mostly lower-budget movies, Columbia was increasing its television production and was weathering a dip in revenue, and Republic ceased theatrical operations altogether to concentrate on television.

The spate of mid-1950s blockbuster films set new expectations for financial return. The negative cost for *The Ten Commandments* was over $13 million. A reviewer of the film wrote, "In the enthusiastic language of the trade, a blockbuster is, currently, a tall revenue feature. When a picture grosses $10,000,000 or near it's blockbusting. But look how tall *Commandments* must grow before it's out of the red!"[62] Designations of this kind are an ever-changing feature of the entertainment business, with its ordinary inflation of expectations. And most of the films documented here that carried the title of "blockbuster," or had it appended to them, did not hit that level of revenue, so we should treat this definitional claim with skepticism. But the point being made in this review was that the expansion of production expenses meant that even elevated revenue might not make the film as profitable as desired. This "tall revenue feature" needed to become even taller to make money.

The Ten Commandments, by the way, did just fine.

As a new approach to motion picture production and promotion, "super-blockbusters" like *The Ten Commandments* posed an accounting problem. These unusually large investments had a theatrical longevity that saw their returns accrue over longer stretches of time, well beyond conventional fiscal time frames. As a result, in the short term, some of the most successful titles could appear on the books as failures, depending on the period in which the cost and the revenue were accounted for. This apparent lag worried studios because it was possible that potential investors, ignorant of these conditions, might hold back on financial commitments due to erroneous perceptions of poor performance.[63]

While the longevity of these assets befuddled studio accountants, another element played as a distributor advantage with blockbusters. Their sheer attractiveness to exhibitors meant that the studios found themselves with additional bargaining power. With the might of *The Ten Commandments*, Paramount required drive-ins to charge per person rather than per car, which encroached on the divorcement decree's restriction of distributor influence on admission prices.[64] This effort, too, sprang from the growing box-office potential of "ozoners," the term for drive-ins in *Variety*'s lingo. The same "super-blockbuster" circulated with a skillfully exclusive set of runs, beginning with seventy weeks in a relatively small number of houses, then moving to average runs of four to six weeks at smaller-market theaters.[65] The ability to dictate changing clearances, which was the range within which no other theater could show the same film at the same time, and availability to second-run exhibitors came only with an extraordinary hit. And while exhibitors benefited from hits, distributors welcomed the supplementary control over their product, especially in the context of federally enforced limits. Theater owners in smaller cities found that the new terms demanded by distributors for their blockbusters (including higher percentages of box-office revenue), some of which were also being demanded for nonblockbusters, were making many films unprofitable for exhibitors, even if the film was a big hit.[66] Blockbusters, then, were a path to revenue generation but also renewed market power for the studios.

The upward trajectory encountered other bumps. Some theater owners found that they were waiting for authentic blockbusters, ones that had unusual staying power in terms of popularity and length of theatrical run, which were quite few in number. They complained to distributors when the next *The Ten Commandments* or *The Bridge on the River Kwai* (1957) was not on the horizon. Another observation sparked doubt about the general reorientation toward such films: each Cinerama release stayed in theaters for fewer weeks than the previous one.[67] This observation led to the question, was this a symptom of exhaustion of that particular format or of the blockbuster strategy more generally?

Raising further questions about blockbusters, *Gigi* (1958), *The Ten Commandments*, and *The Bridge on the River Kwai* all saw ticket prices going up to an exorbitant $3. Average admission prices had been 49.7¢ in 1956, up from 34¢ in 1946.[68] *Around the World in 80 Days* and the Cinerama films demanded similar jumps in admission prices. Distributors saw these hikes as fundamental extensions of the type of film they were supplying: "bigger admission scales are to be required if the 'blockbuster policy' is to shape as economically sound."[69] The very concept of a "blockbuster policy" gives us a sense of the clarity of the path being pursued by the studios. Executive Samuel Goldwyn was pointedly direct about this tactic, saying, "'Hollywood's future welfare lies in the production of 50 blockbusters a year,'" and hence the ability to make such financial demands on moviegoers.[70]

So as the blockbuster was proving to stir excitement, theater owners had specific concerns about the associated costs and the limited number of available films. This was even more pronounced for smaller-market houses, where the high-end roadshow did not land. These more modest theaters needed films, too, and distributors woke up to the fact that blockbusters would not provide them with what they needed. With a long-term view, maintaining favorable relations with exhibitors, big and small, had additional advantages. Having a range of films, with different production and promotional budgets, placed differing pressures on box-office expectations, making films affordable to owners of smaller theaters and less challenging for distributors to break even on.[71] For this reason, attention to blockbusters kept open the countervailing attention to the low-budget or gimmick film, with AIP and UA smartly feeding this end of the market. As sensible and successful as this tactic appeared to be, the allure of the big payoff led to the ongoing development of extravagant movies, with stratospheric budgets, by the big studios and the most ambitious of independent producers.

The consolidation of industry practice around the blockbuster meant that other films had to be positioned accordingly. Exhibitors, as we have seen, complained about the lack of smaller films for their theaters. But still, the bulk of the studio libraries consisted of nonblockbusters. Designation as a nonblockbuster had significant implications. Just as the blockbuster strategy for theatrical exhibition was settling in, a new market was opening for these old films, which had previously been considered as having little, if any, economic value: television. Despite initial reluctance, as Eric Hoyt documented, "by the end of the decade, all of the studios had licensed their pre-1948 film libraries to television; some, such as M.G.M., United Artists, and Columbia, had even come to embrace film-to-television distribution as a business essential to their health."[72] Ranking films by budget and appeal became a vehicle for selling Hollywood's film libraries to broadcasters. For its sales, the MGM film library divided films into five categories: AAA, AA, A, B, and C movies. *Thirty Seconds over Tokyo* (1944), *Treasure Island* (1950), and *A Tale of Two Cities* (1935) were AAA films, while the Marx Brothers movies and *Lassie Come Home* (1943) were in the AA category. A different price tag was affixed to each category, such that it was more costly to broadcast a AAA film than a lesser-rated film. Broadcasters, as a result, were judicious, and budget conscious, when scheduling films from each of these categories, effectively meaning they would simply not show the best films all the time. This more gradual flow of high-quality films also meant slightly less competition for fresh blockbuster offerings in theaters.[73]

Soon, though, broadcasters had exhausted the pre-1948 films and were looking to post-1948 films, expressing a willingness to pay for blockbusters and to give select films a blockbuster push for their television screenings.[74] The Theatre Owners of America, in a move to slow the flow of films to television, floated the idea of setting up a trust to purchase post-1948 films themselves, though they knew it would likely not fly by the U.S. Justice Department, as attentive as it then was to collusion. Nonblockbusters attracted special attention in that some way to categorize films would be needed; the future value of blockbusters, and their relation to other films, was understood as significant and in need of special handling.[75] For instance, Screen Gems sold a package of seventy-eight films from Columbia and Universal to television in 1958, branded as a "Powerhouse" slate entirely made up of "blockbusters." The films, of course, were nothing of the sort and included such titles as *The Killers* (1946), *Here Comes Mr. Jordan* (1941), and *The Man from Colorado* (1948).[76]

As the MGM film library shows, production budget alone did not determine secondary market ideas about what a "blockbuster" was, which was how those triple-A films were described; the hierarchical ranking of films involved other features of cultural and economic value. This held true for exhibitors just as it did for broadcasters. As we've already seen, even less extravagant productions might be sold to exhibitors as potential blockbusters. The Frank Sinatra vehicle *The Joker Is Wild* (1957) promised to be "the blockbuster that sets off Paramount's autumn of record-busters!," a claim that appeared in an eight-page advertisement in *Daily Variety*.[77] Not only did the star mark the considerable box-office prospects for the film—and images of Sinatra dominate five entire pages—but the ad promoted *The Joker Is Wild* as part of a full slate of releases, naming nine upcoming films, plus two Dean Martin/Jerry Lewis reissues, and reminded exhibitors that *The Ten Commandments* was still in circulation. The ad also continued Paramount's push for their special screen technology, VistaVision, which merited two mentions.

Gestures such as these were a way to ease relations between distributors and exhibitors. The anxiousness of investors certainly was matched by that of theater owners, who pressed Hollywood for better and distinctive product, and more of it. Promotional material in the trade press provides evidence. For example, a *Daily Variety* advertisement for *April Love* (1957) includes the following statement, in small type near the bottom: "Again 20th answers the demands of exhibitors for a blockbuster Thanksgiving attraction!" The copy again takes pride in pointing out the prestigious technological features of the film: CinemaScope, DeLuxe Color, and stereophonic sound. It even clarifies Twentieth Century Fox's distribution strategy: "Watch for more than 30-theatre saturation opening in L.A. area."[78] Twentieth Century Fox took out a four-page trade advertisement informing exhibitors of the four blockbusters to be released over the 1957 Christmas and New Year's season, *A Farewell to Arms* (1957), *Peyton Place* (1957), *Kiss Them for Me* (1957), and *The Enemy Below* (1957). All four uniformly featured CinemaScope, DeLuxe Color, and MagOptical stereophonic sound.[79]

In a comparable advertisement, UA was even more explicit and tried to convince exhibitors that the advertisement itself was a sign of their epic commitment to theater owners, stating in bold block letters across the top of two pages: "This ad is an event! Fulfillment of the basic need of all exhibitors!" With this promotion, UA not only announced sixteen films and their release dates, carefully lined up to provide a consistent flow of product through 1958, but proclaimed that the films represented a "backlog of blockbusters."[80] They also reminded exhibitors of their biggest smash, still in theaters at the time, *Around the World in 80 Days*. A year later, UA ran a similar trade campaign, four pages celebrating their 1958 success, previewing upcoming films for 1959, and asking exhibitors to "look forward to the biggest lineup of blockbusters

FIGURE 5.3 United Artists advertisement promising future blockbusters, 1959

ever," arriving in 1960 (figure 5.3). Again, mention was made of the continuing draw of *Around the World in 80 Days*.[81]

For 1957, UA planned a steady stream of ten blockbusters, including Stanley Kramer's *The Pride and the Passion*.[82] They did the same thing in subsequent years, promising a staggered release of eleven blockbusters for 1959, in addition to increased global marketing, with international revenue counting for 45 percent.[83] In other contexts, UA said it had planned up to twenty-four blockbusters, or double-A films, for 1959, which shows how the exigencies of promotion kept the category in flux.[84] The company claimed to have been the first to space out the releasing of their blockbusters, offering exhibitors a reliable schedule of quality material.[85] Such scheduling became standard practice across the board, with blockbusters an essential part of a distributor's stable by then. When Columbia did not fare so well through most of 1957, it was blockbusters they were missing, with *Pal Joey* (1957) and *The Bridge on the River Kwai* just around the corner at the end of the year to help their financial standing.[86] Ultimately, the fiscal year 1957 showed that half of Columbia's grosses came from just five of their forty-six releases. Such lopsided returns led to questions about the value of those many nonblockbuster efforts.[87] All the studios were waking up to comparable numbers.

And the larger the production, the larger the promotional schemes. For the most elaborate of cinematic works, promotion expanded beyond the film itself to highlight the film's state-of-the-art technological features and the celebrated talents involved. The blockbuster, now widely agreed on as the future of film despite the aforementioned downsides, equally promoted the entire industrial sector. One broad industry promotional event was Twentieth Century Fox's *The Big Show* (1957), a cross between a behind-the-scenes promotional film, a compilation of clips, and a feature-length trailer for the studio's entire slate of upcoming releases. It presented what Fox called their blockbusters, great pictures, and showmanship films, about fifty in all to be released over the next year. A three-page promotion in *Daily Variety* read, "You are invited to *The Big Show*, the most important industry presentation in the history of 20th Century-Fox and your theatre! Presenting the new look in motion picture achievement dedicated to the prosperity of exhibitors everywhere!"[88] The film title replaced Twentieth Century Fox's name on its familiar art deco logo with the sweeping searchlights. The copy represented exhibitors as a primary audience for the advertisement and the film, and publicly declared the company's responsibility for exhibitor "prosperity." Described as "a parade of blockbusters for 1957," and timed just before the summer months, the screening was open to "exhibitor staff, press, stockholders, motion picture councils and organizations, civic leaders and opinion-makers."[89] The promotional invitation lists forty specific theaters in different cities across Canada and the United States with the date and start time for the screening. *The Big Show* was a trade tool, screened for exhibitors as well as stockholders, two thousand of whom showed up at 9:15 a.m. to see it at the Roxy in New York City. Again, such efforts aimed to bolster confidence in financiers, doing so not just for Fox but, reportedly, for all of Hollywood.[90]

About this time, critics and columnists were using the term "blockbuster" more freely, generally capturing an impressive film or performance. In 1955, gossip columnist Hedda Hopper said Alan Ladd's new film would be "a blockbuster of a picture," and theater critic Dorothy Kilgallen expected Lena Horne's Broadway debut "to be a blockbuster."[91] Later, in 1958, Kilgallen described Cecil B. DeMille's follow-up to *The Ten Commandments*, *The Buccaneer* (1958), as his "new blockbuster," and to explain the appropriateness of this designation, she parenthetically noted that the cast of 12,160 made the casting log two pounds heavier than the script.[92] For the Marilyn Monroe–Laurence Olivier vehicle *The Sleeping Prince*, which eventually appeared as *The Prince and the Showgirl* (1957), it was expected that the star power of the actors could make it a blockbuster.[93] These articles project ahead to notable impacts in the near future, making such claims an expression of buzz rather than actual performance.

Popular film critics who celebrated a cinematic success by calling a film a blockbuster saw their comments added as endorsements to advertisements. In his *Daily News* appraisal, in 1958, Ed Sullivan declared *A Farewell to Arms* to be "a blockbuster that rivals *Gone with the Wind*" (the latter movie has since been casually and anachronistically discussed as a shining example of Hollywood blockbusting).[94] A review of *The Brothers Karamazov* (1958) had its enthusiastic assessment of the film as "a blockbuster" featured among other endorsements in newspaper advertisements.[95] Entertainment news asserted that a blockbuster film could be one that displayed both box-office might and production excesses. For example, A. H. Weiler reported on the spectacular box office of "Cecil B. DeMille's blockbuster *The Ten Commandments*" a year and a half after its initial roadshow release. In the article the film itself was a blockbuster, with an unusual length of three hours and forty minutes; Weiler also associates this quality with actual grosses.[96] A few weeks later, Weiler commented on the unusually long run of *The Bridge on the River Kwai* at the Palace in New York City, where "this blockbuster" was entering its twentieth week at the mixed live stage and movie house.[97]

This Is Cinerama (1952), with its special technological environment, enjoyed even longer runs of over two years, and the Todd-AO *Around the World in 80 Days* stretched to eighteen months and more in some locations. Conversion to these special formats and viewing conditions typically reduced the number of seats, as side views left the picture too distorted, and the running time of the films limited the number of screenings. Still, premium ticket prices and sheer audience volume made films in these formats exceptionally lucrative for about a decade, into the early 1960s. As reporter Milton Esterow noted, writing about the surprising revitalization and reorientation of moviegoing, the roadshow of the mid-1950s was a product of both new features of cinema technology and a particular type of film, the blockbuster. The cinema culture that resulted included a high end for American movies, pushing out the more modest "in-between" movies, as they were called, but also left open a market for more obscure and international film tastes, with art houses finally coming into their own, increasing in number and experiencing unprecedented audience traffic.[98]

But, as mentioned earlier, fewer of these midbudget films were coming from the studios, like *Chase a Crooked Shadow* (1958), which critic Richard L. Coe praised for being a film that understands its own generic appeal as a classic in-betweener; it "modestly doesn't try to be a blockbuster or off-beat," despite being directed by Michael Anderson of *Around the World in 80 Days* fame.[99] The privileging of blockbusters created a very different exhibition landscape. Not only were those in-betweeners squeezed out, with fewer booking spots available, less production attention, and insubstantial promotional support, but the low- or middle-budget films that were being produced were heading directly to television.[100] Manny Farber cast a jaundiced eye on this situation, seeing in-betweeners as "the muddlebrow's mock-serious pride in creativity."[101] The pretenses of cultural elevation identified by Farber, but also evident in the blockbusters of the period, bespoke the cultural taste hierarchies that Pierre Bourdieu pinpointed in the formation of class stratification in France of the 1960s.[102] A key element here was that these pretenses, and the differing film forms that embodied and satisfied them, were solidly planted as the magnetic north for the American film business, its investment rationale, and its assumptions about what drove audiences to theater seats.

The Hollywood American Federation of Labor (AFL) Film Council, which represented thirty-one unions active in the film industry, commissioned a report on the state of the business in an effort to understand the ramifications of the industrial upheaval that had transpired since the end of World War II. *Hollywood at the Crossroads: An Economic Study of the Motion Picture Industry* was a synthetic portrait, one that documented dire financial straits but also provided cautious optimism for the future. Labor had taken a hit in pay, and the average number of production workers employed in Southern California on average had fallen over 42 percent from 1946 to 1956.[103] Employment at the major studios had fallen by more than 43 percent over the same years.[104] Author Irving Bernstein produced a succinct yet comprehensive document that charted the decline of revenues, profits, film releases, and labor conditions, doing so with wry commentary uncharacteristic of such sector reports. He began by describing the overall economic decline of the American film industry as "an inescapable fact," writing that the post–World War II economic performance had been "less than colossal. In fact, it has laid an egg."[105] Competition from television accounted for much of the situation, but the Paramount Decree had ruptured the industry's organization of production, distribution, and exhibition. The forced restructuring, designed to break monopolistic practice and limit it in the future, was an economy-wide statement about industrial regulation in the postwar period. Bernstein cited one analyst who wrote that the decision "represent[ed] the most important experiment in vertical disintegration under the Sherman Act."[106] Most extraordinarily, the postwar decline of the film business had transpired during a time of overall growth and health in the American economy. Hollywood was simply not benefiting from the rising affluence of Americans.

As movie attendance dropped precipitously, ticket prices had risen. The number of movies released in theaters rose slightly, from 467 in 1946 to 479 in 1956, but those totals hid a significant reduction in U.S.-produced films (from 378 to 272) and an even more significant rise in the domestic release of foreign films (from 89 to 207).[107] The diversification of the major studios was one tactic that followed, sowing the seeds of the cross-sector media corporations we see today. Diversification also meant that financial statements could not be parsed for specifics about motion pictures. On this point, Bernstein wrote, "There is, in fact, no way to segregate income derived from production and distribution from income arising from theater operations, rental of studio facilities to independent producers, television production, sale of old films to TV, sale of real estate, or oil production, to name only some of the other sources of corporate income."[108] The cross-media activity Bernstein documented emphasized the growth in the production of television programs and commercials, and it highlighted economic activity further afield from the media business, such as the discovery of oil and gas on the Fox studio lot. Additionally, Fox owned theaters abroad, created television content through TCF Television Productions, and distributed films for television through its 50 percent control of National Television Associates. Paramount had diversified into DuMont Laboratories, Famous Players theaters in Canada, television station ownership, Chromatic Television Laboratories, the early pay-TV experiment International Telemeter, and Dot Records. Warner owned over a third of Associated British Pictures, a chain of U.K. cinemas, as well as a number of music and television production and distribution entities. Columbia developed its television interests with Screen Gems.[109] It was likely, as Bernstein commented, that these diversifications had helped cushion the fall of motion picture profitability. He took note of a turn toward global film production, what he called "American-interest film made abroad"; the nineteen such films in 1949 had grown to fifty-five by 1957.[110] Table 5.1 provides a comparison of revenue and profits for the decade following World War II.

During the course of the decade, revenue declined by 26 percent, and profits by a dramatic 73.5 percent. As Bernstein commented, "The streets in Hollywood, apparently, are now paved with asphalt."[111] Looking at the companies individually, one finds that it was actually Warner, Fox, and Paramount that experienced major decreases in both revenue and profit, with Loew's (MGM) also suffering a significant decrease in profit. Allied Artists, Columbia, Republic, and Universal all grew their business in terms of revenue, though they saw varying degrees of profit reductions. Whereas RKO withdrew from active operations, Disney expanded and became a major industry force.

Bernstein noted with confidence that despite the economic hardship, "more movies of high quality are being presently produced than at any time in the previous history of the industry."[112] This claim was unmistakably a reference to the big-budget prestige films that were showing considerable profit, drawing critical attention, and offering a glimmer of sunshine in the gloomy situation. He noted both big-budget films and experiments with new exhibition technologies as qualities designed to attract more moviegoers, which he reported as being called the "Battle of the Millimeters." "The theory," he wrote of big-budget productions, "is that the average citizen can be persuaded to desert his television set for the movies only if the attraction is unusual, the rationale of the so-called 'blockbuster,'" elaborating that both majors and independents had pursued this, with *The Ten Commandments* being the "ultimate" illustration.[113] He indicated that "the turn to the 'blockbuster' came

TABLE 5.1 Revenue and Profit for Major American Film Companies after World War II (in millions USD)

	1946		1956	
	Gross revenue	Net profit	Gross revenue	Net profit
Allied Artists	$6.1	$0.4	$16.8	$0.4
Columbia	$46.5	3.5	$91.1	$2.7
Disney	$4.1	$0.2	$27.6	$2.6
Loew's (MGM)	$165.4	$18.0	$166.6	$4.7
Paramount	$193.5	$39.2	$95.3	$8.7
RKO	$120.1	$12.2	n.a.	n.a.
Republic	$24.3	$1.1	$42.2	$0.8
20th Century Fox	$190.3	$22.6	$122.3	$6.2
Universal	$53.9	$4.6	$77.6	$4.0
Warner Bros.	$163.9	$19.4	$77.4	$2.1
Total	$968.1	$121.2	$716.9	$32.2

SOURCE: Irving Bernstein, *Hollywood at the Crossroads: An Economic Study of the Motion Picture Industry* (Hollywood: Hollywood AFL Film Council, 1957), 13–14, 17–18.

NOTE: This table is not comprehensive and is missing data for United Artists and several independent companies like Eagle-Lion, Hecht-Lancaster, Amalgamated, and Michael Todd Productions.

in 1951 and has grown steadily since," a tacit reference to *Quo Vadis* (1951).[114] Comparing 1945 to 1956 to demonstrate the economic importance of the blockbuster, Bernstein cited figures showing how Paramount had reduced productions from twenty-five to ten, but with the average negative cost rising from $1,065,000 to $2,195,000 (the latter number was a conservative measure as it excluded any part of the enormous sums that went into the production of *The Ten Commandments*).[115] He summarized the "unusual exhibition practices" that producers forced upon exhibitors, including "prereleases, special releases, abnormally long showings at first-run houses, reserved seat showings, and higher admission prices," all of which "evoked howls of rage from the independent exhibitors and were largely responsible for the investigations of the industry by the Senate Small Business Committee in 1953 and 1956."[116]

Encouraging signs for the future of the industry, according to Bernstein, included the demographic growth of teenagers, who were turning into active moviegoers, and the expectations economists had for continued prosperity and hence for leisure-time markets. But with regard to the decisions made by the motion picture business, the blockbuster strategy appeared to be working. As Bernstein observed, "The only big money that has been made in Hollywood in recent years has been on individual films that have proved to be smash hits. . . . The public is gradually being educated to accept the notion that going to the movies can be something special, like going to the legitimate theater or a big football game."[117] Moviegoing was settling into its new position, reformulated as an event.

In his comprehensive theoretical examination of genre and its function as a processual organizing schema for texts, producers, critics, and spectators, Rick Altman referred to adjectives being used as nouns in advertisements and criticism. This shift from adjective to noun helps cycles of films become identified as more coherent and recognizable film genres.[118] Something similar occurred as "blockbuster," beginning as a noun, becoming an adjective for explosive impact, then became a noun describing a particular type of film. And yet there is a difference insomuch as blockbusters are not a genre in the way that Altman and others understand the concept. "Blockbuster" references a category of production, marketing, and sensation but not necessarily narrative, characterological, thematic, or setting conventions that would make blockbusters distinct from any other particular generic formation. These features make blockbusters an industrial strategy, rather than a distinctive genre.

As the blockbuster strategy came to rule American film, its adoption was not totalizing or unified. It organized relations with exhibitors and investors and was a mechanism in the redistribution of market power following the Paramount Decree. It experimented with new technology and cross-media operations, making cinema technology and innovations a central part of the entertainment package. And it helped explain film commodities and their value to audiences and investors, being used to name identifiable films while remaining loose enough to be claimed for virtually any work. But the blockbuster strategy was far from the only approach to the movie business, and other entertainments like the televisual realism of *Marty* or the adult drama of *The Man with the Golden Arm* (1955) were popular and celebrated. Competing distributors navigated these assumptions about the American film market and audience with various films and promotional plans. The result was a variegated slate of entertainments in which American cultural tastes found differential forms of expression. The landscape was not just one of hits and misses but of different kinds of hits and misses: slow building (sleepers), instantaneously realized, unexpected, underperforming, and so on. Versions of such differentiation had existed before. But in the 1950s the idea of the blockbuster had become the central organizing pole for these assessments and expectations.

A transformation in Hollywood had taken place. The turn toward the event movie, the expensive production, the technologically advanced experience, the blockbuster, had been completed, and a commitment had been made to this expansive model as the future of the industry. The next few years would be a period of refinement, most notably handling the growing dissatisfaction with the quality of the films being released. But by 1956, the future of Hollywood—with its growing reliance on a few films, ones that extended their ties to other industries and cultural commodities—was agreed to be at the behest of the blockbuster strategy.

(CHAPTER SIX)

COSMOPOLITAN ARTLESSNESS

A letter to *New York Times* drama critics in 1953 chastised them for the limited terms with which they discussed "Negro" plays, resorting repeatedly to "dignity," "honesty," and "moving." The letter writer implied that these descriptions were stereotypical and that they did not connect with the "average Broadway theatregoer." This imagined audience member only understands "a play as a blockbuster or a dud."[1] The result was that interest in more challenging and offbeat plays, in particular ones about the African American experience, would not be generated. This letter suggests that even in 1953 "blockbuster" circulated as a way to describe hit productions and that it then had some currency in the theater trade. It equally shows us that the rather brute binary of hit or miss, success or failure, operated to organize works, in this case live theater, and to identify the limited critical interest of audiences. The hit value was seen as a central characteristic that attracted audiences, and the racialized earnestness critics used to describe alternatives made them that much less appealing. Consequently, audience attention, and hence dollars and attendance, was directed away from more socially engaged or artful productions. This illustration, which referred to the theatrical business rather than movies, presents reasoning that would come to represent much of what we understand of commercial culture and the role of critical assessments, that is, that blockbusters, for all their appeals to universalism, are engines of exclusion.

In this chapter we examine the first years in the United States when the modern concept of the blockbuster movie settled and circulated outside industry trade venues. We see both the efforts to push this direction in Hollywood moviemaking and promotion and also the resistance to it, especially from exhibitors. The shifts taking place in distribution and exhibition continued to normalize the technological change from earlier in the decade. They equally involved more attention to international markets, with blockbusters designed as global enterprises. Most notable is that just as the blockbuster arrived on the scene as the future for Hollywood, critical challenges to this model mounted, many of which concluded that the blockbuster exemplified all that was wrong with the mixing of art and commerce.

However well the blockbuster fit with an industrial common sense about audiences, and however often the investments paid off, there were always counterexamples of failed efforts and critical dissatisfaction. For some, the financial risks were unreasonable. Producers had higher expectations for their fewer, more expensive productions. This meant longer runs in theaters, which had the effect of creating fewer bookings and a shortage of premium screens on which to show featured product. With limited bookings possible, some distributors actually complained they had too many to release at any given time.[2] As Hollywood sought to emerge from its theatrical downturn, films settled into the categories of in-betweeners, blockbuster, and gimmick or teen-oriented exploitation film. A blockbuster was sold as that rare and celebrated film that captured everything proper and uplifting in cultural life. In-betweeners were mid-budget adult or family fare. Quality films included the more challenging, and less well attended, art films. Together, highbrow art films, middlebrow blockbusters, and middlebrow in-betweeners all enjoyed a degree of respectability that lowbrow gimmick pictures did not.

Variety's year-end commentary for 1957 referenced their annual review seven years earlier, when Hollywood had come down with "psychosis televisionitis." Some of that panic about the broadcasting medium remained, but new issues for exhibitors involved the limited kinds of films being provided by distributors. The review declared, "The thing which has discouraged the film trade in recent months has been the failure of 'good' pictures to do expected business. A vacuum area has opened up between blockbusters on the one extreme, with their capital risks, and exploitation cheapies at the other extreme. Understandably many showmen have had trouble adjusting their bearings."[3] With the uncommon performance of *Around the World in 80 Days* (1956), *Giant* (1956), and *The Ten Commandments* (1956), all evidence pointed to continuing vitality for the industry, despite exhibitors' concerns. But questions about the full impact of the blockbuster had begun to appear. Were blockbusters really worth their cost? In 1957 "Hazards in 'Blockbusting'" noticed a turn away from the big-budget strategy, suggesting that foreign and in-betweener films would be more financially advantageous than the expensive blockbusters.[4] This caution in *Variety* appeared next to a report on the surprising successes of nonblockbusters, in particular those that featured promotional or exhibition gimmicks as well as quickie tie-ins to news stories, like the U.S.S.R.'s launch of the Sputnik satellite.[5]

From roughly 1957 on, the criticisms of blockbusters amplified. At the 1957 Cannes Film Festival, which opened with *Around the World in 80 Days*, American film was seen as set apart from other national cinemas. As mentioned earlier, Vanessa R. Schwartz documented the orchestrated globalism of *Around the World in 80 Days*, dealing most elaborately with its appearance at Cannes, as a realization of "the cosmopolitan film."[6] As *Variety* put it, festival favorites tend toward "the unusual, the profound, the different," whereas U.S. films "are boxoffice blockbuster exponents," like *Around the World in 80 Days*. The conclusion of one reporter was that the attitude at Cannes was not so much "anti-American" as "pro-arty."[7] A dichotomy was developing, separating the prestigious cosmopolitan American films from artful cinematic renditions.

But while the American blockbuster still chased the bourgeois audience with trappings of prestige, many understood blockbusters as exactly the opposite, as woefully soulless creatures produced by a soulless system. They were reliant on access to substantial amounts of investment resources; coordination of cross-sector deals and financial advantages; the ability to wait for returns for a relatively long time, weathering fallow periods; and access to new technology or to the means to develop such systems. The blockbuster, in other words, was fundamentally wrapped up with an industrial process, one that could meet its intense needs for capital, available to only the most exclusive of corporations and entrepreneurs. As a result of its own visibility and prominence, the blockbuster was the realization of exactly the kind of culture a highly industrialized system would produce. For all of its pretense of worldliness and state-of-the-art cinematic achievement, the blockbuster was material evidence for the limited and predictable expressions of commercial culture. It became recognized and lambasted as a form of *cosmopolitan artlessness*.

For some producers, the prospects of blockbuster riches made smaller-scale works less desirable, narrowing the range of films in circulation. This reasoning was evident in 1958, when *Variety* reported that "the so-called medium budget pictures—those made at costs of $1,000,000 to $2,500,000—are rated as the most dangerous pictures by the film companies. These entries, lacking the ingredients for blockbuster action and too costly to capture the audience that's available in the current market, are proving to be one of the major headaches of the economy-conscious film companies."[8] Handled properly, a low-budget film costing $500,000 or less could predictably expect a profit between $50,000 and $350,000. The biggest blockbusters had recently proven lucrative, including the less successful ones, like *Raintree County* (1957), which turned a profit once international receipts were in. It was the middle-budget films that created the "headaches."[9]

These midrange-budget films were important because many presumed this was where the "art" of film was found. The less inclined producers were to back such films, the more dire the state of the art, according to critics and audiences. This is the familiar and persistent dream of a tasteful middle, not too cheap but also not too garish or excessive. And the concern about the pursuit of the big as the pursuit of the garish was crossing over to general audiences, with critical assessments of Hollywood appearing in venues like the *New York Times*. There, long-standing film critic Bosley Crowther wrote, "Throughout the Hollywood community, among big producers and small, the one driving ambition today is to make what they call the 'jackpot' film. That is to say, they are all shooting for the picture—the 'blockbuster'—that will be a tremendous attraction and make big profits for all." As a result, "there are very few 'in-betweeners.'"[10] Put differently, in-betweeners were artful and not jackpot films, and jackpot films, that is, blockbusters, were not artistic achievements.

Universal, in contrast, tried to base its brand on such midrange films and kept its focus on in-betweeners. This decision, though, led to skepticism about their ability to thrive. So widely embraced was the blockbuster strategy of big productions with extended runs that pursuing other approaches seemed foolish. Universal released about thirty films a year, most of which were modestly budgeted genre entries of science fiction, action, melodrama, and horror, with their eyes on smaller city markets and tastes.[11] They had recently released additions to two of their popular rural comedy series, *Ma and Pa Kettle at Waikiki* (1955), *The Kettles in the Ozarks* (1956), and *Francis in the Navy* (1955), the last featuring Francis the Talking Mule. Their lineup was not solely cornball comedy, and they received critical acclaim with some of their prestige moneymakers, including *The Glenn Miller Story* (1954), *Magnificent Obsession* (1954), and *Written on the Wind* (1956). Still, their approach stood out primarily as a counterpoint to the more singular focus on blockbusters seen at the larger studios, a focus that ate up media, trade attention, and celluloid.

There were other skeptics of the blockbuster strategy. Exhibitor Leonard H. Goldenson, president of American Broadcasting-Paramount Theatres, Inc., which was then the largest chain in the United States, challenged the orthodoxy that "only the blockbusters do business and the B's and the 'nervous A's' are poison."[12] Exhibitors would be well advised, he declared, to consider other factors, including star power, beyond marketing and production heft. In contrast, Charles B. Moss, who led the B. S. Moss theater chain, predicted that soon exhibition would consist solely of blockbusters. Theatrical releases would, he said, be big productions that ran for ages, and were distinct from the smaller productions and immediacy of television.[13]

Goldenson's skeptical and Moss's more singularly optimistic views aside, after several major successes of big films in 1955, including *Oklahoma!* and *The Bridges at Toko-Ri*, 1956 was the year the organization of epic production and box-office performance fused to typify the blockbuster. *Variety*, applying the term retrospectively, made the lineage seem fluid and obvious. *Gone with the Wind* (1939), the film with the most successful box office in U.S. history, stood as the mark to best, initiating a ranking system that extended beyond single seasons or summers. With the headline "New Group of Potential Blockbusters Rising to Hold Hands with 'GWTW,'" the David O. Selznick classic of 1939 was described as "the all-time blockbuster."[14] Indeed, the ongoing revenue-generating potential of a film was one of the main factors in the idea of the blockbuster. *Variety* characterized it as follows: "As a result of the current blockbuster trend, a group of pictures are emerging that might well be dubbed 'perennials' or 'posterity' films. These are screen classics, produced in such scope that they represent all-time contributions; that is, films that can be played and replayed, after respectable waiting periods, for years and years to come."[15] The examples given included recently released *War and Peace* (1956), *The Ten Commandments*, and *Moby Dick* (1956), as well as the to-be-released *Giant*. And filmed versions of Rodgers and Hammerstein musicals *Carousel* (1956), *Oklahoma!*, and *The King and I* (1956) appeared to have the potential to be perennials, as did the still-being-filmed *South Pacific* (1958). The expectation of ongoing success required a different, long-term conceptualization of the investment incurred, with a quick payoff being counter to the building of a lasting commercial entity. Moreover, the category of "all-time hits" established a cross-decade comparison and ranking, where hits in current release were ranked in relation to hits from the past, presenting a sense of historical continuity and competition for financial impact.

Ideas about what made a perennial film settled on identifiable and already popular works, literary classics, and tales from biblical times. The presentation, from widescreen formats to extended running times, mirrored the emphasis on scope and scale, and the sumptuous presentation invited seriousness and contemplation. All such features designated hierarchies of cultural value, constructing what Pierre Bourdieu would identify as a field of cultural production in which divisions among class formations are reproduced.[16] Flagship works enjoyed uniform critical praise. A consensus culture built around them. They were films for the ages and were treated as a different order of the art of popular film. They were for everyone, discussed and seen by everyone, or, rather, such was the conceit. Moreover, they elicited a sense of duty. They were important, as films and as part of a general education. In this way they helped make coherent dominant ideas about tastefulness and the people who were most at home with those valued cultural qualities. Blockbusters had become an essential part of cultural literacy. Other films might be distracting amusements, artistic explorations, or timely social commentary. Blockbusters were civic responsibilities.

Just as these characteristics settled, another move in the field of cultural production pushed against this category as being industrially tainted. Blockbusters were lavish but also garish and crass. Distinction among a cultured cohort shifted to a developing location, where the in-betweener was artful and tasteful. So, with that impression of duty came attacks on blockbusters' aesthetic value. Early in 1957 writer-director Nunnally Johnson wrote a sardonic piece reminding folks that size does not bespeak entertainment, art, or value. "Oh, Men! Oh, Women! Oh, Slightly Colossal!" plugged the virtues of his "small" comedy, *Oh, Men! Oh, Women!* (1957). Johnson stated flatly that the film would have been "harmed" if they had spent more on it. He wrote, "As every school child knows, there were 68,894 people photographed in 'Around the World,' 112,538 in 'War and Peace,' and the rest of mankind in 'The Ten Commandments.'" He lampooned the production budgets as $6 million for *Around the World in 80 Days*, "seven or eight or nine million" for *War and Peace*, and "a flat rate of $1,000,000 per Commandment." The producer was then "to decide how many [commandments] he wanted at that price."[17] He joked about how punishingly long those films were, saying that his new movie, coming in at ninety minutes, was equivalent to five commandments, just "War" (without peace), and only "40 Days." Johnson's commentary was but one example of a denotative and connotative assuredness about what "blockbuster" meant, circulating ever more widely, in which the blockbuster became a mark against which one could establish the distinctive charms of an in-betweener.

Small, artful, and tasteful, the in-betweener connoted the adult as well. As serious as many of the prestige epics were, and as carefully oriented toward internationalist middlebrow senses of cultural import, blockbusters were for general audiences. Though the running times made them unsuitable for young children, they were films that families could see, sitting side by side, without any sense of embarrassment, save a few raised eyebrows about the formfitting outfits in The Ten Commandments. As Variety observed, there was very little sex in epic releases, for "these are the 'blockbusters' and there's not one among them that could give the moralists cause for concern."[18] Those interested in more mature and sophisticated treatments had to find them elsewhere.

As the definitional form of the blockbuster movie took shape, the role of advertising was key. The sense that a blockbuster was such as a result of being promoted in a particular way made it easy to see blockbusters as cynical and inauthentic works from a faceless commercial machine. Still, the managing editor for Variety, Robert J. Landry, challenged the impression that the moviegoing public was so easily influenced. He argued that the critic and the marketer were not so far apart in that they shared the goal of directing people toward one film and away from another. And while overwrought claims of excellence and failure marked each rhetorical position, the public had the final say and, according to Landry, wielded more power than either. Further, audiences did more than make decisions about movies; they also evaluated the reviews and the promotional campaigns. Moviegoers surveyed the entirety of movie culture and in so doing drew an explicit distinction between the work and its hype. As Landry wrote, the public understood that "a box-office blockbuster is not synonymous with a blockbuster campaign."[19] Or a film with strong support from reviewers might not see a related upswing in business. For Landry, "the ideal parlay is a good picture, a good campaign, a good set of reviews and attendance to match."[20]

Blockbuster promotional heft was showing signs of reduced usefulness. In 1957, Columbia set an explicit goal to streamline their press books, as expenses for printing had been running too high. Press books and kits were the products of marketing units, and they offered stories, information, images, posters, and various merchandise to help exhibitors exploit the film. The standard length had been about twenty pages, but it had been "going as high as 70 pages for so-called blockbuster pictures." Their new length at Columbia was to be roughly an economical six pages. As one Columbia executive commented, the oversized press books had come to be "measured by weight rather than content," packed with "verbiage" and "garbiage."[21]

Other managerial and financial matters arose. The battle for year-over-year predictability continued, and a reduced number of films, each with greater expectations, only exacerbated Wall Street's impression of the industry's radical swings between high times and low. Producer Walter Wanger saw an alternate pathway to assure stability in the business if space in theaters were given over to merchandise of various sorts, like records, cosmetics, and books. Developing a movie-related retail space could provide another revenue stream for exhibitors as well as distributors. Wanger reasoned, "'If this type of merchandising became successful' . . . 'perhaps every picture would not have to be a blockbuster. Then the industry could afford to take chances with experimental films.'"[22] This view built on the promotional merchandise offered to exhibitors by distributors through the press books but saw an expanded function, and retail opportunity, for the smart impresario.

As covered in previous chapters, for every purpose-built blockbuster, there were aspirational productions that described themselves as such. Exhibitors complained that neither they nor producers were equipped to identify what should receive blockbuster promotional treatment, and that the moviegoing public could not always be transparently read for what it would respond to best. This lack of coordination was considered a drawback of divorcement, whereas in the past distributors and exhibitors might have been able to agree on the films that would merit special promotional attention.[23] One curious case experimented with the boundaries of the notion and involved the film *Proud Rebel* (1958). Paramount's advertising unit selected this Alan Ladd drama set in the post–Civil War period to test whether they might promote a small wholesome family film the same way they promoted a big-budget extravaganza. Concentrating on Minneapolis–Saint Paul, the Minnesota Amusement Company, a Paramount subsidiary, invited outstanding students from elementary schools, along with their families, to attend the film. Post-screening photographs of these people, along with testimonials about the film, ran in newspapers. The thinking here was that word of mouth could be created at each of the schools represented.[24] Ultimately, Paramount considered the results unsatisfying, concluding that a nonblockbuster did not benefit from blockbuster-style promotion.[25] Others tried to push nonblockbuster films with over-the-top claims and outsize promotional machinery, but a general truism developed that the film dictated its marketing treatment and that only true blockbusters benefited from hard-sell tactics. As A. D. Murphy put it, "The 'blitzkrieg' school of hard sell seems best reserved for the God-and-Gomorrah type of production."[26]

One of the first strongly positive reviews of *Proud Rebel* was from A. H. Weiler, who championed this little film by describing it as being as emotionally successful as more ambitious productions. He wrote that it avoids special effects and "cleaves to the premise that a 'little' story, honestly told, can be just as persuasive as the sound and fury of a blockbuster."[27] The description of the emotionally honest film, avoiding the inauthenticity of effects and the excesses ("sound and fury") of big-budget productions, drove home the sense that the overstuffing of respectable cinematic quality had tipped over into vapid and loud manufactured culture. Weiler's line was immediately featured in print ads, including one on the very next day: "PERSUASIVE AS A BLOCKBUSTER!" (figure 6.1).[28] Unlike other early appearances of the term "blockbuster," this line did not appear in a list of other enthusiastic statements or in small ad notices, but as a featured, top-of-the-ad, bolded pronouncement with only two other short critical blurbs. This newspaper appearance was arguably the first prominent one for "blockbuster," used to promote a film to the general public, not only to industry agents in trade publications. Importantly, even as this endorsement appealed to an idea about an impactful movie, it equally disavowed the film's association with the blockbuster and marked off a clear value-laden difference: the honest little story versus the sound and fury of the blockbuster. *Proud Rebel* was like this by not being like that; such a statement works with, and fortifies, a semiotic distinction between the modest film and the excessive blockbuster.

At this point, in the summer of 1958, when the term "blockbuster" had been an industry-specific designation for the past decade, there were still few films that had incorporated the term into their ads addressed to the general moviegoing public. But as a category designating a set of characteristics to promise audiences, we had seen this in a minor way with *Ransom!* (1956). So here, with *Proud Rebel*, we find the most complete embrace of the term in a broad public ad campaign to date as a reference to *a particular kind of movie*, and it tells audiences that this film is *not* a blockbuster.

In a less extensive manner, a few months earlier, MGM's *The Brothers Karamazov* (1958) employed a similar promotion in specialized trade magazines. In an ad pushing this "new blockbuster," several highly complimentary quotes from reviews extolled the virtues of the film. Included was a line from

FIGURE 6.1 *Proud Rebel* advertisement, calling the film "persuasive as a blockbuster," 1958

the *Motion Picture Daily* review that the film "stacks up with the blockbusters of the season."[29] Here, too, a point of distinction was being made, one that implied a common reference, namely, that readers knew what those blockbusters were and that *The Brothers Karamazov* was not one of them, and was a greater film for it. The blockbuster, both savior and failure of the industry, was becoming a point of orientation and comparison, from which some films needed to assert their difference.

★ ★ ★ ★

Even as signs pointed to a resurgence for the film business, the future of American moviegoing, given other leisure options available to consumers, continued to be a worry. For a couple of years at the end of the 1950s, *Variety* ran a regular page "Bureau of Missing Business," in which Robert J. Landry assembled and commented on items relevant to market assessment. In one of the first, Landry focused on the "mortgaged masses" whose tight financial situation made their entertainment consumption that much more discretionary. This view, echoed elsewhere, is an important corrective to our unexamined assumptions about the universal affluence of the postwar American consumer. Instead, Hollywood saw a more discriminating and economically careful consumer, one who was in need of very specialized wooing. But, as Landry observed, the recent big-budget extravaganzas had hit on exactly the qualities that would get folks to line up at top-dollar ticket prices. His conclusion was that many still believed in "the myth of the undiscriminating audience," which was never really the case. Now, "showmen seem startled as if the idea that quality alone triumphs was new or strange, whereas, of course, it has prevailed always." Quality, even at additional expense, drew crowds, and for that reason "there is little truly new about the blockbuster idea, save the word."[30]

It was difficult for anyone, critics and investors alike, to verify claims about economic standing, let alone futures. Some assessments of market health were a product of incomplete statistical assumptions, which sometimes underplayed actual activity. For example, the long runs of blockbusters, especially when they were held over from their initial engagements, had the effect of pushing aside other films in the queue for exhibition. The result was that what had been a standard measure of market activity—the number of bookings for a film—now looked meager. Longer runs also meant those prints, tied as they were to a single engagement, were not available for other bookings, making some screening venues wait for desired shows. Indeed, this waiting period was built into the roadshow releasing strategy. Twentieth Century Fox's president, Spyros P. Skouras, saw that what might be advantageous to blockbusters and even to "Regal quickies," a reference to their modest-budget film unit, was detrimental to in-betweeners.[31] Further, Landry pointed out that Twentieth Century Fox had become worried about the reduced booking potential of their CinemaScope films as they waited for some theaters to convert their facilities to accommodate this format. But their tally did not include their RegalScope films, which were lower-budget black-and-white CinemaScope films rebranded so that the company could claim to be maintaining their promise that all CinemaScope films would be in color.[32]

As familiar as it may have been to the history of movie showmanship, at about this moment the contemporary incarnation of the blockbuster idea was being exported, and, most significantly, it was characterized as a defining feature of the time. Gene Moskowitz's report on the French film scene described the embrace of American approaches to film extravagances, including CinemaScope and epic running times. Specifically, Moskowitz wrote that the four-hour *Les Misérables* (1958) was "the French answer to such American blockbusters as *Around the World in 80 Days* and *The Ten Commandments*," though its "ponderous" adaptation did not translate into enthusiastic moviegoing crowds. The film was France's entrance into the "blockbuster era," fortifying the impression that outsize American-style productions and significant audience attention went hand in hand. Moskowitz smartly noted that this turn in France was not prompted by any perceived competition from television, indicating that other motivating factors encouraged the efforts to contribute to the epic end of the international film spectrum.[33]

In Britain the focus on blockbusters was not seen as the savior of the business but as its demise. Producer Michael Forlong laid out the limitations presented by such singularly enormous investments, which required appealing to virtually everyone. The films couldn't but address the "lowest common denominator" in taste, he claimed. Similarly, exhibitor Jim Poole recommended that family films and double bills, made of more modest offerings, would keep the British film industry alive.[34]

The competing definitions of "blockbuster" made general pronouncements about them imprecise and spurious. Universal's general sales manager, Henry H. Martin, commenting on their decision to reduce the number of releases for 1958–1959, claimed that blockbusters were not identified by their budgets but by their performance and their appeal to audiences. The unpredictability of these meant that it was difficult to plan in advance how many films the market would hold, and exhibitors would need, in a given year.[35] Once a hit was identified, runs were extended, wreaking havoc on existing release schedules.

The blockbuster strategy had gripped the major studios so securely that they began to circulate the logic more widely, building a publicly legible rationale that large-scale productions beget large-scale cultural value, which in turn beget large-scale profits. Paramount, for example, enjoyed a particularly strong first three quarters in 1958. Though their revenues essentially matched those of 1957, the studio had cut costs, leaving them with elevated profits. To continue this trajectory, they planned to release at least twenty films in 1959 that would have budgets in excess of $1 million, a significant increase from the fourteen comparable films released in 1958. The total budget for these coming films surpassed $30 million. In a meeting between Paramount executives and theater owners, Paramount vice president Paul Raibourn commented on how challenging it was to promote "very ordinary pictures," while "big pictures, known as 'blockbusters' in the trade, stand to make 'big money.'"[36] Given the audience of trade personnel, it is likely the reference to the trade usage of "blockbuster" was added by the *Wall Street Journal* staff reporter for the benefit of the paper's readers. It does, however, remind us of the transitional period that was continuing through 1958, in which "blockbuster" still maintained its connection to industry lingo and was only just beginning to push into the lexicon of the general reader and the moviegoing public.

Raibourn pointed to Paramount's Academy Award–winning *The Ten Commandments* as solid evidence of the certainty of the blockbuster approach. With a sky-high production budget of $13.7 million, and an additional distribution expense of $10.3 million, Raibourn said the studio expected the two-year-old film to stay in theaters and continue earning through 1961, which is an incredible stretch of time for a film. The projected take by then would be $60 million, making it an unbelievable critical and financial success.[37] The following year, Paramount president Barney Balaban reiterated this view to shareholders, again referencing the ongoing revenue generated by *The Ten Commandments*, especially as it continued playing overseas. According to Balaban, "the movie industry today is highly dependent on the production of high-budget 'blockbusters' for its earnings." He added that they were difficult to produce, and he identified a lack of "'great stories, popular stars and top producers, directors and writers,'" which made blockbusters even pricier, as key talent had to be enticed with a percentage of the profits.[38]

Other studio executives provided comparable depictions of their operations. Joseph R. Vogel, who became president of MGM's parent company, Loew's, in 1956, commented in 1958 on the turnaround that he had overseen, especially noting the studio's coming "blockbusters."[39] At a press conference following a shareholders' meeting at the end of the same year, Columbia vice president Leo Jaffe gave an account that featured the studio's plans to release fewer films, but with larger budgets, saying, "'We're going more and more for the so-called blockbuster type.'" The reasoning was that such films "stand a better chance in today's film market of making money than do many of the smaller-budget, so-called B movies."[40] Increasing certainty about this assessment appeared when Universal released its financial expectations. In a press conference about its real estate and television dealings with MCA, also in December 1958, Universal's president, Milton R. Rackmil, announced a reduction in the number of films to be released in the coming year to twenty-one, down from thirty-seven the year before. Production budgets, however, were to increase, as "blockbusters . . . stand a better chance in today's market of bringing in bigger grosses at the box office than do the smaller-budget films," echoing the report on Columbia from three days earlier.[41]

The reduced number of releases—notwithstanding the occasional increase seen with some studios—continued the exhibitors' problem of a shortage of product. Additionally, the play dates for blockbusters were more tightly controlled, so along with their length limiting the number of performances in a given day, they presented operational difficulties for theater owners and managers. The American Congress of Exhibitors reported that theater owners wanted a range of product, commenting that "Hollywood . . . should be encouraged to make more pictures and not to try to produce a blockbuster each time."[42] It was an issue not only of supply but also of the way theater owners handled material. Blockbusters seized the attention and focus of exhibitors, leaving midrange films to languish. Giving blockbusters more play dates meant fewer dates for other films, making it even more challenging for them to be profitable.[43] The loss of the in-betweener and the "nervous A" was a concern. Some, including Continental Distributing's chair, Walter Reade Jr., presented international financing partnerships as a way to assist in the flow of production funds to these midrange efforts.[44] The savior of the American film industry was not taken as such by everyone.

In his end-of-1958 survey of the state of Hollywood, Thomas Pryor wrote that 1959 was promising to see a historic low in the number of films released by the studios. This turn would result in a more dramatic difference between the budgets of smaller and bigger films, with the "so-called 'nervous A' films" suffering the most. The midrange budgets of between $500,000 and $900,000 were too risky, because, as Pryor reported, "the majority were not strong enough as box office attractions to obtain choice playing time at the big first-run theatres and are too costly for the money they can earn as second features."[45] Pryor even dated the stabilization of the associated rationale as emerging with clarity in 1958, when it became generally accepted that "there are only two really profitable types of movies, the 'blockbuster' that almost everybody deserts television to see at a premium price and the quickie program feature that costs from $100,000 to $300,000."[46] What had been an argument among trade agents had formed into a general understanding about what to expect of motion pictures.

The potential failings of this bifurcated direction for American film were not lost on commentators. Pryor continued his assessment of 1958 by naming the recent midrange film successes that ran counter to the focus on either bigger or smaller productions, including *Marty* (1955), *Twelve Angry Men* (1957), and *The Defiant Ones* (1958). Moreover, the growing cult of the blockbuster resulted in a "warped perspective," with "too many producers endeavoring to inflate small story ideas with bigness in terms of star names, impressive sets and padding plots simply to extend the running time two hours or more."[47] His analysis was in part prompted by earlier expectations that the Hollywood studio system would increase in instability because of the unusually extreme risks they were taking with big-budget films, which would make room for even more powerful influence from independent operations. Pryor concluded that this had not come to pass, nor would it in the near future, as most independents still needed the majors for distribution and as the sale of real estate when the majors were required to divest from theater ownership had in fact made them more financially able to focus on film. As wrongheaded as some elements of the blockbuster strategy may have been, "if movie attendance continues to average about 45,000,000 customers weekly Hollywood no doubt will be able to afford at least its customary quota of costly mistakes in 1959 without collapsing."[48]

Blockbusters had, at least for the moment, performed a key function for the business: they provided investors and stockholders with a measure of financial health.[49] A studio that had a couple of major blockbusters on the horizon was an attractive prospect for investment, whereas one that did not seemed to be out of the high end of this media industry game. Blockbusters also simplified what investors outside of the movie business needed to pay attention to, beyond interest from the average moviegoer. Investors could keep their eyes on a few titles and assume they could predict the return on their investments. These hulking films, after all, were built for unusual success.

Critic Gavin Lambert, writing in *Sight and Sound*, renamed in-betweeners "desperation pictures." Lambert pointed to *I Want to Live* (1958), *The Defiant Ones*, and *God's Little Acre* (1958) as prime examples. These desperation pictures were not blockbusters or low-budget exploitation films but artful, high-minded moderate-budget films that aspired to creative expression and were becoming a rare product in Hollywood. His criticism of blockbusters was a perfect summation of the presumption of artlessness they had come to be associated with, quoted here at length:

> Coming out of a blockbuster is as bad as waking up with a hangover. And there's no pleasure to look back on. The blockbuster isn't just a picture with physical bloat, unless it's dedicated to showing off yet another new process; it has the lure of a Broadway hit or a best-seller behind it, and one or more Top Money-Making Stars. It runs 2–2½ hours, usually in Cinema Scope and colour; it has lavish backgrounds which become foregrounds, and there's a widely advertised set-piece, battle scene, sex scene, bullfight, elephant stampede, etc. It doesn't really matter who directs a blockbuster—you'll find no personal style. It doesn't seem to matter who writes it—the dialogue is mainly reminiscent of subtitles in silent pictures and the characters are strip cartoon. The total effect is traumatic: a jumble of titles . . . of stars wandering around like displaced persons . . . of endless travelogues. . . . In retrospect, the blockbuster period will surely appear as Hollywood's most spectacularly vacant and dull. And not one of these pictures seems like a *movie*.[50]

In the next issue of the same publication, John Gillett reiterated the narrative of Hollywood's downward spiral, noting "the industry's desperate and often debased attempts to hold its audiences through a constant vulgarisation of subject matter and a faith in fabulously expensive blockbusters on ever widening screens. In these circumstances, it is not surprising that the personal film has become even more difficult to achieve."[51] The arrival of the blockbuster, here, was not the savior of the industry but the end of the artful Hollywood film. The mechanistic aspects, the flat dialogue, the impersonal style, and the showcasing of new cinematic processes made these films into something other than movies, as Lambert put it. What these and other critics could not know was that this phase would not be a short one. This approach to industrial moviemaking was digging in for the long haul. As it turned out, Pryor was right about 1959, though the end point of the blockbuster strategy that critics had warned of would eventually come to pass within the next decade, prompting a serious reevaluation of all aspects of the movie business. And yet, in the long run, the blockbuster strategy rebounded in the 1970s and has stayed with us ever since.

The years 1958 and 1959 battled openly for the title of "the year of the blockbuster." Most important, there was no doubt that large productions now ruled Hollywood. From then on, there was no longer any uncertainty about the particularity of this American cinematic form, its cosmopolitanism, its technological exhibitionism, its audience appeal, and its investment status. But its cultural import and impact on the art of cinema remained a source of considerable skepticism. The criticism of blockbusters' cultural value extended even to those who were otherwise champions of middlebrow appreciation, including the prestigious blockbuster. In a commentary that extended the concern about the rise of the blockbuster, Bosley Crowther opined that the loss of habitual moviegoing meant that the small wonders of otherwise-imperfect films were going unnoticed. Pointing to television as a primary factor contributing to the decline of moviegoing, Crowther also blamed "blockbuster merchandise techniques." In other words, the promotional facet as much as the film itself had created a tainted moviegoing environment in which a film had "to be 'terrific' or two hours and thirteen minutes long or dressed up in wide-screen and color with three major and six minor stars in order to make it attractive."[52] Typifying a form of cinephilia that he saw as waning, Crowther wrote that a "rather large and not uncritical clan" did not need their movies to be prestigious, epic, or even especially good. They would devote themselves to particular artists and see everything with Bob Hope, Franklin Pangborn, or Mikhail Rasumny, or directed by John Ford.[53] Here, the indiscriminate cinephile has access to small, hidden pleasures unavailable in the tasteful uniformity of the big blockbuster epic. In Crowther's comments were notes of what Manny Farber later described as the "termite" film, which contrasted the big-issue, self-important "white elephant film" by offering small moments of surprise and insight within an otherwise-imperfect film.[54] Both are critical assessments that emerged from and responded to the rise of the blockbuster strategy.

And that strategy had been nailed into place. When asked, some, like Jerry Wald at Twentieth Century Fox, saw a future of about sixty films being released by each studio annually. Others, like prominent independent producer Samuel Goldwyn, foresaw an industry that made only blockbusters and only about fifty each year in total. In this scenario, television, particularly some sort of pay-TV model, would become the primary platform for all the nonblockbusters produced.[55] *Picturegoer* was direct about the prospect. "This will be the year of the blockbusters," wrote Elizabeth Forrest of 1958, "the kind of free-wheeling, high-scaling, star-studded films that producers calculate are

TABLE 6.1 Top Ten Films by Domestic Box-Office Revenue, 1950–1959

Film	Gross, in 2005 USD (millions)
1. *The Ten Commandments* (1956)	$829.2
2. *Ben-Hur* (1959)	$754.3
3. *Around the World in 80 Days* (1956)	$534.0
4. *The Robe* (1953)	$474.8
5. *Cinderella* (1950)	$379.8
6. *The Bridge on the River Kwai* (1957)	$362.3
7. *The Greatest Show on Earth* (1952)	$349.1
8. *Lady and the Tramp* (1955)	$326.8
9. *From Here to Eternity* (1953)	$326.4
10. *Peter Pan* (1953)	$323.3

SOURCE: Alex Ben Block and Lucy Autrey Wilson, eds., *George Lucas's Blockbusting: A Decade-by-Decade Survey of Timeless Movies Including Untold Secrets of Their Financial and Cultural Success* (New York: ItBooks, 2010).

the only certain incentives to drag you away from the home TV screen," continuing with references to *A Farewell to Arms* (1957), *The Young Lions* (1958), *Legend of the Lost* (1957), *Raintree County*, *South Pacific*, *The Vikings* (1958), and *The Buccaneer* (1958).[56] Looking ahead, Forrest mentioned two blockbusters in production: *Lawrence of Arabia* (1962) and *Ben-Hur* (1959).

A few months later, in October 1958, *Variety* summed up the year similarly: "With 1958 coming into the homestretch, it's now a certainty that this will go down as the 'year of the blockbusters.'"[57] Whereas recent years had had only a hit or two, every studio had its own in 1958. As a point of comparison, *Variety* heralded only two smashes from 1952—MGM's *Quo Vadis* (1951), taking $10.5 million, and Paramount's *The Greatest Show on Earth*, grossing $12 million—and estimated that overall only sixteen titles took in $3 million or more. By contrast, 1958 would have far more movies that did far better. They described the blockbuster approach as "new picture making and thinking."[58] This line of argumentation appeared frequently, for example, in the statement "The guesswork has it that the key to riches in the future lies in the 'blockbuster' type of product for theatres."[59] In this instance, future revenues from television sales were being factored in to justify rising production budgets, a relatively novel idea and accounting. The blockbuster was always too big for the movies alone. It stretched quite naturally into cross-media properties, seeking paths to future revenue streams once the theatrical run had played out.

Gene Arneel continued this assessment of the centrality of the giant production, also writing about 1958 as "the year of the blockbusters," pointing out that the "big" films, prominent as they were, included disappointments like *The Vikings* as well as hits like *The Bridge on the River Kwai* and *Peyton Place*, both released late in 1957 and doing strong business in 1958.[60] *Ben-Hur*'s director, William Wyler, had his 1958 release promoted as a blockbuster: *The Big Country* (1958) carried taglines from adoring critics, one of which was Jay Carmody's superlative "a blockbuster . . . outstanding performances! Runs the gamut of the passions!"[61] This film shared more than its director with *Ben-Hur*; both films starred Charlton Heston.

Stanley Kramer, with a producer-director's view, and thinking specifically about his topical in-betweener *The Defiant Ones*, wrote of "the subliminal blockbuster," arguing that 1958 might be remembered as "the year of the blockbuster" but that for all the successes, the failures were substantial. Quality films on the right topic, Kramer argued, could "blockbust any audience subliminally," even without the promotional advantages of the bigger productions.[62] Other strategies developed, and some wrote of 1958 as the year that TV finally took over Hollywood, with many studio resources given over to TV production. Instead, reported Donovan Pedelty, 1959 would be "the year of the blockbusters."[63] Soon after, Pedelty continued the observation, charting Hollywood's reduced number of releases—325 films in 1957, 225 in 1958, and 200 set for 1959—alongside increasing budgets to argue that the blockbuster had become dominant.[64] Furthering this critical consensus, the publication's editor reiterated a few issues later Pedelty's claim that 1959 would be the year of the blockbuster.[65]

The predictably savvy Farber noted some improvements in blockbuster artistry, referring to a handful of releases in early 1959 as "a victory parade for distinguished tonnage." The films he had in mind were the "new type of big-studio 'Super' that seems conceived at the top of Wall Street by an art board recruited from *Time*, *The New Yorker* and *Partisan Review*, and then baked in a Pittsburgh blast furnace so as to outlast the Easter Island sculptures as monumental art." *The Diary of Anne Frank* (1959), *Compulsion* (1959), and *The Five Pennies* (1959) were prime examples of this for Farber. He commented on the challenges to critics that such "monumental art" posed. "With their high-powered craftsmanship, curious efficiency as art and a Genius-bug that insists on making the 'listing of credits' more costly than an old-time 'B' film," Farber wrote, "these films demand a far-out criticism that is more like bead-reading than aesthetic evaluation." Their stature "suggested a hulking, solemnly evolved Gothic building rather than a mere 'flick.'"[66] The distinction, though, was that a few "new blockbusters are usually steered by a surprisingly hip craftsman," rather than the "romantic dreadnaughts" or "Dreiser-type realists" of the past.[67] As examples, Farber sang the praises of *Compulsion* and *Some Like It Hot* (1959).

The expectations of American moviegoers had shifted. Great, distinctive movies were more like "a hulking . . . Gothic building." The experience was decidedly theatrical, linked with an evening out and the grandeur of state-of-the-art viewing conditions. Moviegoers' tastes may have been as broad as ever, but there was now a relatively narrow band of essential works, films that stood atop the slate of releases as the most elaborate examples of cinematic accomplishment. Some critics, in pushback, directed attention to the more modest dramatic and comedic efforts. They elevated the aesthetic pleasures of the smaller films, the in-betweeners, and the artistry of working with limited resources, including the countervailing approach of Walt Disney and its outstandingly popular animated features. But even in their criticism they affirmed the influence of the hulking status of the blockbuster, that giant monumental movie that filled up the cinematic atmosphere.

The stage was set for *Ben-Hur*, released in 1959. That same year critic Richard L. Coe declared that Billy Wilder's *Some Like It Hot* was a comedy blockbuster owing to its stunning comedic achievement rather than an epic scale of production or financial prowess.[68] Coe's assessment appeared as a newspaper ad endorsement, informing moviegoers, "The sooner you see this rollicking blockbuster—the better."[69] *Billboard*'s review declared of *Some Like It Hot*, "Monroe pic has block-buster aura."[70] And the promotional prose for *A Summer Place* (1959), which was not excerpted from a critic's review, described it as "the dramatic blockbuster of the year" in a small-font short paragraph suggesting a literary connection for the tale (i.e., this was a film for readers).[71] A market assessment at the time commented on rising movie attendance, attributing the increase to the appeal of blockbusters, naming as exemplary *Some Like It Hot* and *The Diary of Anne Frank* as well as the "feminine appeal"

of hits like *Auntie Mame* (1958) and *Separate Tables* (1958).[72] "Blockbuster" circulated at this key moment, then, as a name for a distinctive and uncommonly good film, even as it was most securely understood as referring to a particular type of big production.

Ben-Hur enjoyed significant prerelease buzz, most of which focused on the unfathomable production extravagances mounted for the epic. The film was an adaptation of Lew Wallace's popular nineteenth-century religious novel. It had been filmed at least twice before, including an expansive rendering in 1925 from MGM that garnered substantial praise for its spectacle. The tale had wended its way through popular culture and had a profound influence on how biblical and Roman historical epics were told.[73] For the 1959 version, MGM pulled out all the stops for what they claimed was the most expensive movie ever. Production-related stories replete with numerical evidence circulated: 75 horses, 12 camels, 750 workers building an arena, 200 artists making sculptures, 1,000 suits of armor, and 10,000 costumes. More than a year before its release at the end of 1959, *Ben-Hur* was a "blockbuster."[74] And a full year before it premiered, the film helped improve relations between MGM and "friendly company" exhibitor Loew's, built on a string of successes, but expectations for *Ben-Hur* were so high that many were certain it would transcend other achievements as a "super blockbuster."[75]

Bosley Crowther contributed to the critical fanfare that accompanied the arrival of *Ben-Hur*. Three weeks before its world premiere in New York, Crowther wrote of the elevated expectations for the film and for Hollywood movies in general, observing that on studio lots "optimism appears to be as rampant as pessimism was a few years ago."[76] The New York–based critic's visit to the heart of the American movie business revealed a surprisingly deep faith in the future of theatrical film and a willingness to bank on those fortunes. Crowther noted that not only was *Ben-Hur* generating excitement among studio personnel, but the outsize production pointed the way to further investment.

The promotion for the film featured the many spectacular scenes, especially the chariot race, and made frequent reference to the expansiveness of the production, its cost, and the number of actors involved. The ad layout for posters, lobby cards, and print publications directed attention to two key technological features: Technicolor and MGM Camera 65. Format information of this kind had become a familiar aspect of film promotion by 1959. Camera 65, developed under MGM's supervision in collaboration with Panavision, to which it would be sold in a few short years, offered a larger area on the celluloid for the image than the standard 35 mm, in this way providing a crisper and more visually dense image. Rebranded as Ultra Panavision after 1961, Camera 65 shot on 65 mm stock that was later printed on 70 mm. The remaining 5 mm contained the soundtrack, which could house up to six discrete channels. The result was sound with unprecedented complexity for a mainstream release.[77] *Ben-Hur* was the first product to be filmed and released in MGM's new format. *Raintree County* had been filmed in Camera 65 but was released in CinemaScope. Pleased with the look and sound of their new film, MGM deployed Camera 65/Ultra Panavision for other epic tales, including *The Four Horsemen of the Apocalypse* (1962) and *Cimarron* (1960). The exorbitant expense of the cameras and stock meant, however, that the format was used on only a few big-budget productions. It would soon be shelved until Quentin Tarantino dusted off the cameras for his Panavision chamber piece *The Hateful Eight* (2015).

Ben-Hur reignited a rage for grand biblical and Roman-era tales. It encouraged Fox to follow suit with *The Story of Ruth* (1960), *The Greatest Story Ever Told* (1965), and *Cleopatra* (1963), with the last becoming a counterargument to the blockbuster strategy upon its release once its overextended budget turned the film into a financial disaster, or at least so it seemed at the time. As the eventual release dates show, the optimism Crowther reported with regard to the industrial advantages of superproductions marked out production plans that would take several years to unfold. The running times alone betray the expansiveness of the respective productions, with 150 minutes not uncommon. The scale of the format and length sparked Crowther's comment that each print of *Ben-Hur* was thirty-one reels long, weighing a total of 480 pounds.[78] The prerelease promotional plans included a *New York Times Magazine* pictorial featuring film stills whose headline highlighted the unusually high budget, "The $15,000,000 Chariot Race."[79] Because of the extravagances of its production, commentator Richard Nason described its release, a few days in advance of the opening, "as one of the most important theatrical events in [movie business] history."[80]

Ben-Hur premiered on November 18, 1959, prior to which New York newspapers promoted presales, with ticket purchases possible at the box office of the Loew's State Theatre or by mail order. Tickets went on sale a month earlier on October 26 and offered differential pricing for evenings and matinees as well as by seat placement in the orchestra, mezzanine, and balcony levels. The Loew's State, at Broadway and Forty-Fifth Street, specially refurbished and described in advertisements as "The NEW Loew's State," promised, "During this exclusive engagement BEN HUR will not be shown in any other theatre in this city."[81] The roadshow release itself was an effort on MGM's part to systematize a strategy that had been more haphazardly applied in the recent past for "super-productions."[82] The roadshow promotion for the heavily marketed epic, with special reserved seating, fit seamlessly among the live-theater advertisements, which is where both large and smaller notices for *Ben-Hur* appeared, and not on the movie page. It was a film apart. On the page next to the notices for *Ben-Hur*, the advertisements for two theatrical productions, already in full swing, carried the "blockbuster" designation. Tennessee Williams's *Orpheus Descending* and Robert Penn Warren's *All the King's Men* both featured critical endorsements that consisted of that single word, taken from theater reviews in the *Journal American* and *Cue Magazine*, respectively.[83] The promotional efforts for *Ben-Hur* were as much a matter of orchestrating popular taste as they were mechanisms for attendance. Here the film and the roadshow practices aligned the work with the legitimate theater. And here on the theater page were other blockbusters, described as such for their prestige and accomplishment, and not for their box-office take only. Visibility and prerelease press were sought, having to do with the middlebrow tastefulness of Broadway. This "theatricalization" of the film extended to the choice of a Broadway-adjacent location for the premiere in New York, rather than, say, Grauman's Chinese Theatre in Hollywood. The day after the premiere, the header for *Ben-Hur*'s newspaper notices, still on the live-theater page, was simply "NOW!"[84]

The film's thirty-four-page souvenir program detailed the production extravagances and the cultural significance of *Ben-Hur*. It included two rectangular cutout posters, one of the chariot race and the other broken into five scenes from the film, primarily those intersecting most obviously with the New Testament. These posters, and many pages in the program, were reproductions of specially commissioned drawings and paintings, giving the publication a less-promotional appearance. Sixteen pages of color film stills showed off the splendor of the production and highlighted compositional affinities with Renaissance religious painting. The written text declared the importance of the film, described as "A Momentous Event in Motion Pictures," and provided evidence of the care that went into the production, including the high caliber of the filmmakers. For example, even though Karl Tunberg received the sole screenwriting credit for *Ben-Hur*, the program noted the script contributions from major literary figures S. N. Behrman, Maxwell Anderson, Gore Vidal, and Christopher Fry. The booklet described the historical significance of the source novel and the other film and theatrical versions, with direct references to the superior quality of this newest version. Production notes on the cast, studio shoot, wardrobe, music, and director William Wyler provided a backstage view. The souvenir program devoted a full page to Camera 65, described as "the sharpest, most brilliant image ever seen on the screen."[85] A theme ran through the publication concerning an evolutionary approach to art. The reader was invited to seek out the next crowning achievement in cultural expression, one that surpassed styles and media from earlier works. The implication was that *Ben-Hur* was exactly that next evolutionary development.

Critical confidence about the film spilled over into the financial sector. On the day of the film's premiere, trade publications already declared it a smash hit, one that importantly proved the clarity and viability of the blockbuster strategy. Record-breaking advance ticket sales were in the range of $100,000 for New York City and $150,000 for Los Angeles, Boston, and Philadelphia, where it would open a week later. The film's merchandising palette included over a hundred product tie-ins.[86] Merchandise included such non-Roman, nonbiblical items as cookies, contemporary decor, wallpaper, candy, toys, and baby products.[87] Sears sold figurines and miniature sets of Roman antiquity as "educational."[88]

The generically disparate uses of "blockbuster" to describe a popular film were soon overshadowed by *Ben-Hur* and its advertising, which sealed the blockbuster strategy as an industrial concept embraced by a moviegoing public. *Ben-Hur* was not the only epic to push "blockbuster" toward the public connotative location in which it would come to reside, and we have already seen some earlier examples. The year 1959 also saw the release of Joseph E. Levine's *Hercules*, a film that received significant attention for its novel saturation distribution strategy, opening in five thousand theaters, rather than a more limited and specialized roadshow treatment for a blockbuster. This wide-releasing strategy, for a pulpy rendition of an antiquity-related epic, was an early signal that there were divergent directions for the blockbuster strategy. It was in this less self-consciously prestigious realm that the blockbuster would settle in the 1970s. *Hercules* was a hit that helped reignite a sword-and-sandal film craze and demonstrated a viable releasing alternative that contradicted the common sense of the day. Commentators, however, saw films like *Ben-Hur* and *Spartacus* (1960) as "'blockbusters' . . . in a class separate from movies like *Hercules*."[89]

The reverential treatment of *Ben-Hur*, and the framing of the story as a distinguished cultural work, extended from the middlebrow trappings of upscale theatrical environments and film format to the opening moments of the film itself. For the first time in MGM's history, they permitted their roaring-lion logo to be altered by the filmmakers. The film's prologue includes a Nativity scene, which director William Wyler felt would be distastefully disrupted by the MGM lion's roar, so it was silenced, and sits there, appearing after the six-minute overture that consists of a close-up detail of God reaching for Adam's hand to give him life from Michelangelo's Sistine Chapel painting.[90] While the plentiful merchandising ran counter to such reverence, an artificial sense of importance carried through to the premiere, which deliberately avoided obvious forms of ballyhoo, like star interviews on the red carpet and searchlights. Instead, as *Variety* put it, the film "bowed with dignity. It was a high-hat and highbrow nature first-night audience."[91] *Variety* described "the evidence of boffo boxoffice blockbuster of superlative magnitude."[92] This success was a vindication of the big-budget approach of MGM and its parent company Loew's, which had to convince investors that this brand of spectacularly expensive entertainment would pay off.

Crowther could not contain his enthusiasm for the film. His review carried the headline "'Ben-Hur,' a Blockbuster," a double reference describing the production genre and the aesthetic accomplishment. The opening line, though, clarified that this particular iteration of the blockbuster made up for failings that had become too common with that type of film: "Within the expansive format of the so-called 'blockbuster' spectacle film, which generally provokes a sublimation of sensibility to action and pageantry, Metro-Goldwyn-Mayer and William Wyler have managed to engineer a remarkably intelligent and engrossing human drama in their new production of 'Ben-Hur.'"[93] His endorsement of the film as distinctive among blockbusters considered its weighty attention to drama as effectively equal to the power of the action set pieces. In doing so, he described the film as "respectable" and replete with "artistic quality" and "taste." This review was the source of the leading boldfaced emphatic advertising claim in the days that followed, interestingly still placed among the live-theater notices and not with the film listings, first appearing as simply "A BLOCKBUSTER!" and then "'BEN-HUR' IS A BLOCKBUSTER!" (figure 6.2).[94] "A BLOCKBUSTER!" appeared only two days after the film's release, on November 20, replacing "NOW!"[95] A half-page notice in the *New York Herald Tribune*, still on the live-theater pages until after November 24, had Crowther's "'BEN-HUR IS A BLOCKBUSTER!" across the top and then drew quotes from other critics that included the terms "spectacle" (four times), "giant," "massive," "staggering magnitude," and "enormous."[96] Size clearly mattered, and massively so. The quote declaring "IT'S ENORMOUS" is a direct demonstration of this. No other quality is mentioned, simply largeness. Most

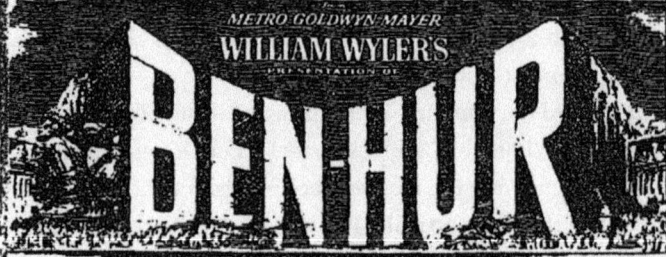

FIGURE 6.2 *Ben-Hur* advertisement, describing it as "a blockbuster," 1959

significantly, never, to this point, had "blockbuster" been so prominently presented to sell a film to the general moviegoing public. The closest had been *Proud Rebel*'s counterpositioning advertisement.

Crowther celebrated the film in part because other recent epics had been so disappointing. He wrote, "We have seen too many botches with big spectacle films." He was direct in his criticism: "Time after time, in many pictures, including most of the 'epics' of Cecil B. DeMille, we have seen dismal taste and gross extravagance overwhelm and desecrate a valid tale." However, he continued, with *Ben-Hur* "the all-too-familiar pattern of gaudy vulgarity is escaped and a drama of real excitement and sober meaning has been made to emerge."[97] *Variety*'s review of *Ben-Hur* echoed Crowther's superlatives and made explicit that the film represented the pinnacle of blockbuster filmmaking. The review began by calling the film a "blockbuster to top all previous blockbusters" and surmised that MGM's "chariot race should result in the biggest payoff in the history of film business."[98] The review's conclusion again reiterated that the film was "a complete vindication of the policies of Vogel and his management team."[99] *Ben-Hur*'s success, correcting the "gaudy vulgarity" of other blockbusters, went beyond the aesthetic and the cinematic; it was corporate and strategic in nature.

Today the chariot race is the best-remembered sequence in *Ben-Hur* (figure 6.3). The sheer scale of the competition, with each thundering chariot pulled by four horses, is breathtaking. But the attention to human drama, the quiet and introspective scenes of doubt and betrayal throughout the rest of the film, stands out just as much. Lost in most discussions of *Ben-Hur* is just how political it is. A key narrative turning point, when the deep friendship between Judah Ben-Hur (Charlton Heston) and Messala (Stephen Boyd) is irreparably shattered, comes when Ben-Hur, a wealthy member of the conquered Jewish people, refuses to pinpoint those who have been grumbling about Roman rule. This matter of principle, not to name names, triggers the imprisonment of Ben-Hur's family and his years of enslavement; the allusion to McCarthyism and the culture of loyalty oaths in contemporary America could not have been clearer. And while technically a tale of Christ, *Ben-Hur* puts Judaism, and the struggles of oppressed Jews, at the front of the story. Our hero and his family are Jewish, unambiguously identified as such. Jesus

FIGURE 6.3 *Ben-Hur*, the spectacular chariot race, 1959

is not named and is instead called the rabbi from Nazareth. Ben-Hur carries a Star of David with him to the chariot race.

At the time, not everyone, of course, was so enthused by the film. *Newsday*'s Ben Kubasik did not overlook the punishing length and the pretentious treatment of the subject matter, with the exception only of the exciting chariot race sequence. In the end, *Ben-Hur* was "nine lively minutes wrapped in 3½ hrs. of nothing."[100] Many might agree with Kubasik today and find *Ben-Hur* dull save a brief spectacular sequence or two.

Despite such misgivings, blockbusters provided a solid financial basis for success. The standard rule was that a film needed to return double its negative cost in order to break even. Following the success of expensive productions like *The Ten Commandments* and *Ben-Hur*, with their high promotional costs, this ratio shifted downward, largely because distribution costs don't scale up as rapidly as the production budget. So, relative to the overall budget, it was cheaper to market a big picture than a little one, or so the dominant thinking went, and indeed still goes. Additionally, at a certain point, with proven box-office performance films sell themselves to exhibitors, who clamor to screen them, thus cutting the need for studio representatives to keep pushing them into theaters.[101]

So other studios chased comparable attention, drawn by the publicity and promise of profits. Late in 1959, Loew's announced its refurbished "NEW Loew's Capitol," only a few blocks from where *Ben-Hur* continued its run at the Loew's State in New York, with an inaugural film, another biblical epic, UA's *Solomon and Sheba* (1959), in Super 70 Technirama and Technicolor.[102] Although UA had been the distributor for the independently produced *Around the World in 80 Days*, they had been reluctant to embrace the blockbuster strategy. Their newspaper promotion described *Solomon and Sheba* as "THE MIGHTIEST MOTION PICTURE EVER CREATED!" The description of the new Loew's venue was equally superlative: "THE WORLD'S MOST SPECTACULAR MOTION PICTURE THEATRE."[103] An additional, smaller notice on the same page provided more detail about the theater, called "A View of the Future" with "panoramic viewing," "fabulous projectors," and "brilliant, non-distorted sharpness. All the better to enjoy the vast spectacle of 'SOLOMON AND SHEBA' starring Yul Brynner and Gina Lollobrigida."[104]

With this illustration we see the pairing of the featured film title, production technology, projection format, and theatrical venue as well as stars and the distributor brand. While individual film titles—or more accurately individual cultural commodities—jockeyed for competitive advantage in a marketplace that included other consumer cultural choices, promotional material bundled an array of formats, technologies, and corporate entities. Consequently, the media environment worked as a flow of appeals that built the entirety of the commercial cultural scene, including the modes of production and circulation. This feature extended beyond blockbuster promotion. Some exhibitors temporarily adopted sensory novelties like Percepto and Emergo in order to offer viewing environments that television could not, but also in order to be "in competition with many of the so-called movie blockbusters with amazing success."[105] In other words, gimmick films recognized the status of the blockbuster while learning from blockbusters' promotional focus on the film performance situation. Whether blockbusters or gimmick films, single titles were excuses to promote an entertainment apparatus.

In attending to an appetite for antiquity, UA was not alone. Independent production company Herts-Lion targeted television with *The Sword and the Cross*, a series of tales set in biblical times told in thirty-minute episodes.[106] Universal saddled *Spartacus* with the responsibility for being a blockbuster.

At $10 million, the film would be the company's most expensive production, with expectations that it would do for Universal what *Ben-Hur* did for MGM and *The Ten Commandments* did for Paramount.[107] And for Paramount itself, still reeling from the death of Cecil B. DeMille in 1959, the lack of a "prestige-blockbuster" on the horizon meant they were losing ground to other studios in the big-budget-feature game.[108]

In the months before the release of *Ben-Hur*, Murray Schumach wrote about "filmland jargon" and discussed the deliberate ambiguity of such terms as "built-in value," "chemistry," and a "plus" or "big plot." Respectively, these terms euphemistically designated selling properties, artistry, and social message. "Blockbuster" appeared as one of the new terms Schumach identified as part of this new promotional hype.[109] Distributors continued to promote their successes, which resulted in metaphoric inflation. Trade advertisements for *Operation Petticoat* (1959) presented it as "A RECORD-BREAKING BLOCKBUSTER!"[110] The military provenance of "blockbuster" resurfaced on occasion, reminding audiences of the destructive legacy signaled by the concept. *Ten Seconds to Hell* (1959) by UA is a tale of a German bomb-disposal unit in postwar Berlin who attempt to decommission the Allied bombs that litter the city. To exhibitors, UA sold the film two months before the release of *Ben-Hur* as "ON THE SCREEN . . . AT THE BOXOFFICE . . . A BLOCKBUSTER!," with deliberate double reference to the explosive subject matter and the revenue-generating potential.[111] The posters for moviegoers with the bold red tagline "BLOCKBUSTER ABOUT TO EXPLODE!" accompanied by a larger and more prominently positioned image of a bomb, referencing directly the military connection. "Blockbuster" was everywhere, as seen in the word's repetition in *The F.B.I. Story*'s (1959) advertisements, which also appeared a few months before *Ben-Hur*'s release but still focused on a trade readership and not the general moviegoing public (figure 6.4).[112]

Neither the hyperbole nor the logic won over everyone. Producer Albert Zugsmith, whose work had recently included the Academy Award–winning *Written on the Wind*, voiced the contrasting approach and clarified that Hollywood producers felt concern about the focus on epic-scale filmmaking. He commented, "There's too much emphasis on so-called blockbusters costing millions. Money and magnitude alone won't make a movie. The story is still the thing."[113]

Of course, sometimes money is the story. In an epic, technological spectacle, sweeping world-historical drama, and investment scale all converge.

FIGURE 6.4 *The F.B.I. Story* advertisement: Symptom of overuse of "blockbuster" among trade papers, 1959

By year's end, *Ben-Hur* typified the blockbuster as the future of American film entertainment. *Ben-Hur* went on to an unprecedented sweep of eleven Oscars, a number that would be matched only decades later by *Titanic* (1997) and then *The Lord of the Rings: The Return of the King* (2003). Many award categories available to those later films had not yet been introduced in 1959, which makes *Ben-Hur*'s eleven Oscars, out of fifteen categories in which it was even eligible to be nominated, a unique achievement. Other accolades were less unambiguous and more contentious. The New York Critics Award had to go to a fifth ballot in order to select *Ben-Hur* as the ultimate winner of best film of 1959. The biblical epic's primary competition, a film that narrowly missed that honor, was the British kitchen-sink drama *Room at the Top* (1959).[114] The contrast between the most expensive film spectacular ever made and the low-budget black-and-white quotidian drama could not have been more striking. Here the American blockbuster and the foreign in-betweener faced each other down and split critical attention and praise.

The 1950s ended with commentary characterizing it as the decade during which Hollywood developed a distinctive global consciousness, technological focus, and obsession with big-budget blockbusters. All of these characteristics were ways to remake the film business in light of the new competitor, television. Hy Hollinger's decade wrap-up called it the "Frantic '50s," "a hectic period of revolution, experimentation, adjustment, deep pessimism and guarded optimism." Describing "blockbuster" as "a trade word of the 1950–60 era," Hollinger identified that "the answer to TV was the blockbuster."[115]

It should also be said that the answer to the blockbuster was television. By 1965 big films had pushed the average price of movies sold for television broadcast up to $400,000 apiece. Columbia sold *The Bridge on the River Kwai* to ABC for a record $2 million in 1966, and ABC then sold all the advertising spots to Ford Motor Company for $1.8 million. When the film premiered on television on September 25, 1966, the first of the 1950s blockbusters to be televised, an estimated 66 million viewers watched, making it one of the most watched single-event broadcasts of all time (it had more viewers than the final episode of *Friends* in 2004 at about 51 million, for instance).[116] There was so much enthusiasm for films on television that the average price for broadcasting films rose dramatically, reaching $800,000 by 1968. The week after the attention-getting broadcast of *The Bridge on the River Kwai*, various networks announced a total of $93 million worth of broadcast rights for 112 films, including blockbusters like *Cleopatra* and *The Longest Day* (1962).[117] Soon ABC followed this up with *The Robe* (1953), for which it had purchased the rights to three showings, the first on Easter 1967, for about $2 million. Ford again bought the right to be the only advertiser for the first two broadcasts. Both the sponsor and the broadcaster had been criticized for regularly interrupting *The Bridge on the River Kwai* with commercials throughout the broadcast, so for *The Robe* they opted for only one advertising break in the 135-minute-long film, rather like an intermission.[118] The widescreen films had to be optically altered to match the shape of television screens, thus losing the horizontal aspect ratio, but this didn't seem to hamper the ratings.[119] In the wake of earlier sales of film libraries to television, a lucrative pathway to ancillary markets had been established, and the value and life span of big, popular, and relatively current motion pictures increased.

Hollinger's recap of the 1950s described a "technical revolution in the film business," naming stereophonic sound, 3-D, CinemaScope, Camera 65, Todd-AO, Panavision, VistaVision, and Technirama 70, as well as gimmicks like Aromarama and Smell-o-Vision.[120] Another notable development was diversification of studio interests, with producers buying TV stations, and theaters buying radio stations; "perhaps the most successful acquisition outside of the amusement business was Stanley Warner's association with the International Latex Corp., manufacturers of baby pants, girdles, bras, rubber gloves and pharmaceutical items. International Latex is said to account for more than 70 percent of SW's income."[121] A surprise such as that encouraged others to look further afield from the entertainment market, a sign of diversification among the major studios that was noted by Irving Bernstein's report, discussed in the previous chapter.[122]

A central development, the 1950s was "the decade of global thinking."[123] Globalism in American entertainment produced competing sensibilities. In one camp, the cosmopolitanism of the blockbuster, its status as the prestige production that pushed forward cinema technology, was the shining example of the accomplishments of the American film business. A vision of universal aesthetic achievement, coupled with the scientific improvement of sensory stimulation, placed blockbusters in a uniquely elevated position. Global culture was best exemplified by the way these hulking technological and middlebrow monuments were constructed and promoted as transcending local differences, articulating an internationalist style. The critical backlash, which tried to direct moviegoer attention away from these mastodons toward subtler dramas and artistic explorations, may have opened up a front on the issue of taste, but it did not tamp down the financial enthusiasm for the blockbuster strategy and its logic that big investment led to big profits worldwide.

Funnily enough, pretty well every subsequent decade has ended with a comparable set of assertions about the "novel" directions of recent years, doing so by highlighting globalism, technological advancement, and blockbuster strategy. These three entwined vectors are now securely lodged in the heart of the American entertainment establishment. They drive decision-making and promotion, and they feed popular sensibilities about the economic and cultural role played by media entertainment. By the end of the 1950s, "blockbuster" had settled in as a feature of both industrial and popular film language, and with it a set of ideas about success, taste, investment, and technology; to echo Lisa Gitelman's framework for media history, it had become part of the normative rules, default conditions, meanings, and hierarchies for motion picture entertainment.[124] This stabilization would not have happened without a transformation in cultural value that included both the elevation of the monumental package and the in-betweener counterpart. The in-betweener was artful and less overwhelming of the senses. Where the latter tended toward a more televisual style of dramatic realism (*Room at the Top*), the former pushed into Technicolor fantasy, there finding an aesthetic of universal cultural duty (*Ben-Hur*).

Shyon Baumann has described the legitimation process through which film came to be considered art. He focused on the post–World War II United States, with television drawing audiences away and then occupying a lower status, paired with a rising appreciation of European film. The increasing selectivity of moviegoing made it appear to be less of a lower- and middle-class habit, in contrast to the democratizing force of television. He wrote that "a status vacuum was created," making consecration of film possible.[125] Festivals, awards, and critics all developed at the time to serve the intermediary function of legitimization. Curiously, though, this account works if one concentrates on the emergence of the international art cinema of the 1950s and 1960s. But the most popular and lucrative films filled that status vacuum with prestige productions—middlebrow in all ways—even though they also slid rapidly to be seen as crass industrial products. The first era of blockbusters initially muddled up the art/commerce divide, and the films became vehicles for simultaneous legitimation and delegitimation. They were consecrated, and adorned with the trappings of middle-class seriousness, but they could only ever be expressions of industrial machinations. Yet their very existence helped consecrate the in-betweeners and the foreign art film by providing an identifiable point of distinction. The "nonblockbuster" appeared to be the "nonindustrial," or at least less industrial, and hence a more authentic artistic expression.

Ben-Hur was both the most advanced example of cinematographic art and technology, lavishly showered in praise and awards, making money hand over fist, and also a prominent example of all that was wrong with Hollywood, its high capital needs, its promotional excesses, and its laminated-postcard approach to history. The hegemony of the blockbuster strategy began to come undone only a few years later. All these features that propelled the industry out of the 1950s led to general collapse in the 1960s. Big-budget flops like *Doctor Dolittle* (1967) and *Star!* (1968) shook the roadshow blockbuster model and hastened a restructuring of the ownership of Hollywood properties. But the resilience of the blockbuster strategy saw to its resurrection a very short time later in the early 1970s with prestige blockbusters like *The Godfather* (1972) and the disaster films *The Poseidon Adventure* (1972), *Airport* (1970), *The Towering Inferno* (1974), and then *Jaws* (1975). Indeed, *Jaws* was both a continuation of the disaster film cycle and a harbinger of the new Hollywood blockbuster that would rule the entertainment world for the coming decades. By the late 1970s, blockbusters were no longer just box-office successes but event movies, films that involved long-term planning, visible throughout their production, especially to investors, and were designed to reassure shareholders and attract capital. As John Izod pointed out, modest-budget sleeper hits that overperform at the box office cannot serve all these functions and do not provide a stable basis for the flow of financing into the system.[126] This function is the province of the blockbuster. Outlining more recent phases of Hollywood history that led to our current situation, Douglas Gomery described the transitional years as going from 1975 to 1982, between *Jaws* and *E.T.*, privileging the role Universal and Steven Spielberg played in shaping the theme, aesthetic, production, and promotion of the contemporary blockbuster. During this time, Gomery claimed, without hyperbole, "the blockbuster reinvented Hollywood."[127] But this was not the first nor last time; the blockbuster had done so in the 1950s, and it would do this again, with the rise of the blockbuster franchise in the 1990s.

And a contradictory operation of cultural value has rested with the blockbuster for the same stretch of time; the blockbuster is all that is wrong with Hollywood, and it is the peak of Hollywood's cultural and technological achievement. The embrace by big-budget films of what had been minor genres and the province of the gimmick film—horror, disaster, and science fiction—was in part a pursuit of the low. If the middlebrow was crass in its own way, why bother with the forced trappings of culture? Sensation had always been the core blockbuster quality, so why not assemble more purely dynamic sensory spectacles? Sensory appeal, in fact, motivated the claims of artlessness. The serious and worldly—the limited cosmopolitan ease described earlier—embodied the aspirational elements of popular culture, but this was dragged down by the unavoidable sensory pleasure of the big screen and stunning production scale of the biggest blockbusters. This was "shock and awe" for cultural commodities. Linda Williams's "body genres," meaning works that elicit physical responses in audiences, could include the blockbuster, whose scale might trigger boredom as much as awe.[128] Though Williams concentrated on pornography, melodrama, and horror, the genres of disaster, action, and science fiction, all of which collided in the comic-book superhero franchises to come in the following decades, offered perfect vehicles for sensory extravaganzas. Prestige blockbusters were still produced and could draw critical attention, for instance, *The Deer Hunter* (1979) and *Reds* (1981). But economic weight, and sheer popularity, had decidedly shifted toward big-budget genre films and franchises. Today a tautological claim rules popular entertainment: the crass commercial blockbuster strives for the summit of cinematic technological achievement, and efforts to realize this lofty goal render a work crass and commercial.

For all its middlebrow pretenses, *Samson and Delilah* (1949) comes across today as a vaguely campy sword-and-sandal movie. The fantastical costuming, the sumptuous sets, and the sensational effects and action sequences are the most memorable elements, very much like its generic spawn ten years later, *Ben-Hur*. These characteristics overshadow by a long shot the staid and didactic educational tone of moral instruction that runs through the story. The alignment of spectacle with sensory thrills is amply evident in this proto-blockbuster released in late 1949. *Jaws*, on this count, is truly a reiteration, and a reinvigoration, of what had become dominant in the 1950s. Grasping these points of continuity, we confront the remarkable stability of an idea about entertainment, spectacle, and technology, one that marked popular understanding and expectations for film as much as it guided investor faith and logic. So powerful has this been that the blockbuster movie remains the most culturally and economically impactful American cultural form.

As the new decade of the 1960s began, exhibitors had been noting that, contrary to much reporting, there was no longer an actual shortage of film, only a shortage of blockbuster spectacles. Otherwise, all markets and audiences were being profitably served.[129] This included overseas territories. In 1959 the improved state of the U.K. film industry was credited to such factors as the new technological screening systems, the popularity of low-budget British horror, and "the Hollywood blockbuster."[130]

The year 1960 had *Ben-Hur* as the top-grossing film, along with other blockbuster productions, including *Can-Can* (1960), *Operation Petticoat*, *Spartacus*, and *Solomon and Sheba*. An absolute surprise, though, was *Psycho* (1960), marketed expertly with carnival-barker flair, ending up one of the top moneymakers of the year. Described as a "freak" success, it was likely the most profitable movie of 1960, given its modest production budget of just over $1 million.[131] Even though the blockbuster strategy was firmly ensconced, the appeal of a faster payoff with low-budget productions encouraged producers to keep filling the teen and horror niches.[132]

The summer of 1963 again confirmed that the American film industry was back in earnest. In May, Columbia took out trade advertisements to celebrate what it called the biggest blockbuster in the company's history, the British-produced *Lawrence of Arabia*.[133] *Film Bulletin* reported in the fall that "both blockbusters and B's rolled up big grosses throughout the country and lifted hopes for the future."[134] The task at hand was to sustain this into the slower moviegoing season of winter, but for all intents and purposes, the fortunes of the past were returning to Hollywood, so much so that Twentieth Century Fox coordinated an unusually elaborate publicity tour in which 126 journalists visited the European production sites of three of the company's upcoming blockbusters. In Austria journalists visited the set of *The Sound of Music* (1965); they saw the Roman set of *The Agony and the Ecstasy* (1965); and in London they toured the production of *Those Magnificent Men and Their Flying Machines* (1965).[135]

Notes of uncertainty could be detected, however. The overproduction of blockbusters began to clutter the media with an advertising haze of supposedly unique cinematic achievements. In 1961, so plentiful were blockbusters, and so familiar the usage of the term, that advertisements for *Exodus* (1960) used a quote from Crowther describing it as "the best blockbuster of the year."[136] These movies now constituted a category of regularly appearing film within which they could be ranked from "the best" downward. In 1962 Wall Street investment analysts began to see the risks of big-budget epic products as extreme, cautioning about coming instability.[137] Costs were running so high (with mention of Twentieth Century Fox's *Cleopatra* and MGM's *Mutiny on the Bounty* [1962]), and the competition among big productions was so intense, that it was not clear how, or when, profits would be realized.[138] As one industry loan officer explained, films like *The Ten Commandments* and *Ben-Hur* were "pioneers of their type and didn't face much competition from other spectaculars. Running five or ten of these big films at the same time is another matter."[139] Sure enough, in spite of *West Side Story* (1961), *Lawrence of Arabia*, and *The Longest Day*, later in the decade there were *Doctor Dolittle*, *Star!*, and *Hello, Dolly!* (1969), which suffered from negative reviews and elevated expenses that impeded profitability. No single work better encapsulated the hazards of big-budget moviemaking than *Cleopatra*, whose budget overruns made it the most expensive film ever produced at that time. That film was the four-hour-long gilded canary in the coal mine, warning that an excess of excess was just around the corner.

This abundance of "extraordinary hits" created a crammed marketplace and led to the abandonment of the roadshow; revenues were significantly below expectations for these large-scale films, they were impractically costly, and they were too regularized to guarantee the special-event status of a roadshow film anymore, at least in the eyes of the moviegoer. Roadshowing was virtually dead by the early 1970s, though aspects of it continued with runs based on box-office performance, scheduled start times, advance ticket sales, and reserved seating or upscale theatrical environments advertised by some locations.

The blockbuster category itself received more criticism. For 1961 Twentieth Century Fox declared it would release twenty-four self-described blockbusters, and independent producer American International Pictures planned twelve of their own. As *Variety* reported, "over-use" had made "blockbuster" "that most tired of all Hollywood euphemisms."[140] Producer-director John Frankenheimer, after observing the scene at the 1962 Cannes Film Festival, commented that American films were too few and too expensive when compared to European productions. What Americans called art films were more straightforwardly seen as "idea" films, meaning "serious pictures centering on contemporary problems of living."[141] His position echoed earlier arguments for the adult in-betweener and against the excessive blockbuster. Champions of the unsung works included critic Kevin Thomas, who mused, "When the full measure of Hollywood's artistic achievement is taken it may be that all those boring blockbusters, heavy-handed sex comedies and pretentious message movies will be bypassed in favor of the taut B-production action films and the imaginative science fiction features."[142] Here Thomas questioned blockbusters and in-betweeners alike, and a glance at the works most discussed by film scholars today confirms that this view was prophetic.

Over the course of about ten years, a popular film form had stabilized. The blockbuster had become an identifiable film type, though not a genre exactly, and the term communicated clear expectations about motion picture entertainment and approaches to filmmaking. British critics Penelope Houston and John Gillett wrote a critical survey about this, titled "The Theory and Practice of Blockbusting," for *Sight and Sound* in 1963. They identified the salient characteristics of this specifically Hollywood form—color, a long running time, roadshow release, and a special exhibition format—and pointed out the "block to be busted: audience resistance."[143] They dated the term as emerging no earlier than 1955—which we have seen is inaccurate—and confirmed that though there were some earlier "superspectaculars," "the systematic construction of blockbusters in bulk, as it were, is something new."[144] The most significant element, they explained, was that blockbusters were the product of an era in which moviegoing was no longer a regular practice. The films, then, were oriented toward people who were not habitual moviegoers. One consequence was that potential audience members had to be informed about the special qualities of the film. It was not enough to present new formats and extravagant sights, but they had to be sold. The escalation of production investment meant that a successful film had to bring in far more spectators, and run far longer, than did modestly budgeted films. This translated into a necessity of seeing entire populations as the target audience for a film. Such universalism produced "neutralised" war films and religious films that "[kept] in mind religious minorities," and it shied away from any theme that "lacks appeal for foreigners."[145] There may have been some sound reasoning in this, they argued, but exactly how many of these "hard ticket" shows could the market stand at one time? They wrote, "If the spectacular becomes the commonplace, where do you then look for your special occasion?"[146]

The real blow, they argued, was to the director. Blockbusters were truly a producer's medium, making the director a cog in a project of risk reduction. The spectacle, the dialogue, and the eye-popping set pieces were all determined in advance, and many of the most elaborate of these were handled by second-unit directors. Houston and Gillett argued that the problem with blockbusters was that directors "may only be present in a supervisory capacity."[147] They did identify the distinctive touch, if only in isolated moments, when the likes of Nicholas Ray, Anthony Mann, and John Ford tried their hands at blockbuster films. And they went further to acknowledge that the tedium experienced by the film critic did not represent the thrill experienced by the family or the child on a school trip, prepared as they would have been for a special and lengthy time at the cinema. Still, they noted that the pressure to please universally, and to reduce individual artistic control, regardless of the talent involved, made the blockbuster an ambiguous statement. *Lawrence of Arabia* was a case in point. A gorgeous and smartly conceived work on one level, it was ultimately unsure of what it was saying about the subject and the historical figure at the center of the tale, leaving more questions than answers in the afterglow of its luminous desert vistas. They wrote, "*Lawrence* was sold, quite brilliantly, as the first blockbuster that *everyone* was going to regard as a great film; and it turned out to be . . . a blockbuster."[148]

While "The Theory and Practice of Blockbusting" did not give the operation and appeal of spectacle its full due, and only briefly considered the significance of the aesthetic specificity of blockbusters' big-screen processes, the essay marked a moment of full realization and recognition of a dominant American filmmaking approach and its exportation abroad. The valorization of a director's cinema and a personal cinema, and hints of disparagement of a lowest common denominator, makes Houston and Gillett's argument an echo of preexisting cultural hierarchies, with denunciations of commerce's contaminating influence on the artist. But this article, now over fifty years old, could have been written yesterday, and most of its claims about blockbusters ring true with later decades of youth-oriented, genre-based franchises. Superheroes supplanted Christian martyrs. Harrison Ford replaced Charlton Heston. The Marvel Universe and DC comics are default sources rather than Bible stories and Greek mythology. And computer-generated imagery does work that would have been done by set dressers, costumers, and extras. But the economic and aesthetic centrality of the ideologically indeterminate, technologically enhanced, globally appealing event entertainment package still rules our popular moving-image culture.

PART III THE TECHNOLOGICAL SUBLIME OF ENTERTAINMENT EVERYWHERE

(CHAPTER SEVEN)

THE END OF JAMES CAMERON'S QUIET YEARS

For many, James Cameron's groan-inducing "I'm king of the world" proclamation during the 1998 Academy Awards broadcast confirmed existing stories of his egomania. His outburst was part of his acceptance speech after winning the Oscar for best director for *Titanic* (1997). Just imagine what he must have been thinking when he got up to accept the best picture award a few moments later. Though he was quoting a line of dialogue he had written for the film, Cameron's triumphant declaration made his status as a less-than-beloved figure, especially among people who had worked for him, evident to a wide television audience. A few weeks after the Academy Awards, Peter Bart wrote an April Fool's editorial in *Variety* that parodied Cameron's megalomania, saying executives had to rent Chasen's Restaurant just to hold a meeting with him, that Cameron insisted no fewer than four studios would be required to back his next project, and that he asked to be addressed as king, beginning all meetings with a few minutes' silence for the victims of the *Titanic*.[1] But for all of his grandiose behavior, imagined or otherwise, let us remember that just before *Titanic*'s release, the film and Cameron were widely ridiculed, with most expecting that his film would be a colossal failure. The production, the financing, and the releasing strategies were so outside industry standards at that time that it was difficult for observers to understand his plan. Doubters were convinced it would be a film that demonstrated, once and for all, the outer limits of the blockbuster strategy that had been dominant since the 1950s. But it wasn't; instead, *Titanic* reaffirmed the blockbuster as an internationalist, technologically enhanced cultural entity that could revitalize theatrical settings. So, that evening at the Academy Awards ceremony, Cameron had reason to gloat.[2]

The prerelease miscalculation about *Titanic* led many critics and industry analysts to take a wait-and-see attitude toward Cameron's more audacious sci-fi project, *Avatar* (2009). Cameron wrote, produced, and directed that expensive 3-D production; he also did uncredited work as director of photography and provided hands-on contributions to virtually every aspect of the film. Critics reserved judgment on what appeared to be a fundamentally insupportable business model, even when some sneak peeks at footage left fans underwhelmed. And once *Avatar*'s record-breaking box-office returns began to roll in, it was clear that this had been a prudent decision. *Avatar*, like *Titanic* before it, injected new life into a sixty-year-old industrial logic at a time when other media and other rationales for culture industries were supposedly supplanting the post–World War II approach to global cultural "shock and awe."

Part II of this book documented the foundation of an industrial logic built around the concept of the blockbuster and the migration of the term via publicity and criticism to public usage. Along the way, the blockbuster connected spectacle, an investment rationale, and ambiguous cultural value, or what I call cosmopolitan artlessness. Those chapters provide the deep historical context for the most recognized blockbuster era, which runs roughly from *Jaws* (1975) through *Jurassic Park* (1993); this, as elaborated in earlier chapters, is a period that has been abundantly addressed by film and media scholars. Those years (1975–1993) saw the flourishing of the blockbuster franchise, born of merging media conglomerates, themselves a result of relaxing restrictions on monopolistic practice.[3] Cameron contributed to that mode with his "Terminator" franchise, launched as a result of the unexpected success of the low-budget first film in the series. So sound was the franchise approach by the 1990s that the success of the big-budget, stand-alone, written-for-the-screen, no-star, overly long *Titanic* was impossible for many to comprehend. But it was a classic blockbuster, imbued with all the international-style features of the theatrically oriented, cosmopolitan technological spectacle. Part III examines how these features of the blockbuster strategy continue to operate in our environment of converged, multimedia, digital industries. The next chapter addresses the technophilic heart of our movie culture, focusing on home-viewing media, theatrical settings, and diegetic accommodation, followed by an epilogue that summarizes my claim about the role the blockbuster strategy has had in building our contemporary technological society. But, first, this chapter shows how the long arc of blockbuster strategy runs through research and development, with a special focus on the years leading up to one of the defining films of our times, *Avatar*.

Concerning the time between Cameron's Oscar achievement in 1998 and the release of *Avatar*, an impression circulated that he was not making movies. For instance, *Variety* titled a brief 2001 update on his career "*Titanic* Titan Takes Time Out."[4] But that period was no hiatus, and his status as an elusive craftsman and perfectionist continued to develop; indeed, this impression expanded even though he was absent from the annual blockbuster slate for over a decade. Despite his counterintuitive career path, he remained popularly understood as a decisive creative force. His cameo in the *émission à clef Entourage* (HBO, 2004–2011) had Cameron playing himself and signing the heartthrob character Vinnie Chase to star in *Aquaman*, a fictional project that seemed to be a plausible Cameron pursuit: he had made water-set action epics and worked to launch the "Spider-Man" franchise before being supplanted. In a telling moment, Cameron notifies the actor of his casting decision while piloting a helicopter. The image of the powerful filmmaker, directing the players from on high, propellers churning in the background, matches the sense that Cameron is rather like a remote and technologically savvy military commander. As Turtle, a member of the show's eponymous entourage, says, "With Cameron directing, you know it's going to be special." This reputation persisted, and his fan base was strong, even though most assumed he had made only six films in the twenty-five years following his breakthrough movie, *The Terminator* (1984). That's roughly the same rate of production that his self-declared creative mentor, the painstakingly slow filmmaker Stanley Kubrick, had from *Spartacus* (1960) to *Eyes Wide Shut* (1999).

In actuality, Cameron was an active filmmaker during the years between *Titanic* and *Avatar*, working as a documentary producer and director as well as a television producer (Fox's *Dark Angel* [2000–2002]), and he did so in his typically outsize way. His documentary turn was unusual for this committed sci-fi action director, to say the least. He was the executive producer of several controversial made-for-cable documentaries, most notably two with revisionist biblical subject matter: *The Exodus Decoded* (2006) and *The Lost*

FIGURE 7.1 James Cameron as popular science documentarian, early 2000s

Tomb of Jesus (2007), both directed by Emmy Award–winning documentarian Simcha Jacobovici, who went on to star in the VisionTV/History Channel series *The Naked Archeologist* (2005–2010). The documentaries that Cameron directed and produced himself are *Expedition: Bismarck* (2002), which he codirected with Gary Johnstone; *Ghosts of the Abyss* (2003); and *Aliens of the Deep* (2005), codirected with Steven Quale, who was later a second-unit director on *Avatar*.

These three Cameron films are large-budget science documentaries involving remote undersea settings. In fact, some claim *Aliens of the Deep*, which included a $14 million expedition, is the most expensive documentary ever made.[5] His penchant for quoting himself reappears in these titles, two of which allude to his features *Aliens* (1986) and *The Abyss* (1989). Beyond these references, the links between these documentaries and his blockbusters are manifold and substantial enough that we should not see them as a radical departure from his oeuvre. In fact, this trilogy solidified Cameron's relationship to ideas about popular science, exploration, and technological innovation. Indeed, his success in building a persona that embodied these traits is such that in 2006, with *Titanic* nine years in the past and *Avatar* still called *Project 880*, Cameron received the Visionary Award from Cinema Expo, an exhibitors' convention, for his special contribution to technological innovation.[6] Two years earlier, he received the Nicola Tesla Award in Recognition for Visionary Achievements in the World of Digital Technology and Sound from the Satellite Awards. Meanwhile, an honorary doctorate from the University of Southampton for his contribution to maritime science, as well as membership on the NASA Advisory Council, marked the degree of recognition he held among scientists. Note that these industry and scholarly recognitions transpired during his supposed hiatus.

Cameron doesn't do anything quietly, and his years of retreat from the mainstream of the Hollywood industry involved some grand exploits. His surprising activity over the twelve years following *Titanic* tells us about financial control, technological innovation, market development in the international film business, and relations among film and other media. In this way we can see how the blockbuster strategy, shaped and tested in the 1950s, continues to have a deep impact on the long-term operations of media production and experimentation, which includes projects far afield from the big-budget tentpole.

In media industries noted for their sprawling and unwieldy character, Cameron stands out as one who succeeds—commercially and, in some quarters, critically—where prevailing logic suggests he shouldn't. With each film, Cameron and his collaborators systematically worked through the problems and possibilities of certain kinds of special filmmaking conditions, special exhibition contexts, and business strategies. Significantly, and this is what I investigate in this chapter, in his projects and persona we can identify the technological imperative lodged in conceptions of the future of cinema. He displays a *technological auteurism*, especially in the popular and industrial representation of his credited innovations. As *Variety*'s Peter Debruge wrote of Cameron, "When 'the King of the World' sets his sights on tomorrow's technology, the rest of the industry takes note."[7]

Through Cameron, we can begin to discern the meaning and implications of "technological achievement" for an industry that invests a considerable amount in the notion. The Academy Awards for technological accomplishment tend to be sectioned off from the primary broadcast, relegated, at best, to a few minutes' recap of an earlier, highly gendered ceremony that typically involves an attractive starlet doling out statues to geeky white men. In actuality, this dimension of the corporate competition for proprietary control over the advancement in moving-image technologies is a major feature of the entertainment industry. By linking Cameron's blockbusters with his documentaries, and by focusing on production and exhibition technology, this chapter shows how Cameron has carefully capitalized on certain unstable technological aspects of the film industry. In a sense, he is an idol of the digital future of cinema. This especially involves his commitment to 3-D film and to the development of 3-D filmmaking processes. Even though such processes have a long history and are associated with countless innovators, Cameron was elevated as a vanguard enthusiast for the technological and economic viability of contemporary 3-D. One biography of Cameron is titled *The Futurist*.[8] To establish his current status as a technological auteur, we begin with the reception of *Avatar* and its use of 3-D.

The jokes about *Avatar* were almost as good as the movie: Pocahontas meets Halo, *Dances with Wolves* in space, James Cameron's *FernGully*, and a recruiting vehicle for Blue Man Group. With the film's juggernaut rollout, such humorous spins were to be expected. But it is one thing to put the promotional engine in high gear, and another to deliver a financially successful, audience-pleasing, and critically respected film to match the hype. By virtually every measure, Cameron did exactly that with his body-swapping, environmentally aware space opera. *Avatar* enjoyed a high cumulative score on the omnibus movie review website Rotten Tomatoes. And audience interest bulked up the film's box office to $760 million domestically and $2.79 billion worldwide, making it for a few years the highest-grossing film of all time.[9]

And like other blockbusters of earlier decades, *Avatar* was a tentpole film; it was the centerpiece of distributor Twentieth Century Fox's slate of releases. Tentpoles, as introduced in chapter 1, typically have large budgets, especially for promotion, and might be expected to launch or continue a film franchise. A major distributor may have a couple of tentpole properties over the course of a year, but they represent a minority of its films. Such movies are mentioned in the annual reports of media corporations, as distributors temporarily bank their corporate fiscal health on the success of those particular releases. With tentpoles drawing the largest theatrical audiences, a distributor fills out its "tent" with films that might be directed toward genre or niche audiences. From the exhibitor's perspective, a tentpole benefits simultaneously released films, as, say, those not wanting to see *Avatar* can take in *Fantastic Mr. Fox* (2009) playing on the screen next door.

But *Avatar* was also something of a different order. It may be a case of absence making the heart grow fonder, but the lead-up to *Avatar*'s release, beginning overseas on December 16 before opening domestically on December 18—dates that acted as a commemorative or superstitious marking of

Titanic's release twelve years earlier—was extraordinary in a number of respects. Online ticket vendors MovieTickets.com and Fandango both started selling tickets in August, four months before the release.[10] Cameron enjoyed a substantial amount of media attention through the fall of 2009, with profiles of his career and the technological innovations of *Avatar* characterizing him as a "man of extremes" who did not let the mundane fiscal realities of a production budget hamper the final product. But these profiles also carefully crafted a kinder, gentler, blue-collar hero whose advancement was the product of ingenuity, hard work, and a faith in scientific discovery.[11]

An air of secrecy around the film's production helped build public anticipation. Entertainment news greeted the release of individual photographs from the set and film stills as just as newsworthy as paparazzi shots of inebriated stars. But a tone of reverence was evident in some of this entertainment journalism, making the publicity photos seem like images of an actual far-flung space station or scientific expedition.[12] The availability of a three-minute trailer for *Avatar* online and in theaters was conventional marketing material. A new trailer premiered during an episode of Fox's *House, M.D.* (November 16, 2009), with advertisements for the trailer broadcast throughout the preceding week. Consider that detail: the promotional machine had reached the point that there were advertisements for upcoming advertisements. Close connections to the gaming industry were sought; Ubisoft developed a 3-D *Avatar* game, released on December 1, 2009, just weeks ahead of the film itself.[13] Not surprisingly, the trailers for the movie and the game were easily confused, and, indeed, this was part of the point. But the decision to show twenty-five minutes of the film in Amsterdam at the exhibitors' convention CineExpo in June, then in Los Angeles at a gathering of two thousand U.S. exhibitors at Grauman's Chinese Theatre, and then at the U.S. comic book and science fiction convention Comic-Con in July in San Diego was highly atypical. The lead-up to the release additionally included surprise clips and a panel discussion at the videogame conference E3 in Los Angeles, as well as a free showing of sixteen minutes on a hundred IMAX 3-D screens on August 21, 2009.[14] Such access to a portion of a highly anticipated film generated a sense of scarcity and word-of-mouth publicity. But these were very risky decisions because the reviews, especially on increasingly influential web-based fan sites, were not uniformly positive.

The most unusual aspect of the months before the film's release was the way *Avatar* was talked about as a revolutionary shift in cinema. Few media products have such elevated expectations as *Avatar* had attributed to it. And these expectations were not only for the film but also for a number of other products and technologies bundled with it to share its revenue-generating glory. Many believed that this film was a game changer for the business of cinema. Steven Soderbergh was one unlikely voice singing the praises of *Avatar* based on footage he had seen during the production process. He went so far as to describe it as a "benchmark" movie, comparable to *The Godfather* (1972) in its day.[15] Similarly, DreamWorks Animation head Jeffrey Katzenberg asserted, "I think the day after Jim Cameron's movie comes out, it's a new world."[16] At the film's premiere, director Michael Mann declared, "'There's before this movie and after this movie.'"[17]

The language about the game-changing impact of *Avatar* is illuminating. First, the film represented stupendous budget aggrandizement and ever more Byzantine accounting procedures. The official budget from Fox and Cameron's production company, Lightstorm Entertainment, was $230 million, up from the initial budget of "close to $200 million" when Fox's participation was first announced in January 2007.[18] So unrestrained was Cameron that that amount soon seemed like a bargain next to unofficial estimates. Once we add all the international distribution and marketing expenses, and the personal financial commitment of individual investors, including Cameron, the figure is estimated to be closer to $500 million.[19] That outlandish figure was not as worrisome for the distributing studio Fox as one might expect, because of its limited liability. Dune Entertainment and Ingenious Media, two private-equity partners, were reportedly in for roughly 60 percent of the budget.[20] That *Avatar*'s grosses rapidly surpassed its record-breaking budget gave industry investors confidence in the financial viability of the top end of the budget spectrum. Take note that a parallel 2009 Hollywood success story was that of the low-budget big hit *Paranormal Activity*. These two films thus laid out two contrasting contemporary blockbuster economies.

The trade and popular press coverage of Cameron's production unfailingly emphasized the intricacy of the technological requirements of the film as part of its game-changing status. Trade publications faithfully repeated that Cameron had sketched the idea for *Avatar* in the mid-1990s, but at that time the technology needed to realize his vision was, according to Cameron, "not advanced enough."[21] He had to wait for the technology to "catch up" to his vision.[22] Frequent mentions of how long this project had gestated presented *Avatar* as the product of a devoted artist. As the story goes, Cameron was so singularly driven by his original vision for the film that he was willing to wait until the cinematic technology matched his imagination, or he impatiently initiated the innovations himself. Cameron, in this representation, willed the future of cinema into being. The trade press emphasized that Cameron was, in a sense, making a movie for a cinematic apparatus that did not yet exist, something that had been suggested at other points in his career, especially related to the groundbreaking computer-generated imagery (CGI) in *The Abyss* and *Terminator 2: Judgment Day* (1991).[23]

Trade pundits and cultural commentators most frequently discussed *Avatar*'s game-changer status in relation to 3-D exhibition. Cameron began production of the film at a time when the conversion of cinemas to digital exhibition—a vast international endeavor to replace traditional celluloid projectors in movie theaters with digital ones—had slowed. Digital theaters were going to be an essential aspect of the film's success, as it required the new 3-D digital projection for which only a fraction of existing digital screens had been equipped. There was a level of blind faith on Cameron's part that the screens would be there by the time he released his film. By April 2009 there were merely two thousand 3-D-ready digital screens in the United States, representing just over 5 percent of all screens.[24] The risk inherent in such a form of production was offset by plans to release regular 2-D versions of the film as well.

Such devotion to a future cinematic era does not always work out. A relatively recent example of such a commitment to a specific vision of technological change was George Lucas's declaration that he would release *Star Wars: Episode I—The Phantom Menace* (1999) exclusively for digital exhibition. At the time he was confident there would be a speedy conversion to hard drives and digital projectors from film reels and celluloid, and doubly confident that his film was so attractive to exhibitors and audiences alike that it would actually encourage that conversion. This did not come to pass for a variety of reasons, including underdeveloped technical standards, shaky security, and a lack of coordination between exhibitors and distributors for the expense of digital conversion, as well as the dire financial straits of exhibitors at that time.

Cameron saw *Avatar* as an engine that would push the overall 3-D technological shift, as much as he and Fox expected to benefit from it, and eventually an influential segment of the industry agreed. A significant difference from Lucas's 1999 effort was that the financial and technical coordination needed for digital exhibition had been resolved, largely through the work of the industry consortium Digital Cinema Initiative. And the exhibition industry was relatively sound, with the 2009 domestic box-office receipts set to reach a record at over $10 billion *before* the December release of *Avatar*. Moreover, the advance word on the film itself was strikingly positive—those tepid online fan reviews of select film segments notwithstanding—something that *The Phantom Menace* did not enjoy.

An industrial agreement had been in process that 3-D was the next phase in cinema technology history. When an opinion piece in the *Los Angeles Times* derided the rush to 3-D, Katzenberg responded in *Variety* to reaffirm the celebration of 3-D technologies and to chastise the author for being a Luddite. As with the turn to color, Katzenberg reasoned, 3-D would eventually be recognized and exploited for its artful potential.[25] His drum banging was in part shilling for his 3-D DreamWorks Animation SKG releases *Monsters vs. Aliens* (2009) and *Shrek Forever After* (2010). But he did show a high level of faith in the general economic viability of this transition. And *Avatar* figured prominently in this cheerleading for 3-D. *Time* concluded its feature on 3-D by describing *Avatar* as a vanguard example of the future of the format.[26] Michael Lewis, head of the leading 3-D exhibition outfit RealD, predictably concurred, saying, "'The industry is looking for its *Citizen Kane* [1941], its definitive work of 3-D, and *Avatar* may be that film.'"[27] Versions of this line had been repeated by this company for several years, a view that gently pushed the responsibility for the conversion to digital 3-D, in particular to their proprietary system for 3-D, back onto filmmakers, who had yet to make an art of the form. Joshua Green, cofounder of RealD, said in 2005, "'We still haven't seen the *Citizen Kane* of 3-D.'"[28] In 2009 his business partner Lewis reiterated, "'*Avatar* is potentially the *Citizen Kane* of this medium.'"[29]

The seizing of milestone moments is one way in which technological change is made comprehensible and inevitable. Investment analyst Lloyd Walmsley predicted that "'3-D stands to reestablish the "experience premium" of movie-going. It's a game changer.'"[30] Trade reports conventionally linked this phase of 3-D with the short-lived fad of the 1950s but went on to cite other lasting changes, like the variety of widescreen processes from the same period, as more relevant comparisons for this exhibition innovation.[31] Lewis maintained that 3-D is "'the killer app of digital. As more and more of these films come out and we see them perform well, there's going to be an even bigger push to get more [digital] screens out there.'"[32] The subtitle of *Variety*'s supplement on Cinema Expo and 3-D in the summer of 2008 was "The Killer App."[33] Thus, 3-D exhibition, which had proven lucrative for animated features over the years just before *Avatar*, was being taken as a driving force for the acceleration of the conversion of theaters to digital exhibition. In this understanding, *Avatar*'s influence extended beyond 3-D to the speeding up of the obsolescence of celluloid projectors.[34]

The "game-changing" hyperbole was manifest in other aspects of the *Avatar* commodity world. Game developer Ubisoft's 3-D *Avatar* game prompted *Variety* to wonder, in a rather weak pun, whether or not it was "a game changer."[35] Ubisoft had been seeking increased involvement in the feature-film business, acquiring prestigious CGI company Hybride, based in St. Sauveur, Quebec. Further complicating the lines between entertainment industries, Cameron contracted Hybride to do effects for *Avatar*, the movie. Panasonic used *Avatar* in an international cross-promotion deal to sell its own new HD 3D Home Theater system.[36] This push linked to the gaming industry, as *Avatar: The Game* required a 3-D-enabled television or monitor for the full 3-D design of the game to work. But it also looked ahead to 3-D television programming. Accordingly, immediately following *Avatar*'s apparent box-office success, several television channels announced plans for conversion to 3-D broadcasting.

To see how Cameron became an industrial avatar in the technological revolution of digital and 3-D cinema, we must look at a period generally thought to be his "quiet years."

Cameron's first foray into 3-D was with *T2–3D: Battle across Time* (1996), made for Universal Studios Theme Parks. This theme park attraction, based on *Terminator 2*, includes a mixture of live action and a twelve-minute multiple-screen film. It extends the action enough to be considered—by Cameron, at any rate—a miniature sequel. The film portion features *Terminator 2* cast members Edward Furlong, Linda Hamilton, Robert Patrick, and Arnold Schwarzenegger. With a budget of $62 million, some have claimed it had the most expensive per-minute cost for a film to date. It is difficult to assess the profitability of this kind of attraction, but its longevity lends some justification to this investment; the exhibit played at Universal Studios Theme Parks in California until 2012 and in Florida until 2017, and it continues to run in Japan.

The *T2–3D* attraction was made through Digital Domain, a company Cameron started with special-effects expert Stan Winston and Steve Ross from Industrial Light and Magic (ILM), along with a 50 percent equity stake from IBM, in 1993. They intended the enterprise to be an artist-centered special-effects shop all under one roof (contra the various boutique companies that made up ILM). That one location was a Frank Gehry–designed retrofitted warehouse in Venice, California, over which the self-described Hollywood renegades fly the Jolly Roger; later they opened offices in Playa Vista and other locations around the world. No pirates ever enjoyed such comfortable digs. Cameron did plunder, literally, the resources of Digital Domain to an extraordinary extent for the making of *Titanic*, such that he almost ran the company into the ground, departing acrimoniously from the board of directors in 1998, though he maintained minority ownership. His parting words to the board were reportedly those of the musicians on the sinking *Titanic*: "Gentlemen, it's been an honor and a privilege playing with you."[37]

The company did not sink; just the opposite, at least until its bankruptcy in 2012. While Digital Domain's work on such films as *Fight Club* (1999), *Apollo 13* (1995), and *X-Men* (2000) garnered most of the praise lavished on the company, it handled roughly three or four films a year. By way of contrast, it did approximately eighty commercials annually. As a result, projects other than features were usually the first testing ground for new software and effects.[38] These smaller works became a point of initiation for new processes, digital and otherwise, only to be highlighted for popular entertainment audiences in subsequent films. It follows that to properly account for the development of new cinematic processes, techniques, and software, we must attend to the industry's full range of audiovisual production, eschewing a singular focus on feature fiction. Accordingly, with Digital Domain, Cameron's first turn toward his current interest in 3-D was not with a feature film or even a documentary but with a theme park exhibit.

While Digital Domain worked on the 3-D CGI effects for *T2–3D*, the challenges of shooting in 3-D included the sheer weight of the dual 65 mm camera unit, which at 450 pounds required a specially constructed cable system to suspend and move the unit during the long motorcycle chase sequence that is the centerpiece of the film (figures 7.2 and 7.3). Cameron and his cinematographer, Russell Carpenter, who also shot *Titanic*, learned—as anyone shooting 3-D realizes—that getting the exact focal length for the point of convergence of the two cameras, and hence our two eyes, was key to reducing eyestrain as well as establishing the best 3-D effect. Crudely put, to be able to cut between an establishing shot and a close-up, you have to change the point at which the audience will focus their eyes, and having a camera system that allows the director of photography to do this as easily as possible is extremely valuable to 3-D filmmakers. This, and the weight of the double-camera unit, became the primary issues addressed by the systems Cameron would help develop. Additionally, slight differences in the positions of frames on each of the two projectors used at the 3-D screenings can ruin the depth effect. This was solved by increasing the frames per second from twenty-four to thirty for both shoot-

FIGURE 7.2 *T2–3D: Battle across Time*, explosions, 1996

ing and projection.[39] More broadly, Cameron became an active campaigner for increasing the accepted standard for all frame rates to above twenty-four frames per second, which has since been used in mainstream releases like the "Hobbit" trilogy and *Billy Lynn's Long Halftime Walk* (2016).[40] He challenged the standards for digital projection because they addressed pixels but not the frame rate; Cameron believed the ideal format would be 3-D, 2K, meaning an image resolution consisting of just over two thousand pixels horizontally, and forty-eight frames per second.[41] The faster frame rate for the T2–3D shoot, in turn, necessitated an extraordinarily bright shooting environment and therefore posed unusual power demands for lighting the set.

So elaborate, and expensive, was the production of this attraction, and so unusual the involvement of such high-profile Hollywood figures, that *Variety* reviewed T2–3D's opening as though it were a film. While most of the review

FIGURE 7.3 *T2–3D: Battle across Time*, heavy camera rig, 1996

recounts the narrative setup for the blended live-action/3-D film performance, there is much reverence for the technical accomplishment. Reviewer Joe Leydon wrote, "The 3-D cinematography and special-effects handiwork are nothing short of astonishing," and "everything about this enterprise has been meticulously thought out and cleverly executed."[42]

After *Titanic*'s release, and following the accolades for that film's technical achievement, especially the integration of CGI with conventional photography in what appeared to be a seamless fashion, Cameron committed to 3-D as a fulfillment of the cinema's promise of totalizing sensory involvement, despite the generally unsatisfying experience shooting *T2–3D*. His ethos as a filmmaker involves popular forms of pleasure via the action/romance genre, which include unfamiliar images (the liquid Terminator in *Terminator 2*), surprising leaps from the intimate to the destructive (the "I'll be back" sequence in *The Terminator*), and powerful female leads.[43] Cameron's action set pieces typically locate the view at the heart of the sequence—in the cab of the truck or police cruiser racing away from a pursuing cyborg, among the soldiers running from aliens, and inside a flooding submersible. In this way the potential of 3-D as a "new" popular action experience met its equal potential to extend the sensation of being surrounded and engulfed by images, as emphasized in many of Cameron's films. The centrality of immersion to the cinematic experience is arguably something Cameron has implicitly grasped well, offering underwater and sci-fi sets that nestle, or claustrophobically entomb, characters and viewers alike.

But as a maker of popular plot-driven entertainments, Cameron is also on record as understanding the limits of immersion, believing that IMAX screens are too large and allow for too much wandering of the spectator's eye to work for strong narrative forms. His approach to 3-D is to direct the eye and to guide the viewer through the narrative experience.[44] Contra claims that *Citizen Kane*'s extensive use of deep-focus cinematography is a good model for 3-D shooting, Cameron said, "I find the opposite is true. Selective focus, created by working at low f-stops with longer lenses, evolved as a cinematic technique to direct the audience's attention to the character of greatest narrative importance at any given moment. With 3-D, the director needs to lead the audience's eye, not let it roam around the screen to areas which are not converged. So all the usual cinematic techniques of selective focus, separation lighting, composition, etc., that one would use in a 2-D film to direct the eye to the subject of interest, still apply, and are perhaps even more important."[45] In addition to an aesthetic and thematic overlap, it is also noteworthy that in our era of an economic tilt toward home theater systems, Cameron's 3-D projects—which include writing, producing, and/or directing four *Avatar* sequels, *Alita: Battle Angel* (2019), and *Sanctum* (2011)—continue a key aspect of the blockbuster strategy: a remarkable faith in moviegoing. Though the bulk of revenue can still be expected to flow from ancillary windows, he makes these films for theatrical exhibition and for the newest iterations of theatrical digital projection.

Two of his documentaries, *Ghosts of the Abyss* and *Aliens of the Deep*, were shot for exhibition in IMAX 3-D, though these were not shot with the IMAX camera system. The opening sequence of *Titanic* includes a dive to the wreck, led by Bill Paxton's character. This sequence serves as a framing device for the

FIGURE 7.4 *Ghosts of the Abyss*, documenting technological access, 2003

story and introduces the film's MacGuffin—the Heart of the Ocean diamond necklace. This opening was the product of an actual dive to the ship's remains, though Digital Domain "improved" that footage later. Cameron returned to the sunken wreck, with Paxton, to shoot *Ghosts of the Abyss* in 2001 (figure 7.4). That time the shoot included a twenty-six-pound lightweight 3-D HD camera developed by Vince Pace, called the Reality Camera System (RCS), and two smaller remote-control vehicles carrying standard video cameras, anthropomorphized as Jake and Elwood, named after the lead characters in *The Blues Brothers* (1980). Pace is an underwater film expert and had worked with Cameron on *The Abyss* and *Titanic*. The expedition also resulted in another documentary, filmed by Russian crew members, and an internet webcast of the descent, with the Buckminster Fuller–esque title *EarthShip.tv*, supervised by Cameron's brother J. D. The other familial connection was brother Mike, an engineer who designed the deep-sea casings for the cameras. Such a thoroughly recorded event, not surprisingly, involved many cameras, including small "lipstick" cameras inside the diving capsules. The final result did not impress reviewers, though they remained taken with the 3-D effect. Tim Cogshell wrote for *Boxoffice*, "*Ghosts of the Abyss* can be too jokey and often outright silly with an overwrought sense of drama. But it's fascinating, especially in 3-D."[46]

Expedition: Bismarck, which chronicles a dive to the famous sunken Nazi battleship, was shot with the same 3-D system, two remote-control cameras, and other cameras, though broadcast on Discovery Channel in the more familiar 2-D.[47] Like *Ghosts of the Abyss*, this film too uses computer graphics

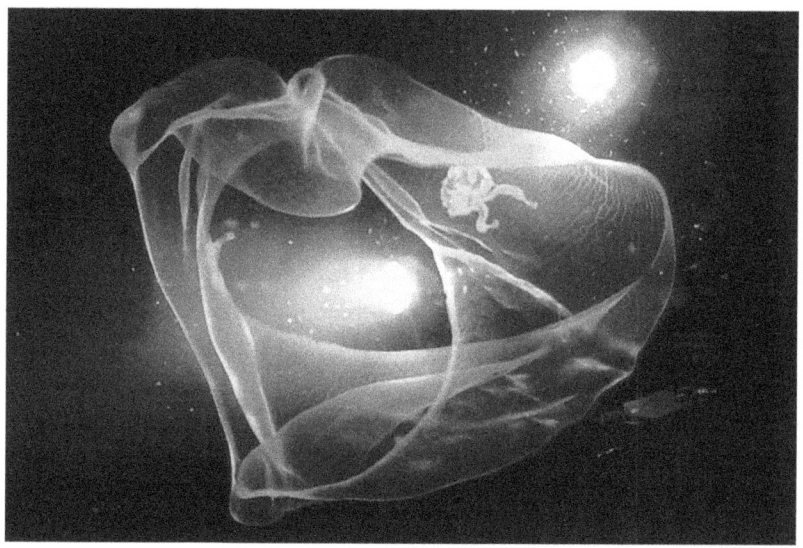

FIGURE 7.5 *Aliens of the Deep*, sea creatures as abstraction, 2005

and reenactments to supplement the raw data of the wreck with speculative accounts of how the ship sank. It was filmed after *Ghosts of the Abyss*, in 2002, but Discovery broadcast it the same year, before the opening of the IMAX 3-D film, making *Bismarck* Cameron's first documentary release. For their efforts, *Bismarck* received five Emmy nominations, winning one.

Aliens of the Deep documents several dives in both the Atlantic and Pacific Oceans but centers on a journey to the so-called Lost City, a deep-sea location with a unique ecosystem of creatures that live without light around hydrothermal vents of 350 degrees Fahrenheit (figure 7.5). For this film, he used the same 3-D cameras, though he and Pace had modified their RCS system to improve things like the zoom, which they put to effective use to record close-ups of some bizarre and relatively unknown creatures, including one called "the ugliest fish in the sea," which it likely is.[48] An otherwise-skeptical review by Jonathan Barnes in *Sight and Sound* still confesses that the film's 3-D experience elicits both "childish delight" and fright, with giant sea creatures "out of H. P. Lovecraft's most inventive nightmares."[49]

Following the *Aliens of the Deep* shoot, Cameron and Pace built the next generation of the camera, now called the Pace/Cameron Fusion System, which made it easier to change the point of convergence between the two cameras for 3-D shooting. Other differences from the earlier RCS included a faster response time, lighter weight (at twenty-two pounds), and better accommodation of sound.[50] Cameron, Pace, and Patrick Campbell (president of the company Pace and a camera assistant on *Ghosts*) received the patent for their system, a "platform for stereoscopic image acquisition," and one for "stereo camera with automatic control of interocular distance."[51] Versions of this camera system were used to shoot the live-action sequences of *Avatar*; concert films for U2, the Jonas Brothers, and Miley Cyrus; and features, including *Final Destination 3D* (2009) and *Journey to the Center of the Earth* (2008). In terms of wider market development, they claimed to have the largest inventory of such 3-D units.[52] This puts Pace (the company) and Cameron and colleagues (the patent holders) in an advantageous position as the making of 3-D movies grows, against competing 3-D camera rigs like Element Technica, Binocle, and P+S Technik.

In April 2011 the Pace company was rebranded as the Cameron Pace Group (CPG) to offer a full range of 3-D products for feature films and for television, sports, commercials, and other specialty events.[53] Along with their Fusion camera system, CPG offered a service it called Slate2Screen to assist in all aspects of 3-D production. Emphasizing its cross-media expansion beyond feature film, it made this announcement of the formation of CPG at the National Association of Broadcasters convention in Las Vegas, rather than at a film industry event. The proponents—by which I mean the company promoting these features—claimed their cameras and systems were "artist-centered" and gave control back to those on the shoots rather than the special-effects team later on. A material consequence was that CPG supplied just two personnel to whoever rented the system—an engineer and a systems supervisor. It didn't supply cinematographers, as its Fusion system was comparable enough to other kinds of high-definition shooting that special training was not necessary.[54]

One feature of Cameron's visual instruments included a way to produce immediate and on-set approximations of how 3-D and performance capture would look. He did the motion-capture portions of *Avatar* with a "virtual camera," basically a handheld monitor on which he and others could watch the performers. This screen was fed by a grid of a hundred HD cameras, and by moving the screen, he could record the camerawork he desired, including pans, tilts, and tracking.[55] There was no lens to look through, no actual tracks laid for camera movement, and no individual lighting setups. For the live-action portions of *Avatar*, Cameron experimented with the "Simulcam," developed with performance-capture company Giant.[56] This allowed people on set to see, when looking through the camera eyepiece, takes with mock-ups of green-screen and motion-capture elements. A limitation for CGI-driven shoots is the separation between filming personnel and digital craft workers, whose enhancements to the film appear much later. The Simulcam gave directors and directors of photography the ability to see a rough approximation of effects that will eventually be integrated, and thus they had an immediate basis for on-set decision-making.

Regardless of the actual location of creative energy, the innovation and services offered by CPG at the very least reasserted a conventional hierarchy for filmmaking. They allowed for the existing networks of filmmaking labor to continue. Mark Deuze has documented the importance of networks of connections among personnel as they travel from job to job.[57] These informal relationships, he shows, are central to maintaining a steady flow of work and building a reputation. New production technology that can be introduced without disrupting these working relationships is therefore of premium value. Cameron's own stable of personnel travels across his films, and some have established a special expertise with the Fusion system (e.g., *Avatar* second-unit director Steven Quale directed the 3-D *Final Destination 5* [2011]). In sum, one of the advantages of Cameron's 3-D and performance-capture systems was that they supplemented, and hence reinforced, existing commitments to CGI, relations among crew, and digital exhibition concurrently.

There are many telling commonalities across Cameron's three documentaries. First, it is important to note that the deep-sea locations build on the underwater experience Cameron had shooting not only *Titanic* but also his earlier film *The Abyss*, which was an especially arduous and expensive feature about alien life-forms, nuclear terror, and labor politics. The making of that film produced an ample supply of the definitive stories of Cameron's monomania on set. He was reportedly so insensitive to the conditions of actors that several claimed to have nearly drowned, which Cameron denied.[58]

In *The Abyss*, the film's subject—undersea oil workers realizing they are pawns in the company's operations—represents an ideologically advanced critique that appears to contradict the actual working conditions Cameron himself created. His films routinely offer complex, if contradictory, depictions of abuses of technological power. *The Terminator* is best known for its dystopian views, depicting the lead-up to a devastating nuclear holocaust precipitated by initially benign but ultimately fateful decisions on the part of corporate managers and military contractors (like Cyberdyne's Miles Dyson, played by Joe Morton). *Aliens*, even with its visual fetish for weapons and their accessories, is a story of the fallibility of military command and corporate colonial ambitions. As James Kendrick has suggested, whereas most Hollywood films are superficially radical but internally conservative, Cameron's films are "superficially conservative, internally radical."[59]

Yet these currents of ideological critique battle the mode of representation, which figures on-screen in characters' facility with technological apparatuses and improvisation. In her classic feminist reading of time travel in *The Terminator*, Constance Penley noted the "tech noir" aesthetic that includes representation of the everyday abundance of machines running the gamut from hairdryers to automated factory equipment.[60] Typical Cameron scenes include the crew in *Aliens*, under siege by the creatures, scouring blueprints of the colony facilities on illuminated screens, trying to hatch an escape plan, and Kyle Reese (Michael Biehn) in *The Terminator* teaching Sarah Connor (Linda Hamilton) how to make explosive devices from everyday materials. There is a recurrent image of technological investment and improvisation for narrative action in these films. The acquisition, construction, and operation of machines and devices drive stories forward and set up relations among characters. A case in point is Corporal Hicks (Michael Biehn) outfitting Ripley (Sigourney Weaver) with various weapons and explosives in preparation for one of her final battles with the Alien Queen creature in *Aliens*, which amounts to an unusually tender moment. Notably, this investment mixes the advances of new technological capabilities and a survivalist DIY approach to low-tech devices (e.g., Ripley's use of duct tape). This theme, in particular, reappears in *Avatar*, where the conceit of the drama is that part of the planet on which the majority of the action transpires is so humid and has such a strong magnetic field that some advanced weaponry is inoperable. Or, as Cameron confessed, "'It's all an excuse to do helicopters versus pterodactyls.'"[61]

These features display considerable thematic and aesthetic connections to Cameron's documentaries, where a brand of technofetishism, both improvised and cutting-edge, also drives the tales.[62] Annette Kuhn has suggested that the attention to special effects makes science fiction films a notable genre in which the state of the cinematic art is expected to be encountered.[63] Cameron extends this aspect of sci-fi to his documentaries. To say that each of Cameron's documentaries is about undersea exploration captures only part of their subject matter. Each equally focuses on the technological means by which the images were captured. It's not just that the cameras needed specially designed titanium casings to withstand the high-pressure environment of deep-sea shooting locations and that accommodations for the lighting conditions underwater had to be made; it is that the films announce these and comparable features repeatedly. The films become documentaries about the inventiveness of the filmmakers-cum-explorers and the complexity of the hardware as much as the purported subject of marine life and shipwrecks.

Ghosts of the Abyss presents the core theme of visual technology in the first moments of the film, opening with a poetic camera tracking movement in an early twentieth-century stereoscopic slide viewer, displaying several black-and-white period scenes of the famous ocean liner, with a slight tremor shaking the image as though a crude mechanism is flipping it to the next (figures 7.6 and 7.7). On the final image of this sequence, the figures in the slide begin to move, and the background dissolves to color and to the film's title. To remind viewers of the passing of media history, the film returns to these stereoscopic slides later on. One finds comparable techniques in other moments of technological transformation, including Al Jolson's opening declaration in *The Jazz Singer* (1927) that "you ain't heard nothing yet," and Tom Ewell's direct address about stereophonic sound, color, and the aspect ratio in the credit sequence of *The Girl Can't Help It* (1956), in which the screen's edges were pushed out horizontally to a widescreen format. Transitions of this sort carry spectators through a short evolutionary narrative about media format, proffering improvements for the audiences' appreciation.

These stereoscopic images in *Ghosts* are computer generated from archival images, constructed to appear to be antique slides. Similarly, postproduction involved converting the various resolutions from the different cameras to a uniformly high resolution acceptable for IMAX screens. This conversion also involved software to approximate 3-D effects for the images captured from the regular HD cameras, as well as those images produced in postproduction. And some shots of the wreck are in fact composite images, based on the technology "used by NASA" to produce complete images of planets and solar systems, as stated in one DVD extra. Invoking the imprimatur of NASA suggests that the technology is state of the art and that it is not really manipulation of the visual record, which of course it actually is. In the end, the viewer is watching a composite image, rather like a mosaic or a David Hockney gridlike Polaroid portrait, but with the seams between the smaller images rendered invisible.[64]

In addition, Cameron has actors play out scenes from the sinking ship superimposed on these composite images of the wreck. These "ghosts" re-create

FIGURE 7.6 *Ghosts of the Abyss*, historical mechanisms for immersive viewing, 2003

FIGURE 7.7 *Ghosts of the Abyss*, dissolve to contemporary CGI immersive viewing, 2003

FIGURE 7.8 *Ghosts of the Abyss*, interior of the wreck with camera-carrying ROV, 2003

the event of the sinking on the "actual" deck and in the "actual" cabins, though these sets are not to be found at the bottom of the North Atlantic and appear only with CGI manipulations. One dramatic sequence involves a CGI representation of *Titanic*'s sinking with a fast-paced collage of photographic portraits of the victims falling into the wreck, as though being sucked again into the vortex (figure 7.9). Cameron's efforts to scrape together as proximate a representation as possible of the actual disaster here replay the calamity using the only indexical traces remaining—places where passengers stood, pieces of objects they touched, and family photographs. The film wants to situate the spectator as a "witness to tragedy," as one crew member puts it. This impulse is driven home when, during their expedition, they receive news of the September 11, 2001, attacks. This prompts several comparisons between the two events and sparks the crew's resolve to memorialize the ninety-year-old disaster by laying a plaque on the ocean floor.

Much of the adventure of *Ghosts* involves the cameras, getting them to the wreck and providing adequate lighting. The film displays not just the wreck but the special remote-control cameras that get to the interior of the *Titanic*. Emphasizing the premium placed on technological presence, one of the dramatic episodes of the film involves the recovery of a remotely operated vehicle

FIGURE 7.9 *Ghosts of the Abyss*, images of victims being dragged again into the wreck, 2003

FIGURE 7.10 *Ghosts of the Abyss*, Cameron's cameras, 2003

(ROV) that lost power—Elwood, incidentally. During this interlude the ROV is described as one of the crew members, and a military credo is evoked that no one gets left behind (ignoring the fact that the credo isn't "don't leave broken hardware behind"). For a good portion of the dive segments, we see several smaller inset images of the crew, including Cameron and Paxton, observing and operating cameras and submersibles (figure 7.10). In fact, these inset images obscure direct visual access to the wreck, as they lie on top of the pictures of the sunken ship.[65] While it is not exactly a film about cameras, there is enough attention to them that parts might have been called *Cameron's Cameras*.

All three films present comparable thematic priorities. *Bismarck* is about the special submersibles that get people and cameras to the remains of the Nazi battleship. The submersibles receive special attention in each film, with rollicking sequences of the Russian "Zodiac cowboys" who have to attach the cables that will lift the submersibles back onto the ship by riding on top of them when they surface. Completing this task in rough seas is visually exciting, enhanced by a fast and dramatic musical score.

Aliens of the Deep is the most aesthetically ambitious of these three films. The opening presents a series of portraits of individuals and animals, including some crowd-pleasing 3-D tricks like an elephant unfurling its trunk directly at the camera and audience. We see an urban street corner, a dance club, and then fireballs in space. A few shots of suburban life follow with a slow-motion IMAX-size 3-D image of kids playing in a sprinkler and a chubby boy eating a messy hamburger in a fenced-in backyard, while a cow moos on the soundtrack. This sequence of a calculatedly spectacular ordinary sets up the animal-human, and terrestrial-extraterrestrial, connection that the rest of the film pursues. Several young scientists accompany Cameron, though the lead is Dijanna Figueroa, an African American doctoral student in marine animal physiology from the University of California, Santa Barbara. In a surprising, perhaps ill-considered, turn, this film ends with speculative sequences about meeting mothlike alien beings, which in tone and appearance seem to appropriate the angel creatures from *The Abyss*. One sequence depicts a hypothetical method for melting through thick layers of ice with a nuclear-heated torpedo, as well as a journey down through an extraterrestrial ocean by a fictional remote-control vehicle, presumably several generations more advanced than Jake or Elwood.

The film ends with Figueroa and Kevin Hand, an astrobiologist, greeting an imaginary sea creature on that ocean floor through the glass of a submersible. "We have new friends," Figueroa says in this *E.T.*-like moment of interspecies harmony, blending the real and the invented. Cameron's documentary aesthetic does not hesitate to borrow from science fiction filmmaking to approximate the actuality of a scene or argument. The film advances a universalist idea about experience and knowledge, reasoning that the similarities between life-forms warrant extrapolating what we feel and know to others. This, for Cameron, includes creatures that do not exist, which is a fine conceit for a science fiction writer but not sound argumentation for a documentarian.

With *Aliens of the Deep*, *Ghosts of the Abyss*, and to a lesser extent *Expedition: Bismarck*, documentary realism stretches to include CGI. In this case, documentary is not the recording, or the creative representation, of reality but a display genre for visible effects. Importantly, not all effects are equally visible; some do not announce themselves as such and take a trained eye to be identified. Others are obvious and signposted, often by the narrator, with the effect of making each film a document of CGI representational strategies. Others form the basis of DVD extras. In a way, the extreme locations and the presence of the filmmakers in these extraordinary places—places that relatively few humans have ever visited—become the guarantor of authenticity for what, in the end, are constructed computer-based post-production moving-image works.

Here we see a link between moving-image innovations and other technological materials. Cameron's particular brand of celebrity activism involves "gee-whiz" popular science and an environmentalism that embraces technological progress. Within weeks of the Deepwater Horizon oil spill in 2010, Cameron had convened a panel of experts and quickly produced a recommendation on how to stop up the well. He not only offered his own state-of-the-art submersibles but was willing to do it himself. And in March 2012 he successfully shot, diving in his newly designed submersible, some of the *Avatar* sequel and a new 3-D documentary in what is known to be the world's deepest point, eleven kilometers (6.8 miles) under the Pacific Ocean in the Mariana Trench, a place where only two people had ever been before.[66] That's far fewer people than have climbed Mount Everest and fewer than have been to the moon. Cameron's investment in exploration vehicles for extreme shooting conditions might seem like the polar opposite of his investment in the virtuality of digital cinema, simultaneously plunging as deep as one can go into extraordinary location shooting and into simulation. But in fact they are products of the same impulse, both foregrounding the scientific-technological apparatus. Whereas Sean Cubitt points to the neobaroque cinema of Cameron and others as involved in creating and presenting simulated worlds closed off from history and the social, we see here that the attention to unusual shooting locations and production processes—including pulleys, power sources, lights, ROVs, and performance-capture software—stretches us well beyond that virtual seal.[67]

These documentaries all involve Cameron as a central figure. He is on camera and is guiding the expedition as much as the narrator in each. *Ghosts* has Paxton, and *Bismarck* has Lance Henriksen, both part of Cameron's stable of actors, as nonexpert narrators whose journey and introduction to the subject matter are written to mirror those of the audience. Paxton's amateur status is especially emphasized; his arrival on the ship involves a staged comical interaction with a Russian crew member who speaks only in Russian, making Paxton appear that much more on unfamiliar territory. He describes his nervousness about the upcoming dive and later treats IMAX spectators to big-screen vomit upon his return to the surface. *Aliens of the Deep* uses student scientists to fill this amateur role. These figures serve to bolster Cameron's experience and command of both the filmmaking and expeditionary situations.

By building his persona as a champion of science, explorer, and technological wizard, Cameron is, after a fashion, part of the long history of the expedition film, which often involved the anthropologist, or quasi-anthropologist, filmmakers of primarily European lineage traveling to some outlying location and population, returning with images of some strange earthly wonders. Cameron often refers to Jacques Cousteau as a major influence, but he is also not that far from the likes of Merian C. Cooper and Ernest B. Schoedsack, the explorer/showmen making *Grass* (1925) and the hybrid ethnographic/fiction feature *Chang* (1927), who then include the explorer/showman as a central part of their fiction films; remember that the original *King Kong* (1933), aside from the gorilla-girl love story, is about filmmaking and show business.[68]

Cameron's expedition trilogy asserts multiple times that we are watching the absolute cutting edge of imaging and transportation technology, with the newest and most complex gadgets, some custom made for the demands of these enterprises. And one can understand the appeal of this approach for the science museum context of many IMAX screens and for the Discovery Channel. On this point, each film presents Cameron as a cruel technological taskmaster who is "totally reliant on technology" (*Aliens of the Deep*), dealing with state-of-the-art machines that "push the limits of technology" (*Ghosts of the Abyss*). These three documentaries construct a relationship between technological and natural wonders: extreme machines for extreme shoots. Indeed, the *National Geographic* companion volume to *Aliens of the Deep* says this exactly.[69] If there is an environmental ethic, especially evident in *Aliens of the Deep*, it is one of awe, where viewers experience the eye-popping, jaw-dropping spectacular vistas of unusual natural wonders. Robert Koehler wrote that *Ghosts* "is nearly overwhelmed by incessant chatter and expression of wonder by crew members," and Ronnie Scheib wrote of *Aliens of the Deep*, "As many 'wows' and 'gee whizzes' abound as do albino shrimp."[70] But the natural world is not meant to hold a monopoly on the aesthetic of awe; these films extend this affect to the world of advanced technology. Beneath their titular subject matter, this expedition trilogy is essentially a series of "making-of" documentaries promoting the ingenuity and resourcefulness of the filmmakers/explorers in the seizing of remote sites for audiences back on dry land.

Some commentators, including Thomas Schatz and Edward J. Epstein, point out that a core element in the contemporary media business is intellectual property, especially the ownership of stories and characters and control of the multiple products that come out of franchises.[71] This facet explains the arrangements between Disney and Marvel for the former to gain access to the latter's stable of comic book characters, and then Disney's acquisition of "Star Wars" home LucasFilm and "Avatar" home Twentieth Century Fox. It explains the focus of the Motion Picture Association of America on piracy in recent years. Companies exist to help others exploit their intellectual property. For example, Starlight Runner Entertainment specializes in the development and coordination of story worlds and mythologies, including characters, chronologies, geography, and weapons, with the intention of orchestrating "transmedia" incarnations of franchised works. They have done this work for "Pirates of the Caribbean" and "Avatar." As outlined in *Variety*, "now that the franchise has replaced the blockbuster as Hollywood's holy grail, a new tool has emerged to help those who want to extend film and TV properties across multiple platforms"—the "megabible."[72]

To this extension of media format and text we should add the intellectual property associated with technological systems. U.S. media history has been profoundly shaped by technological patents, starting with Edison, but continuing with Michael Todd (Todd-AO), Jerry Lewis (video assist technology), and George Lucas (various proprietary processes developed at ILM). But any technological apparatus still turns on content, especially as a way to sell the advantages and improvements of one format or process over another. Consequently, we can find notable occasions in which specially designated content is linked quite directly to new media systems. This link is not about firsts but about logjam breakers, forgers, and tipping points. For example, Discovery Channel used *Expedition: Bismarck* to promote its high-definition format, doing so with a mobile HD screen and theater installed temporarily at retail locations, like Best Buy, where new HD televisions were available to consumers. In such instances the exact item being promoted is lost in the confluence of television channel, high-definition format, big-budget documentary, star director, and consumer electronics retailer.[73]

And this was where *Avatar* was a standout work. It was conventional in story and characterization, and it had the conventional transnational economic impact of its production, spanning corporate participants from Quebec's Hybride to New Zealand's Weta Studios. But *Avatar* was celebrated and promoted as a flagship work beckoning the next wave of industrial and consumer technologies and entertainments. Chapter 1 introduced the example of Panasonic's international cross-promotion deal in which the first 3-D home version of *Avatar* was available only on Blu-ray and compatible only with Panasonic's Viera sets from the end of 2010 to early 2012.[74] With *Avatar* we had 3-D filming processes, 3-D exhibition, digital exhibition, and 3-D home entertainment all banking on the film's appeal. This was yet again an instance of a blockbuster acting as a prototype for the future of moving-image technology, advancing requirements for new skills, production conditions, and exhibition environments.[75] *Avatar* was a *technological tentpole*, under which not only commodities but also media formats slid into our lives.[76] One report even described Cameron's film in exactly this fashion, as a tentpole for digital 3-D.[77] Technological tentpoles introduce and promote hardware and media systems; such entities advance the very notion of a perpetually reconstructed cinematic apparatus, as well as a wider audiovisual environment. As discussed in chapter 1, *Avatar*'s platform-conscious advertising invited audiences to see the film "everywhere" and "every*way*."

The varieties of media materiality have ample representation in Cameron's vision of the future. *Avatar* is replete with screens on-screen: 3-D screens, topographical screens, video screens, computer screens, touch screens, handheld digital tablets, and curved screens. The thematic center of the film—the conversion of our human characters into their respective avatars as giant blue extraterrestrial creatures, the Na'vi—appears as a form of transportation, with abstract blazing lights moving through a tube to some distant material body, like a cross between teleportation and long-distance communication. *Avatar* is so embellished with interstellar cutting-edge media culture that one might be surprised to discover that it tells an anticolonial tale of an indigenous population's resistance to the exploitation of minerals on their home planet, Pandora, by invading Earthlings. For Cameron, the devastation of colonialism includes the consequences of technological change. Stating this theme directly, he said, "'We're basically telling the story of the Americas and to a certain extent some of the other areas in the world that were conquered by the British, Dutch and so on, but we're really telling the story of what happens when a technologically superior culture comes into a place with resources that the conquerors want.'"[78] As a political parable, it is a thinly veiled critique of imperial adventures by armed forces, ostensibly U.S. in appearance and style (with at least one shot of Old Glory in the background). Bombastic dialogue about natives as terrorists, "preemptive attacks," "daisy cutters," and "shock and awe" tactics takes what might have been a John Milius film—for instance, *Farewell to the King* (1989), of which *Avatar* is in many ways a remake—and reframes it as a critique of the U.S. invasion and occupation of Iraq.

As influential as his work has been for nonconventional gender depictions, especially his muscularization of female action characters, the limits of Cameron's imagination are apparent in his racial politics. In *Avatar* the species-specific divide presented on Pandora is recognizably driven by familiar earthly notions of difference. His extraterrestrial indigenous peoples are a version of the noble savage, living harmoniously with their environment until greedy colonial invaders disrupt their spiritual bond with nature. Even as the drama directs audiences to cheer for the spiritually advanced and environmentally aware Na'vi, we confront stereotypical gestures and appearances of tribal peoples. Moreover, the actors behind the virtual costumes and makeup are suitably ethnicized to perform the "blueness" of the Na'vi. African American actors C. C. H. Pounder and Laz Alonso and Cherokee actor and activist Wes Studi play lead Na'vi characters, and Dominican/Puerto Rican American actor Zoe Saldana plays hero Jake Sully's love interest. Pointedly, only White folk, like our lead Sully, get to cross over into their Na'vi avatars to live among the natives. Sully's story, then, is a "Na'vi like me" tale of passing. The core of the film is a "blueface" performance, which draws this film closer thematically to the other most referenced game-changing film, the breakthrough talkie *The Jazz Singer*, in which Al Jolson's stage persona is *his* racialized avatar.

The world of the noble savage offers ideologically safe contact with the natural and the archaic, that is, civilization's other. In Cameron's case, the environmental ethos of the Na'vi, while reiterating the trope of nobility, is equally a way to present harmonious connections among all beings, using contemporary technological references to do so. Characters describe Pandora as a complex and complete data network, where even plant life has communicative capabilities. The Tree of Souls, the spiritual heart of the ecosystem (female, of course), holds records of all feelings, expressions, and memories. It is, ostensibly, a colossal organic server. Flying into battle, individual Na'vi can communicate across distances by placing thumb and forefinger on either side of their throat, like a mimed handless mobile phone. Several scenes show the temporary intertwining of animal and humanoid as a kind of jacking in of electrical filaments. The moments of these fusings are, in many ways, the most erotic renderings in the film, with abundant rolling eyes and pleasurable gasps. Talk about fidelity follows, too. Once selected, connected, and tamed, the pterodactyl-like flying creatures serve as your permanent transportation vehicle, a kind of interspecies monogamy.

As figured, the Na'vi are not merely representations of an ancient and superstitious worldview; they offer an image of a superior technological system. Pandora is worth defending, then, as an example of perfect synergy across beings and devices, with integration a racial, environmental, and technological concept simultaneously. This planet offers a world of natural networks. So when Sully, permanently "avatared" as Na'vi at the end of the film, remains behind on Pandora after winning the battle against the invading colonial forces, this is not a refusal of technological enhancement for some form of native spiritual awareness but a full acceptance of what might be called technological naturalism. This unambiguously anticolonial story, by the end, sneaks in the true colonists, those hybrid avatars. The technological game-changing film is a tale of full acceptance and assimilation, at the level of the genetic, with an even more advanced game-changing technological system. In a moment of corporate reflexivity, it should not go unnoticed that the logo for Cameron's production company Lightstorm—a thin, angular blue individual readying a bow and arrow—bears an uncanny resemblance to the ten-foot-tall creatures populating Pandora.

Cameron does not fit the mold of what we expect of a Hollywood A-list director. And this ultimate insider-outsider had not had any Hollywood agent from the early 1990s until 2009, when he signed with Creative Artists Agency, ostensibly to represent him as the "Avatar" franchise develops and as his technological processes are marketed.[79] There are easier ways to make money in the film business than trying to find a way to light the pitch darkness at the bottom of the ocean, designing camera containers to withstand the pressure of deep-sea shooting conditions, and changing the frame rate to improve a 3-D effect. *Ghosts of the Abyss* cost about $13 million and brought in a little over $22 million for its worldwide box office, a tidy sum for a documentary but hardly an IMAX record, let alone an example of Cameron's stratospheric moneymaking prowess.[80]

The point here is that it is easy to get caught up in the conventionality of Hollywood—buy a recognizable property, construct a star-driven vehicle with the appropriate smattering of romantic interest and international appeal, plan a big opening, and follow through with releases of related commodities, then the disc, streaming, and TV versions, and so on. With Cameron, we see that there are different, and influential, ways to navigate the demands of the media industry. It would be easy to skip over documentaries such as Cameron's, thinking of them as side projects and inconsequential labors of love. And yet there is continuity through his entire oeuvre. Recognizing this, we see an extraordinary range of corporate investments and priorities, which produce a greater cross-sector industrial beast and a fundamentally unstable technological apparatus. Cameron is an exemplar of the current phase of Hollywood history, in which the business of film is bound up with a range of media products, technological forms, and types of intellectual property. John Caldwell argues that not only is every script a business plan, it is also a branding opportunity.[81] With Cameron the technological auteur, a script is equally a plan for the remaking of the cinematic apparatus and conventional modes of industrial and technological practice.

Most impressively, the language of a revolutionary shift is not new; indeed, it has been a persistent feature in the film business. Never content with an existing apparatus, Hollywood competitors have battled over formats, technologies, and processes as much as stars, directors, and movie franchises. Declarations of "game changing" and "technological revolution" are forms of competition at the level of hardware and software. We might see figures like Todd, Lewis, Lucas, and Cameron as the carnival barkers of the technological tentpoles, rather than as inventors. The benefits to becoming a new industry standard are immeasurable, and they can include markets beyond films in a number of other industrial sectors. In this way an individual audiovisual entertainment like *Avatar*, with a technological exhibitionism that echoes earlier blockbuster periods, works to reinstate the dominance of key corporate participants, making technological change appear inevitable and natural. At one level, even with all the local instances of innovation—and yes, to be sure, the entertainment business is shifting dramatically—the language of "game changing" is another way to talk about business as usual.

(CHAPTER EIGHT)

THE TECHNOLOGICAL HEART OF MOVIE CULTURE

What does cinephilia mean now that cinema practice crosses so many media configurations? Cinephiles, after all, are cut from a very particular cloth. They are an audience that has a special relationship to the world of motion pictures and are imagined as different from the ordinary viewer. They don't just watch movies—sorry, films. They inhale the atmosphere of the theater, they single-mindedly seek out allusions to other films, and they dream of hushed audiences and passionate conversation after the end credits roll. They learn a little French. Cinephiles invest emotionally in the idea of the cinematic, as though there is a unique and spectacular world that only the elect may visit. Their commitment to cinephilia ranges from mild to intense, and their numbers are legion.

Cinephilia, no different from any cultural activity and experience, is materialized in practices and in media forms. Those conditions include the situations, occasions, infrastructures, and institutions in which moving images are encountered, and they include venues for criticism, inventories of information, publishing, merchandise, and ephemera. Some practices have receded from use and memory. In Pierre Bourdieu's seminal work on class formation through manifestations of taste, *Distinction*, he made a brief observation that cinephiles spend a lot of time "transcribing film credits onto catalogue cards."[1] That was France, and that was the 1960s, but this lost practice is intriguing, and it tells us something about the period. For Bourdieu, the then-novel elevation of talk about film and jazz was symptomatic of a new class faction, one in which the acquisition of cultural knowledge not taught in schools correlated with educational levels and was a generational wedge against an older version of a middle-class faction. Here, the absence of formal materials for the enrichment of connoisseurship about film and jazz provided the conditions for the production of a new class position. Bourdieu said practices building new cultural connoisseurship were ways to assure the vitality of social strata, hence to assure the reproduction of class divisions. The success of the academic discipline of film studies was evidence that a new class faction had solidified.

Let me propose another underappreciated instrument of film culture: the television guide. No single resource was more important to my own education than the now-residual printed magazine-format television guide, and I venture to claim this was the case for the majority of other film fans coming of age in the 1970s—though no doubt for years before and after, too. Each issue provided a weekly menu of movie possibilities. Beyond the schedule of movies to see or eventually record for the building of a home video library, television guides provided brief descriptions of plots, release dates, genres, stars, and ratings. If you were lucky, there was a page of weekly recommendations from a film critic. Note that, typically, movies were given a star rating, not television shows. In my family the guide arrived free with the Saturday newspaper; I would nab it and pore over the movie options for the week ahead, circling the ones of interest, and then coordinate my time accordingly. It was much later, as an adult, that I discovered this was how committed film authorities treat festival programs.

Not so long ago, the dominant discourse in the world of film scholarship and fandom was about scarcity; we live now with a dominant discourse of cultural abundance. From the 1980s on, we confronted a new era of filmic plenitude, which required assistance in organizing the possibilities. Today, internet scholars and policymakers say that cultural plenitude results in a problem of "discoverability." This was the case in the VCR era of video rental and purchase, and accordingly guidebooks proliferated: *Leonard Maltin, Roger Ebert, Videohound, Psychotronic*, and then, finally, Amazon's IMDb. Given all the information available in later years, the television guide no longer holds ay, February 16 • Primetime

W	E	V	6 p.m.	6:30	7 p.m.	7:30	8 p.m.	8:30	9 p.m.	9:30	10 p.m.	10:30	1
4	4	02	Le Téléjournal	P'tite vie "Le retour de Rod"	En direct de l'univers Invité(es): Denise Bombardier (N)		Downton Abbey "Secrets dévoilés" (N)		Dre Grey, leçons d'anatomie "Un pas de trop" (N)		Le Téléjournal	NouvellesSports/:40 Infoman	:10 Ap
21	21	53	Channel 3 News	CBS Saturday Evening News	Entertainment Tonight Weekend		Person of Interest "Firewall"		Criminal Minds "Through the Looking Glass"		48 Hours "Honor and Dishonor" (N)		Chan News
23	18	52	Newschannel 5	NBC Nightly News	Jeopardy! Weekend	Wheel of Fortune	American Ninja Warrior "Best of the Southwest"		Chicago Fire "Warm and Dead"		Law & Order: Special Victims Unit		News
13	13	06	CBC News: Montreal	Hockey Tonight Live	Hockey NHL Philadelphia Flyers vs. Montréal Canadiens From: Bell Centre - Montreal, Que. Live						Hockey NHL Colorado Avalanche vs. Edr Place - Edmonton, Alta. Live		
-	-	10	CTV News		W5 (N)		★★★ Harry Potter and the Chamber of Secrets (Family, '02) Harry Potter returns to Hogwarts only to find the school plagued by mysterious attacks. Rupert Grint, Daniel Radcliffe.						CTV News
7	7	04	TVA nouvelles	★★ Nuit et jour (Action, '10) La vie d'une femme est bouleversée lorsqu'un agent secret fait surface. Cameron Diaz, Tom Cruise.				:35 ★★ Course à la mort Joan Allen, Jason Statham.				:40 TVA nouvelles	:10 peau
11	11	07	CTV News		W5 (N)		★★★ Harry Potter and the Chamber of Secrets (Family, '02) Harry Potter returns to Hogwarts only to find the school plagued by mysterious attacks. Rupert Grint, Daniel Radcliffe.						CTV News
8	8	03	Les Dalton	Dis-moi tout	Planète bleue "La reine des tigres"		Les francs-tireurs		Belle et Bum (N)			★★★ Lettre ouvert Blunt, Maria Bello.	
22	22	51	ABC World News	ABC 22 News	TMZ		★★★ Harry Potter and the Chamber of Secrets (Family, '02) Harry Potter returns to Hogwarts only to find the school plagued by mysterious attacks. Rupert Grint, Daniel Radcliffe.						ABC
57	6	55	The Lawrence Welk Show "Love Songs"		As Time Goes By	Mulberry	Waiting for God	Keeping Up Appearances	Midsomer Murders "Ring Out Your Dead"		Austin City Limits "Gary Clark Jr./ Alabama Shakes" (N)		Infini Jenny
5	5	05	District V	★★ La fièvre des planches L'histoire d'un groupe d'étudiants qui fréquente une école artistique à New York. Asher Book, Kristy Flores.				La chute de l'ange (Comédie fantaisiste, '97) Un détective affronte un démon qui, après s réincarne dans un autre corps. John Goodman, Denzel Washington.					
46	36	54	Two and a Half Men	Two and a Half Men	The Big Bang Theory	The Big Bang Theory	Auto Racing Sprint Cup Series NASCAR Sprint Unlimited From: Daytona International Speedway - Daytona Beach, Fla. Live				FOX 44 News at 10 p.m.	Family Guy	The F
3	3	08	Evening News	Global National	Border Security	Border Security	Global Currents "Sabrina's Law"		Chicago Fire "Warm and Dead"		Very Bad Men "The Deadly Messiah"		News
24	40	50	Art Express	New York NOW	Mountain Lake Journal	Borderless North	Antiques Roadshow	Antiques Roadshow	Lark Rise to Candleford		DCI Banks Chief Superintendent Gerry R Banks to find his missing teenage daugh		
14	14	14	Murdoch Mysteries "Rich Boy, Poor Boy"		Get Stuffed	Out There	Murdoch Mysteries "Rich Boy, Poor Boy"		Phantom Racer (Action, '09) A racecar driver tries to outrun a car that is possessed by an angry spirit. Chad Willett, Greg Evigan.				The E
39	66	66	5:30 Scared "Follow-up Special"		Storage Wars	Storage Wars	Storage NY	Storage NY	Storage NY	Storage NY	Storage NY	Storage NY	Stora
58	58	25	MixedBlessings	Animism	Health Nutz	By the Rapids	Bionic Bannock	Contain Nuts	★★★ Don Juan DeMarco Johnny Depp, Marlon Brando.				
31	31	31	5:00 Juste la TV	Comme magie	Pour l'amour du country		Lumière "Béatrice Picard" (N)		Un gars, une fille, une aventure			Un gars, une fille	
130	130	131	Holmes in New Orleans		Property Virgin	Property Virgin	Double Your House		Top Gear		Holmes in New Orleans		Prope
162	162	162	Caitlin's Way	Caitlin's Way	4 O'Clock Club	Horrible His.	K9	K9	Robin Hood	:50 Creature	4 O'Clock Club	Horrible His.	K9
124	124	124	BET Now			BET Now	BET Honors				Music		
153	153	153	Change/ Life	Most Amazing	Quon Dynasty	Extraordinary	Biography Teri Hatcher		I Survived...		Mobsters "The Westies"		Wom
34	69	69	Missing "This Is Your Life"		The Listener "Eye of the Storm"		Castle "Reality Star Struck"		★★ The Wedding Planner Jennifer Lopez.				:15
20	20	36	Enchères	Enchères	Grand Rire de Québec		Grand Rire de Québec		Comédie Club "Réal Béland"		Michel Barrette 1/2		Ench
36	27	62	The Situation Room		CNN Newsroom		MLK: Words/ Changed		Piers Morgan Tonight		CNN Newsroom		MLK:
127	127	127	Match Game	Match Game	Just for Laughs		The Simpsons	The Simpsons	Red, White and Brown		Match Game	Match Game	Just
44	35	35	Vendre ou rén. "Julia et Sub"		Premier flip "Le clan Bradford"		Maigrir/mourir "Mike" Pt. 1 de 2		Défi sucré		Patron clandes. "Mack Trucks"		Mais
37	37	64	Cash Cab	How It's Made	Cash Cab	Cash Cab	Auction Kings	Auction Kings	Canada's Greatest Know it All		Sons of Guns "Jesse James Gun"		Gold
137	137	137	Married, Child	Married, Child	All in Family	All in Family	P. Stranger	P. Stranger	Roseanne	Roseanne	Due South "Odds"		Due
55	216	216	5:40 ★★ Matinee John Goodman.			★★ The Man With Two Brains Steve Martin.			★★★ Bad Boys Martin Lawrence, Will Smith.				★★
160	160	160	Good Luck ...	Really Me	Wizards	Life on Deck	Sonny Chance	So Random!	★★★ Princess Protection Program			★★ The Cheetah G	
102	102	102	Food Factory	Food Factory	Eat St.	Eat St.	Restaurant "Sapori D'Italia"		Chopped "A Gut Reaction"		Chopped		Gotta
107	107	107	Universe "UFO: The Real Deal"		The Universe		The Universe		History of the World in Two Hours				The U
212	212	212	5:30 CKrevia.	:45 Rock and Roll Hall of Fame "2012 Induction Ceremony"					Beyonce: Life Is But a Dream			Boxing HBO World Cha	
29	103	103	Holmes "Headroom Headache"		House Hunters	House Hunters	House Hunters	House Hunters	Income Prop. "Jeff and Kirsti"		Leave...Bryan	Leave...Bryan	Home
47	74	74	Canadian Pickers "Screeched In"		Ice Pilots NWT "Dark Skies"		Air Aces "Gabby Gabreski"		★★★ Saving Private Ryan Matt Damon, Tom Hanks.				
211	211	211	5:10 ★★★ Contagion		★★★ Dolphin Tale Ashley Judd, Morgan Freeman.				★★★ The Lucky One Zac Efron.			:45 The Mechanic Ja	
35	67	67	★★★ Dodgeball: A True Underdog Story Vince Vaughn.				★★ Dude, Where's My Car? Ashton Kutcher.				MuchMusic Countdown		
48	32	32	5:00 ★★★ Le fantôme de l'opéra Minnie Driver, Gerard Butler.				:55 Artiste "Bobby Bazini"		Haute coiffure		Q'viva		Tops,
30	30	30	Le décompte Musique Plus				Danse ou crève!		Snooki	Pauly D	Buzz	Cliptoman	L'ADI
129	129	129	Chicago Fire		NCIS: Los Angeles		NCIS "Royals and Loyals"		Copper "The Empty Locket"		Museum Secrets "The Louvre"		Urba
25	48	63	The National	One on One	Nat. Things "Meet the Coywolf"		5th estate "Runaway Fighter"		The National	Marketplace	Doc Zone "My Thai Bride" (N)		Doc
-	-	218	The Office	The Office	Seinfeld	Seinfeld	★★★ The Bourne Identity Franka Potente, Matt Damon.					★★★ The Bourne U	
19	19	19	La Semaine verte		RDI en direct	Artisans	Découverte		Le Téléjournal	Les grands report		La Facture	Le Té
33	33	33	Sports 30	Hockey 360°	Hockey LNH Flyers de Philadelphie c. Canadiens de Montréal En direct					:45 L'antichambre		Sports 30	Cana
38	38	81	Sportsnet Connected		The Ultimate Fighter		Mixed Martial Arts UFC Barao vs. McDonald				Sportsnet Connected		Poke
232	232	232	Tim McCarver	Seinfeld	The Big Bang	The Big Bang	★ Showtime Eddie Murphy, Robert De Niro.				CSI: Miami "Mommie Deadest"		Lever
201	201	201	Cinéma	:45 Cinq ans de réflexion Jason Segel, Emily Blunt.					★★★★ Ça, c'est mon gars Andy Samberg, Adam Sandler.				★★
40	76	76	★ Deadly Skies Rae Dawn Chong, Antonio Sabato Jr..				Recoil Serinda Swan, Steve Austin.				★★ Iron Man 2 Don Cheadle, Robert		
73	73	73	Housewives Vancouver		Housewives Vancouver		King of the Nerds "Supernerds"		Four Weddings Canada		Teen Wedding	Teen Wedding	Mom
32	70	70	5:00 Twister Valley		Primeval 1/2 cont'd Feb 23		Merlin (N)		Ripper Street (N)		:10 ★★★ The Day After Tomorrow D		
27	39	65	Lottery "Millionaire Bachelor"		Lottery "Janitor Millionaire"		Cake Boss "Road to the Finale"		Cake Boss: Next Great Baker "Vegas Baby!"			Cake Boss	Cake
250	250	250	Magnifica	Magnifica	Wine Trails	Wine Trails	Rhodes Across Italy		Two Greedy Italians		The Godfather		
49	71	71	Detentionaire	★★ Nanny McPhee Returns Maggie Gyllenhaal.					★★ Starsky and Hutch Owen Wilson, Ben Stiller.				
45	34	34	Les Simpson	Têtes-Claques	★★ Anastasia Voix de John Cusack, Meg Ryan.				Les Simpson	American Dad	Family Guy	South Park	Les S
161	161	28	Octonauts	Mike the Kni	Toopy & Binoo	Cat in the Hat	Big Big Friend	Harry	Toopy & Binoo	Mike the Kni	Franklin	Cat in the Hat	Big B
122	122	122	Eat St.	Eat St.	Instant Cash	Instant Cash	Friends	Friends	Friends	Friends	Eat St.	Eat St.	Insta
28	28	60	SportsCentre		Curling Draw 2 Tournament of Hearts Live						SportsCentre		
15	15	37	:55 Champion	Journal FR	GPS Monde	À table!	Variété du samedi soir						TV5
77	77	77	Allan Gregg	The Interviews	Orca Killing School		:05 Ajami Nisrine Rihan, Fouad Habash.				:10 ★★★★ Do the Right Thing Spike		
75	75	75	Gaunda	Dharkan	Sanjha Punjab	Masti	Intezar	Jee Aayan Nu	Des Pardes		Aikam		Taur
101	101	101	Movie	★★ The Break Up Jennifer Aniston, Vince Vaughn.					★★★ The Bounty Hunter Gerard Butler, Jennifer Aniston.				
231	231	231	Living Healthy	Chicago's Best	Two and Half	Friends	Phunny Business: A Black Comedy				WGN News at Nine		30 R
18	44	72	Zoink'd	Splatalot	XBabysitting	Zoink'd	★★ A Cinderella Story Chad Michael Murray, Hilary Duff.				Zoink'd	Splatalot	XBab

FIGURE 8.1 Television guide listings, 2013

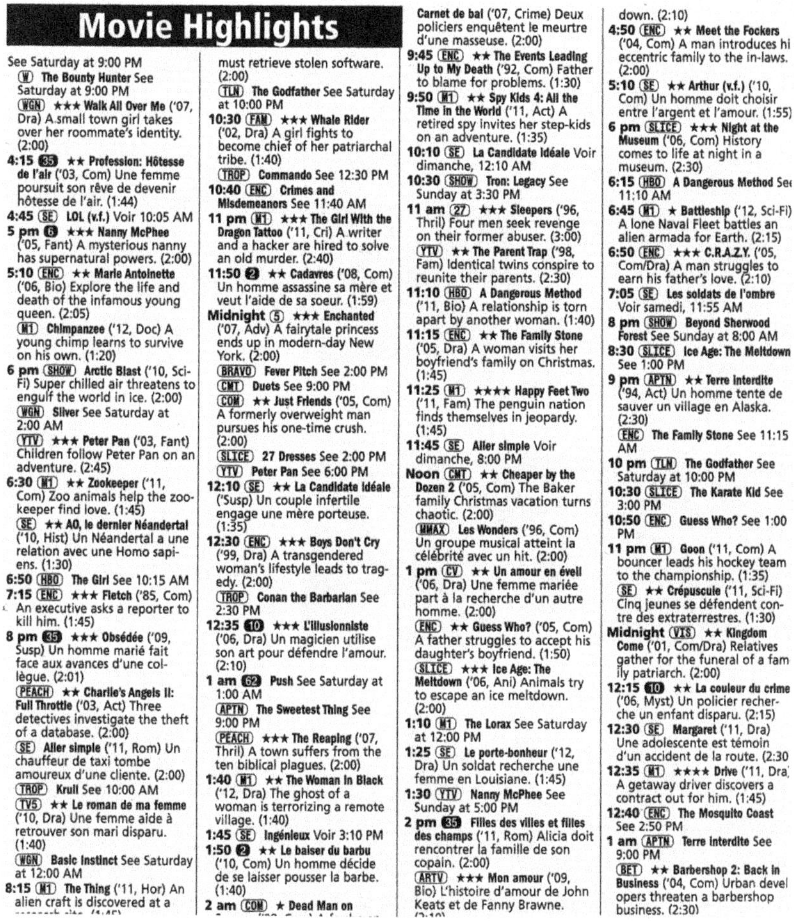

FIGURE 8.2 Television guide movie recommendations, 2013

the same status as a film resource that it did a few decades ago, but the offerings are still there in print or on interactive listings. Here are some entries from 2013: *Goin' down the Road*, three stars, 1970, drama, "two young drifters from east travel to Toronto"; *Klute*, three stars, 1971, suspense, "detective falls for call-girl"; *Permanent Record*, three stars, 1988, drama, "friend plagued by guilt." There is a haiku-like simplicity to these descriptions, and they were once indispensable, even tantalizing, morsels.

The other notable contribution to my formation as a movie-crazed adolescent—less generalizable than the television guide—was Richard J. Anobile's books that reproduced classic films on the printed page, shot by

FIGURE 8.3 Richard J. Anobile's print version of the opening of *The Maltese Falcon*, 1974

shot, with the dialogue appearing as captions under the appropriate image (figure 8.3). These books were like reading a graphic novel, but they decidedly avoided the more cartoonlike renditions of the French variants. These were serious and true to the text, taking a thousand-plus stills to reproduce *Casablanca* (1942), *Frankenstein* (1931), *Stagecoach* (1939), *The Maltese Falcon* (1941), and *Psycho* (1960), and over two thousand for *The General* (1926). Each of these I knew well, having *read* them over and over again—the dialogue, the face of every actor, the composition of every shot—long before I actually *saw* the movies they were depicting. For me, the shower scene, Peter Lorre's face, John Ford's landscapes, these were initially features of the printed page, not the silver screen.

If we take our cue from what Bourdieu said of such practices as transcribing film credits on index cards, these practices and materials are similarly evidence of class reproduction in the training of how taste and culture are to be treated. Again, seeking out what is not taught in school becomes a form of autodidacticism that is ever more necessary as one moves up educational and social hierarchies.[2] As a more recent example, we've clearly just passed the turning point at which the autodidacticism of video gamers can be cashed in as cultural capital; they can be connoisseurs, experts, of something, with a burgeoning scholarly legitimacy that, not long ago, was dismissed and not part of the curriculum. But the more rudimentary point is that these illustrations demonstrate the ordinariness of what might at first seem to be unconventional ways to enter and live with movie culture, namely, through publishing, vernacular inventories, mass-readership newspapers, and television. As someone who has been elated and energized by the promise of the world of movies ever since it hit me that the names of actors and directors were important to remember, I understand deeply the impulse to valorize one's constellation of cinema superstars. But my practices engaged with TV, not the cinematheque, and had more to do with Hollywood's lower genres than international prestigious or personal films, leaving me removed from the orbit of the tasteful cinephile. The ordinariness of the practices described here is an essential part of cultural life. It would grossly misrepresent people's immediate and passionate commitments if we were to ignore them or to see these illustrations as substandard cultural expressions.

The basic elements described here remind us of the material and cross-media determinants of moving-image culture. The observation that cultural expression emerges from varieties of media is even more evident today as we are living through a period in which some conceive of the varieties of moving-image fandom as threats to the wholesomeness of a true love of cinema. Whether as feature films, television shows, or amateur video clips, the easy availability of movies in multiple formats has prompted the presumption that people are indifferent to how they view such works. This view strategically forgets how important television had been in the enlivening of movie culture for decades, though it had to weather charges of being an agent of cultural barbarism. Today convenience is said to be of primary importance, pushing adoption of new media platforms. There are, of course, few things that violate dominant understandings of what art is supposed to be more than the accusation of ease. The true love of cinema is wholesome, robust, and difficult to chew, whereas the new love is nutritionally vacant but convenient fast food. As James Quandt dispiritedly puts it, "the new cinephilia . . . champion[s] ubiquity over purity."[3] Guess which one he approves of. Let us be attentive to the connotations of purity: the pristine, the untouched, the perfect. Any additional element—in this case, ubiquity—must be a move away from that heavenly state.

Accordingly, there has been a veritable industry of cinephilic pleading, horrified at the denigration of the cinematic apparatus at the hands of screen-centered convenience. Pleading of this kind has worked hard to establish the barricades needed to reassert the boundaries between the precious artful medium and those lowly encroaching pixel pretenders. Susan Sontag's 1996 essay "The Decay of Cinema" has been cited as the font for many facsimile essays; it notably turns to suggest that it was in fact cinephilia, and not the cinema, that was in decline in the 1990s.[4] Cinephiles have tended to invest heavily in dreams of decay and loss, and many of them seem entranced by their own poetry, like the tortured romanticist, as though there is a competition for the most ornamental declarations of devotion ("I love you more; no, *I* love *you* more"). Thomas Elsaesser describes this tortured pose as the "disenchantment" that runs wild in the cinephilic imagination. Cinema just keeps letting us down.[5]

Proponents might see the flourishing of essays and books on cinephilia as Minerva's owl taking flight in the gathering dusk, but presumptions of cultural privilege run rampant in cinephilic rhapsodies, making them seem more like the actions of the art-loving bully waving gang colors in the face of the new kid at school. There is no small amount of masculinist territoriality involved in some strains. For this reason, Janet Staiger sees cinephilia as a secret masculinist enterprise, one that displaces the feminized fan-driven affections with the respectability of author-based connoisseurship and relegates women to the domestically situated television set.[6] Aboubakar Sanogo reminds us that for Africans, cinema was entwined with colonialism, freighting cinephilia with an aggressive ideological force.[7] We would have to be utterly blind not to recognize similar colonizing efforts elsewhere. Bourdieu's effective demonstration of the formation of class-based hierarchies through cultural capital can inform our understanding of gender and ethnic divisions. What's love got to do with *that*? Cinephilia has been just as much a license to hate—television, cultureless peoples, Hollywood, low genres, and blockbusters. Why can't "fandom" capture what "cinephilia" references? It can, and should, but the fact remains that most of the voluminous writings about cinephilia don't see it that way.

The roots of cinephilia are found in one of the most lasting dispositions toward art: appreciation. It operates not only to educate and analyze but to set up the terms and rituals of tasteful understanding. Consequently, the cinephilic outlook has worked hard to devalue other sorts of cultural engagements as insufficiently reverential. But the multitude of forms of and occasions for moving-image encounters far outnumber the more reified, and increasingly "museumified," cinema situations. Screen variety and the plentitude of moving images expose and unsettle exclusionary ventures. We have moved far from the counterpoised choice of roadshow and art house. The two volumes of *Cinephilia in the Age of Digital Reproduction: Film, Pleasure and Digital Culture* are symptomatic efforts to take seriously the actuality of multimedia moving-image culture.[8] Elsaesser describes a generationally specific "take two" reboot of cinephilia, which involves the remastering, repurposing, and reframing of images. He describes the new cinephilia of DVDs, the internet, fragments, and textual reworkings, concluding that they have "un-Frenched" more conventional forms of cinephilia. Yes, though the first generation still reigns and brandishes the weapon of the tasteful art over the artless technology. On this count, Jeffrey Sconce's essay "Trashing the Academy: Taste, Excess, and an Emerging Politics of Cinematic Style" remains a key work that opens consideration of a fuller range of film practices to challenge traditional hierarchies of cinema value. His "paracinema" of low genres, cycles, and auteurs is, in the end, an argument about cinephilia and connoisseurship, written through the subcultural fandom of the *Psychotronic Encyclopedia*, the bootleg videotape, the camp classic, and the gory work of Herschell Gordon Lewis.[9]

Elsaesser's generational split is echoed by Francesco Casetti and Mariagrazia Fanchi, who propose a distinction that one version of cinephilia is about textual appreciation and knowledge, invested in rarity, and the other is about technology, which is code for TV/digital formats.[10] But this divide is a messy one, if only because of the long entwinement of cinema and television, and other media, especially at the level of practice. Here, as in other appraisals, Casetti and Fanchi's cinephilia proposes one marked by a residual appellation for medium singularity, where in actuality format variation has been historically dominant.

Of course, one only dreads losing what one truly adores. And the purity of cinema was only ever possible to theorize if the technological apparatus was imagined as essential and stable. Commentary has been populated with work that wonders whether the art of film is a thing of the past. In many ways the cinephile understands that the triumph of moving images has been the death of cinema. Even the most casual digging reveals that concern about impending doom has popped up with surprising regularity throughout the history of the cinematic arts: color versus black and white, Academy ratio versus widescreen, silent film versus synchronous sound, and, of course, the greatest movie killer of all time, television. The most recent rendition, and it has been a deep wound-inducing attack, has been digital cinema's vanquishing of celluloid.

Technological change has been a feature of every conceivable era of cinema history and film fandom. The blockbuster exaggerated the technological dimensions of popular entertainment, bringing them into the center of promotional and business arenas, putting them on display. Our current age of technological instability, in which new platforms seem to redefine our relationship to cultural life regularly, has made the fact of technological and textual mutability even more of a focal point. The contemporary environment of entertainment includes works designed for particular formats but squeezed and stretched into others. Texts are Silly Putty, which for some is an inconsequential cost of convenience and frugality, but for others is an abomination. Either way, some films are produced with paths of media migration in mind, designed to be stretched and squeezed, giffed and guillotined. The result is that media platforms have an accented role in industrial strategy and a higher visibility for audiences. Navigating platform plenitude has made technological reflexivity prominent. One does not watch a movie on an iPad. One watches an iPad showing a movie.

Regardless of the specialized taste formations of cinephiles, and what we call platform plenitude, there has always been a range of spectatorial occasions that must be accounted for whenever we make claims about moving images. "Occasion" refers to the spaces, times, geographies, architectures, mobilities, and distractions that create vastly different kinds of media experiences. The internationalized flows of images and sounds productively trouble efforts to imagine a universal media experience, making the specificity of media occasions all the more central to our analytic purpose. Varied formats, textual features, distribution paths, and viewing experiences don't exist as a set of equally available options; they constitute hierarchies of taste, knowledge, and money, and hence they organize and fortify class formations and power distribution. Configurations of these features become sites for the operation of cultural and symbolic capital, for the reconstruction of hierarchies around technology: theater, home, car, plane, e-cinema, d-cinema, 35 mm, 16 mm, 2K, 4K, HD, DVD, Blu-ray, 3-D, 2-D, frame rate, refresh rate, plasma, LCD, aspect ratio, full screen, letterbox, and on and on. What may be presented as features of consumer choice—with blockbusters and franchises the most purposely built mutable properties—become vectors along which distinctions are made: affordability, access, and prestige.

Taste is something that one wants to defend; it compels one to say, "My taste is beautiful and true; yours is, frankly, embarrassing." Bourdieu lastingly demonstrated that this association with character is an ideological mask for the way taste is in fact a correlate of class position. My argument here is that a Bourdieuian analysis of dispositions toward culture needs to include dispositions toward technology, format, and platform. Cinephile purists may scoff at the contemporary blockbuster, but they still long for the theatrical environment that the blockbuster privileges as a point of entry into cultural life, with its theater-specific state-of-the-art sound and projection systems. Cultural value corresponds to technological specifications. Cinema traditionalists hold a special affection for celluloid, bright projection, sound-controlled settings, and author-authorized digital transfers, and for them cultural value corresponds to technological specifications. In short, *the secret life of the cinephile is that of the technophile.*[11]

Even as it continued the technological exhibitionism of the blockbuster strategy, *Avatar* (2009) played an important contemporary role in advancing consciousness about different formats, beyond the actual development and promotion of new systems for production and exhibition, as seen in the previous chapter. Consider the DVD/Blu-ray collector's edition of *Avatar*. "Extend the journey" is one of the taglines for this second home video release of the film, on November 16, 2010. This journey isn't just a reference to James Cameron's sci-fi blockbuster. It describes the layers of packaging one must deal with to get to the actual discs inside: plastic wrapping, cardboard sleeve, hard cardboard cover, booklike bound folder, and finally pullout tabs for each of the three discs. This object, with its luminescent blue color scheme and images of the film's Na'vi creatures from Pandora—no live-action scenes are reproduced on the packaging—is a jewel box designed to impart a sense of preciousness to an already amply familiar movie. For all the technological sophistication of compressed digital storage to be read by lasers, let's remember the importance of folded cardboard and plastic casings in the augmentation of value.

The DVD release is one of many predictable stops on a journey through the iterative world of moving-image commodities. With regard to the most recent DVD/Blu-ray edition of *Avatar*, "extend the journey" can also be seen as a description of the core business plan for a nascent film franchise, which requires additional films (with more *Avatar* installments reportedly coming after long delays in December 2021, December 2023, and onward) and exploitation of multiple merchandising opportunities. But a new film episode is only one way to expand a blockbuster saga; with this particular DVD/Blu-ray release, we see that the movie itself is elastic. New chapters supplement the original work, such that what we think of as *Avatar* is in fact a mutable and varying entity, a work in progress.

Avatar is not a single finished film with defined boundaries. Though it is not officially the title, much advertising material refers to the movie as *James Cameron's Avatar*, an auteurist conceit that carries the stamp of brand predictability. His name is a guarantor of generic and technological quality. Moreover, the titular presence of Cameron highlights the ongoing involvement of his creative hand. This is *his* film and franchise, and he will do with it what he wishes. Notably on the November 2010 DVD/Blu-ray release, the phrase "director's cut" is nowhere to be seen. This set is the "Extended Collector's Edition." One can confidently assume that there will be a "director's cut" at some point, which means that the textual variations of this particular film are not yet finished. Most obviously, this release did not offer the primary feature of the theatrical releases—3-D—meaning that that capability for home viewing had to wait a bit longer.

The packaging promises that with the DVD we "journey deeper into *Avatar*," not Cameron's fictional universe but *Avatar* the film (figure 8.4). In this way the line hails us to engage more fully with the film as an industrial product rather than directly inviting us back to Pandora with the colonizing Earthlings. Similarly, the outermost sleeve asks us to "experience the complete filmmaker's journey with 3 discs and 3 versions of the film!" This ambiguous statement presents the entire package as a making-of documentary, which it isn't. Nonetheless, with three versions of the film included, among other offerings, this DVD set provides a highly selective window into an ongoing production process.

One of the three versions of the film is the original theatrical release from December 18, 2009 (162 minutes), which had previously appeared as an unadorned DVD on Earth Day (April 22) in 2010 to capitalize on the film's environmental ethos. In a marketing decision indicative of the transition period between DVD and Blu-ray, a two-disc package of both of those formats was also released at that time, which was the only way one could purchase a Blu-ray version. The other two versions of the film on the "Extended Collector's Edition" set are the "special edition re-release," which appeared in theaters on August 27, 2010 (170 minutes), and, exclusive to this set, the "collector's extended cut" (178 minutes). So, by the third version, the film is sixteen minutes longer than the original release. The preference options provide demographically sensitive adaptability: Spanish and French audio tracks in addition to the original English, English and Spanish subtitles, closed-captioning, and a family audio option that removes "objectionable language."

The three versions of *Avatar* are split across two discs. The second disc also includes *A Message from Pandora* (twenty minutes), a documentary short that

FIGURE 8.4 *Avatar* DVD "Extended Collector's Edition" release insert, 2010

chronicles Cameron's involvement with the environmentalist organization Amazon Watch, depicting actions taken against a massive Brazilian dam project, but that does so by establishing parallels between the indigenous people of the Amazon and Pandora's Na'vi. The third disc, called "Filmmakers' Journey" (note the possessive subtly but generously acknowledging the collaborative nature of the enterprise), includes a making-of documentary, *Capturing Avatar* (ninety-eight minutes), as well as forty-five minutes of deleted scenes, that is, *additional* additional footage. These are not bloopers. They are scenes that are "never-before-seen" with "unfinished footage" in various stages of completion. In viewing them, one can extrapolate the extra layers of construction needed to polish each clip—green screens filled in, performance-capture footage fully rendered, and the soundtrack finished. Still, the term "scene" suggests a degree of completeness, making these oddly legitimate parts of the film, or at least of the filmmaking process, despite their lowly "extra" status. What would it take to move these from the hierarchically subordinate third disc to the body of the text? Or are they only ever to appear as adornment to the main feature(s), no matter how mutating and expansive they may be? Certainly, the status of a clip as "never-before-seen" ends with the moment of release. The third disc also conveniently offers in a single location the sixteen minutes of additional scenes added to the main features. One need not wade through each entire version of the film in order to spot what's new.

These clips amount to three hours of additional material in this DVD set. That's nothing. The simultaneously released Blu-ray format of this "Extended Collector's Edition" boasts eight hours of extras, including extensive behind-the-scenes production footage, an archive of production material, and interactive production information, some of which was live for a limited time.

What is this material called "extra footage" and "deleted scenes," now conventional options on DVD/Blu-ray menus? These inclusions differ from other forms of extras in that they are explicitly supplements to the world of the film. If they appear with authorial validation, and are inserted into a film, the new and improved version becomes a more fully realized cinematic vision. Examples include such key moments in contemporary Hollywood as Steven Spielberg's 1980 rerelease of *Close Encounters of the Third Kind*, which featured footage inside the alien mothership at the end that did not appear in the first release, or Ridley Scott's 1992 rerelease of *Blade Runner* (1982) as *the* director's cut. A less successful effort, but one that marked the coming malleability of digital cinema, was George Lucas's digital insertion of creatures and scenes into the 1997 rerelease of *Star Wars: Episode IV—A New Hope* (1977), which, obvious and distracting as they are, look like rub-on transfers of dinosaurs from the bottom of a box of Sugar Crisp.

While these films were theatrical rereleases, as was Cameron's first lengthened edition of *Avatar* a few months after the original release, the storage capacity of DVD and Blu-ray prompts even more ambitious expansions. These formats allow us to buy footage in bulk. Fill the bucket to the brim, and whether you fill it with vinegar or wine is not as important as the sheer volume. The measure of this volume is minutes, and more minutes equal more value.

One template for DVD extras is Criterion's cinephilic material of historical relevance to the artistic value of the main feature. Their edition of *Breathless* (1960) includes a booklet with the film's original treatment, video essays, trailer, and interviews with Jean-Luc Godard and lead actors, as well as a making-of documentary. All these extras bolster the unique and stable work of Godard's masterpiece, presenting it as timeless. Even the transfer is approved by the film's cinematographer, Raoul Coutard, lest cinephiles worry about the digitization of a beloved classic.

But the *Avatar* model puts less stock in the singular prestige of the unified film. Instead, Cameron's endlessly expanding imagination, as represented by the seemingly bottomless archive of filmed material and iterations, is the focus. Both DVD and Blu-ray home entertainment formats sell a peek into the film's production that has resulted in this deep catalogue of footage, a peek that is especially attentive to the newest forms of cinema technology involved, including 3-D shooting and performance capture. In this way the expandable text is a romance with a particular mode of blockbuster cultural production defined by an engagement with new technological materials and processes.

An activist spirit slips out of the film. For all the utterly conventional racial motifs, and its ideological limitations on other counts, *Avatar* is a fable of exploitation and an explicit critique of colonial adventure. As such, it is not surprising to see that it was mobilized by Palestinians to protest Israeli barriers; they dressed and inhaled tear gas as the fictional Na'vi. Canadian and indigenous environmentalists used the popular tale to draw attention to the developing catastrophe of the Alberta oil sands projects, placing a notice in *Variety* to voice support for *Avatar*'s campaign for the Oscar for best picture (figure 8.5).[12] In response, Cameron toured the northern Alberta site. He met with politicians and business leaders who themselves hoped to win Hollywood's blessing for their enterprise. But Cameron did not disappoint the activists, and he has, to date, steadfastly condemned the energy project.

As a dominant theme in *Avatar* that is further evident in the documentary extra *A Message from Pandora*, political engagement has also served as a way to promote the film. Accordingly, newspaper advertising called the "Extended Collector's Edition" a "revolution," a term that simultaneously referred to the uprising depicted in the film, referenced descriptions of *Avatar*'s innovative 3-D filming processes, and described the work that went into the DVD/Blu-ray sets themselves.[13] Part of the November 2010 DVD rerelease was a flyer for "an activist survival guide" book tie-in, which was "a confidential report on the biological and social history of Pandora."

As energizing as the dream of revolution may be, actually at issue is a set of expectations about the importance of technological innovation in moving-image industries. *Avatar*, with an ongoing rerelease schedule that alternates among platforms and an expandable text and paratext, represents a refinement

FIGURE 8.5 Environmentalist promotion of *Avatar* for Academy Awards in order to advance concerns about fossil fuel extraction, 2010

of franchise operations in the context of digital production and distribution. And the value of the new scenes added to a new *Avatar* iteration goes beyond narrative extension, character elaboration, or thematic depth. Amassing more material to cram into the film, or to file away as a sidebar, marks a salient difference from previously available versions, thus warranting the additional release. But it is also evidence of the epic proportions of the production and the capability of digital manipulations of a text. In this way the dominant topic of each rerelease is a celebration of technological processes and the expansiveness of the blockbuster strategy itself.

The dream of theatrical darkness haunts moviegoing. In actuality, moving images have always been experienced with some degree of illumination, even if it was only the projector beam or reflective screen. Auditoriums usually have some level of ambient light as well. Pesky safety requirements keep the reassuring red glow of exit signs peripherally visible throughout screenings. Only the most obscure and exclusive efforts to build the "perfect" black box for film viewing ever came remotely close to the sensory-deprivation idea of the cinematic apparatus imagined by some of the more mystifying strains of film theory. But these fictions were short-lived and had almost no meaningful impact on actual moviegoing.

Some level of illumination has always been the norm, and this is even more so today. The general brightness of our terminally electric era means that film and television programming mostly arrive, and are watched in, well-lit locations, frequently on devices that themselves shine like torches. Cinema has moved definitively into daylight. Daylight—including the artificial daylight of the electrified night—is a permanent and stable part of moving-image entertainment and information, only partially responded to with the dimming of lights in bedrooms and living rooms. And with light comes distraction. Glowing electronic screens populate our sensory field, and the ordinary expectation is that moving-image works will have to battle other competitors for that most precious modern human resource, attention. The bright world tempts with distractions, relentlessly. "Second screens," which became an accepted industry term to reference simultaneous media engagement by television viewers in the early 2000s, seem appropriate to media experience and continuous with the conviction that permanent technological connection has been accepted as a brand of civic and occupational responsibility. Moving images, all images and texts, enter a context that does not shift or alter in any substantive way to accommodate their arrival. Images and sounds are perpetually appearing, a flow that opens up with the miniscule labor of a pushed button. So what? Big deal. Immediacy and convenience in media culture, after all, translate into the blasé.

And yet the dream of darkness, contra this informalization of cinematic wonder, has not vanished. Indeed, this elusive dream may have intensified; it is ever more precious. The dream of darkness, at root, is a technological aspiration, a conception of constructed, mediatized environments. The dream is, after all, about an unencumbered relationship with the screen. It is a contemplative dream of zero distraction. On this count we find "new" expectations for virtual reality, which has been burdened with what in the end is a long-standing, and often retrograde, idea about immersion. Movie theaters prod patrons as forcefully as they dare with pleading notices to turn cell phones off and refrain from texting, to be quiet and respectful. For the technological exhibitionism of the blockbuster strategy to work, theaters must be controlled technological environments. The notices can be sleek and expensive, and can be taken up as a branding opportunity for the theater chain or a corporate partner. Some chains incorporate these requests into their preshow, an increasingly important source of revenue for exhibitors, by first encouraging smartphone usage through trivia games and then, while phones are in hand, asking patrons to turn them off in preparation for the show. Canadian exhibitor Cineplex has done this with their TimePlay app, which allows those present in an auditorium to test their movie knowledge against that of other moviegoers. TimePlay gets audience members to play a range of games, many of which link their questions to current or upcoming movies, thus serving a direct promotional function. It additionally allows Cineplex to collect data about the audience members, to be monetized at some later date. The TimePlay portion of the preshow ends with a request to put the device in your hand away. While surreptitious texters can be witnessed during the screening of films, my experience is that most people actually comply or at least make a genuine effort to do so. After all, everyone present has paid a premium price for this special theatrical situation. Everyone has a relatively comparable incentive to make the most of their investment. The movie theater, in our era, offers a moment of uninterrupted cultural engagement. This temporary retreat from the media web and from the second screen, this momentary cord cutting, is strangely rare. Theatrical moviegoing today is an elaborately orchestrated effort to specify media attention and coordinate this with others who are immediately present, as one shares in a short-lived technological bracketing with fellow patrons. Like the dream of darkness, these procedures work to define and distinguish the situation and the technological elements of the theatrical event.

Film purists and fans elevate, and pine for, particular contours and technological arrangements of cinema in which artificially enforced darkness has a high value. Preshow pleas to participate in the specialness of the theatrical environment—the dream of darkness, the dream of contemplation, and what amounts to a ticket surcharge for theatrical occasions—reveal that these features are a shared ideal. The actuality of broken concentration and multiple appeals for our attention has pushed the focused moving-image situation into the province of luxury. The quiet, respectful, and darkened auditorium, this is how we used to live with and appreciate film, right? Well, no. But no matter, a pleasing warmth radiates from the idea that there was such a time and that there may still be an opportunity to escape the annoyances of immediacy and convenience, of duty to our insistently bright gadgets and what they represent, and to engage and concentrate fully on a carefully crafted work of media culture. Even if technological distraction pulls our attention away, we sense, deep down, that there will be rewards if we can only just watch and listen closely.

The theatrical environment, however, is not itself a technological retreat; it is its own technological system. The big and the loud of theatrical splendor offer an unreproducible experience, even as the same works circulate to different media formats in our brightened homes, offices, and transport. The theater's volume cuts out competing sounds. The colors lock in gazes. Whatever sensory battles are fought at later stages of the audiovisual commodity cycle, here, with the first-run theatrical release of a movie, the spectacular achievement of the big and the loud rules.

What is the state of theatrical splendor? That phrase is a legacy of the movie-palace era a century ago, when the trappings of legitimate theater, the architectural ornamentation, and the prestige of top-dollar prices for middlebrow entertainments all made "splendor" an appropriate descriptor. The Egyptian motifs, the Hellenic forms on painted ceilings, the heralds woven into velvet curtains, and the uniformed ushers together embellished filmed entertainment as worthy of a lavish night on the town. This was exploited most fully with the roadshow and its upscaled blockbuster strategies in the 1950s and 1960s. Such trappings live in the memories of older cinephiles. There are a few venues that still make these efforts—ArcLight Cinemas and

Alamo Drafthouse, for instance—but these tend to be museum, cinematheque, or specialty houses, targeting a select and well-heeled audience of connoisseurs.

The marks of "splendor" today are cup holders and extensive branded concessions, large seats with high backs with stadium raking, extra legroom and curved screens. The branding of the lobby has pushed the precinema space of the theater closer to the food court and the arcade. On your way to your auditorium, you walk through a garden of cardboard advertisements and electric signage. Minimum-wage theater employees take tickets, casually direct patrons to the appropriate screen, and conduct narrowly defined problem solving (e.g., helping locate a bathroom, finding a lost hat or child). Anything involving the actual quality of the screening requires more specialized intervention. Employees are engaged as cleanup crews who quickly sweep the auditorium between screenings. And with minimal labor rights protections, and precarious subcontracting, the people who clean theaters at the end of the day can be paid less than minimum wage, work unreasonable hours, and enjoy no job benefits like sick leave and holidays.[14] Splendor, it seems, is a close cousin of tidy and exploitative.

The features of the megaplex cinema—the most costly form of mainstream audiovisual entertainment—are not distinct from what one might expect at an upscale mall or theme park: cleanliness, comfort, easy flow of people, and shared orientation (in the theater's case, a movie screening). "Splendor" seems less and less like an appropriate term to describe theatrical environments, even the most expensive of them. "Comfort" is more accurate.

We still marvel at the same scientific tricks that we did more than a century ago: the magic of electricity, the unsettling experience of images animated, the auditory hallucination of hearing absent voices. As naturalized, normalized, and miniaturized as these aspects may be—after all, they populate the most mundane and unmagical facets of daily routine today—the sheer strangeness and delight moving images and distant sounds can generate prompt a spark of recognition of magical possibility. While we may attend theatrical film screenings with decreasing frequency, happy as we are with our personalized and insulated media spaces, sufficient numbers continue to return to the cinema and the theme park to make these sound cultural economic sectors. We do so for many reasons, one of which is to surrender to technological wonder. The app store provides miniaturized versions of moving-image and audio wonder, but smartphones will never engulf collectives in the sensory tidal wave that auditorium-size media performances do.

The particularities of the theater, of these movie-specific public-performance situations, are located in the technological and architectural structures of that media environment. These features include plush seats; subdued auditory cushioning; a curved screen; clear sight lines; fully operational high-resolution projectors; computer control of the volume, lights, and temperature; and sound systems with speakers and directionality that can be experienced virtually nowhere else. As such, cinemas are built to present the most complete manifestation of the contemporary motion picture sound and image. They are environments in which one experiences directly and purposefully state-of-the-art audiovisual technology, and as such they try to bring us face-to-face with a technological sublime. The technological motors of this sublime are on display, just as they are themselves vehicles for display and cinematic performance. In short, the blockbuster—the big, the loud, the expensive, the spectacular—is an economic and aesthetic form suited to that environment and to the advancement of that technological system.

Blockbuster movies are built to be wondrous. Joyous, terrifying, dramatic, or revelatory. Whatever emotional impact they actually produce, they appeal to awe and wonder. Blockbusters are at home in movie theaters. They are cultural forms that are produced explicitly and deliberately with that location in mind. Audiences, producers, and distributors accept that works are viewed at home and on less-than-epic screens by larger numbers of spectators. Still, the orchestration of a filmed entertainment for cinemas, for out-of-home viewing, for temporarily limited access and availability, for time-sensitive exclusivity, remains a foundational part of the American movie business and its blockbuster strategy. For everything else that it did and signaled, *Avatar* was a conscious declaration of faith in the theatrical specificity of the blockbuster, as were *Star Wars: Episode VII—The Force Awakens* (2015), *Wonder Woman* (2017), *Avengers: Endgame* (2019), and so on.

Blockbusters, more than any other type of entertainment, are designed to premier at and feature the theatrical environment. This environment boasts of audio, projection, and architectural elements that are rarely found elsewhere, if at all. The theatrical setting is a showroom for future technology, for the future of media experiences. Surely, not all futures presented take off as standard for cinemas and then later in more quotidian settings. But the idea that the state-of-the-art cinemas, the prestige venues, display the best of our technological innovations alongside new films, themselves built to feature the technological architecture of theaters, has been a lasting and stable part of popular cinematic entertainment, most explicitly foregrounded in the rise of the blockbuster strategy in the 1950s, as we saw in earlier chapters. The exhibition industry orients a good deal of its energy toward conceptualizing, renovating, and promoting special aspects of the theatrical setting. The elaborate branding of the features—special seats, sound systems, projectors, resolutions, speeds, aspect ratios, concessions, services, and comforts—helps exhibitors in the pursuit of distinction among competing media and entertainment options.[15] An overall impression is that when entering the media space of the contemporary cinema, we enter a forward-looking manifestation of technological promise.

I expect you can see that I have a particular idea about motion picture exhibition in mind. There are plenty of terrible, substandard, and downright shoddy exhibition venues. Many can make you long for your home viewing context, where you have more immediate control over the volume and program. I write here of the mainstream first-run theater chain, which is essentially the most costly, most exclusive, and least accessible of cinema venues. They are a widely exported ideal, as in the aggressive international wave of megaplex building from the mid-1990s onward, which radically increased the screens and services at single theatrical locations, attempted to control the quality of the commercial cinema experience, and in the process made moviegoing more in tune with event-movie distribution.[16] Big multiscreen theater locations are plentiful enough to count as ordinary parts of urban life: more plentiful than theme parks but less plentiful than museums and art galleries. Additionally, efforts to standardize screening quality have been an ongoing part of the operation of chains, and they succeeded in making flagship sites the gold standard for quality in the film business today, worldwide.

I address the variety of media formats and occasions, of which the theatrical context is itself a varying set of conditions and experiences, in order to emphasize a position that runs in opposition to those who suggest that the specificities of format are immaterial to contemporary media entertainment. David Denby decried the conditions of "platform agnosticism," describing it as emblematic of the deteriorating value of the theatrical setting for motion pictures.[17] "Platform agnosticism" has been taken up and repeated by critics, scholars, and fans alike, and cinema traditionalists are alarmed. Yet there is no evidence for it. In fact, all evidence points to the contrary. Many media entertainment decisions surely conclude that it does not matter how a particular title is seen, whether it is broadcast on TV, streamed on a tablet, or viewed via a DVD borrowed from a library. But behind every lineup at a film's opening night, every moviegoer sitting cramped in a thick crowd or sprawling out over several seats at a poorly attended screening, and every date or special occasion that ends up at a multiplex, there is a calculated and deliberate decision that the theatrical screening situation is the one that matches the needs of the moment. Those needs could be social ("I didn't pick this movie, but everyone else wants to go") or more directly aesthetic ("THIS is a big-screen movie"), or the choice could reflect an absence of other options ("I need to get out of the house, but what can I do? Okay, I'll see a movie"). These conclusions contain some vague conceptualization of the difference between movie theaters and other venues. Whereas so many scholars and critics have downplayed the significance of medium specificity, I propose that a more detailed and direct accounting for the varying qualities of media occasions is appropriate. The interchangeability and plenitude of formats have magnified the differences between media occasions, not erased them.

Among the features of that "future-oriented" technology platform called the movie theater, first and foremost is the fact that moviegoers find themselves sitting in a land of giants. In front of them, above them, are giant faces and sweeping vistas, giant hands and planetary realizations, giant eyes and city streets. Nothing is small in a movie theater, even in the tiny and nearly extinct multiplex screening rooms from the 1980s. For a blockbuster, the small is either not there or it works as a counterpoint to the appearance of an even larger entity. Plates of pasta, fingernails, acorns, microchips, car wheels, paper clips, seagulls—whatever appears, it appears to be immense. Close-ups can be truly grotesque inflations of scale. Even tiny specks—a battleship on the horizon—communicate extreme distance and the impossible expanse of deep space.[18]

The price of admission, then, includes a tour of the land of giants, a visit to a strange superhuman country. It is also a peek at the miraculous machinery realizing this giganticism. Moviegoers effectively experience their own diminished state and the celebration of the creative and technological prowess that generates this imagistic world that is so much greater than our own. Outside the theater, when we watch at a subtheatrical scale on television, computers, tablets, and smartphones, we access but the suggestion of this sensory awesomeness. Narrative and character may be presented intact. But their relationship to the state of the art of filmed entertainment—more precisely, to reigning ideas about the state of the art—is only intimated. Subtheatrical contexts are marvels of state-of-the-art distribution, but not of sound and image.

Home theaters attempt to reproduce theatrical giganticism with ever more booming sound systems and bigger monitors. Typically, large electronic devices cram into rooms designed for family life, obscuring windows and personalized decor. As a result, off-balance, large flat-screen monitors colonize wall space and hover precariously over human-scale furnishings, except for the most expansively wealthy who can afford to devote theater-size space to their personal screening rooms. The overstuffed electronic domestic deck is not just an aesthetic matter; the number of children injured by falling television sets has risen sharply since the rush to larger flat-screen sets began in the early 2000s. The U.S. Consumer Product Safety Commission reported in 2012 that falling television sets had killed two hundred children since 2000 and injured eighteen thousand people a year.[19]

Movies participate in the organization of the experience of scale. Roland Barthes wrote "The Romans in Films" in the early 1950s, commenting on *Julius Caesar* (1953) and "the label of Roman-ness," specifically noting the fringed haircuts and the sweating, gleaming bodies of the actors in this American production. He concluded that they produced a "degraded spectacle, which is equally afraid of simple reality and of total artifice."[20] The film tries to strike a balance between the intellectual and the visceral but ends up producing "a duplicity which is peculiar to bourgeois art . . . a hybrid, at once elliptical and pretentious, which is pompously christened 'nature.'"[21]

The focus of Barthes's commentary is a middlebrow adaptation of Shakespeare's celebrated play, a black-and-white rendering that conveyed its dramas with stagey composition and few epic vistas. But the observations extend to the grander biblical epics of *The Ten Commandments* (1956) and *Ben-Hur* (1959), in which religious contemplation and political intrigue blend with gleaming skin and the American authority of Charlton Heston's profile, accent, and stubble.[22] Buried in the splendors of cinematic immensity are tiny suggestions of humanness that make the sensory palette move between overwhelming vistas and delicate intimacies. The film epic is not only a "land of giants"; it is a movement or relationship between large and miniature scales of representation.

The contemporary blockbuster's version of Barthes's "elliptical and pretentious" hybrid is the humor of deflation. Lucas, Spielberg, and virtually all the major figures of post-studio-era blockbuster Hollywood—with the possible exception of Cameron—rely on instances of light humor that peek through even the most portentous scenes. Spielberg has been appropriately identified as a heavy user of "eyes of wonder" shots. His special-effects set pieces typically include cuts to diegetic spectators, wide-eyed and open-mouthed as they (pretend to) witness the same stunning event that the audience sees. *Close Encounters of the Third Kind* is replete with scenes of this kind, encompassing major and minor characters. Expressions of awe, faces reflecting the glowing lights of the phenomenon before them, mirror and prompt audience experiences. These inserts place our characters in the same space as the cinematic effect as it unfolds, putting them on the same physical scale, dumbstruck by the marvels they observe. Seeing their responses is a form of verification for the spectacle, which, thus, doesn't unfold for the spectator alone but for the characters, too. It naturalizes the visual and auditory effect, inflates the scene, and depicts the wonder it has been designed to spark. Diegetic audience cuing the nondiegetic audience turns the externalization of wonder into part of the proceedings, not simply a consequence of them.

The humor of deflation is another technique with a different impact, one that does not support the spectacle but undercuts it, transforms it into an opportunity for ridicule, brazenness, or cowardice. Deflationary humor also winks at the audience, saying, "I'm with you in your assessment of how absurd this is." It releases the tension, and it rescues the spectator from a possibly humiliating total identification with the absurd and the fake. Analogously, Siegfried Kracauer said that the ornamentation of the movie palace of the 1920s was "to rivet the viewers' attention to the peripheral, so that they will not sink into the abyss," and that details in the architectural design were "like *life buoys*."[23] Where Kracauer's life buoys distract from the realist pull of narrative cinema, and have affinities with Brechtian distanciation, the small joke/big spectacle situation nudges attention to human scale apart from spectacular display.

The Platonic instance is perhaps Butch's fight with a challenger over who would lead the Hole in the Wall gang in *Butch Cassidy and the Sundance Kid* (1969). Just as rules are being laid down for the fight, Butch surprisingly kicks his opponent in the testicles and quickly finishes the contest. The suddenness of the kick, and the cut-on action to a long shot showing the recipient keel over in pain, perfectly captures the cheeky irreverence and underhandedness of the character, as well as the easy repartee between Butch and Sundance as they improvise on the rules of the fight to Butch's advantage. Variations of this physical repartee appear in other American films: Indiana Jones (Harrison Ford) lazily dispatching a sword-wielding would-be attacker with a single pistol shot in *Raiders of the Lost Ark* (1981); Steve Hiller (Will Smith) punching an alien senseless in *Independence Day* (1996). There is no nobility in these heroes, only the trickster dispatching his challenger efficiently, if brutally. The character type is that of the American slacker rebel saying, "Who cares? Whatever."[24]

Comic violence is only one path followed by deflationary humor. A notable example is in *Jaws* (1975), when Hopper's response to Quint's easy crushing of a beer can is to crush a Styrofoam cup dramatically. The action pokes fun at Quint's masculine display, shows Hopper's evasion of the challenge, and winks at the audience. It is also an instance, as Tom Shone has observed, in which we see improvisational and naturalistic acting at work. Spielberg gave room in the film for such idiosyncratic characterizations and ironic counterpoint alongside the shocks of the thrill ride. Effectively, even as *Jaws* discarded middlebrow cultural value for genre entertainment, it still kept hints of it in the acting.[25] Cheap and corny one-liners in the face of extreme dangers operate on a similar wavelength, melding irreverence with bravado. These small moments deflate the epic proceedings with a contrasting human-scale attitude. They equally bolster a character type that used to be found on the fringes of an ensemble as comic relief but that is now more centrally figured, often in the primary hero: the American smart aleck. "Yippee-ki-yay." There was a time when the American rebel occupied a more existentialist and critical position, but the American smart aleck is far less disruptive and is ultimately invested in maintaining or restoring a broken or threatened community. A conservative ethos seeps into the proceedings. Everyone on the *Orca* wants to kill the shark and make Amity Island's beaches safe for citizens and vacationers; everyman John McClane from *Die Hard* (1988) wants to free the hostages, return the corporate tower to its rightful owners, and save Christmas and his marriage; and narratives of alien invasion—including the "Transformers" series, *Independence Day*, and *War of the Worlds* (2005)—invariably represent saving the world as saving a vision of American family life led by "ordinary" men.

Nonetheless, gentle obnoxiousness places the American smart aleck in a realm slightly apart from the conventions implied by the tale that is unfolding. The irreverence, the "whatever," points to the proceedings of the story, as though the multimillion-dollar set pieces can only elicit a "blah" response. The American smart aleck, the blasé face of perpetual dissatisfaction, is the inverse of the faces of wonder, though they can appear in the same film, even the same scene. The smart alecks present themselves as cool, distancing themselves from the million-dollar sound-and-light shows that, in the end, are crowd-pleasing extravagances and are often precisely the reason audiences have gathered together. They expose a sequence as recognizable and then signal to the audience this recognition. They say, "We are in the know. We are on the same page."

Though the smart aleck gets center stage, we must not lose sight of the fact that blockbusters conventionally draw out a communitarian spirit. So the contemporary blockbuster might be better described as the education of the American smart aleck. Our leads, usually white men or a surrogate family of diverse smart alecks (the "Marvel Cinematic Universe" and "The Fast and the Furious" films, for instance), are awakened to the necessity of acting in order to benefit others. The roguish Indiana Jones is a prime exhibit as a rugged individualist, beholden to no one, and yet, simultaneously, a teacher, a champion of historical value, a colonial plunderer, and a committed interventionist for nationalist American purposes. Han Solo travels on similar terrain.

The Bourne Identity (2002) provides an illuminating counterexample. It emphasizes a step-by-step realist approach to action in order to depict to full advantage how our confused title character gets through each challenge. The tamping down of bravura shortcuts means the film progresses without the expected character flair. Following an exciting car chase through the streets of Paris—notably he drives a Mini Cooper and not a souped-up racer—Bourne and his passenger arrive in a parking lot. Consider how few chaotic car chases resolve in a parking space, with the vehicle parked in an orderly and appropriately positioned manner. There is a beat, an extended quiet moment, and this is where the audience expects the smart-alecky one-liner to appear. It doesn't come. The effect is positively shocking. Bourne says robotically that they can never return to the car, after which is more step-by-step planning. To underplay the moment in this way runs absolutely counter to audience expectations for blockbuster action and lead character responses to that action.

Exceptions notwithstanding, the smart aleck has become the prime example of what appears to be the most elevated form of evaluation for contemporary culture: relatability, which is our version of what Barthes called "nature" in "The Romans in Films." Here, naturalism is not about Bourne-like seriousness. Instead, American naturalistic acting with its slouching posture, slurred diction, casualness, and realist cinematic techniques—designed to appear observational and unobtrusive for whatever strange and implausible events are being depicted—has become a vehicle to validate snappy, irreverent, immodest, and mildly disrespectful behavior. To relate to a character and their behavior is to imagine a responsive parallelism. What distinguishes relating from identifying? To identify, one is drawn out of one's life, into the temporary conditions of an Other. To relate, one applies a familiar set of normative experiences, drawing the representational figure into one's own life. Valuing relatability in realist cinema is a way to naturalize depictions as obvious and true, timeless and sensible, while deflating the drama to a scale matching an impression about what is everyday and what is not.

In this respect, relatability is a powerful ideological purveyor of hidden norms. It is especially prominent in post-studio-era Hollywood, perhaps a convenient outgrowth of the myth-deflating New Hollywood films, where the point of view of the little person in historical situations made the antihero a fine volley against a larger oppressive system. Examples include *Easy Rider* (1969), *Little Big Man* (1970), *McCabe and Mrs. Miller* (1971), and *Shampoo* (1975), all New Hollywood classics, with the antihero/little man representing generational complaint. But it extends to the more conspiratorially minded of that era's tales, including *Chinatown* (1974), *Parallax View* (1974), *Three Days of the Condor* (1975), *Winter Kills* (1979), and *All the President's Men* (1976). Here the hapless but ethically superior smart aleck is swept away by the machinations of closed organizational powers. Each protagonist is a midlevel employee, doing his job as a journalist, CIA bureaucrat, or small-business owner, as with the detective agency in *Chinatown*, but they soon find out that greater and complex forces bind their ability to act decisively and effectively. Only Redford is able to eke out successful disruption in *Three Days of the Condor* and *All the President's Men*, both times with full reliance on that most American of institutions, the Fourth Estate.

In many ways, the smart aleck is a primary mode of American masculine ordinariness. Smart alecks are not defined as extraordinarily talented, whether physically or mentally. They are the Richard Dreyfuss and Dustin Hoffman nebbish, the Jack Nicholson humorous jerk, and the Harrison Ford and Bruce Willis smirker. For a younger generation, our nebbishes are hobbits (Sean Astin, Elijah Wood), our humorous jerks are Johnny Depp and Robert Downey Jr., and basically everyone else is a version of the smirker (Mark Wahlberg, Will Smith, Hugh Jackman, Vin Diesel, Dwayne Johnson, Angelina Jolie, etc.). Those last two aside, most leading actors appear as audience representatives precisely because they portray accessibility and are easily imagined as part of one's life as relatives, friends, and intimates. Robert Redford, Warren Beatty, and Denzel Washington were always exceptions, given how much of their star personas are meshed with an idea of beauty and seriousness. Contemporary versions of these ethical beauties are Jennifer Lawrence, Matt Damon, Ben Affleck, and Tom Cruise, who all stand out as predictably sincere figures and generally humorless action heroes, unless they are specifically doing shtick. These figures are personifications of an American idea of liberalism, ethical fortitude, and civic responsibility. Smart-alecky behavior in boys is endured and accepted, even encouraged, and the few women performers who have taken this up (say the blockbuster comedy stars Melissa McCarthy, Amy Schumer, and Kristen Wiig) show that there is a gendered challenge to be made. Smart-alecky behavior is mostly an expression of entitlement as a tolerated minor disruption that goes unchecked. Smart alecks are not antiheroes; they are charmingly obnoxious but harmless pains in the ass. When such behavior appears in adults, we have cooled the seriousness of a critical and contradictory voice, making it juvenile and cute. Dennis the Menace becomes the urtext for post-studio-era blockbuster masculinity. Break stuff, indiscriminately and spectacularly, but expect an affectionate pat on the head. The ur-joke is, "Sorry about the window, Mr. Wilson. Can I have my ball back?"

The age of blockbuster superheroes has changed some of this, but much of the smart aleck continues. Testosterone-injected stories are designed to feature muscle and mayhem alongside humanizing jokes and one-liners. Arnold Schwarzenegger, Sylvester Stallone, Bruce Willis, Vin Diesel, Robert Downey Jr., Milla Jovovich, Keanu Reeves, and Dwayne Johnson all smirk their way through even the most punishing of set pieces. Christian Bale, Ben Affleck, Henry Cavill, and Brandon Routh are more focused on dour seriousness for their superhero characterizations. Partly a function of the DC universe, but also a function of their neogothic treatment in recent films, they bend away from the ordinariness of the blockbuster hero toward the extraordinary epic masculine protagonist. They suggest superhuman, even divine, connections and float aloft above humanity. Director Zack Snyder, involved in the production of many of the DC universe film installments, commits the contemporary blockbuster sin of taking his subject matter too seriously. Gal Gadot in *Wonder Woman* (2017) changed only a little of this, despite the gender flip of the superhero, shuffling smart-aleck duties to Chris Pine's character. These DC characterizations are closer to the religious epics of the 1950s, and they are examples of what Susan Sontag called "fascinating fascism."[26]

The key point here, and the reason I've spent time on this discussion, is that the American smart aleck is a distancing device, moving the character ever so slightly out of the film world, not quite breaking the fourth wall with a direct acknowledgment of the viewer but knocking on it, drawing audience attention to it. The attitude invites the viewer to share with the character the experience of representational excesses. Like a tour guide, with a smirk and a wink and a shoulder shrug, the American smart aleck points out the attractions of CGI, physical-effect, and narrative ostentation. The smart aleck assures we don't miss those signposts of our sublime creative, industrial, and technological world that realizes the moving-image performance.

The event movie arrives as an obligation, exhaling an air of self-importance. One must see this film or that film. If you see one film this year, this one or that one is it. The historical moment requests attention from all, and if you are to be au courant, then attendance, or at least an opinion, is required. Calls for civic participation and duty are seen in many forms of cultural practice, so this summons is not unique. Most prominent today is "quality" television, in which conversations seem to circle back to a relatively narrow band of supposedly abundant outstanding works. There is a darker command behind the vaguely authoritarian must-see popular entertainment, pointing to forms of widespread, even global, synchronization in cultural life. Sean Cubitt observed something comparable, concluding that we were experiencing "a shift from cultural capital to consumer discipline."[27] Cubitt continued, "The obligation to consume communication (rather than to communicate) supersedes citizenship, even economic exchange, as pure being."[28]

This obligation extends to the infrastructure. One consumes not only the event but also the technological elements that constitute its eventness: the sound system, the star system, the cinema system, the distribution system, and so on. The "elliptical and pretentious" figure of the smart aleck is a dominant trope in blockbusters that humanizes, makes "relatable," this environment. It is both a part of and above the spectacle. Platform plenitude proffers everywhere entertainment, and with it, the hardware of display devices is experienced as a modern necessity. Cinephilic modes of engagement provide a language of distinction among platforms, connecting connoisseurs to historical hierarchies of cultural value while hiding their own investment in the infrastructure their taste supposedly can see through—"just another predictable artless blockbuster." One might challenge Cubitt to say that our newer forms of social media have been emancipatory in their capacity to encourage expression and communication rather than consumption of messages. But this is a limited response, and the so-called democratic potential of social media has been smothered by the promotional, branding, and commercial exercises that circumscribe the world building of the biggest platforms. Neobaroque cinema has stretched into neobaroque commercial publics. The obligation, and display performance, of participation—have a Facebook profile, subscribe to Twitter, join LinkedIn, subscribe to Netflix, shop on Amazon, listen to Spotify, build a YouTube channel, meet via Zoom—is in fact an obligation to participate in our own consumer discipline. Motion pictures have been major contributors to our acceptance of the inevitability of this version of technological society, and none more so than the American blockbuster with its appended formats and theatrical accouterments. The blockbuster convention of jokey deflations diminishes the absurdities of manufactured spectacle, making the technological apparatus pleasing and appear to be benign.

(EPILOGUE)

EXHAUSTED ENTERTAINMENT

American blockbuster movies have played a key role in debates about film and popular entertainment, art and commerce, since the 1950s. In one respect, they are vanguard manifestations of the state-of-the-art moving-image spectacle. They do not represent the totality of movie culture; they are but one circuit of motion picture entertainment, and there is a myriad of alternatives, generic and geographic, to the blockbuster's international style. But the American blockbuster has been set up as the most highly capitalized embodiment of what is possible with moving-image entertainment. They are supremely engrossing, wonderous, and fun. Communities can be sparked to celebrate and challenge, to rework and enjoy, the movies that come and go and the franchises that never stop. Blockbusters are equally evidence of everything that is wrong with commercial culture, and are products of the stunted imagination that comes with huge moneyed interests in cultural commodities: predictability, built on spurious and pseudoscientific interpretations of audience desire, and shaped in relation to the return on investments, asset growth, and brand extensions. They are worthy of emotional engagement, and they are soulless distractions. This range of evaluations and apparent contradictions maps our contemporary sensibilities about pleasure and critique in popular culture.

Toward the end of the summer season of 2016, a season that did not meet the typically inflated box-office expectations, a twist on the persistent theme of cinematic disappointment appeared. Instead of the death of the cinema—the technology, the culture, the art—popular and industry observers began to write about the death of the movies.[1] Audiences, so the reasoning went, were tired of sequels—"sequelitis" was one diagnosis—and time-tested popular filmmakers like Steven Spielberg couldn't guarantee a hit, as seen in the reportedly poor performance of *The BFG* (2016).[2] And there was so much on television to watch. In fact, the abundance of exceptional shows available at home—HBO's *The Night Of* (2016) and Netflix's *Stranger Things* (2016–) earned repeated mentions, but there was a healthy supply of other lauded titles, too—seemed to be a root cause of the dwindling audience and box-office numbers. No longer was television stealing moviegoing audiences because it was free and convenient; it was stealing them because it was better. Still, by the end of the year, at $11.3 billion, *2016 was the biggest domestic box-office year of all time*.[3] The persistence of disappointment is so engrained that even historic levels of revenue generation are an afterthought. Financial expectations echo perennial dissatisfaction: blockbusters make money, but shouldn't they make more?

A similar dynamic unfolded in 2019, when in the context of continuing industrial complaints about declining moviegoing, *Avengers: Endgame* (2019) and its astonishing revenue generation demonstrated, yet again, the potential for massive interest in theatrical screenings and the economic vitality of the "Marvel Cinematic Universe," which Disney used as one of the technological tentpoles to launch their Disney+ streaming service in November 2019. After only a few months in release, *Avengers: Endgame* became the highest grossing theatrical release of all time, with a take of nearly $2.8 billion worldwide.[4] Martin Scorsese used that franchise to decry the detrimental cultural impact of blockbusters, declaring that they are not cinema. He valorized instead, predictably enough, an auteurist cinema, one that he suggested had at least found a new home with streaming services.[5] The anxiety about the loss of a tasteful middle—what were called in-betweeners in the 1950s—continued to be voiced, echoing Scorsese, with again blockbusters identified as the culprit for greedily occupying so much theatrical real estate.[6]

The standard frames for the most visible and lucrative franchises may describe their creative feats as world building, but they spend a good deal of screen time engaged in world destroying. "Harry Potter," "Avatar," "Star Wars," "James Bond," "Star Trek," "Hunger Games," "Marvel Cinematic

Universe," and so on provide multifilm, global- or interplanetary-scale dramas in which the lead characters and entire civilizations are taken through existential threats and punishing demolitions. Franchises literalize "creative destruction," representing a popular management slogan related to radical business upheaval as citywide, countrywide, or planetwide conflagration. Susan Sontag's essay "The Imagination of Disaster," from 1965, speaks with remarkable precision to this aspect of the American blockbuster of today. In it, she focused on the contrasting scale of national and global military emergencies depicted in science fiction film, mostly the alien monster kind, and the individualized human dramas and ethical simplicity that ensue. She offered a generic formula that included (1) the arrival of a "thing"; (2) confirmation of the hero's understanding of the situation; (3) declaration of a national emergency, as the authorities jump into action; (4) atrocities but, most important, danger to the hero's family and/or girlfriend; and (5) a final strategy using some ultimate weapon, though the endings hint at the possibility that more atrocities may still come.[7] This broad structure replays in so many blockbusters, and in virtually every superhero movie, where the ultimate weapons can be the superheroes themselves, which can have the effect of taking the mystery out of the proceedings as the audience sits and waits for the superhero to be, well, super. The five-part formula Sontag identified was made strikingly appealing by advancing cinematic techniques, all the better to realize the sights and sounds of destruction. And she saw the structure and aesthetic as providing a simplified moral choice that allowed extreme actions—whether use of atomic weaponry, widespread warfare, or experimental scientific means—to be taken without consideration of their full consequences. Invariably, "a technological view" is reinforced, in which solutions to emergency situations can be resolved with fast deployment of technological force.[8]

This technological view is an argument about the promise of the triumph of technology that supplements the blockbuster strategy more generally. Not only do we witness spectacular displays of technological resolutions to world-threatening conflicts, but these technological priorities have been embedded in exhibition contexts, modes of production, mechanics of circulation, and blockbuster paratexts. The blockbuster strategy is at the center of American moving-image entertainment, morphing products into an extensive multimedia lifecycle that reinforces technological infrastructure as much as it promotes particular franchise story worlds. While commentary laments the loss of the tasteful middle due to blockbuster aesthetics and economic rationale, in the process advancing a conventional cultural hierarchy, the deep ideological work of popular movie culture of the last seventy years continues: the normalizing and stabilizing of our technological infrastructure.

The technological society we inhabit has been built and fortified with concerted economic, scientific, philosophical, and cultural work. Expectations for better conditions for existence, a less cumbersome lot in life, and a more healthy and productive world shared by more people have kept hopes in the possibilities of progress high. But blind faith in technology's ability to serve up those ideals has periodically led to tremendous horrors. Lewis Mumford's late-career critiques revealed the technological obsessions of contemporary society, where "machine-mindedness" has blotted out our understanding of actual human progress.[9] The perpetual failure to realize those dreams of human and planetary advancement, and the introduction of even more complex environmental and ethical problems, has not decelerated the drive toward innovation and the faith in progress. We have taken for granted that remaking our world with new materials and ideas, however untested, is worth the risk.

No single force has created and re-created the technological society, but our popular entertainment has been a compelling motor for legitimization. Popular forms tell us stories about progress, demonstrate new social arrangements, and display technological promise. And they do so even when productively, sometimes radically, critiquing and unsettling the ideological certainty of technological progress. This is because, in consuming popular forms, we are invited to play and experiment with new devices and to experience changing versions of the pastimes and pleasures we seek. Legitimizing technological society is not the only thing entertainment does; it also inspires, energizes, gives us reasons to live and hope, and provides us with tools for critique. Yet, through our enjoyment, we find ourselves adapting to the very conditions we may wish to keep at bay.

In the arena of technological display, motion pictures have been influential since their earliest years as a medium of mass entertainment. A product of nineteenth-century mechanical innovations, and a source of experiential wonder, movies became a deliberate focal point for technological exhibitionism, a feature that entered a new phase of format spectacularization in the 1950s. The movies, and most specially movie exhibition contexts, have been akin to localized versions of world's fairs and industrial exhibitions, demonstrating a technological structure that did not yet exist elsewhere. The second- and third-tier theatrical circuits—the decrepit auditoriums, the torn or bug-ridden seats, the suspiciously sticky floors, the poorly tended image—may be the most familiar movie conditions for many. But every motion picture era produced a premier, showcase tier of cinema environment, one designed to be married to new productions that themselves have been designed for those high-end spaces. With color processes, synch sound, large screen size, stereo sound, 3-D, elevated frame rates, high-definition digital projections, and so on, one stratum of movie theaters has been, and continues to be, made up of future-oriented halls of technology and marvels of new media.

The blockbuster became the dominant Hollywood form for this function after World War II, and it has, with some bumps in the road, remained there ever since. And with this dominance, the story of the blockbuster movie was also the story of the settlement of movie-based technological exhibitionism. On this topic, J. P. Telotte has explored the technological orientation of Disney, showing their long engagement with cinematic innovations, television, and theme parks. And while Disney has been especially vigorous in its balanced pursuit of new technology and nostalgia, Telotte understood how widespread the links between entertainment and technology had come to be. He wrote, "Examining that Disney negotiation with technology as a pattern for many others in the entertainment industry can thus provide the perspective we need to understand how entertainment and technology have arrived at the sort of partnership that typifies today's media environment and, indeed, much of contemporary life."[10] With Hollywood's adoption of the blockbuster strategy, which negotiated ideas about investment and audience predilections, a narrativized and spectacularized version of the future arrived on display at a theater near you. Blockbusters are the Sturm und Drang of popular entertainment as technological spectacle.

In his famous essay "The Work of Art in the Age of Mechanical Reproduction" from the 1930s, Walter Benjamin cited André Breton evocatively stating that "the work of art is valuable only in so far as it is vibrated by the reflexes of the future."[11] Blockbusters hum with this vibration. They are only one possible moneyed future. There are, of course, a variety of other experiments and innovations that push moving-image art in different directions: virtual reality, augmented reality, biological art, human-machine hybrid forms, and so on. Most centrally, blockbusters, the exhibition apparatus they make viable, and the extended stream of multimedia iterations they produce, show us the financial and cultural priorities placed on the fractiously twinned art and industry. They exhibit the way we understand and resolve a battle between taste and economy, between movies and capitalism.

The World War II blockbuster bombs, two tons of destructive power, promoted as accurate and efficient instruments that assured victory in that most expansive and totalizing of industrial wars, were actually more a supporting cast player to the incendiaries that produced the indiscriminate deadly monster of the firestorm. The incendiaries too were prototypical of modern war, fought from above with scientific know-how and with disregard for the distinction between civilian and military targets. Those guiding the conflict equally orchestrated the description and representation of military operations. A double attack took place, and a double effectiveness was expected, namely, that the moment of assault was also an event to be reported and represented elsewhere, to friendly and enemy eyes alike, through the various filters of journalism, advertising, and government offices. The horrifying bureaucratic mentality of such bombings appears in Joseph Heller's novel *Catch-22* (1961), in which a U.S. general complains that a bombing run didn't produce the right photographs.[12] The pattern of destruction captured by the cameras mounted on bombers didn't meet expectations. As a consequence, the general concluded the mission was a flop. In the novel the imagistic representation of destruction determined outcomes, resulted in adjustments to operations, and left the actual devastation pushed further into the distance in military minds. The air campaign, as Heller satirically saw it, was designed to produce not just destruction and death from above but good photographic records.

The entwining of technological and representational imperatives, even with all the advancements and insights offered, has served a dark divisive need of civilization: to advance in ways that produce comfort and security for affiliate populations and not for others. While the actual technological function may be backstage and unseen, as with the small incendiary bombs, display technology impresses with its physical dimensions and impact. Display technology has a representational drive, a spectacular core, with a symbolic efficiency and clarity. World's fairs and vacuum noise—they are similar semiotic pronouncements that this technology is working, is working for me, or is going to be working for all of us in a near and accessible future. Such exhibitionism clouds our ability to ask the questions we must about inevitability, necessity, ecology, and humanity.

Blockbusters are an expressive mode of technological exhibitionism. They are the big, loud, and declarative voices that echo through the very fabric of our lives and reverberate down to more microscopic experiences with technology. Blockbusters fill up exhibition spaces and then continue their long life as they splinter and travel through various other media and commodity iterations. They are easily located on a lower rung of the cultural hierarchy, and their cosmopolitan artlessness gives people a comfortable wedge, a distancing device through which blockbusters can be experienced without consequence: "that's mass taste, not mine." But say what you will about the tedium of yet another blockbuster, we find enough of them to be impressive, fun, and awe-inspiring, such that their cultural and economic heft continues to power our entertainment landscape.

As part of a vast complex of social and cultural orientation, blockbusters do not stand alone as singularly determining forces. Significantly, technological innovation is a major and expanding industrial sector, one that shapes life beyond the sparkle of entertainment; it is a dominant category of education and labor, as well as leisure. One need not look further than the smartphone revolution of the past decade. Gadget-wise citizens now truck around neighborhoods, performing reigning ideas about mobility and freedom, risking vehicular mayhem and collisions with sidewalk obstacles. Conspicuous connectivity is the primary message delivered by such visible activity. The swift thumbing on tablets and smartphones can be play, a familial or community responsibility, or work. Whatever tasks public individualized technological practitioners are completing, the material presence of the device signifies, "I am gadget-wise. I am connected in a modern way. This device makes me so." It has a display function, a performative value, and the prayer-book posture of smartphone users signals the reverence with which technological connectivity is understood. Where the automobile was the display technology of the Fordist economic regime, handheld conspicuous connectivity is the defining display technology of the current phase of the post-Fordist economy.

One key unsettling hidden term, as with all consumer capitalist structures, is obsolescence. The kernel of truth, the economic rationale that makes the gadget world spin, is the limited time frame for any device's use. Planned obsolescence, propelling ongoing cycles of purchase, disposal, and environmental damage, has been accelerated with the rote argument that digital technology must keep changing and improving—and fast. We are currently at an obscene pace in which components have limited interchangeability, software updates require newer operating systems, and materials are assembled to last but a handful of years at best. Most astonishingly, it is an obscenity that has been embraced as common sense. While this track of perpetual digital gadget shopping may provoke frustration, the response has not been enough to generate a more extreme refusal to participate in the status realm of the shiny device. As bound up in the new as conspicuous connectivity may be, every purchase heralds the looming obsolete and plants the seed of a future purchase. Conspicuous connectivity is conspicuous obsolescence; gadget-wise is garbage-wise.

The perpetual gadget shopping spree, the endless technological consumer cycles—these features, perhaps more than any others, pushed me to approach the American blockbuster as I did. The assembly of such a deep and powerfully embedded common sense requires more than the immediate convenience of mobile computing to settle and fix itself so surely in our lives. It requires decades of building a technologically warmed and readied citizen. This is an enterprise that unfolded on numerous fronts, including education, public policy, resource extraction, and scientific experimentation. The front I've addressed is the most visible form of large-scale public entertainment—the blockbuster movie—to show the cultural work the very idea of moving-image extravaganzas has done to set the stage for the culture of technological innovation.

The bright sun of progress makes us gasp. It steals our breath and plumbs the imagination. It makes wonder something that appears in time and in front of us. Behold! The greater the awe, the more it eclipses what came before, making history a bit more difficult to access. As we marvel at spectacular technological achievement, we face a feature that is a distinctive part of the modern world, one that we seem to embrace and adore even as legions of critics challenge it: we worship the notion that human advancement springs from technological innovation. Whether the fascination materializes as wondrous entertainment or murderous hardware, as inspiring sensation or environmental disaster, those applications sprout from the sparks of our technological imagination and imperative. In so many ways, we have taken up roles as C. Wright Mills's "cheerful robots," marshalling the resources to make push-button armaments and gadgets.[13] The capacity of technology to diminish misery and augment collective well-being keeps alive our investment in innovation, and considerable achievements, though unequally shared, demonstrate that some of that promise might reasonably be realized. And yet, we find that the technological imagination has moved closer to determining our consciousness.

Why is this the case? Because we are sold the rewards, benefits, and sensations that technological society might offer as the only path forward. The drumbeat of progress, advancement, and amusement is incessant and exhausting. Of the many drummers, the American blockbuster is one of the most globally audible, even pleasurable, smoothing the way for the next generation of utopian technologists to join the band.

(NOTES)

CHAPTER 1 **BLOCKBUSTER BALLYHOO**

1. Richard Dyer, "Entertainment and Utopia" (1977), in *Movies and Methods Volume II*, ed. Bill Nichols (Berkeley: University of California Press, 1985), 220–232.
2. Box-office returns, accessed December 23, 2019, www.imdb.com.
3. Eileen R. Meehan, "Ancillary Markets—Television: From Challenge to Safe Haven," in *The Contemporary Hollywood Film Industry*, ed. Paul McDonald and Janet Wasko (Oxford: Blackwell, 2008), 106–119.
4. Thomas Schatz, "The Studio System and Conglomerate Hollywood," in McDonald and Wasko, *Contemporary Hollywood Film Industry*, 13–42.
5. Constance Balides, "Jurassic Post-Fordism: Tall Tales of Economics in the Theme Park," *Screen* 41 (2000): 139–160; and J. D. Connor, *The Studios after the Studios: Neoclassical Hollywood (1970–2010)* (Stanford, CA: Stanford University Press, 2015).
6. Fredric Jameson, "Reification and Utopia in Mass Culture" (1979), in *Signatures of the Visible* (New York: Routledge, 1992), 25.
7. Roland Marchand, *Advertising the American Dream: Making Way for Modernity, 1920–1940* (Berkeley: University of California Press, 1986).
8. Thomas Schatz, "The New Hollywood," in *Film Theory Goes to the Movies*, ed. Jim Collins, Hilary Radner, and Ava Preacher Collins (New York: Routledge, 1993), 3–36.
9. Thomas Schatz, "Seismic Shifts in the American Film Industry," in *The Wiley-Blackwell History of American Film*, ed. Cynthia Lucia, Roy Gundmann, and Art Simon (London: Blackwell, 2012), 1–21.
10. Schatz, "New Hollywood."

11. Jon Lewis, "Following the Money in America's Sunniest Company Town: Some Notes on the Political Economy of the Hollywood Blockbuster," in *Movie Blockbusters*, ed. Julian Stringer (New York: Routledge, 2003), 61–71.
12. An important survey of the wider media integration of American film is found in Janet Wasko, *How Hollywood Works* (Thousand Oaks, CA: Sage, 2003).
13. Steve Neale, "Hollywood Blockbusters: Historical Dimensions," in Stringer, *Movie Blockbusters*, 47–60; and Sheldon Hall and Steve Neale, *Epics, Spectacles, and Blockbusters: A Hollywood History* (Detroit: Wayne State University Press, 2010).
14. Geoff King, "Spectacle, Narrative, and the Spectacular Hollywood Blockbuster," in Stringer, *Movie Blockbusters*, 114–127.
15. Peter Krämer, "'Want to Take a Ride?': Reflections on the Blockbuster Experience in *Contact* (1997)," in Stringer, *Movie Blockbusters*, 128–140.
16. Yvonne Tasker, *Spectacular Bodies: Gender, Genre and the Action Film* (New York: Routledge, 1993), 5. See also Yvonne Tasker, "Dumb Movies for Dumb People: Masculinity, the Body, and the Voice in Contemporary Action Cinema," in *Screening the Male: Exploring Masculinities in Hollywood Cinema*, ed. Steven Cohan and Ina Rae Hark (New York: Routledge, 1993), 230–244.
17. Tom Shone, *Blockbuster: How Hollywood Learned to Stop Worrying and Love the Summer* (New York: Simon and Schuster, 2004), 26.
18. King, "Spectacle, Narrative," 124.
19. Michael Allen, "Talking about a Revolution: The Blockbuster as Industrial Advertisement," in Stringer, *Movie Blockbusters*, 101–113.
20. Michelle Pierson, *Special Effects: Still in Search of Wonder* (New York: Columbia University Press, 2002), 63.
21. Scott Bukatman, *Matters of Gravity: Special Effects and Supermen in the 20th Century* (Durham, NC: Duke University Press, 2003), 113.
22. Bukatman, *Matters of Gravity*, 114.
23. Bukatman, *Matters of Gravity*, 28.
24. Kristen Whissel, "Tales of Upward Mobility: The New Verticality and Digital Special Effects," *Film Quarterly* 59, no. 4 (2006): 23–34; and Kristen Whissel, "The Digital Multitude," *Cinema Journal* 49, no. 4 (2010): 90–110.
25. Sean Cubitt, *The Cinema Effect* (Cambridge, MA: MIT Press, 2004), 247.
26. Cubitt, *Cinema Effect*, 250.
27. Cubitt, *Cinema Effect*, 268.
28. For a study of the contemporary dimensions of this, see my essay "Consumer Electronics and Building an Entertainment Infrastructure," in *Signal Traffic*, ed. Lisa Parks and Nicole Starosielski (Urbana: University of Illinois Press, 2015), 246–278.
29. Pierson, *Special Effects*, 61.
30. J. P. Telotte, *The Mouse Machine: Disney and Technology* (Urbana: University of Illinois Press, 2008), 2.
31. "Panasonic and Twentieth Century Fox Team for Global Promotion of James Cameron's *Avatar*," *Asia Corporate News Newswire*, August 21, 2009, en.acnnewswire.com;

and "Panasonic Rolls with HD 3-D Home Theater Truck Tour," *Entertainment Close-Up*, September 5, 2009, www.highbeam.com.

32 Mark Raby, "Avatar Blu-ray 3D Tied to Panasonic until 2012," *TG Daily*, December 14, 2010, www.tgdaily.com.

33 The materiality of media forms, and their variability, has been importantly advanced as "format theory," which challenges ideas about the stable technological coherence of media. See Jonathan Sterne, *MP3: The Meaning of a Format* (Durham, NC: Duke University Press, 2012); and Haidee Wasson, "Formatting Film Studies," *Film Studies* 12 (Spring 2015): 57–61.

34 Thomas Elsaesser, "The New New Hollywood: Cinema beyond Distance and Proximity," in *Moving Images, Culture and the Mind*, ed. Ib Bondebjerg (Luton, UK: University of Luton Press, 2000), 187–203.

35 Alexander Huls, "Child's Play: The Degeneration of Blockbusters," Roger Ebert, January 8, 2014, www.rogerebert.com.

36 Slavoj Žižek, "*Avatar*: The Return of the Natives," *New Statesman*, March 8, 2010.

37 Stéphane Delorme and Jean-Philippe Tessé, Interview with Slavoj Žižek, *Cahiers du Cinéma*, April 2010.

38 Katie Ellis, *Disability and Popular Culture: Focusing Passion, Creating Community and Expressing Defiance* (New York: Routledge, 2016).

39 Peter Biskind, *Easy Riders, Raging Bulls: How the Sex-Drugs-and-Rock 'n' Roll Generation Saved Hollywood* (New York: Touchstone, 1998); and Peter Biskind, *Down and Dirty Pictures: Miramax, Sundance, and the Rise of Independent Film* (New York: Simon and Schuster, 2004).

40 Janet Maslin, "Golden Age: Just Before They Invented the Blockbuster," *New York Times*, May 1, 1994.

41 Julie Turnock, *Plastic Reality: Special Effects, Technology, and the Emergence of 1970s Blockbuster Aesthetics* (New York: Columbia University Press, 2015), 106.

42 Pierre Bourdieu, "The Field of Cultural Production, or: The Economic World Reversed" (1983), in *The Field of Cultural Production*, trans. Richard Nice (New York: Columbia University Press, 1993), 40.

43 Sherry B. Ortner, *Not Hollywood: Independent Film at the Twilight of the American Dream* (Durham, NC: Duke University Press, 2013).

44 Ortner, *Not Hollywood*, 30.

45 See Thomas Schatz, "Film Industry Studies and Hollywood History," in *Media Industries: History, Theory, and Method*, ed. Jennifer Holt and Alisa Perren (Malden, MA: Wiley-Blackwell, 2009), 45–56.

46 Julian Stringer, "Introduction," in Stringer, *Movie Blockbusters*, 7.

47 Bourdieu, "Field of Cultural Production," 36.

48 Stringer, "Introduction," 13.

49 For example, AMC's "Film Terms Glossary" notes, "The term was first applied to Steven Spielberg's *Jaws* (1975), often acknowledged as the first blockbuster." AMC, Film Terms Glossary, http://www.filmsite.org/filmterms3.html.

50 Frank Eugene Beaver, *Dictionary of Film Terms: The Aesthetic Companion to Film Art* (New York: Peter Lang, 2007); Susan Hayward, *Cinema Studies: The Key Concepts*, 2nd ed. (New York: Routledge, 2000); and Ephraim Katz and Ronald Dean Nolen, *The Film Encyclopedia: The Complete Guide to Film and the Film Industry*, 7th ed. (New York: Harper Collins, 2012).

51 Steve Blandford, Barry Keith Grant, and Jim Hillier, *The Film Studies Dictionary* (New York: Arnold, 2001).

52 Key contributions include Kevin Sandler and Gaylyn Studlar, eds., *Titanic: Anatomy of a Blockbuster* (New Brunswick, NJ: Rutgers University Press, 1999); Kristin Thompson, *The Frodo Franchise: The Lord of the Rings and Modern Hollywood* (Berkeley: University of California Press, 2007); Stringer, *Movie Blockbusters*; and Justin Wyatt, *High Concept: Movies and Marketing in Hollywood* (Austin: University of Texas Press, 1994).

53 John Sanders, *The Film Genre Book* (Leighton Buzzard, UK: Auteur, 2009), 9.

54 Sanders, *Film Genre Book*, 389.

55 Sanders, *Film Genre Book*, 389.

56 Neale, "Hollywood Blockbusters," 47.

57 Marco Cucco, "The Promise Is Great: The Blockbuster and the Hollywood Economy," *Media, Culture, and Society* 31, no. 2 (2009): 215.

58 Sheldon Hall, "Pass the Ammunition: A Short Etymology of 'Blockbuster,'" in *The Return of the Epic Film: Genre, Aesthetics and History in the 21st Century*, ed. Andrew B. R. Elliott (Edinburgh: Edinburgh University Press, 2014), 147–166.

59 "Film Review: Quo Vadis," *Variety*, November 14, 1951, 6.

60 Hall and Neale, *Epics, Spectacles, and Blockbusters*, 139.

61 Alex Ben Block and Lucy Autrey Wilson, eds., *George Lucas's Blockbusting: A Decade-by-Decade Survey of Timeless Movies Including Untold Secrets of Their Financial and Cultural Success* (New York: ItBooks, 2010), 348–349.

62 "Film Review: Quo Vadis."

63 "'Pix Safe from TV for 4 Years'; Both in Eventual Co-op, Sez Schary," *Variety*, November 7, 1951, 1, 22.

64 Hal Wallis, "No Fan Has Yet Stopt to Ask a Mgr., 'How Much Did This Film Cost?'; Blockbusters Are OK but the Main Thing Is 'Is It a Good Show?,'" *Variety*, January 2, 1952, 7; and Stanley Kramer, "Pix Can't Live by Bigness Alone," *Variety*, January 2, 1952, 53.

65 James R. Grainger, "Can't All Be Blockbusters, but 'A' or 'B' Every Pic Must Be Sold," *Variety*, January 2, 1952, 28.

66 Charles P. Skouras, "Chas. Skouras Sees a Big Theatre TV in the Future of the Picture Business," *Variety*, January 2, 1952, 14; and Jeff Jefferis, "Voice from the Stix," *Variety*, January 2, 1952, 14.

67 George Sidney, "An 18-Year-Old Marine Stirs Some Memories," *Variety*, January 2, 1952, 53.

68 James Naremore, *More Than Night: Film Noir in Its Contexts* (Berkeley: University of California Press, 1998).

69 Stringer, "Introduction," 3.

70 Lisa Gitelman, *Always Already New: Media, History, and the Data of Culture* (Cambridge, MA: MIT Press, 2006), 6, 7.
71 Gitelman, *Always Already New*, 7.
72 Johanna Drucker, "Digital Humanities: From Speculative to Skeptical" (public talk for Project Arclight and Media History Research Centre, Concordia University, Montreal, October 9, 2015).
73 For a discussion of the Arclight app, and a contextual survey of the intersection between digital humanities and media history, see Eric Hoyt, Kit Hughes, and Charles R. Acland, "A Guide to the Arclight Guidebook," in *The Arclight Guidebook to Media History and the Digital Humanities*, ed. Charles R. Acland and Eric Hoyt (Brighton, Sussex: REFRAME Books in association with Project Arclight, 2016), 1–29.
74 Charles R. Acland and Fenwick McKelvey, "Terminological Traffic in the Movie Business," in Acland and Hoyt, *Arclight Guidebook*, 238–248.
75 Charles R. Acland, *Swift Viewing: The Popular Life of Subliminal Influence* (Durham, NC: Duke University Press, 2012).
76 Raymond Williams, *Marxism and Literature* (New York: Oxford University Press, 1977).
77 Bourdieu, "Field of Cultural Production," 37.

CHAPTER 2 INDUSTRIAL REGIMES OF ENTERTAINMENT

1 Antonio Gramsci, *Selections from the Prison Notebooks*, ed. and trans. Quintin Hoare and Geoffrey Nowell Smith (New York: International Publishers, 1971), 306.
2 For a study of other kinds of globally circulating visual materials, see Bishnupriya Ghosh, *Global Icons: Apertures to the Popular* (Durham, NC: Duke University Press, 2011).
3 Miriam Hansen, "The Mass Production of the Senses: Classical Cinema as Vernacular Modernism," in *Reinventing Film Studies*, ed. Christine Gledhill and Linda Williams (London: Arnold, 2000), 333.
4 Hansen, "Mass Production of the Senses," 340.
5 Hansen, "Mass Production of the Senses," 341.
6 For an expansive account of the entwinement of American media, industrial, and state institutions in the service of capitalism, focusing on the interwar period, see Lee Grieveson, *Cinema and the Wealth of Nations: Media, Capital, and the Liberal World System* (Oakland: University of California Press, 2017).
7 Thomas Elsaesser, "The Blockbuster," in *The End of Cinema as We Know It: American Film in the Nineties*, ed. Jon Lewis (New York: New York University Press, 2001), 11–22.
8 For the standard measure of box-office returns, see "Top 2016 Movies at the Domestic Box Office," www.the-numbers.com.
9 David A. Garvin, "Blockbusters: The Economics of Mass Entertainment," *Journal of Cultural Economics* 5, no. 1 (1981): 8.

10 Chris Anderson, *The Long Tail: Why the Future of Business Is Selling Less of More* (New York: Hyperion, 2006).
11 Malcolm Gladwell, "The Science of the Sleeper: How the Information Age Could Blow Away the Blockbuster," *New Yorker*, October 4, 1999, 48–50, 52–55.
12 Anita Elberse, "Brighter Than Ever," *Variety*, October 8, 2013, 49–51; and Peter Bart, "The Blockbuster Model That Ate Hollywood," *Variety*, December 3, 2013, 17.
13 Anita Elberse, *Blockbusters: Hit-Making, Risk-Taking, and the Big Business of Entertainment* (New York: Henry Holt, 2013), 1.
14 Quoted in Elberse, *Blockbusters*, 1.
15 Elberse, *Blockbusters*, 9.
16 Elberse, *Blockbusters*, 35–42.
17 Elberse, *Blockbusters*, 186.
18 Gady Epstein, "Winner Takes All: Mass Entertainment," *Economist*, February 11, 2017, 6.
19 Jean Baudrillard, "The Ecstasy of Communication," in *The Anti-aesthetic: Essays on Postmodern Culture*, ed. Hal Foster (Port Townsend, WA: Bay, 1983), 131.
20 For more on the history of information overload and the educational response, see Charles R. Acland, *Swift Viewing: The Popular Life of Subliminal Influence* (Durham, NC: Duke University Press, 2012).
21 Slavoj Žižek, *Trouble in Paradise: From the End of History to the End of Capitalism* (Brooklyn, NY: Melville House, 2014), 11–12.
22 Jodi Dean, *Blog Theory: Feedback and Capture in the Circuits of Drive* (Malden, MA: Polity, 2010), 5.
23 Dean, *Blog Theory*, 6.
24 Dean, *Blog Theory*, 6.
25 Dean, *Blog Theory*, 7.
26 Dean, *Blog Theory*, 7.
27 Dean, *Blog Theory*, 7.
28 Jodi Dean, *The Communist Horizon* (New York: Verso, 2012).
29 Žižek, *Trouble in Paradise*, 233–238.
30 Quoted from *John Mulaney: Kid Gorgeous at Radio City* (2018).
31 José van Dijck, *The Culture of Connectivity: A Critical History of Social Media* (New York: Oxford University Press, 2013), 4, emphasis added.
32 David Bordwell, *The Way Hollywood Tells It: Story and Style in Modern Movies* (Berkeley: University of California Press, 2006).
33 Bukatman, *Matters of Gravity*, 114.
34 Van Dijck, *Culture of Connectivity*, 14.
35 Whissel, "Digital Multitude."
36 For research on the contemporary logistics in international media production, see Kay Dickinson, "'Make It What You Want It to Be': Logistics, Labour and the Financialization of Land Via the Globalized Free Zone Studio," in *In the Studio: Visual Creation and Its Material Environments*, ed. Brian R. Jacobson (Oakland: University of California Press, 2020).

37 For an examination of the archeological rediscovery of the set for DeMille's first version of *The Ten Commandments* (1923) at Guadalupe Dunes, California, and the implications of these artifacts for film history, see Vivian Sobchack, "What Is Film History?, or, the Riddle of the Sphinxes," in *Reinventing Film Studies*, ed. Christine Gledhill and Linda Williams (London: Arnold, 2000), 300–315.
38 Lewis, "Following the Money," 63.
39 Sheldon Hall, "Tall Revenue Features: The Genealogy of the Modern Blockbuster," in *Genre and Contemporary Hollywood*, ed. Steve Neale (London: BFI Publishing, 2002), 22.
40 Scott Roxborough and Jonathan Landreth, "Private Equity Changing Face of Film Industry," *Hollywood Reporter*, May 23, 2007, www.hollywoodreporter.com; for an in-depth examination of the rising influence of financial firms on American media industries at that time, see Andrew deWaard, "Derivative Media: The Financialization of Film, Television and Popular Music, 2004–2016" (PhD diss., University of California, Los Angeles, 2017).
41 *Broadway League Economic Impact Report*, quoted in Ken Davenport, "What's the Average Cost of Putting On a Broadway Show?," *The Producer's Perspective*, June 7, 2012, www.theproducersperspective.com.
42 Vanessa R. Schwartz, *It's So French! Hollywood, Paris, and the Making of Cosmopolitan Film Culture* (Chicago: University of Chicago Press, 2007), 159. Writing about the 1960s, Keir Keightley has importantly advanced a related argument that certain forms of emergent world music, such as bossa nova, made cosmopolitan popular culture a brand of "adult modernity." Keir Keightley, "*Un Voyage Via Barquinho* . . . Global Circulation, Musical Hybridization, and Adult Modernity, 1961–9," in *Migrating Music*, ed. Jason Toynbee and Byron Dueck (New York: Routledge, 2011), 112–126.
43 For a detailed and insightful examination of the links between the Chinese and American movie businesses, see Aynne Kokas, *Hollywood Made in China* (Oakland: University of California Press, 2017).
44 Stringer, "Introduction," 10.
45 For the full report, see Charles R. Acland, *From International Blockbusters to National Hits: Analysis of the 2010 UIS Survey of Feature Films* (Montreal: UNESCO Institute of Statistics, 2012), www.uis.unesco.org.
46 For more on the temporality of the current cinema, see my work in Acland, *Screen Traffic: Movies, Multiplexes, and Global Culture* (Durham, NC: Duke University Press, 2003); and Acland, "'Opening Everywhere': Multiplexes, E-Cinema and the Speed of Cinema Culture," in *Going to the Movies: Hollywood and the Social Experience of Movie-Going*, ed. Robert Allen, Richard Maltby, and Melvyn Stokes (Exeter, UK: University of Exeter Press, 2007), 364–382.
47 Cassie Foss, "Report—'Iron Man 3' Generated $179.8m in Spending, 2,043 Jobs," *Star News*, April 30, 2013.
48 Michael Thom, "Lights, Camera, but No Action? Tax and Economic Development Lessons from State Motion Picture Incentive Programs," *American Review of Public Administration* 48, no. 1 (2018): 33–51.

49 Yvonne Villarreal, "MPAA Blasts USC over Film Tax Credit Report," *Los Angeles Times*, September 14, 2016. For a study of the cultural geography of location shooting in Louisiana, including a discussion of economic impact measures, see Vicki Mayer, *Almost Hollywood, Nearly New Orleans: The Lure of the Local Film Economy* (Oakland: University of California Press, 2017).
50 Stringer, "Introduction," 5.
51 Richard Maltby, *Hollywood Cinema*, 2nd ed. (Malden, MA: Blackwell, 2003).
52 Quoted in Maltby, *Hollywood Cinema*, 40; quote originally in Amy Taubin, "Art and Industry," *Village Voice*, July 9, 1991.
53 Lewis Mumford, *The Myth of the Machine* (New York: Harcourt Brace Jovanovich, 1967–1970), 1:22.
54 Mumford, *Myth of the Machine*, 1:134.
55 Mumford, *Myth of the Machine*, 2:18–19.
56 Ross Melnick, *American Showman: Samuel "Roxy" Rothafel and the Birth of the Entertainment Industry, 1908–1935* (New York: Columbia University Press, 2012).

CHAPTER 3 DELIVERING BLOCKBUSTERS

1 "O.W.I. Exhibit of Axis Terror Is Opened Here: 2,500 Throng Rockefeller Center Promenade, Hear Powell, Eve Curie, Swing," *New York Herald Tribune*, May 18, 1943.
2 "Many See Exhibits of War's Horrors; Tableaux in Rockefeller Center Depict Six Phases of 'The Nature of the Enemy'; Maimed Victim Speaks," *New York Times*, May 18, 1943.
3 "O.W.I. Exhibit of Axis Terror," 17; U.S. Office of War Information, "Release," Washington, DC, May 26, 1943, 5, New York Public Library; and "'Nature of Enemy' Show Thronged at Opening," *New York Post*, May 17, 1943.
4 *The Nature of the Enemy* was the second open-air OWI display in Rockefeller Plaza that year. In March 1943 *United Nations* was the first of a series called "This Is Our War." Whereas *The Nature of the Enemy* concentrated on the evils of fascism, and its threat to democratic values, the first exhibit educated the public about the Allies—"who we are fighting with" rather than "why we fight." *United Nations* consisted of individual information panels on each country contributing to the war effort. The angled design of the panels created a layered "V" for "Victory."
5 "Many See Exhibits of War's Horrors."
6 "A Block Buster on Fifth Avenue," *New York Times*, May 14, 1943.
7 *Desperate Journey* (1942) press book, Film Press Book Collection, University of California–Santa Barbara.
8 "More Areas of Berlin Wrecked," *Times* (London), December 31, 1943.
9 W. R. Hirsch, "Agriculture Goes to War at Louisiana State Fair," *Billboard*, January 2, 1943, 114, 121.
10 "Atlanta Sees Banner Year," *Billboard*, October 14, 1944, 40–41.
11 IBM, "Privilege," advertisement, *Brooklyn Daily Eagle*, June 3, 1943.

12 U.S. Office of War Information, "The Four Freedoms," pamphlet, Washington, DC, 1942, n.p., New York Public Library.
13 "Many See Exhibits of War's Horrors."
14 MOMA, Sarah Newmeyer to City Editors, *Road to Victory* exhibit, press release, May 13, 1942, 1, New York Public Library.
15 For context on the changing role of photography in exhibition practices, with a special focus on MOMA, see Mary Anne Staniszewski, *The Power of Display: A History of Exhibition Installations at the Museum of Modern Art* (Cambridge, MA: MIT Press, 1998); see also Fred Turner, *The Democratic Surround: Multimedia and American Liberalism from World War II to the Psychedelic Sixties* (Chicago: University of Chicago Press, 2013).
16 "Million Strong, City Salutes American Day; Central Park Throng Hears Wallace Urge Freedom for All 'Plain People,'" *New York Herald Tribune*, May 17, 1943.
17 James F. Bender, "Thirty Thousand New Words," *New York Times Magazine*, December 2, 1945, 12.
18 Robert P. Post, "12 of Raiders Lost; Night Fighters Met over German City—Large Fires Set; Nazis Gun British Towns," *New York Times*, December 23, 1942; and "He Who Strikes Last," *New York Times*, April 15, 1943.
19 "Four-Ton Bombs Used," *New York Times*, December 11, 1942.
20 "Day Air Offensive Reaches Berlin; Targets in Germany and Air Bases in France Hit; R.A.F. Now Using Five-Ton Bombs," *Times* (London), March 4, 1944.
21 In some estimates the Allies dropped 68,000 blockbusters, 750,000 medium-capacity bombs, and 800,000 high-explosive bombs. Jörg Friedrich, *The Fire: The Bombing of Germany, 1940–1945* (2002), trans. Allison Brown (New York: Columbia University Press, 2006), 9–10.
22 Bob Trout, letter to the editor, *American Speech* 19, no. 4 (1944): 293; and H. L. Mencken, "War Words in England," *American Speech* 19, no. 1 (1944): 3–15.
23 Raymond Daniell, "50 Two-Ton Bombs Plaster Duisburg; 300 R.A.F. Planes Unload Havoc on Reich Inland Port—Russians Hit Koenigsberg; Invasion Coast Visited; British Spitfires Pound Areas in France and Netherlands—Cologne Damage Described," *New York Times*, July 23, 1942.
24 "RAF 'Block Busters' Blast Hamburg," *Reading Eagle*, July 27, 1942.
25 John Collingwood Reade, "The War Today—German Tactical Lines in Russia More Dangerous," *Globe and Mail*, August 5, 1942.
26 Joe Alex Morris, "Allies Deliver Heavy Blows," *Berkeley Daily Gazette*, August 1, 1942.
27 "Who's Who? Twenty Questions. What's What?," *New York Times*, August 9, 1942.
28 "Heavy Bombers," *Life*, September 28, 1942, 45–48.
29 Sidney M. Shalett, "Air Magic Shown at Wright Field," *New York Times*, December 30, 1942.
30 "Allied Bombs Smash Nazi War Planes," *Victory* 1, no. 5 (1943): 54–56.
31 Peter Sloterdijk, *Spheres*, vol. 1, *Bubbles* (1998), trans. Wieland Hoban (Los Angeles: Semiotext(e), 2011).

32 For a complete historical overview of the ethical rationale that has regularly produced the atrocities of bombing campaigns, see Yuki Tanaka and Marilyn B. Young, eds., *Bombing Civilians: A Twentieth-Century History* (New York: New Press, 2009).
33 Mumford, *Myth of the Machine*, 2:252.
34 Most standard histories describe the British air strategy as one of more intensive saturation bombing while the American strategy was the more limited precision bombing. In actuality, the two air forces flew in support of each other and participated in similar tactics, such that a clear demarcation between the two Allies is impossible. For more on this, see Ronald Schaffer, "The Bombing Campaigns in World War II: The European Theater," in Tanaka and Young, *Bombing Civilians*, 30–45.
35 For details on World War II bombing and its ethics, see Jörg Arnold, *The Allied Air War and Urban Memory: The Legacy of Strategic Bombing in Germany* (New York: Cambridge University Press, 2011); Tanaka and Young, *Bombing Civilians*; and A. C. Grayling, *Among the Dead Cities: The History and Moral Legacy of the WWII Bombing of Civilians in Germany and Japan* (London: Bloomsbury, 2006).
36 Friedrich, *Fire*, 24–25.
37 John Steinbeck, *Bombs Away: The Story of a Bomber Team* (1942; New York: Penguin Books, 2009).
38 Friedrich, *Fire*, 86–87.
39 John W. Dower, *Cultures of War: Pearl Harbor/Hiroshima/9-11/Iraq* (New York: W. W. Norton/New Press, 2010), 172–173.
40 Friedrich, *Fire*, 61–62. Friedrich's book has been very controversial in Germany, sparking a debate about German suffering during World War II. Many have claimed that it has been seized on by right-wing nationalists. The book is written with metaphoric power, and some question the more novelistic writing style. In humanizing the civilians bombed, Friedrich wrote more about cities and villages than the entirety of the country or Nazis. The debate in Germany is an essential one, but it should not distract us from the raw historical evidence Friedrich presented, much of which comes from the Allies' own post–World War II assessment of their bombing campaign, nor from his general claim, which is that civilian targeting is a war crime. For a cogent critique of Friedrich, one that ultimately argues that *The Fire* covered old ground with more dramatic narrativization, see Robert G. Moeller, "The Bombing War in Germany, 2005–1940: Back to the Future?," in Tanaka and Young, *Bombing Civilians*, 46–76.
41 For a study showing how matters of aerial targeting and surveillance construct a contemporary "vertical hegemony," see Lisa Parks, *Rethinking Media Coverage: Vertical Mediation and the War on Terror* (New York: Routledge, 2018).
42 Dower, *Cultures of War*, 156.
43 W. G. Sebald, *On the Natural History of Destruction* (1999), trans. Anthea Bell (Toronto: Vintage Canada, 2003), 4.
44 Randall T. Wakelam, *The Science of Bombing: Operational Research in R.A.F. Bomber Command* (Toronto: University of Toronto Press, 2009), 118.
45 "He Who Strikes Last."

46 Friedrich, *Fire*, 98.
47 Edward R. Murrow, "The Target Was to Be the Big City" (1943), in *Reporting World War II: Part One, American Journalism, 1938–1944* (New York: Literary Classics of the United States, 1995), 713–714.
48 Murrow, "Target Was to Be the Big City," 715.
49 Murrow, "Target Was to Be the Big City," 716.
50 Murrow, "Target Was to Be the Big City," 717.
51 "Bomber's View of Berlin; Murrow of CBS Describes Bursts of Blockbusters, Merging of Fires," *New York Times*, December 4, 1943.
52 Murrow, "Target Was to Be the Big City," 717.
53 Murrow, "Target Was to Be the Big City," 718–719.
54 Murrow, "Target Was to Be the Big City," 719.
55 Murrow, "Target Was to Be the Big City," 719.
56 *United States Strategic Bombing Survey Summary Report (European War)*, (Washington, DC: U.S. Government Printing Office, 1945).
57 "Notes on Science," *New York Times*, December 9, 1945.
58 Dower, *Cultures of War*.
59 Castle Films, advertisement, *New York Times*, November 23, 1943.
60 "The Bomb as Pedagogue," *New York Times*, September 26, 1943.
61 Friedrich, *Fire*, 97.
62 Friedrich, *Fire*, 484.
63 Alexander P. de Seversky, "Air Power and the War," *New York Times*, December 15, 1943.
64 *One of Our Aircraft Is Missing* press book, Film Press Book Collection, University of California–Santa Barbara.
65 Hall, "Pass the Ammunition," 150.
66 *Bombardier*, advertisement, *Oswego Palladium-Times*, July 23, 1943.
67 Nat Green, "The Crossroads," *Billboard*, July 24, 1943, 47.
68 *The Memphis Belle: A Story of a Flying Fortress*, advertisement, press kit, Margaret Herrick Library and Archives, Los Angeles (henceforth called the Margaret Herrick Library).
69 Lockheed, advertisement, *Victory* 1, no. 6 (1943): 55.
70 Roland Marchand, *Creating the Corporate Soul* (Berkeley: University of California Press, 1998), 317.
71 Inger L. Stole, *Advertising at War: Business, Consumers, and Government in the 1940s* (Urbana: University of Illinois Press, 2015), 122–138.
72 Theodor Adorno, *Minima Moralia: Reflections from Damaged Life* (1951), trans. E. F. N. Jephcott (New York: Verso, 1974), 53.
73 Bankers Trust Company, advertisement, *New York Times*, September 22, 1943.
74 Bank of New York, advertisement, *New York Times*, January 26, 1943.
75 Marshall Berman, *All That Is Solid Melts into Air: The Experience of Modernity* (New York: Simon and Schuster, 1982).
76 Consolidated Vultee Aircraft, advertisement, *New York Times*, April 20, 1944.
77 "Popular Items," *Billboard*, March 29, 1943, 51.

78 "Secret Explosive Is Demonstrated; Nature of Ingredients Going into 'Blockbusters' Bared with U.S. Approval; Other Processes Shown; Du Pont Plant Experts Reveal New Silver-Plate Method at E Award Fete," *New York Times*, June 4, 1943.

79 Clifford Kennedy Berryman, "Maybe You Should Have Said It Louder, Chief," cartoon, *Evening Star*, January 20, 1943, available online at https://www.loc.gov/item/acd1996000562/PP/.

80 "The Block Buster?," editorial cartoon, *New York Times*, December 31, 1944.

81 "New Uni-Int Set Up," *Daily Variety*, August 14, 1946, front page.

82 Allison Danzig, "Sports Carry On, but the Picture Changes," *New York Times Magazine*, May 23, 1943, 16.

83 "Fair Grounds Entries," *New York Times*, February 2, 1943.

84 Gillette Blades, advertisement, *Washington Post*, January 11, 1946; and Arthur Daley, "Fighter of the Year," *New York Times*, January 15, 1953.

85 *The Air Offensive against Germany*, advertisement, *New York Times*, February 18, 1943.

86 *Thirty Seconds over Tokyo*, advertisement, *New York Times*, July 13, 1943.

87 Review of *Thirty Seconds over Tokyo*, *Farm Journal* 69 (1945): n.p.

88 *Kaiser Wakes the Doctors*, advertisement, *New York Times*, September 26, 1943.

89 *American Dilemma*, advertisement, *New York Times*, March 6, 1944.

90 *The Curtain Rises*, advertisement, *New York Times*, March 19, 1944; and *The Curtain Rises*, advertisement, *New York Times*, April 2, 1944.

91 *The Road to Serfdom*, advertisement, *New York Times*, April 8, 1945.

92 "Blockbuster Hail Stones Cost Theatreman $150 for New Roof," *Showmen's Trade Review*, July 3, 1943, 4.

93 Theodore Strauss, "Miss Bankhead Back from the Sea," *New York Times*, December 5, 1943.

94 "Review: *No Time For Love*," *Boxoffice*, November 13, 1943, 100; *No Time for Love*, advertisement, *Daily Variety*, January 18, 1944, 8–9.

95 *Brazil*, advertisement, *Daily Variety*, November 15, 1944, 4–5.

96 "What the Newspaper Critics Say," *Film Bulletin*, February 5, 1945, 31.

97 Richard L. Coe, "'Holiday in Mexico,' M-G-M's Melting Pot, Sadly Needs Refining," *Washington Post*, September 26, 1946.

98 *There's a Waar On*, advertisement, *The Stage*, August 19, 1943, 6.

99 John Chapman, "Children Capture a Pirate Ship in Charming 'Innocent Voyage,'" *New York Theatre Critics' Review* 4 (1943): 224 (originally published in *New York Daily News*, November 16, 1943).

100 Frank Gill, review of *Carmen Jones*, *Billboard*, December 11, 1943, 28.

101 Francis Drake and Katharine Drake, "Our Next Pearl Harbor?," *Atlantic*, October 1947, 24.

102 Susan Sontag, "The Imagination of Disaster," *Commentary* 40, no. 4 (October 1965): 42–48.

103 Hanson W. Baldwin, "The Atomic Weapon; End of War against Japan Hastened but Destruction Sows Seed of Hate," *New York Times*, August 7, 1945.

104 Baldwin, "Atomic Weapon," 10.
105 "What's Going On at Du Mont Tele? Retrenchment Blues Evident," *Billboard*, November 24, 1945, 15.
106 WOR, advertisement, *Billboard*, November 1, 1947, 11.
107 This critique has been elaborated by Leo Marx and Bruce Mazlish, eds., *Progress: Fact or Illusion?* (Ann Arbor: University of Michigan Press, 1996); and Mumford, *Myth of the Machine*.
108 "This Month . . . ," *American Gas Journal* 173, no. 4 (1950): 3.
109 Drake and Drake, "Our Next Pearl Harbor?," 24.

CHAPTER 4 **THE BUSINESS OF BIG**

1 Thomas Schatz, *Boom and Bust: American Cinema in the 1940s* (Berkeley: University of California Press, 1997), 392.
2 Schatz, *Boom and Bust*, 392.
3 Quoted in Schatz, *Boom and Bust*, 394.
4 Schatz, *Boom and Bust*, 392.
5 John Izod, *Hollywood and the Box Office, 1895–1986* (New York: Columbia University Press, 1988), 64.
6 Peter Lev, *The Fifties: Transforming the Screen, 1950–1959* (Berkeley: University of California Press, 2003), 162–168.
7 Antonio Gramsci, *Selections from the Prison Notebooks*, ed. and trans. Quintin Hoare and Geoffrey Nowell Smith (New York: International Publishers, 1971), 306.
8 Susan Sontag, "Fascinating Fascism," *New York Review of Books*, February 15, 1975.
9 Leo Marx, "Does Improved Technology Mean Progress?," *Technology Review* 90, no. 1 (January 1987): 32–41.
10 Leo Marx, *The Machine in the Garden: Technology and the Pastoral Ideal in America* (New York: Oxford University Press, 1964).
11 David Nye, *American Technological Sublime* (Cambridge, MA: MIT Press, 1994), 282.
12 See, for example, Judy Wajcman, *Feminism Confronts Technology* (Cambridge: Polity, 1991).
13 Mumford, *Myth of the Machine*, 1:168.
14 Haidee Wasson, *Everyday Movies: Portable Projectors and the Transformation of American Culture* (Oakland: University of California Press, forthcoming).
15 Susan Stewart, *On Longing: Narratives of the Miniature, the Gigantic, the Souvenir, the Collection* (Durham, NC: Duke University Press, 1993), 71. For a discussion of the gigantic in relation to the history of visual culture, see Alison Griffiths, *Shivers down Your Spine: Cinema, Museums, and the Immersive View* (New York: Columbia University Press, 2008).

16 The most reliable and comprehensive treatment of these formats remains John Belton, *Widescreen Cinema* (Cambridge, MA: Harvard University Press, 1992); see also John Belton, Sheldon Hall, and Steve Neale, eds., *Widescreen Worldwide* (New Barnet, UK: John Libby, 2010).

17 Ariel Rogers, *Cinematic Appeals: The Experience of New Movie Technologies* (New York: Columbia University Press, 2013).

18 "Let's Go! It's Movietime, U.S.A. . . . ," advertisement, *New York Times*, October 3, 1951.

19 Dave Levadi, "B&K's Slogan Is: 'No Slogans'—Wallerstein Reaction to Golden Jubilee Fiasco—Consistent, Point-of-Sale Showmanship Pays," *Variety*, November 13, 1957, 5, 13.

20 Irving Bernstein, *Hollywood at the Crossroads: An Economic Study of the Motion Picture Industry* (Hollywood: Hollywood AFL Film Council, 1957), 2.

21 Izod, *Hollywood and the Box Office*, 98–99.

22 Izod, *Hollywood and the Box Office*, 119, 124.

23 Izod, *Hollywood and the Box Office*, 124.

24 Izod, *Hollywood and the Box Office*, 124.

25 "'Sick' Screen Given Senatorial Advice," *New York Times*, August 5, 1953; and U.S. Congress, Senate Select Committee on Small Business, *Problems of Independent Motion Picture Exhibitions*, Report of the Select Committee on Small Business, 83rd Cong., 1st sess., August 3, 1953.

26 Simon N. Whitney, "The Impact of Antitrust Laws: Vertical Disintegration in the Motion Picture Industry," *American Economic Review* 45, no. 2 (May 1955): 491–498.

27 Leo A. Handel, *Hollywood Looks at Its Audience: A Report of Film Audience Research* (Urbana: University of Illinois Press, 1950), 98.

28 Handel, *Hollywood Looks at Its Audience*, 98.

29 Whitney, "The Impact of Antitrust Laws," 495.

30 "Blockbusters Coming—but When?," *Variety*, November 3, 1954, 10.

31 Kim R. Holston, *Movie Roadshows: A History and Filmography of Reserved-Seat Limited Showings, 1911–1973* (Jefferson, NC: McFarland, 2013), 271. For more detail on this history and its relationship to other distribution practices, see Hall, "Tall Revenue Features," 11–26.

32 For example, "Holdovers Heftiest among L.A. 1st Runs; 'SAC' 66G in Second Round in 10 Sites," *Daily Variety*, July 12, 1955, 3.

33 A fine survey of these exhibition technologies appears in Lev, *Fifties*, 107–125, as well as in Belton, *Widescreen Cinema*.

34 Manny Farber, "The Robe" (1953), in *Farber on Film: The Complete Film Writings of Manny Farber*, ed. Robert Polito (New York: Library of America, 2009), 451.

35 Farber, "The Robe," 451.

36 Farber, "The Robe," 453.

37 Manny Farber, "Movie Gimmicks; Seven Films of 1953" (1954), in *Farber on Film*, 458.

38 Roland Barthes, "Cinemascope" (1954), in *Essays and Interviews*, vol. 4, *Signs and Images: Writings on Art, Cinema and Photography*, trans. and ed. Chris Turner (New York: Seagull Books, 2016), 12.

39 Roland Barthes, "Cinemascope," 12.
40 Audience Research Inc., "Survey of Reactions to Three Dimension Pictures, Wide Screen, and Stereophonic Sound" (July 1953), in "Gallup Looks at the Movies: Audience Research Reports 1940–1950" (Wilmington, DE: Scholarly Resources, 1979).
41 Audience Research Inc., "Survey of Reactions," 5.
42 Audience Research Inc., "Survey of Reactions," 6.
43 Audience Research Inc., "Survey of Reactions," 7–7b.
44 Audience Research Inc., "Survey of Reactions," 60.
45 "ABC Fusing Friday TV Blockbuster," *Daily Variety*, May 27, 1953, 1, 14.
46 "Nitery Reviews," *Daily Variety*, December 17, 1954, 6.
47 Marjorie B. Snyder, "Much-Touted 'Story in 3-D' Would Interest Dr. Kinsey," *Washington Post*, September 20, 1953.
48 "Advertising and Marketing," *New York Times*, January 22, 1954.
49 "Studios Star-Stud Pix to Bolster Limp Box-Office," *Daily Variety*, April 27, 1948, 3, 8.
50 "$119 Million for 65 Pix; High Priced Films Lined Up for '49," *Daily Variety*, December 2, 1948, 14.
51 "'12 O'Clock' Wow $34,000 in Philly," *Variety*, February 1, 1950, 11.
52 Mike Connolly, "Just for Variety," *Daily Variety*, December 19, 1950, 4.
53 Mike Connolly, "Just for Variety," *Daily Variety*, August 19, 1951, 2.
54 *The Atomic City*, advertisement, *Daily Variety*, May 8, 1952, 5.
55 Paramount Pictures Production Records, 18.f-220 *The Atomic City*—Production 1951–1952, Margaret Herrick Library.
56 *Daily Variety*, June 4, 1952, explained the odd retitling decision as done "in the hopes that new tag will generate grosses in keeping with the film's critical acclaim as a 'sleeper.'" Press clipping in Paramount Pictures Production Records, 18.f-220 *The Atomic City*—Production 1951–1952, Margaret Herrick Library.
57 *The Atomic City*, advertisement, Paramount Pictures Press Sheets, *The Atomic City*—Pressbook, 1951–1952, Margaret Herrick Library.
58 "UA's Gross for 1952 up by 50 Per Cent," *Boxoffice*, January 17, 1953, 16.
59 *Ransom!*, advertisement, *Daily Variety*, December 28, 1955, 15; and *Ransom!*, advertisement, press kit, 1955, MGM, Margaret Herrick Library.
60 *Ransom!*, advertisement, *Saratogian*, February 4, 1956; and *Ransom!*, advertisement, *Lockport Union-Sun and Journal*, May 31, 1956.
61 *Thirty Seconds over Tokyo*, advertisement, *Times-News*, February 9, 1956.
62 Army Archerd, "Just for Variety," *Daily Variety*, November 6, 1953, 2.
63 "Report 300G Payoff by Col for 11 Kramer Pix; Includes 'Caine Mutiny,'" *Daily Variety*, November 24, 1954, 21.
64 "'Caine' Wow $40,000, Det.; 'Apache' Smash 27G, 'High' Lofty $35,000," *Variety*, July 7, 1954, 8.
65 Lev, *Fifties*, 122–123.
66 Joe Schoenfeld, "Time and Place," *Daily Variety*, August 18, 1955, 2.
67 Joe Schoenfeld, "Film Review—*Oklahoma!*," *Daily Variety*, October 11, 1955, 3.

68 "Holiday Bix Here SRO for 'Okla.,' 'G&D,' Cinerama," *Daily Variety*, November 25, 1955, 1, 3.
69 "All-Time B.O. Champs," *Variety*, January 8, 1958, 6, 60; and "Selznick's Top-Money-Film Crown Threatened by '57 Blockbusters," *Variety*, January 8, 1958, 6.
70 "All Par '56 Pix to Be in VistaVision," *Daily Variety*, November 25, 1995, 1.
71 "Review: War and Peace," *Variety*, August 22, 1956, 6.
72 For more on CinemaScope and its use of stereo sound systems, see Matthew Malsky, "The Grandeur(s) of CinemaScope: Early Experiments in Cinematic Stereophony," in *Living Stereo: Histories and Cultures of Multichannel Sound*, ed. Paul Théberge, Kyle Devine, and Tom Everrett (London: Bloomsbury, 2015), 207–222.
73 Lev, *Fifties*, 212.
74 Robert F. Hawkins, "19 Nations with 32 Pix in Venice Film Fest; 'Thief,' 'Kentuckian' from U.S.," *Variety*, August 24, 1955, 2, 75.
75 Fred Hift, "Music Films' Hard-Sell Abroad; Foreigners Like Plenty o' Plot," *Variety*, November 30, 1955, 1.

CHAPTER 5 **HOLLYWOOD'S RETURN**

1 Izod, *Hollywood and the Box Office*, 124.
2 Izod, *Hollywood and the Box Office*, 125.
3 Bill Brogdon, "L.A. Theatres' Sock Year," *Daily Variety*, October 17, 1955, 295.
4 Quoted in Lev, *Fifties*, 211.
5 Izod, *Hollywood and the Box Office*, 142.
6 "48-Pix, $40,000,000 UA Program; 12-Month Slate to Include Monthly 'Blockbusters'; US Prez Bullish on Future," *Daily Variety*, August 2, 1954, 1, 5.
7 "48-Pix, $40,000,000 UA Program," 1.
8 "48-Pix, $40,000,000 UA Program," 5.
9 AIP, advertisement, *Variety*, August 29, 1956, 21; and AIP, advertisement, *Boxoffice Barometer*, February 9, 1957, 55.
10 AIP, advertisement, *Variety*, January 8, 1958, 57.
11 "Action-and-Horror Staple Stuff; 20,000,000 Thrill-Seekers (12 to 25) Backbone of Exploitation Pix," *Variety*, March 6, 1957, 20.
12 Quoted in "Action-and-Horror Staple Stuff," 20.
13 Quoted in "Action-and-Horror Staple Stuff," 20.
14 Whitney, "The Impact of Antitrust Laws," 494.
15 Quoted in "Nicholson Scores 'Dollar Snobbery,' 'Provincialism,'" *Independent Film Journal*, October 26, 1957, 22.
16 "Sees Blockbusters as Boost to Short Films," *Variety*, December 18, 1957, 12.
17 "Your Business Will Continue to Thrive in 'Fifty-Five with More Blockbusters from Paramount," advertisement, *Variety*, January 5, 1955, 26.
18 *The Bridges at Toko-Ri*, advertisement, *Daily Variety*, January 21, 1955, 5–14.

19 *The Seven Little Foys*, advertisement, Paramount Pictures Press Sheets, *The Seven Little Foys*—Pressbook, 1955, Margaret Herrick Library.
20 *We're No Angels*, advertisement, *Variety*, July 6, 1955, 14.
21 Quoted in "Steve Broidy Turns the Tables on Exhibs, Pins Blame on Them for Pix Shortage," *Daily Variety*, March 23, 1955, 1, 4.
22 "In Quest of an Alibi," *Variety*, December 7, 1955, 3.
23 "'Glass Slipper' Glides to Shimmering Start at B'w'y B.O. despite Bad Weather," *Daily Variety*, March 28, 1955, 3.
24 "'Blackboard Jungle' Eyes 180G Wk. Here," *Daily Variety*, May 16, 1955, 1.
25 "'Stranger' Mighty 40G, Pitt; 'Lady' 25," *Daily Variety*, July 27, 1955, 8.
26 "WB Blockbusters for TV Series; Brochure Names 'Casablanca,' 'King's Row,' 'Cheyenne,' in TV Plans; Prep Aviation Series," *Daily Variety*, April 8, 1955, 1, 13.
27 Frank Scully, "Scully's Scrapbook," *Variety*, April 25, 1956, 77.
28 "'56 Oscar a $1,000,000 Baby; Will Add That to 'Marty' Take," *Variety*, March 28, 1956, 5, 15.
29 "Line Up Big Films in the Summer Alleys (with Blockbusters Included)," *Variety*, May 2, 1956, 13.
30 "'Trapeze' Swings toward $7,000,000 for U.S. and Canada," *Variety*, August 15, 1956, 4.
31 Robert J. Landry, "Fight 'Greater TV' Season," *Variety*, July 2, 1958, 13.
32 Gene Arneel, "Pix Prosperity in for a Run; Television Fades as B.O. Heavy," *Variety*, August 24, 1955, 75.
33 "It May Be Filmdom's Best Year," *Picturegoer*, December 24, 1955, 18.
34 Freeman Lincoln, "The Comeback of the Movies," *Fortune*, February 1955, 127.
35 "All-Time B.O. Champs," 6, 60.
36 "Selznick's Top-Money-Film Crown Threatened," 6.
37 "C'Scope Anni," *Daily Variety*, September 3, 1954, 3.
38 Lincoln, "The Comeback of the Movies," 128, 129, 130.
39 Denise Mann, *Hollywood Independents: The Postwar Talent Takeover* (Minneapolis: University of Minnesota Press, 2008), 122.
40 Gary R. Edgerton, *American Film Exhibition and an Analysis of the Motion Picture Industry's Market Structure, 1963–1980* (New York: Garland, 1983), 22. At the time, the top national distributors were Buena Vista (Disney), Columbia, Loew's (MGM), Paramount, Twentieth Century Fox, UA, Universal, and Warner Brothers along with Allied Artists and AIP. Two others, RKO and Republic, were in the process of ceasing distribution operations at the time.
41 Television as a popular everyday cultural practice has been explored in key works in television studies, including David Marc, *Demographic Vistas: Television in American Culture* (Philadelphia: University of Pennsylvania Press, 1984); and Horace Newcomb and Paul M. Hirsch, "TV as a Cultural Forum," *Quarterly Review of Film Studies* 8, no. 3 (Summer 1983): 45–55. For a comprehensive study of the settlement of the television industry in the 1950s, see William Boddy, *Fifties Television: The Industry and Its Critics*

(Urbana: University of Illinois Press, 1990). For an examination of the emergent forms of citizenship that developed as shaped by television, see Anna McCarthy, *The Citizen Machine: Governing by Television in 1950s America* (New York: New Press, 2010).

42 "'Matinee' Call for 4,000 Actors; NBC-TV's 5-a-Week Using No Producers and No Big Names," *Daily Variety*, July 21, 1955, 23.

43 Thomas M. Pryor, "Film Men Report on TV Competition: Studio Chiefs Hear Box Office Didn't Succumb to Sunday's 'Diamond Jubilee' Telecast," *New York Times*, October 29, 1954.

44 "Blockbuster Features Cause Greater Rating Fluctuations," *Billboard*, May 13, 1957, 20.

45 Leon Morse, "CBS-TV Skeds Blockbuster Million-Dollar Features," *Billboard*, August 6, 1955, 2.

46 Walter F. Kerr, "Review: *No Time for Sergeants*," *New York Herald Tribune*, October 21, 1955; and *No Time for Sergeants*, advertisement, *New York Times*, October 22, 1955.

47 Hy Hollinger, "'Lost Audience': Grass vs. Class—Sticks Now on 'Hick Pix' Kick," *Variety*, December 5, 1956, 1, 86.

48 George McCall, "Sticks Nix Hick Pix: Not Interested in Farm Drama," *Variety*, July 17, 1935, 1, 51.

49 Hollinger, "'Lost Audience,'" 86.

50 Susan Ohmer, *George Gallup in Hollywood* (New York: Columbia University Press, 2006); and Handel, *Hollywood Looks at Its Audience*.

51 *Giant*, "Motion Picture Audience Action Index," November 15, 1956, file 703, George Stevens Papers, Margaret Herrick Library, 1–2.

52 Fred Goldberg to Bill Blowitz, memorandum, February 25, 1957, file 675, George Stevens Papers, Margaret Herrick Library, 1; Fred Goldberg to Bill Blowitz, memorandum, February 27, 1957, file 675, George Stevens Papers, Margaret Herrick Library, 1–2; and "Sindlinger Finds Movie Growth Sparked by Success of 'Giant,'" March 4, 1957, file 675, George Stevens Papers, Margaret Herrick Library, 1–4.

53 "Study of 'Giant': Killer of B.O. Blues—Sindlinger Poses Science of Blockbuster 'Know-About' and 'Talk-About' Factors Unique Case History Startled Showmen," *Variety*, March 6, 1957, 7.

54 "Study of 'Giant.'"

55 "Japanese Gross on 'War' to Top 'Roman Holiday'; 'Giant' Another Socko," *Variety*, March 20, 1957, 16.

56 "Study of 'Giant,'" 7.

57 Albert Sindlinger, "Take Them Straight!," *Independent Film Journal*, June 26, 1958, 180, 208.

58 Ivan Spear, "Impressive Production Outlook for 1957," *Boxoffice Barometer*, February 9, 1957, 15.

59 "Warners Zingy First Quarter, up 70%; but Second Won't Be Comparable; Blockbusters Swell the Total," *Variety*, February 13, 1957, 4.

60 Gene Arneel, "Hail to a Still-Hale Film Industry (Run Down of 'So What's Good?')," *Variety*, March 20, 1957, 12.

61 Arneel, "Hail."
62 "Review: *The Ten Commandments*," *Variety*, October 10, 1956, 6.
63 "Blockbusters' Fallout Risk," *Variety*, May 7, 1958, 3.
64 "Par Nixes '10c' Free Rides; All Must Pay at Drive-Ins," *Variety*, May 14, 1958, 5.
65 "Precedental Policy Certain to Echo as Others Follow 'Ten Commandments,'" *Variety*, May 14, 1958, 5.
66 "Blockbuster Terms in Smaller Situations," *Variety*, December 17, 1958, 15.
67 "How Does Trade Top Blockbusters?," *Variety*, May 14, 1958, 4.
68 Bernstein, *Hollywood at the Crossroads*, 4.
69 "No More a Poor Man's Show; 'Kwai' in Newark as $3 Hard Tic," *Variety*, May 28, 1958, 7.
70 Quoted in "No More a Poor Man's Show."
71 "Blockbusters vs. Main Street; 'B' (for Budget) Films Return," *Variety*, February 6, 1957, 5, 22.
72 Eric Hoyt, *Hollywood Vault: Film Libraries before Home Video* (Berkeley: University of California Press, 2014), 176.
73 "Hoarding the Blockbusters; Dictated by Payment Plan," *Variety*, February 13, 1957, 67.
74 "Post'48 'Blockbusters' as Panacea for Dwindling Pre-'48 Features," *Variety*, April 29, 1959, 29, 46.
75 "TOA Pushing Idea of Exhibs' Buy of Post-1948 Video Residuals; Might Then Sell Nonblockbusters," *Variety*, October 22, 1958, 5.
76 Screen Gems, "Powerhouse" advertisement, *Variety*, December 10, 1958, 24–25.
77 *The Joker Is Wild*, advertisement, *Daily Variety*, September 17, 1957, 7–14.
78 *April Love*, advertisement, *Daily Variety*, November 6, 1957, 14.
79 20th Century Fox, advertisement, *Variety*, October 30, 1957, 11–14.
80 United Artists, advertisement for 1958 releases, *Daily Variety*, December 3, 1957, 8–9.
81 United Artists, advertisement for 1959 releases, *Boxoffice Barometer*, February 16, 1959, 3–6.
82 "UA List Promises 10 'Blockbusters,'" *Variety*, February 20, 1957, 7.
83 "UA Boast: Blockbusters in Bunches," *Variety*, February 18, 1959, 5, 14.
84 Arthur B. Krim, "No Fixed Limits," *Independent Film Journal*, June 26, 1958, 62, 216.
85 William J. Heineman, "Merchandise Counts," *Independent Film Journal*, June 26, 1958, 110, 162.
86 "Columbia Big Need: Another Blockbuster," *Variety*, October 2, 1957, 4.
87 "Blockbuster Age Economics as Pain during Transition," *Variety*, April 30, 1958, 3.
88 *The Big Show*, advertisement, *Daily Variety*, May 1, 1957, 5.
89 *The Big Show*, advertisement, 7.
90 Hy Hollinger, "20th-Fox Wallopy 'Giant Trailer' Stimulating Entire Film Trade," *Variety*, May 15, 1957, 15.
91 Hedda Hopper, "Cagney's Ready to Bust—Junior's a Football Hero," *Washington Post and Times Herald*, November 27, 1955; and Dorothy Kilgallen, "No Journey's End without a Loan," *Washington Post and Times Herald*, June 28, 1955.

92 Dorothy Kilgallen, "Bid Runs High for Sanders Story," *Washington Post and Times Herald*, November 17, 1958.
93 Thomas M. Pryor, "Warners to Back Movie by Monroe," *New York Times*, March 2, 1956.
94 *A Farewell to Arms*, advertisement, *New York Times*, January 30, 1958.
95 *The Brothers Karamazov*, advertisement, *Washington Post and Times Herald*, March 20, 1958.
96 A. H. Weiler, "View from a Local Vantage Point," *New York Times*, April 13, 1958.
97 A. H. Weiler, "Passing Picture Scene," *New York Times*, May 4, 1958.
98 Milton Esterow, "Adult Films, New Comfort Revive City's Moviegoing," *New York Times*, May 5, 1958.
99 Richard L. Coe, "'Chase's On at the Met," *Washington Post and Times Herald*, May 10, 1958.
100 "Only Blockbusters Get Theatre Bally Attention; In-Betweener's Slapped," *Variety*, April 30, 1958, 3, 20; and Abel Green, "Kalmenson's WB Lowdown; Trouble Is an Exec Veep's Biz," *Variety*, July 16, 1958, 3, 10.
101 Manny Farber, "Three Art-y Films" (1959), in *Farber on Film*, 506.
102 Pierre Bourdieu, *Distinction: A Social Critique of the Judgement of Taste*, trans. Richard Nice (1979; Cambridge, MA: Harvard University Press, 1984).
103 Bernstein, *Hollywood at the Crossroads*, 31–32.
104 Bernstein, *Hollywood at the Crossroads*, 34.
105 Bernstein, *Hollywood at the Crossroads*, i, 1.
106 Whitney, "The Impact of Antitrust Laws," 492, cited in Bernstein, *Hollywood at the Crossroads*, 20.
107 Bernstein, *Hollywood at the Crossroads*, 9.
108 Bernstein, *Hollywood at the Crossroads*, 12.
109 Bernstein, *Hollywood at the Crossroads*, 25–26.
110 Bernstein, *Hollywood at the Crossroads*, 49.
111 Bernstein, *Hollywood at the Crossroads*, 19.
112 Bernstein, *Hollywood at the Crossroads*, i.
113 Bernstein, *Hollywood at the Crossroads*, 27.
114 Bernstein, *Hollywood at the Crossroads*, 28.
115 Bernstein, *Hollywood at the Crossroads*, 27.
116 Bernstein, *Hollywood at the Crossroads*, 28.
117 Bernstein, *Hollywood at the Crossroads*, 77.
118 Rick Altman, *Film/Genre* (London: BFI Publishing, 1999).

CHAPTER 6 COSMOPOLITAN ARTLESSNESS

1 Samuel A. Boyea, letter to the drama editor, *New York Times*, October 25, 1953.
2 "Modesty (in Budgets) Returns; All-Blockbuster Plan Too Risky," *Variety*, June 27, 1956, 3, 7.

3 "Perspective vs. Hysterics," *Variety*, December 18, 1957, 4.
4 "Hazards in 'Blockbusting,'" *Variety*, November 6, 1957, 3.
5 "'Gimmicks' Did Well in 1957—Sputnik Latest 'Of Monsters,'" *Variety*, November 6, 1957, 3, 36.
6 Schwartz, *It's So French!*
7 "Not 'Anti-American'—but 'Pro-Arty,'" *Variety*, May 15, 1957, 5.
8 "Production's Fiscal Danger Zone Is between 'Lil' and 'All-Out' Budgets," *Variety*, July 2, 1958, 20.
9 "Production's Fiscal Danger Zone."
10 Bosley Crowther, "Communique from Hollywood and Vine," *New York Times*, February 3, 1957.
11 "Universal's Money-Making Habit vs. Industry Blockbuster Theory," *Variety*, October 24, 1956, 28.
12 Abel Green, "Pix Pioneering—'56 Style; Goldenson Takes New B.O. Slant," *Variety*, August 22, 1956, 16.
13 "C.B. Moss Sees Future Films Priced and Handled a la Legit," *Variety*, October 3, 1956, 24.
14 "New Group of Potential Blockbusters Rising to Hold Hands with 'GWTW,'" *Variety*, August 29, 1956, 1.
15 "New Group of Potential Blockbusters."
16 Bourdieu, "The Field of Cultural Production," 29–73.
17 Nunnally Johnson, "Oh, Men! Oh, Women! Oh, Slightly Colossal!," *New York Times*, February 17, 1957.
18 "H'wood Not Romancing Sex," *Variety*, September 12, 1956, 5.
19 Robert J. Landry, "Appraising the Judges: Inscrutable Public Has the Last Word in Determining Movie Attendance," *New York Times*, February 24, 1957.
20 Landry, "Appraising the Judges."
21 "Less 'Verbiage' (Translate 'Garbiage') as Columbia Updates Press Books," *Variety*, August 7, 1957, 20.
22 Quoted in Hy Hollinger, "Semi-annual Hysterics in Film Trade 'No Way to Run a Business'—Wanger," *Variety*, October 23, 1957, 75.
23 "Need Exhibitors in Production—Fabian: Producers Don't Figure, Theatres Don't Recognize Blockbusters Ahead of Time," *Variety*, March 6, 1957, 13.
24 "Hardsell—Will It Payoff If Release Is Less Than a B.O. Blockbuster?," *Variety*, June 25, 1958, 18.
25 "'Proud Rebel' Tested," *Variety*, July 2, 1958, 20.
26 A. D. Murphy, "Hard-Sell and Skid Row Blockbuster," *Variety*, December 9, 1959, 19.
27 A. H. Weiler, "Moving Sentiment," *New York Times*, July 2, 1958.
28 *Proud Rebel*, advertisement, *New York Times*, July 3, 1958; and *Proud Rebel*, advertisement, *New York Times*, July 11, 1958.
29 *The Brothers Karamazov*, advertisement, *Independent Film Journal*, March 1, 1958, 2.
30 Robert J. Landry, "Films May Be Doing Dandy, Taking into Account Mortgaged Masses in a Dead-Centre Calm," *Variety*, July 2, 1958, 13.

31 "Long-Run-Short-Week Woe; 20th's Big List Needs More Time," *Variety*, July 16, 1958, 5.
32 Robert J. Landry, "Statistics Never Very Reliable in Film Biz Anyhow, and Today's Changes Easily Misread," *Variety*, July 2, 1958, 20.
33 Gene Moskowitz, "Films along the Seine: 'Les Miserables' Ushers Blockbuster Era into France—Other Matters," *New York Times*, April 20, 1958.
34 "Brit.'s-Eye View of Blockbusters," *Variety*, September 24, 1958, 7.
35 "Universal Cuts Size of Program; Martin Details Present Strategy," *Variety*, July 16, 1958, 3.
36 "Paramount Pictures Says Operating Net for 9 Months Tops '57: Cost-Cutting at Movie Studios Cited; 20 'Million Dollar Plus' Films Slated for '59," *Wall Street Journal*, September 30, 1958.
37 "Paramount Pictures Says."
38 "Paramount Considers Acquiring Companies outside Movie Field: Balaban Tells Meeting There May Be Some Announcements 'during 1959–60 Period,'" *Wall Street Journal*, June 3, 1959.
39 Thomas M. Pryor, "Hollywood Vista: Three Authoritative 'Reporters' Add Background to Production Picture," *New York Times*, October 26, 1958.
40 "Columbia Pictures Sees Second Fiscal Period about Breaking Even: Movie Maker Had $395,000 Loss in December '57; Profit Expected for Half," *Wall Street Journal*, December 16, 1958.
41 "Universal Pictures to Sell, Lease Back Real Estate, Studios: MCA, Inc., TV Show Producer and Talent Agency, to Buy Them for $11,250,000," *Wall Street Journal*, December 19, 1958.
42 "Puzzle: 'How' Get 'More' Films; Playdate-Bank Idea Up Anew," *Variety*, December 17, 1958, 7.
43 "Call Blockbusters an 'Over-eagerness,'" *Variety*, October 21, 1959, 4.
44 "Distributor Bids to Finance Films: Walter Reade Jr. Would Aid U.S. Productions—Isabel Jeans in 'Olympia,'" *New York Times*, April 9, 1959.
45 Thomas M. Pryor, "Hollywood Review: Year's Problems Faced by Hopeful Industry," *New York Times*, January 4, 1959.
46 Pryor, "Hollywood Review."
47 Pryor, "Hollywood Review."
48 Pryor, "Hollywood Review."
49 "Blockbuster a Romantic Word to Wall Street," *Variety*, July 1, 1959, 1.
50 Gavin Lambert, "From a Hollywood Notebook," *Sight and Sound* 28, no. 2 (Spring 1959): 71.
51 John Gillett, "The Survivors," *Sight and Sound* 28, nos. 3/4 (Summer/Autumn 1959): 152.
52 Bosley Crowther, "Raisins in the Pies: On Looking for the Particularly Tasty Things in Films," *New York Times*, May 24, 1959.
53 Crowther, "Raisins in the Pies."
54 Manny Farber, "White Elephant Art vs. Termite Art" (1962), in *Farber on Film*, 533–542.

55 "Two Views on Filmdom's Future," *Picturegoer*, August 2, 1958, 8.
56 Elizabeth Forrest, "The Blockbusters Are Coming," *Picturegoer*, March 15, 1958, 14.
57 "Antidote for Pessimists; Contrasting 1958 to '52 for Moral," *Variety*, October 15, 1958, 3.
58 "Antidote for Pessimists."
59 "WB Policy: 12–14 a Year, All Big; Vidpix Uses Up Studio Facilities," *Variety*, November 12, 1958, 4.
60 Gene Arneel, "1958: Year of Blockbusters," *Variety*, January 7, 1959, 9, 50.
61 *The Big Country*, advertisement, *New York Times*, August 28, 1958.
62 Stanley Kramer, "The Subliminal Blockbuster," *Independent Film Journal*, June 26, 1958, 128, 160.
63 Donovan Pedelty, "The Year of the Blockbusters," *Picturegoer*, December 27, 1958, 20–21.
64 Donovan Pedelty, "The Shape of Films to Come," *Picturegoer*, February 7, 1959, 6–7.
65 "Viewpoint," editorial, *Picturegoer*, March 7, 1959, 4.
66 Manny Farber, "Big-Studio 'Supers'—Monumental Art Baked in a Pittsburgh Blast Furnace" (1959), in *Farber on Film*, 515.
67 Farber, "Big-Studio 'Supers,'" 516.
68 Richard L. Coe, "Wild, Witty and All-Wool," *Washington Post and Times Herald*, March 18, 1959; and Richard L. Coe, "Capitol Comedy Is Many-Faceted Hit," *Washington Post and Times Herald*, March 22, 1959.
69 *Some Like It Hot*, advertisement, *Washington Post and Times Herald*, March 25, 1959.
70 Howard Cook, "Monroe Pic Has Block-Buster Aura," *Billboard*, March 23, 1959, 23.
71 *A Summer Place*, advertisement, *New York Times*, October 21, 1959.
72 "Business Bulletin: A Special Background Report on Trends in Industry and Finance," *Wall Street Journal*, April 9, 1959.
73 For impressively comprehensive documentation of the multiple versions of *Ben-Hur*, see John Solomon, *Ben-Hur: The Original Blockbuster* (Edinburgh: Edinburgh University Press, 2016).
74 Morgan Hudgins, "'Ben-Hur' Rides Again; New Film of the Lew Wallace Classic Generates Wide Interest in Italy," *New York Times*, August 10, 1958.
75 "B.O. Winners Give Loew's Mgmt. Better Chance to Win Proxy Fite," *Variety*, September 28, 1958, 1, 4.
76 Bosley Crowther, "Optimists Galore: High Hopes and Plans Flood Hollywood," *New York Times*, November 1, 1959.
77 Crowther, "Optimists Galore"; "'Roadshow' Keys Metro Thinking," *Variety*, November 18, 1959, 3, 86; and Martin Hart, "Solving the Mysteries of MGM Camera 65 and Ultra Panavision 70," *Widescreen Museum*, 1997/2002, www.widescreenmuseum.com.
78 Crowther, "Optimists Galore."
79 Seymour Peck, "The $15,000,000 Chariot Race," *New York Times Magazine*, November 8, 1959, 26–27.
80 Richard Nason, "On 'Ben-Hur's' Record," *New York Times*, November 15, 1959.
81 *Ben-Hur*, advertisement, *New York Times*, October 25, 1959.
82 "'Roadshow' Keys Metro Thinking," 3, 86.

83 *Ben-Hur*, *Orpheus Descending*, and *All the King's Men*, advertisements, all appearing in the *New York Times*, November 14, 1959.

84 *Ben-Hur*, advertisement, *New York Post*, November 19, 1959. The same ad ran on the same day in the *New York Daily News*, *Newsday*, the *New York Herald Tribune*, the *New York Post*, and the *New York Times*.

85 Metro-Goldwyn-Mayer, *The Story of the Making of Ben-Hur: A Tale of the Christ* (New York: Random House, 1959).

86 "Wall Street and Society Predominate Audience at Dignified 'Ben-Hur' Bow," *Variety*, November 18, 1959, 86.

87 Murray Schumach, "Hollywood Teams: The Promotional Pairing of Pictures and Products Is Popular Practice," *New York Times*, November 22, 1959.

88 "History Comes to Life with . . . *Ben-Hur*," advertisement, *New York Daily News*, November 22, 1959.

89 Richard Nason, "'Hercules' Starts Flood of Movies: Levine's Success Is First of Many Spectaculars on Way—New Bill at Cameo," *New York Times*, October 24, 1959.

90 Murray Schumach, "Metro Stills Leo for the First Time: Famous Roaring Lion Kept Silent in 'Ben-Hur' to Save Religious Mood of Opening," *New York Times*, November 26, 1959.

91 "No Carny Hokum, Open 'Ben-Hur' on Dignified Plane," *Variety*, November 25, 1959, 17.

92 Abel Green, "Towering B.O. Stature of 'Ben-Hur' Vindicates Joe Vogel's Metro Team," *Variety*, November 18, 1959, 1.

93 Bosley Crowther, "'Ben-Hur,' a Blockbuster," *New York Times*, November 19, 1959.

94 *Ben-Hur*, advertisement, *New York Herald Tribune*, November 22, 1959; *Ben-Hur*, advertisement, *New York Times*, November 25, 1959; and *Ben-Hur*, advertisement, *New York Times*, November 29, 1959.

95 *Ben-Hur*, advertisement, *New York Post*, November 20, 1959.

96 *Ben-Hur*, advertisement, *New York Herald Tribune*, November 24, 1959.

97 Bosley Crowther, "The New 'Ben-Hur': Old Story of the Heroic Judean Is Made into a Fine and Pertinent Film," *New York Times*, November 22, 1959.

98 "*Ben-Hur*: Film Review," *Variety*, November 18, 1959, 6.

99 "*Ben-Hur*: Film Review," 6.

100 Ben Kubasik, "'Ben-Hur' Is Nine Lively Minutes Wrapped in 3½ Hrs. of Nothing," *Newsday*, November 19, 1959.

101 "'Ben-Hur' Payoff Quicker Than Tis Said in Trade?," *Variety*, December 2, 1959, 7, 13.

102 *Solomon and Sheba*, advertisement, *New York Post*, December 27, 1959.

103 *Solomon and Sheba*, advertisement, *New York Times*, December 24, 1959.

104 New Loew's Capitol, advertisement, *New York Times*, December 24, 1959.

105 "Gimmicks Pay Off in Box-Office War: Audiences Are Insured, Feel Tingly and See Skeletons at William Castle Films," *New York Times*, October 26, 1959.

106 "'Sword and Cross' TV Series Themed to Blockbusters," *Variety*, December 16, 1959, 22.

107 "Universal Pictures Says Net Shows Sharp Gains," *Wall Street Journal*, December 22, 1959.

108 Gene Arneel, "Paramount Needs Another DeMille to Compete in Blockbuster Era," *Variety*, April 22, 1959, 1, 86.
109 Murray Schumach, "Filmland Jargon Vital, Ambiguous: If a Movie Fails, It's 'Built-In Values' Were Misused, Say Boldly Cautious Aides," *New York Times*, June 22, 1959.
110 *Operation Petticoat*, advertisement, *Variety*, December 30, 1959, 17.
111 *Ten Seconds to Hell*, advertisement, *Variety*, September 2, 1959, 14.
112 *The F.B.I. Story*, advertisement, *Motion Picture Daily*, September 14, 1959, 4–5.
113 Hedda Hopper, "This Man Zugsmith Is the Talk of the Trade," *Washington Post and Times Herald*, December 20, 1959.
114 "N.Y. Critic's 'Bests': 'Ben-Hur,' Audrey Hepburn, Jas. Stewart, Zinnemann," *Variety*, December 30, 1959, 1, 46.
115 Hy Hollinger, "No Biz Like Pix Biz Was Then as Frantic '50's End an Era," *Daily Variety*, December 30, 1959, 1.
116 Tino Balio, ed., *The American Film Industry*, revised ed. (Madison: University of Wisconsin Press, 1985), 435; "Best News: Uptrends Continue," *Broadcasting*, December 26, 1966, 45; Paige Albiniak, "The Long Goodbye," *Broadcasting and Cable*, May 10, 2004, 3.
117 "$93 Million Week's Film Jackpot," *Broadcasting*, October 3, 1966, 25–27.
118 "Ford Buys 'Robe'; Will Have One Break Spot," *Broadcasting*, January 9, 1967, 42.
119 "How Wide-Screen Movies Fit the 21-Inch Tube," *Broadcasting*, October 3, 1966, 27.
120 Hollinger, "No Biz like Pix Biz," 7.
121 Hollinger, "No Biz like Pix Biz," 7.
122 Bernstein, *Hollywood at the Crossroads*.
123 Hollinger, "No Biz like Pix Biz," 7.
124 Gitelman, *Always Already New*, 6, 7.
125 Shyon Baumann, *Hollywood Highbrow: From Entertainment to Art* (Princeton, NJ: Princeton University Press, 2007), 10.
126 Izod, *Hollywood and the Box Office*, 181.
127 Douglas Gomery, "The Hollywood Blockbuster: Industrial Analysis and Practice," in Stringer, *Movie Blockbusters*, 81.
128 Linda Williams, "Film Genres: Gender, Genre, and Excess," *Film Quarterly* 44, no. 4 (Summer 1991): 2–13.
129 "Shortage?—Only of Blockbusters," *Variety*, November 9, 1960, 15.
130 "Signs of Better Times for Films," *Financial Times*, November 10, 1959.
131 Gene Arneel, "Blockbusters of 1960; Emerging 'New Economics,'" *Variety*, January 4, 1961, 5, 47.
132 Thomas W. Bush, "More Producers Buck 'Blockbuster' Trend, Make Low-Cost Films," *Wall Street Journal*, January 17, 1961.
133 *Lawrence of Arabia*, advertisement, *Variety*, May 29, 1963, 14.
134 "Exhibitors Need Product NOW," *Film Bulletin*, September 2, 1963, 7.
135 Don Mersereau, "Newsmen See Simultaneous Filming of Three 20th-Fox Blockbusters," *Boxoffice*, June 22, 1964, 6.

136 *Exodus*, advertisement, *Lockport Union-Sun and Journal*, August 2, 1961.
137 "Blockbuster Doubts," *Variety*, October 31, 1962, 18.
138 Stanley W. Penn, "Blockbuster Movies: Outlays Soar as Firms Gamble for Big Returns from Fewer Pictures," *Wall Street Journal*, April 2, 1962.
139 Penn, "Blockbuster Movies," 1.
140 "'Blockbuster' as Trade's Bad Joke via Mimeograph," *Variety*, May 3, 1961, 3; and "20th Century-Fox Plans One Blockbuster Monthly," *Boxoffice*, November 6, 1961, 5.
141 "Europe Contrary on Blockbusters," *Variety*, May 30, 1962, 7.
142 Kevin Thomas, "Robinson Crusoe as a Stranded Astronaut," *Washington Post*, August 23, 1964.
143 Penelope Houston and John Gillett, "The Theory and Practice of Blockbusting," *Sight and Sound* 32, no. 2 (Spring 1963): 69.
144 Houston and Gillett, "Theory and Practice of Blockbusting," 69.
145 Houston and Gillett, "Theory and Practice of Blockbusting," 70.
146 Houston and Gillett, "Theory and Practice of Blockbusting," 69.
147 Houston and Gillett, "Theory and Practice of Blockbusting," 71.
148 Houston and Gillett, "Theory and Practice of Blockbusting," 74.

CHAPTER 7 THE END OF JAMES CAMERON'S QUIET YEARS

1 Peter Bart, "An Audience with the King," *Variety*, March 30, 1998, 4, 37.
2 Justin Wyatt and Katherine Vlesmas argued that the public drama of the budget and production problems played a key role in the marketing, and ultimately the success, of *Titanic*. Wyatt and Vlesmas, "The Drama of Recoupment: On the Mass Media Negotiation of *Titanic*," in Sandler and Studlar, *Titanic*, 29–44.
3 Of the many assessments of American film in the 1980s, especially comprehensive is Stephen Prince, *A New Pot of Gold: Hollywood under the Electronic Rainbow, 1980–1989* (Berkeley: University of California Press, 2000); and for more on entertainment franchises, see Derek Johnson, *Media Franchising: Creative License and Collaboration in the Cultural Industries* (New York: New York University Press, 2013).
4 Dade Hayes, "*Titanic* Titan Takes Time Out," *Variety*, December 17, 2001, 4.
5 Joseph MacInnis, *James Cameron's "Aliens of the Deep"* (Washington, DC: National Geographic, 2004), 27.
6 Christopher Pickard, "Visionary Award: James Cameron," *Variety*, June 19, 2006, A6.
7 Peter Debruge, "'Chicken' Eggs on Cameron and 3-D Bet," *Daily Variety*, April 21, 2006, A1.
8 Rebecca Keegan, *The Futurist: The Life and Films of James Cameron* (New York: Crown, 2009).
9 Figures from www.boxofficemojo.com, accessed November 22, 2019.

10 "Are James Cameron Fans the Type Who Buy Tickets Four Months in Advance?," *National Post*, August 29, 2009.
11 Two prominent profiles are David Browning, producer, "Cameron's *Avatar*," *60 Minutes*, aired November 22, 2009, on CBS; and Dana Goodyear, "Man of Extremes: The Return of James Cameron," *New Yorker*, October 26, 2009, 54–67.
12 For example, "New *Avatar* Behind-the-Scene Photos," *Coming Soon*, January 12, 2009, www.comingsoon.net.
13 "Ubisoft and Fox Team for *Avatar* Game," *Coming Soon*, July 24, 2007, www.comingsoon.net.
14 Pamela McClintock, "King of the 3-D World," *Variety*, July 20, 2009, 3, 30.
15 "Exclusive: Soderbergh Gives *Avatar* High Praise," *Coming Soon*, April 30, 2009, www.comingsoon.net. Cameron was a producer for Soderbergh's *Solaris* (2002), so it is possible they had a closer relationship than was evident from their different filmmaking personas.
16 Quoted in Goodyear, "Man of Extremes," 67.
17 Quoted in Bill Higgins, "All Eyes on *Avatar*; Fellow Directors Shower Praise on Cameron," *Variety*, December 18, 2009, www.variety.com.
18 Sharon Waxman, "Computers Join Actors in Hybrids on Screen," *New York Times*, January 9, 2007.
19 Michael Cieply, "Eyepopping, in Many Ways," *New York Times*, November 9, 2009.
20 Cieply, "Eyepopping, in Many Ways."
21 James Rampton, "James Cameron: King of All He Surveys," *Independent* (London), December 19, 2006.
22 Gabriel Snyder and Nicole LaPorte, "Cameron Gets *Avatar* Going," *Variety*, January 8, 2007, www.variety.com.
23 Three superior studies of special effects and cinema technology that include analyses of Cameron's specific impact are Stephen Prince, *Digital Visual Effects in Cinema: The Seduction of Reality* (New Brunswick, NJ: Rutgers University Press, 2012); Pierson, *Special Effects*; and Cubitt, *Cinema Effect*.
24 David S. Cohen, "Goggles Galore: The Studios Have a New 3-D Vision: Their Film Libraries," *Variety*, April 6, 2009, 1, 38.
25 Jeffery Katzenberg, "Katzenberg Defends 3-D as Format of the Future," *Variety*, September 29, 2008, 7, 11.
26 Josh Quittner, "The Next Dimension," *Time*, March 30, 2009, 54–62.
27 Quoted in Goodyear, "Man of Extremes," 67.
28 Quoted in Rick Merritt, "Popcorn, Soda and Two Aspirin," *Electronic Engineering Times*, August 1, 2005, 13.
29 Quoted in Browning, "Cameron's *Avatar*."
30 Quoted in Charlotte Huggins, "The Three Dimensions of 3-D," *Produced By*, Spring 2008, 25.
31 Jonathan Bing, "Will Gizmos Give Biz New Juice? Cameron Says Digital 3-D Could Get Auds out of the House and Back to the Multiplex," *Variety*, March 21, 2005, 10.

32 Quoted in Peter Debruge, "Heavy Hitters Bet Big on Third Dimension; Plexes Feel Compelled to Upgrade with Top Directors and Studios behind Format," *Variety*, June 18, 2007, A5.
33 "Cinema Expo/3-D: The Killer App," *Variety* (supplement), June 9, 2008, A1.
34 It is curious that 3-D was being interpreted as a catalyst for digital exhibition because the digital 3-D systems required screens that made conventional 2-D digital projections darker and less sharp. Huggins, "Three Dimensions of 3-D," 25.
35 Chris Morris, "A Game Changer? *Avatar* Looks to Alter H'w'd Vidgame Push," *Variety*, June 15, 2009, 4, 12.
36 See "Panasonic and Twentieth Century Fox Team"; and "Panasonic Rolls."
37 Seth Lubove, "Sinking Ship," *Forbes*, November 14, 2005, 161–165.
38 Piers Bizony, *Digital Domain: The Leading Edge of Visual Effects* (New York: Billboard Books, 2001).
39 Bizony, *Digital Domain*, 221–222.
40 David S. Cohen, "Film Not Ready to Cede to Tape," *Variety*, April 18, 2005, 7.
41 David S. Cohen, "James Cameron Supercharges 3-D; *Avatar* Helmer Reveals the Art and Science of Stereo," *Variety*, April 10, 2008, www.variety.com.
42 Joe Leydon, "*Terminator 2* 3-D," *Variety*, May 6, 1996, 82.
43 For a full analysis of this feature of Cameron's films, see Peter Krämer, "Women First: *Titanic*, Action-Adventure Films, and Hollywood's Female Audience," in Sandler and Studlar, "*Titanic*," 108–131.
44 Debruge, "'Chicken,'" A6.
45 Quoted in Cohen, "James Cameron Supercharges 3-D."
46 Tim Cogshell, "Under the Sea: *Ghosts of the Abyss*," *Boxoffice*, June 2003, 60.
47 Julia McKay, "TV Doc Visits Sunken *Bismarck*," *Kingston Whig-Standard*, December 7, 2002.
48 John Calhoun, "Voyage to the Bottom of the Sea," *American Cinematographer* 83, no. 3 (2005): 58–62, 64–66, 68–69.
49 Jonathan Barnes, "Aliens of the Deep," *Sight and Sound* 15, no. 3 (March 2005): 40.
50 Matt Hurwitz, "Exposure: Vince Pace," *International Cinematographers Guild Magazine*, 2009, 30, 32, 34.
51 Respectively, patent no. 7,643,748, filed June 2, 2006, received January 5, 2010, and patent no. 7,899,321 B2, filed October 13, 2009, received March 1, 2011.
52 Hurwitz, "Exposure: Vince Pace," 32.
53 Carolyn Giardina, "James Cameron, Vince Pace Announce New 3D Venture," *Hollywood Reporter*, April 11, 2011, www.hollywoodreporter.com.
54 Hurwitz, "Exposure: Vince Pace," 32.
55 Jody Duncan and Lisa Fitzpatrick, *The Making of "Avatar"* (New York: Abrams, 2010); and Jody Duncan, "The Seduction of Reality," *Cinefex*, no. 120 (2010): 68–146.
56 Carl DiOrio, "*Avatar* House Is Motion-Capture Giant," *Hollywood Reporter*, July 15, 2009, www.hollywoodreporter.com; and Carolyn Giardina, "3D Spotlight," *Hollywood Reporter*, October 26, 2009, www.hollywoodreporter.com.

57　Mark Deuze, *Media Work* (Cambridge: Polity, 2007).
58　Nicole Lampert, "Has James Cameron, Hollywood's Scariest Man, Blown £200 Million on the Biggest Movie Flop Ever?," *Daily Mail*, December 11, 2009.
59　James Kendrick, "Marxist Overtones in Three Films by James Cameron," *Journal of Popular Film and Television* 27, no. 3 (1999): 38.
60　Constance Penley, "Time Travel, Primal Scene and the Critical Dystopia," *Camera Obscura* 5, no. 3 (15) (1986): 66–85.
61　Quoted in Goodyear, "Man of Extremes," 66.
62　Cameron's technofetishism is dealt with by Alexandra Keller in her study of him as a blockbuster auteur; see Keller, *James Cameron* (New York: Routledge, 2006).
63　Annette Kuhn, "Introduction: Cultural Theory and Science Fiction Cinema," in *Alien Zone: Cultural Theory and Contemporary Science Fiction Cinema*, ed. Annette Kuhn (New York: Verso, 1990), 7.
64　Debra Kaufman, "A Team Effort Finishes *Ghosts*," *American Cinematographer* 84, no. 7 (2003): 64–65.
65　When asked what he learned from this shoot, Cameron replied that the dives were so expensive that focusing on the divers is "counter-productive"; "'It's stupid to be turning the camera around inside and pointing it at the people, when you should be focusing on the marine life and the geology.'" Quoted in Matt Hurwitz, "Beyond the Sea," *Empire*, March 2005, 62.
66　David S. Cohen, "Helmer Kept on Top of Things during Deep-Sea Dive," *Variety*, April 2, 2012, 6.
67　Cubitt, *Cinema Effect*.
68　In this respect *Avatar* seems to be a direct attempt to take the jungle expedition film from the 1920s and 1930s into outer space. Cameron has said, "It's an old-fashioned jungle adventure with an environmental conscience," and he has cited as a primary inspiration Edgar Rice Burroughs's John Carter in his Mars (Barsoom) series. Quoted in Rampton, "James Cameron"; see also Jeff Jensen, "Great Expectation," *Entertainment Weekly*, January 15, 2007.
69　MacInnis, *James Cameron's "Aliens of the Deep*," 20.
70　Robert Koehler, "*Ghosts of the Abyss*," *Variety*, April 14, 2003, 20; and Ronnie Scheib, "*Aliens of the Deep*," *Variety*, February 7, 2005, 67.
71　Schatz, "Studio System"; and Edward J. Epstein, *The Big Picture: Money and Power in Hollywood* (New York: Random House, 2006).
72　Peter Caranicas, "Bibles Hold Tentpole Revivals; Biz Moves Backstory to Forefront," *Variety*, June 29, 2009, 5, 11.
73　"Hendricks's Wide World at HDTV: Discovery Chief Focuses In on a New Platform," *Multichannel News*, May 5, 2003, 4A; and "ESPN, Discovery Plug HD at Retail: Basic Networks Look to Drive Penetration for Local Ops' New Offerings," *Multichannel News*, June 9, 2003, 38.
74　Raby, "*Avatar* Blu-ray 3D Tied to Panasonic."
75　Elsaesser, "New New Hollywood," 191.

76 Along the same lines, the handheld device industry has followed the iPhone's lead on "apps" as a way to designate the special, indispensable aspects of its product. While many are amusing, many also reproduce information that is not especially hidden (temperature, location, time, cultural recommendation, game, etc.), albeit in an immediate and miniaturized form. Though many competing companies offer apps, note that the term offers a clumsy pun, referencing "applications" and "Apple Corporation." The measure of worth of this function is not the single, breakthrough utility of any one but the quantity of them. Apps are valuable because there are so many of them, over 2.2 million as of 2019 offered for the iPhone alone. Their relation to the movement and expansion of the handheld electronic market is not that of the technological tentpole. Instead, they are *technological tent-pegs*.

77 Dade Hayes and Jill Goldsmith, "Glum and Glummer," *Variety*, March 31, 2008, 1, 37.
78 Quoted in Ruben V. Nepales, "Will James Cameron Be 'World's King' Again?," *Philippine Daily Inquirer*, August 8, 2009, services.inquirer.net.
79 "Titanic Helmer Docks with CAA," *Variety*, June 8, 2009, 2.
80 Laura M. Holson, "Director of *Titanic* Turns to 3-D Film Ventures," *New York Times*, March 31, 2003.
81 John Caldwell, *Production Culture: Industrial Reflexivity and Critical Practice in Film and Television* (Durham, NC: Duke University Press, 2008).

CHAPTER 8 THE TECHNOLOGICAL HEART OF MOVIE CULTURE

1 Pierre Bourdieu, *Distinction: A Social Critique of the Judgement of Taste* (Cambridge, MA: Harvard University Press, 1984 [1979]), 28.
2 Bourdieu, *Distinction*, 24.
3 James Quandt, "Everyone I Know Is Stayin' Home: The New Cinephilia," *Framework* 50, nos. 1/2 (Spring–Fall 2009): 209.
4 Susan Sontag, "The Decay of Cinema," *New York Times Magazine*, February 25, 1996, 60–61.
5 Thomas Elsaesser, "Cinephilia or the Uses of Disenchantment," in *Cinephilia: Movies, Love, and Memory*, ed. Marijke de Valck and Malte Hagener (Amsterdam: Amsterdam University Press, 2005), 27–43.
6 Janet Staiger, "Matters of Taste, Subjects of Rank," *Framework* 45, no. 2 (Fall 2004): 76–80.
7 Aboubakar Sanogo, "Regarding Cinephilia and Africa," *Framework* 50, no. 1/2 (Spring–Fall 2009): 226–228.
8 Scott Balcerzak and Jason Sperb, eds., *Cinephilia in the Age of Digital Reproduction: Film, Pleasure and Digital Culture*, 2 vols. (London: Wallflower, 2009–2012).
9 Jeffrey Sconce, "Trashing the Academy: Taste, Excess, and an Emerging Politics of Cinematic Style," *Screen* 36, no. 4 (1995): 371–393; and Michael Weldon, *Psychotronic Encyclopedia of Film* (New York: Ballantine Books, 1983).

10 Francesco Casetti and Mariagrazia Fanchi, "Cinephilia/Telephilia," *Framework* 45, no. 2 (Fall 2004): 38–41.
11 See Charles R. Acland, "The Crack in the Electric Screen," *Cinema Journal* 51, no. 2 (2012): 167–171. Barbara Klinger's work on the DVD technophile is an important development of this line of inquiry. Barbara Klinger, *Beyond the Multiplex: Cinema, New Technologies, and the Home* (Berkeley: University of California Press, 2006).
12 "Canada's Avatar Sands," advertisement, *Daily Variety*, March 5, 2010, 19.
13 *Avatar* DVD/Blu-ray release, advertisement, *New York Times*, November 14, 2010.
14 Gene Maddaus, "Dirty Business: How the Country's Biggest Exhibition Chains Exploit the Men and Women Who Clean Their Theaters," *Variety*, March 26, 2019, 45–47.
15 This angle has been best explored in Paul Grainge, *Brand Hollywood: Selling Entertainment in a Global Media Age* (New York: Routledge, 2008).
16 The story of the megaplex is the focus of my book *Screen Traffic: Movies, Multiplexes, and Global Culture*.
17 David Denby, "Big Pictures," *New Yorker*, January 8, 2007, 54–63.
18 For a sharp analysis of the aesthetics of widescreen and *East of Eden* (1955), see Rogers, *Cinematic Appeals*.
19 Kim Painter, "Falling TVs Can Kill, but Few Parents Aware of Risks," *USA Today*, December 13, 2012.
20 Roland Barthes, "The Romans in Films" (1957), in *Mythologies*, trans. Annette Lavers (New York: Hill and Wang, 1972), 28.
21 Barthes, "The Romans in Films," 28.
22 A sharp bit of dialogue in *Planet of the Apes* (1968) captures this. Toward the end of the film, just before the shocking apocalyptic closing shot, Heston's character Taylor shaves the beard he has sported for most of the film, saying that where he came from, only young people had beards. The talking monkey Lucius replies that he looks less intelligent without the facial hair. True enough, Heston's key roles in *The Ten Commandments* and *Ben-Hur* involved character development and gravitas signaled by beard growth.
23 Siegfried Kracauer, "Cult of Distraction" (1927), in *The Mass Ornament: Weimar Essays*, ed. and trans. Thomas Y. Levin (Cambridge, MA: Harvard University Press, 1995), 326.
24 An elaboration of blockbuster blasé, commenting specifically on the penchant for characters to walk nonchalantly away from powerful explosions, is Jeffrey Sconce, "Explosive Apathy," in *B Is for Bad Cinema: Aesthetics, Politics, and Cultural Value*, ed. Claire Perkins and Constantine Verenis (New York: SUNY Press, 2014), 21–41.
25 Shone, *Blockbuster*, 33.
26 Sontag, "Fascinating Fascism."
27 Cubitt, *Cinema Effect*, 269.
28 Cubitt, *Cinema Effect*, 270.

EPILOGUE

1. See Matthew Jacobs, "Not to Be Melodramatic, but Movies as We Know Them Are Dead," *Huffington Post*, June 9, 2016, www.huffingtonpost.ca.
2. Brooks Barnes, "Hollywood's Summer of Extremes: Megahits, Superflops and Little Else," *New York Times*, September 4, 2016.
3. Brent Lang and James Rainey, "Revenue Record for U.S. Box Office," *Variety*, January 3, 2017, 21–22.
4. "All Time Worldwide Box Office," accessed November 24, 2019, www.the-numbers.com.
5. Martin Scorsese, "I Said Marvel Movies Aren't Cinema. Let Me Explain," *New York Times*, November 5, 2019.
6. Brooks Barnes, "In Blockbuster Era, No Room at the Box Office for the Middlebrow," *New York Times*, November 23, 2019.
7. Sontag, "Imagination of Disaster," 42–43.
8. Sontag, "Imagination of Disaster," 45.
9. Mumford, *Myth of the Machine*, 2 vols.
10. Telotte, *Mouse Machine*, 188.
11. Quoted in Walter Benjamin, "The Work of Art in the Age of Mechanical Reproduction" (1936), in *Illuminations: Essays and Reflections*, ed. Hannah Arendt, trans. Harry Zohn (New York: Schocken, 1969), 249.
12. Joseph Heller, *Catch-22* (New York: Simon and Schuster, 1961).
13. C. Wright Mills, "Culture and Politics" (1963), in *The Sixties: Art, Politics, and Media of Our Most Explosive Decade*, ed. Gerald Howard (New York: Paragon House, 1991), 83.

(FILMOGRAPHY)

The Abyss. James Cameron, 1989.
Act of Violence. Fred Zinnemann, 1948.
Admiral. Andrey Kravchuk, 2008.
The Adventures of Pluto Nash. Ron Underwood, 2002.
The African Queen. John Huston, 1951.
The Agony and the Ecstasy. Carol Reed, 1965.
Airport. George Seaton, 1970.
Aliens. James Cameron, 1986.
Aliens of the Deep. James Cameron and Steven Quale, 2005.
Alita: Battle Angel. Robert Rodriguez, 2019.
All the President's Men. Alan J. Pakula, 1976.
American Graffiti. George Lucas, 1973.
Angels and Demons. Ron Howard, 2009.
Apocalypse Now. Francis Ford Coppola, 1979.
Apollo 13. Ron Howard, 1995.
April Love. Henry Levin, 1957.
Around the World in 80 Days. Michael Anderson, 1956.
Asterix at the Olympic Games (Astérix aux jeux olympiques). Frédérick Forestier and Thomas Langmann, 2008.
The Atomic City. Jerry Hopper, 1952.
Auntie Mame. Morton DaCosta, 1958.
Avatar. James Cameron, 2009.
The Avengers. Joss Whedon, 2012.
Avengers: Endgame. Anthony Russo and Joe Russo, 2019.
The Bad Seed. Mervyn LeRoy, 1956.

Bambi. James Algar, Sam Armstrong, David D. Hand, Graham Heid, Bill Roberts, Paul Satterfield, and Norman Wright, 1942.
Bathory. Juraj Jakubisko, 2008.
Batman. Tim Burton, 1989.
The Beautiful Blonde from Bashful Bend. Preston Sturges, 1949.
Ben-Hur. Fred Niblo, Charles Brabin, Rex Ingram, Christy Cabanne, and J. J. Cohn, 1925.
Ben-Hur. William Wyler, 1959.
The BFG. Steven Spielberg, 2016.
The Big Country. William Wyler, 1958.
The Big Show. 1957 (Twentieth Century Fox promotional feature).
Billy Lynn's Long Halftime Walk. Ang Lee, 2016.
Black Panther. Ryan Coogler, 2018.
Blackboard Jungle. Richard Brooks, 1955.
The Black Rose. Henry Hathaway, 1950.
Blade Runner. Ridley Scott, 1982 (rerelease, 1992).
Block Buster. Wallace Fox, 1944.
Blood of Dracula. Herbert L. Strock, 1957.
The Blues Brothers. John Landis, 1980.
Bolt. Byron Howard and Chris Williams, 2008.
Bombardier. Richard Wallace, 1943.
Bomber Command. 1950 (unreleased).
The Bourne Identity. Doug Liman, 2002.
The Bourne Ultimatum. Paul Greengrass, 2007.
Brazil. Joseph Stantley, 1944.
Breathless. Jean-Luc Godard, 1960.
The Bribe. Robert Z. Leonard, 1949.
The Bridge on the River Kwai. David Lean, 1957.
The Bridges at Toko-Ri. Mark Robson, 1954.
The Brothers Karamazov. Richard Brooks, 1958.
The Buccaneer. Anthony Quinn, 1958.
Butch Cassidy and the Sundance Kid. George Roy Hill, 1969.
The Caine Mutiny. Edward Dmytryk, 1954.
Can-Can. Walter Lang, 1960.
Captain America: Civil War. Anthony Russo and Joe Russo, 2016.
Carousel. Henry King, 1956.
Casablanca. Michael Curtiz, 1942.
The Champion. Mark Robson, 1949.
Chang. Merian C. Cooper and Ernest B. Schoedsack, 1927.
Chase a Crooked Shadow. Michael Anderson, 1958.
Cheyenne. Raoul Walsh, 1947.
Chinatown. Roman Polanski, 1974.
The Chronicles of Narnia: Prince Caspian. Andrew Adamson, 2008.

Cimarron. Anthony Mann, 1960.
Cinderella. Clyde Geronimi, Wilfred Jackson, and Hamilton Luske, 1950.
Cinerama Holiday. Robert L. Bendick and Philippe de Lacy, 1955.
Citizen Kane. Orson Welles, 1941.
Cleopatra. Joseph L. Mankiewicz, 1963.
Close Encounters of the Third Kind. Steven Spielberg, 1977 (rerelease, 1980).
Command Decision. Sam Wood, 1948.
Compulsion. Richard Fleischer, 1959.
Contact. Robert Zemeckis, 1997.
Cowboys and Aliens. Jon Favreau, 2011.
The Dam Busters. Michael Anderson, 1955.
The Dark Knight. Christopher Nolan, 2008.
A Date with Judy. Richard Thorpe, 1948.
Days of Wine and Roses. Blake Edwards, 1962.
Deadpool. Tim Miller, 2016.
The Deer Hunter. Michael Cimino, 1979.
The Defiant Ones. Stanley Kramer, 1958.
Demetrius and the Gladiators. Delmer Daves, 1954.
Desperate Journey. Raoul Walsh, 1942.
The Diary of Anne Frank. George Stevens, 1959.
Die Hard. John McTiernan, 1988.
Doctor Dolittle. Richard Fleischer, 1967.
Down to the Sea in Ships. Henry Hathaway, 1949.
Easter Parade. Charles Walters, 1948.
East of Eden. Elia Kazan, 1955.
Easy Rider. Dennis Hopper, 1969.
Empties (Vratné lahve). Jan Svěrák, 2007.
The Enemy Below. Dick Powell, 1957.
E.T. the Extra-Terrestrial. Steven Spielberg, 1982.
Exodus. Otto Preminger, 1960.
The Exodus Decoded. Simcha Jacobovici, 2006.
Expedition: Bismarck. James Cameron and Gary Johnstone, 2002.
Eyes Wide Shut. Stanley Kubrick, 1999.
Falling Hare. Bob Clampett, 1943.
Fantastic 4: Rise of the Silver Surfer. Tim Story, 2007.
Fantastic Mr. Fox. Wes Anderson, 2009.
A Farewell to Arms. Charles Vidor and John Huston, 1957.
Farewell to the King. John Milius, 1989.
Fast & Furious. Justin Lin, 2009.
The F.B.I. Story. Mervyn LeRoy, 1959.
Fight Club. David Fincher, 1999.
Fighter Squadron. Raoul Walsh, 1948.

Final Destination 3D. David R. Ellis, 2009.
Final Destination 5. Steven Quale, 2011.
Finding Dory. Andrew Stanton, 2016.
The Five Pennies. Melville Shavelson, 1959.
The Four Horsemen of the Apocalypse. Vincente Minnelli, 1962.
Francis in the Navy. Arthur Lubin, 1955.
Frankenstein. James Whale, 1931.
From Here to Eternity. Fred Zinnemann, 1953.
Furious 7. James Wan, 2015.
The General. Buster Keaton and Clyde Bruckman, 1926.
Ghosts of the Abyss. James Cameron, 2003.
Giant. George Stevens, 1956.
Gigi. Vincente Minnelli, 1958.
The Girl Can't Help It. Frank Tashlin, 1956.
Girls in Prison. Edward L. Cahn, 1956.
The Girl Who Played with Fire. Daniel Alfredson, 2009.
The Girl with the Dragon Tattoo. Niels Arden Oplev, 2009.
The Glenn Miller Story. Anthony Mann, 1954.
The Godfather. Francis Ford Coppola, 1972.
The Godfather: Part II. Francis Ford Coppola, 1974.
God's Little Acre. Anthony Mann, 1958.
Goin' down the Road. Donald Shebib, 1970.
Gone with the Wind. Victor Fleming, 1939.
Grass. Merian C. Cooper and Ernest B. Schoedsack, 1925.
Gravity. Alfonso Cuarón, 2013.
The Greatest Show on Earth. Cecil B. DeMille, 1952.
The Greatest Story Ever Told. George Stevens, David Lean, and Jean Negulesco, 1965.
Guardians of the Galaxy. James Gunn, 2014.
Guess Who's Coming to Dinner. Stanley Kramer, 1967.
The Guns of Navarone. J. Lee Thompson, 1961.
Guys and Dolls. Joseph L. Mankiewicz, 1955.
Hancock. Peter Berg, 2008.
The Hangover. Todd Phillips, 2009.
The Harder They Fall. Mark Robson, 1956.
Harry Potter and the Deathly Hallows: Part 2. David Yates, 2011.
Harry Potter and the Half-Blood Prince. David Yates, 2009.
Harry Potter and the Order of the Phoenix. David Yates, 2007.
Harry Potter and the Sorcerer's Stone. Chris Columbus, 2001.
The Hateful Eight. Quentin Tarantino, 2015.
Hello, Dolly! Gene Kelly, 1969.
Hercules. Joseph E. Levine with Pietro Francisci, 1959.
Here Comes Mr. Jordan. Alexander Hall, 1941.

High Noon. Fred Zinnemann, 1952.
Holiday in Mexico. George Sidney, 1946.
Hot Rod Girl. Leslie H. Martinson, 1956.
How to Marry a Millionaire. Jean Negulesco, 1953.
I Am Legend. Francis Lawrence, 2007.
Ice Age: Dawn of the Dinosaurs. Carlos Saldanha, 2009.
Independence Day. Roland Emmerich, 1996.
Indiana Jones and the Kingdom of the Crystal Skull. Steven Spielberg, 2008.
Inglourious Basterds. Quentin Tarantino, 2009.
Inherit the Wind. Stanley Kramer, 1960.
Intolerance. D. W. Griffith, 1916.
Iron Man. Jon Favreau, 2008.
Iron Man 3. Shane Black, 2013.
The Irony of Fate 2 (Ironiya sudby. Prodolzhenie). Timur Bekmambetov, 2007.
I Served the King of England (Obsluhoval jsem anglického krále). Jirí Menzel, 2006.
It's a Mad, Mad, Mad, Mad World. Stanley Kramer, 1963.
I Want to Live. Robert Wise, 1958.
I Was a Teenage Frankenstein. Herbert L. Strock, 1958.
Jaws. Steven Spielberg, 1975.
The Jazz Singer. Alan Crosland, 1927.
John Mulaney: Kid Gorgeous at Radio City. Alex Timbers, 2018.
The Joker Is Wild. Charles Vidor, 1957.
Journey to the Center of the Earth. Eric Brevig, 2008.
Judgment at Nuremberg. Stanley Kramer, 1961.
Julia Misbehaves. Jack Conway, 1948.
Julius Caesar. Joseph L. Mankiewicz, 1953.
The Jungle Book. Jon Favreau, 2016.
Jurassic Park. Steven Spielberg, 1993.
Jurassic World. Colin Trevorrow, 2015.
The Karate Kid. Harald Zwart, 2010.
The Kettles in the Ozarks. Charles Lamont, 1956.
The Killers. Robert Siodmak, 1946.
The King and I. Walter Lang, 1956.
King Kong. Merian C. Cooper and Ernest B. Schoedsack, 1933.
King Kong. John Guillermin, 1976.
King's Row. Sam Wood, 1942.
Kiss Them for Me. Stanley Donen, 1957.
Klute. Alan J. Pakula, 1971.
Kung Fu Panda. Mark Osborne and John Stevenson, 2008.
Lady and the Tramp. Clyde Geronimi, Wilfred Jackson, and Hamilton Luske, 1955.
Lassie Come Home. Fred M. Wilcox, 1943.
Lawrence of Arabia. David Lean, 1962.

Legend of the Lost. Henry Hathaway, 1957.
Les Misérables. Jean-Paul Le Chanois, 1958.
Lifeboat. Alfred Hitchcock, 1943.
Little Big Man. Arthur Penn, 1970.
Live Free or Die Hard. Len Wiseman, 2007.
Logan's Run. Michael Anderson, 1976.
The Lone Ranger. Gore Verbinski, 2013.
The Longest Day. Ken Annakin, Darryl F. Zanuck, Andrew Marton, Bernhard Wicki, and Gerd Oswald, 1962.
The Lord of the Rings: The Fellowship of the Ring. Peter Jackson, 2001.
The Lord of the Rings: The Return of the King. Peter Jackson, 2003.
The Lost Tomb of Jesus. Simcha Jacobovici, 2007.
Lydia Bailey. Jean Negulesco, 1952.
Ma and Pa Kettle at Waikiki. Lee Sholem, 1955.
Madagascar: Escape 2 Africa. Eric Darnell and Tom McGrath, 2008.
Mad Max: Fury Road. George Miller, 2015.
Magnificent Obsession. Douglas Sirk, 1954.
The Maltese Falcon. John Huston, 1941.
Mamma Mia! Phyllida Lloyd, 2008.
The Man from Colorado. Henry Levin, 1948.
The Man with the Golden Arm. Otto Preminger, 1955.
The Mark of Zorro. Fred Niblo, 1920.
The Martian. Ridley Scott, 2015.
Marty. Delbert Mann, 1955.
McCabe and Mrs. Miller. Robert Altman, 1971.
The Memphis Belle: A Story of a Flying Fortress. William Wyler, 1944.
Michael Jackson's This Is It. Kenny Ortega, 2009.
Mission: Impossible—Ghost Protocol. Brad Bird, 2011.
Mission: Impossible—Rogue Nation. Christopher McQuarrie, 2015.
Mister Roberts. John Ford and Mervyn LeRoy, 1955.
Moby Dick. John Huston, 1956.
Mogambo. John Ford, 1953.
Monsters vs. Aliens. Rob Letterman and Conrad Vernon, 2009.
Mr. Bean's Holiday. Steve Bendelack, 2007.
The Mummy: Tomb of the Dragon Emperor. Rob Cohen, 2008.
Mutiny on the Bounty. Lewis Milestone and Carol Reed, 1962.
Nashville. Robert Altman, 1975.
The News Parade of 1943. Albert S. Rogell, 1943.
Night at the Museum. Shawn Levy, 2006.
Night at the Museum: Battle of the Smithsonian. Shawn Levy, 2009.
Not as a Stranger. Stanley Kramer, 1955.

No Time for Love. Mitchell Leisen, 1943.
No Time for Sergeants. Mervyn LeRoy, 1958.
The Number One (released as *The Magnificent Matador*). Budd Boetticher, 1955.
Ocean's Thirteen. Steven Soderbergh, 2007.
Oh, Men! Oh, Women! Nunnally Johnson, 1957.
Oklahoma! Fred Zinnemann, 1955.
One from the Heart. Francis Ford Coppola, 1981.
One of Our Aircraft Is Missing. Michael Powell and Emeric Pressburger, 1942.
On the Beach. Stanley Kramer, 1959.
On the Waterfront. Elia Kazan, 1954.
Operation Burma. Raoul Walsh, 1945.
Operation Petticoat. Blake Edwards, 1959.
Pal Joey. George Sidney, 1957.
Parallax View. Alan J. Pakula, 1974.
Paranormal Activity. Oren Peli, 2009.
Patterns. Fielder Cook, 1956.
Permanent Record. Marisa Silver, 1988.
Peter Pan. Clyde Geronimi, Wilfred Jackson, and Hamilton Luske, 1953.
Peyton Place. Mark Robson, 1957.
Pirates of the Caribbean: At World's End. Gore Verbinski, 2007.
Planet of the Apes. Franklin J. Schaffner, 1968.
The Poseidon Adventure. Ronald Neame, 1972.
Prelude to War. Frank Capra, 1942.
Price of Foxes. Henry King, 1949.
The Pride and the Passion. Stanley Kramer, 1957.
The Prince and the Showgirl. Laurence Olivier, 1957.
The Proposal. Anne Fletcher, 2009.
Proud Rebel. Michael Curtiz, 1958.
Psycho. Alfred Hitchcock, 1960.
Quantum of Solace. Marc Forster, 2008.
Quo Vadis. Mervyn LeRoy, 1951.
Raiders of the Lost Ark. Steven Spielberg, 1981.
Raintree County. Edward Dmytryk, 1957.
Ransom! Alex Segal, 1956.
Ratatouille. Brad Bird, 2007.
Reds. Warren Beatty, 1981.
The Robe. Henry Koster, 1953.
Rogue One: A Star Wars Story. Gareth Edwards, 2016.
Room at the Top. Jack Clayton, 1959.
Rules Don't Apply. Warren Beatty, 2016.
Runaway Daughters. Edward L. Cahn, 1956.

Rush Hour 3. Brett Ratner, 2007.
Samson and Delilah. Cecil B. DeMille, 1949.
Sanctum. Alister Grierson, 2011.
The Secret Life of Pets. Chris Renaud, 2016.
Separate Tables. Delbert Mann, 1958.
The Seven Little Foys. Melville Shavelson, 1955.
Sex and the City. Michael Patrick King, 2008.
Shake, Rattle and Rock! Edward L. Cahn, 1956.
Shampoo. Hal Ashby, 1975.
Shane. George Stevens, 1953.
Shrek Forever After. Mike Mitchell, 2010.
Shrek the Third. Chris Miller, 2007.
Silent Running. Douglas Trumbull, 1972.
The Simpsons Movie. David Silverman, 2007.
Skyfall. Sam Mendes, 2012.
Slumdog Millionaire. Danny Boyle, 2009.
The Snake Pit. Anatole Litvak, 1948.
Solaris. Steven Soderbergh, 2002.
Solomon and Sheba. King Vidor, 1959.
Some Like It Hot. Billy Wilder, 1959.
The Sound of Music. Robert Wise, 1965.
South Pacific. Joshua Logan, 1958.
Soylent Green. Richard Fleischer, 1973.
Spartacus. Stanley Kubrick, 1960.
Spider-Man 3. Sam Raimi, 2007.
Stagecoach. John Ford, 1939.
Star! Robert Wise, 1968.
Star Wars: Episode I—The Phantom Menace. George Lucas, 1999.
Star Wars: Episode IV—A New Hope. George Lucas, 1977 (rerelease, 1997).
Star Wars: Episode VII—The Force Awakens. J. J. Abrams, 2015.
The Story of Ruth. Henry Koster, 1960.
Suicide Squad. David Ayer, 2016.
Sully. Clint Eastwood, 2016.
A Summer Place. Delmer Daves, 1959.
Sun in the Morning. 1948.
A Tale of Two Cities. Jack Conway, 1935.
Taxi 4. Gérard Krawczyk, 2007.
The Ten Commandments. Cecil B. DeMille, 1923.
The Ten Commandments. Cecil B. DeMille, 1956.
Ten Seconds to Hell. Robert Aldrich, 1959.
The Terminator. James Cameron, 1984.

Terminator Salvation. McG, 2009.
Terminator 2: Judgment Day. James Cameron, 1991.
Thirty Seconds over Tokyo. Mervyn LeRoy, 1944.
This Is Cinerama. Merian C. Cooper, Ernest B. Schoedsack, and Mike Todd Jr., 1952.
Those Magnificent Men and Their Flying Machines. Ken Annakin, 1965.
Three Days of the Condor. Sydney Pollack, 1975.
300. Zack Snyder, 2007.
Titanic. James Cameron, 1997.
To Catch a Thief. Alfred Hitchcock, 1955.
The Towering Inferno. John Guillermin, 1974.
Transformers. Michael Bay, 2007.
Transformers: Age of Extinction. Michael Bay, 2014.
Transformers: Revenge of the Fallen. Michael Bay, 2009.
Trapeze. Malcolm Arnold with Carol Reed, 1956.
Treasure Island. Byron Haskin, 1950.
Trouble in Paradise. Ernst Lubitsch, 1932.
T2–3D: Battle across Time. John Bruno, James Cameron, Keith Melton, Stan Winston, 1996.
Twelve Angry Men. Sidney Lumet, 1957.
Twelve O'Clock High. Henry King, 1949.
The Twilight Saga: New Moon. Chris Weitz, 2009.
2001: A Space Odyssey. Stanley Kubrick, 1968.
2012. Roland Emmerich, 2009.
Up. Pete Docter, 2009.
Vespers in Vienna. George Sidney, 1948.
Victory through Air Power. Clyde Geronimi, Jack Kinney, James Algar, and H. C. Potter, 1943.
The Vikings. Richard Fleischer, 1958.
WALL-E. Andrew Stanton, 2008.
Wanted. Timur Bekmambetov, 2008.
War and Peace. King Vidor, 1956.
War of the Worlds. Steven Spielberg, 2005.
Welcome to the Sticks (*Bienvenue chez les Ch'tis*). Dany Boon, 2008.
We're No Angels. Michael Curtiz, 1955.
West Side Story. Jerome Robbins and Robert Wise, 1961.
The Wild Wild West. Barry Sonnenfeld, 1999.
Winter Kills. William Richert, 1979.
Wonder Woman. Patty Jenkins, 2017.
Written on the Wind. Douglas Sirk, 1956.
X-Men. Bryan Singer, 2000.
The Young Lions. Edward Dmytryk, 1958.
Zootopia. Byron Howard and Rich Moore, 2016.

FRANCHISES

"Avatar"
"Batman"
"Bourne"
"DaVinci Code"
"Die Hard"
"The Fast and the Furious"
"The Godfather"
"Harry Potter"
"Hunger Games"
"Ice Age"
"Indiana Jones"
"James Bond"
"Jurassic Park"
"Lord of the Rings/The Hobbit"
"Marvel Cinematic Universe"
"Matrix"
"Mission Impossible"
"Pirates of the Caribbean"
"Spider-Man"
"Star Trek"
"Star Wars"
"Superman"
"Terminator"
"Toy Story"
"Transformers"
"Twilight"
"X-Men"

(BIBLIOGRAPHY)

"ABC Fusing Friday TV Blockbuster." *Daily Variety*, May 27, 1953, 1, 14.
Acland, Charles R. "Consumer Electronics and Building an Entertainment Infrastructure." In *Signal Traffic*, edited by Lisa Parks and Nicole Starosielski, 246–278. Urbana: University of Illinois Press, 2015.
Acland, Charles R. "The Crack in the Electric Screen." *Cinema Journal* 51, no. 2 (2012): 167–171.
Acland, Charles R. "The End of James Cameron's Quiet Years." In *International Encyclopedia of Media Studies*, vol. 6, *Media Studies Futures*, edited by Kelly Gates, 269–295. London: Blackwell, 2013.
Acland, Charles R. *From International Blockbusters to National Hits: Analysis of the 2010 UIS Survey of Feature Films*. Montreal: UNESCO Institute of Statistics, 2012. www.uis.unesco.org.
Acland, Charles R. "'Opening Everywhere': Multiplexes, E-Cinema and the Speed of Cinema Culture." In *Going to the Movies: Hollywood and the Social Experience of Movie-Going*, edited by Robert Allen, Richard Maltby, and Melvyn Stokes, 364–382. Exeter, UK: University of Exeter Press, 2007.
Acland, Charles R. *Screen Traffic: Movies, Multiplexes, and Global Culture*. Durham, NC: Duke University Press, 2003.
Acland, Charles R. *Swift Viewing: The Popular Life of Subliminal Influence*. Durham, NC: Duke University Press, 2012.
Acland, Charles R., and Fenwick McKelvey. "Terminological Traffic in the Movie Business." In *The Arclight Guidebook to Media History and the Digital Humanities*, edited by Charles R. Acland and Eric Hoyt, 238–248. Brighton, Sussex: REFRAME Books in association with Project Arclight, 2016.

"Action-and-Horror Staple Stuff; 20,000,000 Thrill-Seekers (12 to 25) Backbone of Exploitation Pix." *Variety*, March 6, 1957, 20.

Adorno, Theodor. *Minima Moralia: Reflections from Damaged Life*. 1951. Translated by E. F. N. Jephcott. New York: Verso, 1974.

"Advertising and Marketing." *New York Times*, January 22, 1954.

The Air Offensive against Germany. Advertisement. *New York Times*, February 18, 1943.

Albiniak, Paige. "The Long Goodbye." *Broadcasting and Cable*, May 10, 2004, 3.

Allen, Michael. "Talking about a Revolution: The Blockbuster as Industrial Advertisement." In *Movie Blockbusters*, edited by Julian Stringer, 101–113. New York: Routledge, 2003.

"Allied Bombs Smash Nazi War Planes." *Victory* 1, no. 5 (1943): 54–56.

"All Par '56 Pix to Be in VistaVision." *Daily Variety*, November 25, 1955, 1.

All the King's Men. Advertisement. *New York Times*, November 14, 1959.

"All-Time B.O. Champs." *Variety*, January 8, 1958, 6, 60.

"All Time Worldwide Box Office." Accessed November 24, 2019. www.the-numbers.com.

Altman, Rick. *Film/Genre*. London: BFI Publishing, 1999.

American Dilemma. Advertisement. *New York Times*, March 6, 1944.

American International Pictures. Advertisement. *Boxoffice Barometer*, February 9, 1957, 55.

American International Pictures. Advertisement. *Variety*, August 29, 1956, 21.

American International Pictures. Advertisement. *Variety*, January 8, 1958, 57.

Anderson, Chris. *The Long Tail: Why the Future of Business Is Selling Less of More*. New York: Hyperion, 2006.

"Antidote for Pessimists; Contrasting 1958 to '52 for Moral." *Variety*, October 15, 1958, 3.

April Love. Advertisement. *Daily Variety*, November 6, 1957, 14.

Archerd, Army. "Just for Variety." *Daily Variety*, November 6, 1953, 2.

"Are James Cameron Fans the Type Who Buy Tickets Four Months in Advance?" *National Post*, August 29, 2009.

Arneel, Gene. "Blockbusters of 1960; Emerging 'New Economics.'" *Variety*, January 4, 1961, 5.

Arneel, Gene. "Hail to a Still-Hale Film Industry (Run Down of 'So What's Good?')." *Variety*, March 20, 1957, 12.

Arneel, Gene. "1958: Year of Blockbusters." *Variety*, January 7, 1959, 9, 50.

Arneel, Gene. "Paramount Needs Another DeMille to Compete in Blockbuster Era." *Variety*, April 22, 1959, 1, 86.

Arneel, Gene. "Pix Prosperity in for a Run; Television Fades as B.O. Heavy." *Variety*, August 24, 1955, 75.

Arnold, Jörg. *The Allied Air War and Urban Memory: The Legacy of Strategic Bombing in Germany*. New York: Cambridge University Press, 2011.

"Atlanta Sees Banner Year." *Billboard*, October 14, 1944, 40–41.

The Atomic City. Advertisement. *Daily Variety*, May 8, 1952, 5.

Audience Research Inc. "Survey of Reactions to Three Dimension Pictures, Wide Screen, and Stereophonic Sound." July 1953. In "Gallup Looks at the Movies: Audience Research Reports 1940–1950." Wilmington, DE: Scholarly Resources, 1979.

Avatar DVD/Blu-ray release. Advertisement. *New York Times*, November 14, 2010.
Balcerzak, Scott, and Jason Sperb, eds. *Cinephilia in the Age of Digital Reproduction: Film, Pleasure and Digital Culture*. 2 vols. London: Wallflower, 2009–2012.
Baldwin, Hanson W. "The Atomic Weapon; End of War against Japan Hastened but Destruction Sows Seed of Hate." *New York Times*, August 7, 1945.
Balides, Constance. "Jurassic Post-Fordism: Tall Tales of Economics in the Theme Park." *Screen* 41 (2000): 139–160.
Balio, Tino, ed. *The American Film Industry*. Rev. ed. Madison: University of Wisconsin Press, 1985.
Bankers Trust Company. Advertisement. *New York Times*, September 22, 1943.
Bank of New York. Advertisement. *New York Times*, January 26, 1943.
Barnes, Brooks. "Hollywood's Summer of Extremes: Megahits, Superflops and Little Else." *New York Times*, September 4, 2016.
Barnes, Brooks. "In Blockbuster Era, No Room at the Box Office for the Middlebrow." *New York Times*, November 23, 2019.
Barnes, Jonathan. "*Aliens of the Deep*." *Sight and Sound* 15, no. 3 (March 2005): 40.
Bart, Peter. "An Audience with the King." *Variety*, March 30, 1998, 4, 37.
Bart, Peter. "The Blockbuster Model That Ate Hollywood." *Variety*, December 3, 2013, 17.
Barthes, Roland. "Cinemascope." 1954. In *Essays and Interviews*, vol. 4, *Signs and Images: Writings on Art, Cinema and Photography*, translated and edited by Chris Turner, 10–13. New York: Seagull Books, 2016.
Barthes, Roland. "The Romans in Films." 1957. In *Mythologies*, translated by Annette Lavers, 26–28. New York: Hill and Wang, 1972.
Barthes, Roland. "Visualization and Language (an Interview by Philippe Pilard)." 1966. In *Essays and Interviews*, vol. 4, *Signs and Images: Writings on Art, Cinema and Photography*, translated and edited by Chris Turner, 70–81. New York: Seagull Books, 2016.
Baudrillard, Jean. "The Ecstasy of Communication." In *The Anti-aesthetic: Essays on Postmodern Culture*, edited by Hal Foster, 126–134. Port Townsend, WA: Bay, 1983.
Baumann, Shyon. *Hollywood Highbrow: From Entertainment to Art*. Princeton, NJ: Princeton University Press, 2007.
Beaver, Frank Eugene. *Dictionary of Film Terms: The Aesthetic Companion to Film Art*. New York: Peter Lang, 2007.
Belton, John. *Widescreen Cinema*. Cambridge, MA: Harvard University Press, 1992.
Belton, John, Sheldon Hall, and Steve Neale, eds. *Widescreen Worldwide*. New Barnet, UK: John Libby, 2010.
Bender, James F. "Thirty Thousand New Words." *New York Times Magazine*, December 2, 1945.
Ben-Hur. Advertisement. *New York Herald Tribune*, November 22, 1959.
Ben-Hur. Advertisement. *New York Herald Tribune*, November 24, 1959.
Ben-Hur. Advertisement. *New York Post*, November 19, 1959.
Ben-Hur. Advertisement. *New York Post*, November 20, 1959.

Ben-Hur. Advertisement. *New York Times*, October 25, 1959.
Ben-Hur. Advertisement. *New York Times*, November 14, 1959.
Ben-Hur. Advertisement. *New York Times*, November 25, 1959.
Ben-Hur. Advertisement. *New York Times*, November 29, 1959.
"*Ben-Hur*: Film Review." *Variety*, November 18, 1959, 6.
"'Ben-Hur' Payoff Quicker Than Tis Said in Trade?" *Variety*, December 2, 1959, 7, 13.
Benjamin, Walter. "The Work of Art in the Age of Mechanical Reproduction." 1936. In *Illuminations: Essays and Reflections*, edited by Hannah Arendt, translated by Harry Zohn, 217–252. New York: Schocken, 1969.
Berman, Marshall. *All That Is Solid Melts into Air: The Experience of Modernity*. New York: Simon and Schuster, 1982.
Bernstein, Irving. *Hollywood at the Crossroads: An Economic Study of the Motion Picture Industry*. Hollywood: Hollywood AFL Film Council, 1957.
Berryman, Clifford Kennedy. "Maybe You Should Have Said It Louder, Chief." Cartoon, *Evening Star*, January 20, 1943. https://www.loc.gov/item/acd1996000562/PP/.
"Best News: Uptrends Continue." *Broadcasting*, December 26, 1966, 45.
The Big Country. Advertisement. *New York Times*, August 28, 1958.
The Big Show. Advertisement. *Daily Variety*, May 1, 1957, 5–7.
Bing, Jonathan. "Will Gizmos Give Biz New Juice? Cameron Says Digital 3-D Could Get Auds out of the House and Back to the Multiplex." *Variety*, March 21, 2005, 10.
Biskind, Peter. *Down and Dirty Pictures: Miramax, Sundance, and the Rise of Independent Film*. New York: Simon and Schuster, 2004.
Biskind, Peter. *Easy Riders, Raging Bulls: How the Sex-Drugs-and-Rock 'n' Roll Generation Saved Hollywood*. New York: Touchstone, 1998.
Bizony, Piers. *Digital Domain: The Leading Edge of Visual Effects*. New York: Billboard Books, 2001.
"'Blackboard Jungle' Eyes 180G Wk. Here." *Daily Variety*, May 16, 1955, 1.
Blandford, Steve, Barry Keith Grant, and Jim Hillier. *The Film Studies Dictionary*. New York: Arnold, 2001.
Block, Alex Ben, and Lucy Autrey Wilson, eds. *George Lucas's Blockbusting: A Decade-by-Decade Survey of Timeless Movies Including Untold Secrets of Their Financial and Cultural Success*. New York: ItBooks, 2010.
"The Block Buster?" Editorial cartoon. *New York Times*, December 31, 1944.
"Blockbuster Age Economics as Pain during Transition." *Variety*, April 30, 1958, 3.
"Blockbuster a Romantic Word to Wall Street." *Variety*, July 1, 1959, 1.
"'Blockbuster' as Trade's Bad Joke via Mimeograph." *Variety*, May 3, 1961, 3.
"Blockbuster Doubts." *Variety*, October 31, 1962, 18.
"Blockbuster Features Cause Greater Rating Fluctuations." *Billboard*, May 13, 1957, 30.
"Blockbuster Hail Stones Cost Theatreman $150 for New Roof." *Showmen's Trade Review*, July 3, 1943, 4.
"A Block Buster on Fifth Avenue." *New York Times*, May 14, 1943.

"Blockbusters Coming—but When?" *Variety*, November 3, 1954, 10.

"Blockbusters' Fallout Risk." *Variety*, May 7, 1958, 3.

"Blockbusters vs. Main Street; 'B' (for Budget) Films Return." *Variety*, February 6, 1957, 5, 22.

"Blockbuster Terms in Smaller Situations." *Variety*, December 17, 1958, 15.

Boddy, William. *Fifties Television: The Industry and Its Critics*. Urbana: University of Illinois Press, 1990.

Bombardier. Advertisement. *Oswego Palladium-Times*, July 23, 1943.

"The Bomb as Pedagogue." *New York Times*, September 26, 1943.

"Bomber's View of Berlin; Murrow of CBS Describes Bursts of Blockbusters, Merging of Fires." *New York Times*, December 4, 1943.

Bordwell, David. *The Way Hollywood Tells It: Story and Style in Modern Movies*. Berkeley: University of California Press, 2006.

Bourdieu, Pierre. *Distinction: A Social Critique of the Judgement of Taste*. 1979. Translated by Richard Nice. Cambridge, MA: Harvard University Press, 1984.

Bourdieu, Pierre. "The Field of Cultural Production, or: The Economic World Reversed." 1983. In *The Field of Cultural Production*, translated by Richard Nice, 29–73. New York: Columbia University Press, 1993.

Boutell, Clip. "Betty Smith Still Prefers Brooklyn." *New York Times*, January 28, 1945.

"B.O. Winners Give Loew's Mgmt. Better Chance to Win Proxy Fite." *Variety*, September 28, 1958, 1, 4.

Boyea, Samuel A. Letter to the drama editor. *New York Times*, October 25, 1953.

Brazil. Advertisement. *Daily Variety*, November 15, 1944, 4–5.

Breznican, Anthony. "'The Avengers': Your First Look at the Dream Team!" *Entertainment Weekly*, September 30, 2011.

The Bridges at Toko-Ri. Advertisement. *Daily Variety*, January 21, 1955, 5–14.

"Brit.'s-Eye View of Blockbusters." *Variety*, September 24, 1958, 7.

Brogdon, Bill. "L.A. Theatres' Sock Year." *Daily Variety*, October 17, 1955, 295.

The Brothers Karamazov. Advertisement. *Independent Film Journal*, March 1, 1958, 2.

The Brothers Karamazov. Advertisement. *Washington Post and Times Herald*, March 20, 1958.

Browning, David, producer. "Cameron's *Avatar*." *60 Minutes*. Aired November 22, 2009, on CBS.

Bukatman, Scott. *Matters of Gravity: Special Effects and Supermen in the 20th Century*. Durham, NC: Duke University Press, 2003.

Bush, Thomas W. "More Producers Buck 'Blockbuster' Trend, Make Low-Cost Films." *Wall Street Journal*, January 17, 1961.

"Business Bulletin: A Special Background Report on Trends in Industry and Finance." *Wall Street Journal*, April 9, 1959.

"'Caine' Wow $40,000, Det.; 'Apache' Smash 27G, 'High' Lofty $35,000." *Variety*, July 7, 1954, 8.

Caldwell, John. *Production Culture: Industrial Reflexivity and Critical Practice in Film and Television*. Durham, NC: Duke University Press, 2008.

Calhoun, John. "Voyage to the Bottom of the Sea." *American Cinematographer* 83, no. 3 (2005): 58–62, 64–66, 68–69.

"Call Blockbusters an 'Over-eagerness.'" *Variety*, October 21, 1959, 4.

"Canada's *Avatar* Sands." Advertisement. *Daily Variety*, March 5, 2010, 19.

Caranicas, Peter. "Bibles Hold Tentpole Revivals; Biz Moves Backstory to Forefront." *Variety*, June 29, 2009, 5, 11.

Casetti, Francesco, and Mariagrazia Fanchi. "Cinephilia/Telephilia." *Framework* 45, no. 2 (Fall 2004): 38–41.

Castle Films. Advertisement. *New York Times*, November 23, 1943.

"C.B. Moss Sees Future Films Priced and Handled a la Legit." *Variety*, October 3, 1956, 24.

Chapman, John. "Children Capture a Pirate Ship in Charming 'Innocent Voyage.'" *New York Theatre Critics' Review* 4 (1943): 224. Originally published in *New York Daily News*, November 16, 1943.

"China Hiccup Drives Down Global B.O." *Variety*, January 24, 2017, 19–21.

Cieply, Michael. "Eyepopping, in Many Ways." *New York Times*, November 9, 2009.

"Cinema Expo/3-D: The Killer App." *Variety* (supplement), June 9, 2008, A1.

Coe, Richard L. "Capitol Comedy Is Many-Faceted Hit." *Washington Post and Times Herald*, March 22, 1959.

Coe, Richard L. "'Chase's On at the Met." *Washington Post and Times Herald*, May 10, 1958.

Coe, Richard L. "'Holiday in Mexico,' M-G-M's Melting Pot, Sadly Needs Refining." *Washington Post*, September 26, 1946.

Coe, Richard L. "Wild, Witty and All-Wool." *Washington Post and Times Herald*, March 18, 1959.

Cogshell, Tim. "Under the Sea: *Ghosts of the Abyss*." *Boxoffice*, June 2003, 60.

Cohen, David S. "Film Not Ready to Cede to Tape." *Variety*, April 18, 2005, 7.

Cohen, David S. "Goggles Galore: The Studios Have a New 3-D Vision: Their Film Libraries." *Variety*, April 6, 2009, 1, 38.

Cohen, David S. "Helmer Kept on Top of Things during Deep-Sea Dive." *Variety*, April 2, 2012, 6.

Cohen, David S. "James Cameron Supercharges 3-D; *Avatar* Helmer Reveals the Art and Science of Stereo." *Variety*, April 10, 2008. www.variety.com.

"Columbia Big Need: Another Blockbuster." *Variety*, October 2, 1957, 4.

"Columbia Pictures Sees Second Fiscal Period about Breaking Even: Movie Maker Had $395,000 Loss in December '57; Profit Expected for Half." *Wall Street Journal*, December 16, 1958.

Connolly, Mike. "Just for Variety." *Daily Variety*, December 19, 1950, 4.

Connolly, Mike. "Just for Variety." *Daily Variety*, August 19, 1951, 2.

Connor, J. D. *The Studios after the Studios: Neoclassical Hollywood (1970–2010)*. Stanford, CA: Stanford University Press, 2015.

Consolidated Vultee Aircraft. Advertisement. *New York Times*, April 20, 1944.

Cook, Howard. "Monroe Pic Has Block-Buster Aura." *Billboard*, March 23, 1959, 23.

Crowther, Bosley. "'Ben-Hur,' a Blockbuster." *New York Times*, November 19, 1959.

Crowther, Bosley. "Communique from Hollywood and Vine." *New York Times*, February 3, 1957.
Crowther, Bosley. "The New 'Ben-Hur': Old Story of the Heroic Judean Is Made into a Fine and Pertinent Film." *New York Times*, November 22, 1959.
Crowther, Bosley. "Optimists Galore: High Hopes and Plans Flood Hollywood." *New York Times*, November 1, 1959.
Crowther, Bosley. "Raisins in the Pies: On Looking for the Particularly Tasty Things in Films." *New York Times*, May 24, 1959.
"C'Scope Anni." *Daily Variety*, September 3, 1954, 3.
Cubitt, Sean. *The Cinema Effect*. Cambridge, MA: MIT Press, 2004.
Cucco, Marco. "The Promise Is Great: The Blockbuster and the Hollywood Economy." *Media, Culture, and Society* 31, no. 2 (2009): 215–230.
The Curtain Rises. Advertisement. *New York Times*, March 19, 1944.
The Curtain Rises. Advertisement. *New York Times*, April 2, 1944.
Daley, Arthur. "Fighter of the Year." *New York Times*, January 15, 1953.
Daniell, Raymond. "50 Two-Ton Bombs Plaster Duisburg; 300 R.A.F. Planes Unload Havoc on Reich Inland Port—Russians Hit Koenigsberg; Invasion Coast Visited; British Spitfires Pound Areas in France and Netherlands—Cologne Damage Described." *New York Times*, July 23, 1942.
Danzig, Allison. "Sports Carry On, but the Picture Changes." *New York Times Magazine*, May 23, 1943.
Davenport, Ken. "What's the Average Cost of Putting On a Broadway Show?" *The Producer's Perspective*, June 7, 2012. www.theproducersperspective.com.
"Day Air Offensive Reaches Berlin; Targets in Germany and Air Bases in France Hit; R.A.F. Now Using Five-Ton Bombs." *Times* (London), March 4, 1944.
Dean, Jodi. *Blog Theory: Feedback and Capture in the Circuits of Drive*. Malden, MA: Polity, 2010.
Dean, Jodi. *The Communist Horizon*. New York: Verso, 2012.
Debruge, Peter. "'Chicken' Eggs on Cameron and 3-D Bet." *Daily Variety*, April 21, 2006, A1–A2.
Debruge, Peter. "Heavy Hitters Bet Big on Third Dimension; Plexes Feel Compelled to Upgrade with Top Directors and Studios behind Format." *Variety*, June 18, 2007, A5–A6.
Delorme, Stéphane, and Jean-Philippe Tessé. Interview with Slavoj Žižek. *Cahiers du Cinéma*, April 2010.
Denby, David. "Big Pictures." *New Yorker*, January 8, 2007.
de Seversky, Alexander P. "Air Power and the War." *New York Times*, December 15, 1943.
Deuze, Mark. *Media Work*. Cambridge: Polity, 2007.
deWaard, Andrew. "Derivative Media: The Financialization of Film, Television and Popular Music, 2004–2016." PhD diss., University of California, Los Angeles, 2017.
Dickey, Josh. "'Avatar's' True Cost and Consequences." *TheWrap*, March 17, 2010. www.thewrap.com.

Dickinson, Kay. "'Make It What You Want It to Be': Logistics, Labour and the Financialization of Land via the Globalized Free Zone Studio." In *In the Studio: Visual Creation and Its Material Environments*, edited by Brian R. Jacobson. Oakland: University of California Press, 2020.

DiOrio, Carl. "*Avatar* House Is Motion-Capture Giant." *Hollywood Reporter*, July 15, 2009. www.hollywoodreporter.com.

"Distributor Bids to Finance Films: Walter Reade Jr. Would Aid U.S. Productions—Isabel Jeans in 'Olympia.'" *New York Times*, April 9, 1959.

"Domestic Top 250 of 2010." *Variety*, January 10–16, 2011, 12–13.

"Domestic Top 250 of 2011." *Variety*, January 9–15, 2012, 22–23.

"Domestic Top 250 of 2012." *Variety*, January 7–13, 2013, 10–11.

Dower, John W. *Cultures of War: Pearl Harbor/Hiroshima/9-11/Iraq*. New York: W. W. Norton/New Press, 2010.

Drake, Francis, and Katharine Drake. "Our Next Pearl Harbor?" *Atlantic*, October 1947.

Drucker, Johanna. "Digital Humanities: From Speculative to Skeptical." Public talk for Project Arclight and Media History Research Centre, Concordia University, Montreal, October 9, 2015.

Duncan, Jody. "The Seduction of Reality." *Cinefex*, no. 120 (2010): 68–146.

Duncan, Jody, and Lisa Fitzpatrick. *The Making of "Avatar."* New York: Abrams, 2010.

Dyer, Richard. "Entertainment and Utopia." 1977. In *Movies and Methods Volume II*, edited by Bill Nichols, 220–232. Berkeley: University of California Press, 1985.

Edgerton, Gary R. *American Film Exhibition and an Analysis of the Motion Picture Industry's Market Structure, 1963–1980*. New York: Garland, 1983.

Elberse, Anita. *Blockbusters: Hit-Making, Risk-Taking, and the Big Business of Entertainment*. New York: Henry Holt, 2013.

Elberse, Anita. "Brighter Than Ever." *Variety*, October 8, 2013, 49–51.

Ellis, Katie. *Disability and Popular Culture: Focusing Passion, Creating Community and Expressing Defiance*. New York: Routledge, 2016.

Elsaesser, Thomas. "The Blockbuster." In *The End of Cinema as We Know It: American Film in the Nineties*, edited by Jon Lewis, 11–22. New York: New York University Press, 2001.

Elsaesser, Thomas. "Cinephilia or the Uses of Disenchantment." In *Cinephilia: Movies, Love, and Memory*, edited by Marijke de Valck and Malte Hagener, 27–43. Amsterdam: Amsterdam University Press, 2005.

Elsaesser, Thomas. "The New New Hollywood: Cinema beyond Distance and Proximity." In *Moving Images, Culture and the Mind*, edited by Ib Bondebjerg, 187–203. Luton, UK: University of Luton Press, 2000.

Epstein, Edward J. *The Big Picture: Money and Power in Hollywood*. New York: Random House, 2006.

Epstein, Gady. "Winner Takes All: Mass Entertainment." *Economist*, February 11, 2017.

"ESPN, Discovery Plug HD at Retail: Basic Networks Look to Drive Penetration for Local Ops' New Offerings." *Multichannel News*, June 9, 2003.

Esterow, Milton. "Adult Films, New Comfort Revive City's Moviegoing." *New York Times*, May 5, 1958.

"Europe Contrary on Blockbusters." *Variety*, May 30, 1962, 7.

"Exclusive: Soderbergh Gives *Avatar* High Praise." *Coming Soon*, April 30, 2009. www.comingsoon.net.

"Exhibitors Need Product NOW." *Film Bulletin*, September 2, 1963, 7.

Exodus. Advertisement. *Lockport Union-Sun and Journal*, August 2, 1961.

"Fair Grounds Entries." *New York Times*, February 2, 1943.

Farber, Manny. "Big-Studio 'Supers'—Monumental Art Baked in a Pittsburgh Blast Furnace." 1959. In *Farber on Film: The Complete Film Writings of Manny Farber*, edited by Robert Polito, 515–519. New York: The Library of America, 2009.

Farber, Manny. "Movie Gimmicks; Seven Films of 1953." 1954. In *Farber on Film: The Complete Film Writings of Manny Farber*, edited by Robert Polito, 457–460. New York: The Library of America, 2009.

Farber, Manny. "*The Robe*." 1953. In *Farber on Film: The Complete Film Writings of Manny Farber*, edited by Robert Polito, 451–453. New York: The Library of America, 2009.

Farber, Manny. "Three Art-y Films." 1959. In *Farber on Film: The Complete Film Writings of Manny Farber*, edited by Robert Polito, 506–509. New York: The Library of America, 2009.

Farber, Manny. "White Elephant Art vs. Termite Art." 1962. In *Farber on Film: The Complete Film Writings of Manny Farber*, edited by Robert Polito, 533–542. New York: The Library of America, 2009.

A Farewell to Arms. Advertisement. *New York Times*, January 30, 1958.

The F.B.I. Story. Advertisement. *Motion Picture Daily*, September 14, 1959, 4–5.

"'56 Oscar a $1,000,000 Baby; Will Add That to 'Marty' Take." *Variety*, March 28, 1956, 5, 15.

"Film Production and Distribution: Steady Growth Continues in World Feature Film Output." *Screen Digest*, July 2007, 205.

"Film Review: *Quo Vadis*." *Variety*, November 14, 1951, 6.

Fleming, Mike, Jr. "How 'The Secret Life of Pets' Beat 'Deadpool' and 'Rogue One'—the Data behind the Dollars." *Deadline*, April 4, 2017. deadline.com.

Fleming, Mike, Jr. "No. 1 'Transformers: Age of Extinction' Is 2014's Most Valuable Blockbuster." *Deadline*, March 13, 2015. deadline.com.

Fleming, Mike, Jr. "No. 3 'Jurassic World'—2015 Most Valuable Movie Blockbuster Tournament." *Deadline*, March 28, 2016. deadline.com.

Fleming, Mike, Jr. "No. 5 'Furious 7'—2015 Most Valuable Movie Blockbuster Tournament." *Deadline*, March 23, 2016. deadline.com.

Fleming, Mike, Jr. "No. 5 'Guardians of the Galaxy'—2014 Most Valuable Blockbuster Movie Tournament." *Deadline*, March 13, 2015. deadline.com.

Fleming, Mike, Jr. "No. 8 'Captain America: Civil War' Box Office Profits—2016 Most Valuable Movie Blockbuster Tournament." *Deadline*, March 28, 2017. deadline.com.

Fleming, Mike, Jr. "2013 Most Valuable Blockbuster Championship Game—#1 'Iron Man 3' vs. #3 'Despicable Me 2.'" *Deadline*, March 27, 2014. deadline.com.

"Ford Buys 'Robe'; Will Have One Break Spot." *Broadcasting*, January 9, 1967, 42.

Forrest, Elizabeth. "The Blockbusters Are Coming." *Picturegoer*, March 15, 1958, 14.

"48-Pix, $40,000,000 UA Program; 12-Month Slate to Include Monthly 'Blockbusters'; US Prez Bullish on Future." *Daily Variety*, August 2, 1954, 1, 5.

Foss, Cassie. "Report—'Iron Man 3' Generated $179.8m in Spending, 2,043 Jobs." *Star News*, April 30, 2013.

"Four-Ton Bombs Used." *New York Times*, December 11, 1942.

Frankel, Daniel. "Get Ready for the Biggest 'Potter' Opening Yet." *TheWrap*, November 17, 2010. www.thewrap.com.

Friedrich, Jörg. *The Fire: The Bombing of Germany, 1940–1945*. 2002. Translated by Allison Brown. New York: Columbia University Press, 2006.

Garvin, David A. "Blockbusters: The Economics of Mass Entertainment." *Journal of Cultural Economics* 5, no. 1 (1981): 1–20.

Ghosh, Bishnupriya. *Global Icons: Apertures to the Popular*. Durham, NC: Duke University Press, 2011.

Giardina, Carolyn. "James Cameron, Vince Pace Announce New 3D Venture." *Hollywood Reporter*, April 11, 2011. www.hollywoodreporter.com.

Giardina, Carolyn. "3D Spotlight." *Hollywood Reporter*, October 26, 2009. www.hollywoodreporter.com.

Gill, Frank. Review of *Carmen Jones*. *Billboard*, December 11, 1943, 28.

Gillett, John. "The Survivors." *Sight and Sound* 28, nos. 3/4 (Summer/Autumn 1959): 150–155.

Gillette Blades. Advertisement. *Washington Post*, January 11, 1946.

"'Gimmicks' Did Well in 1957—Sputnik Latest 'Of Monsters.'" *Variety*, November 6, 1957, 3, 36.

"Gimmicks Pay Off in Box-Office War: Audiences Are Insured, Feel Tingly and See Skeletons at William Castle Films." *New York Times*, October 26, 1959.

Gitelman, Lisa. *Always Already New: Media, History, and the Data of Culture*. Cambridge, MA: MIT Press, 2006.

Gladwell, Malcolm. "The Science of the Sleeper: How the Information Age Could Blow Away the Blockbuster." *New Yorker*, October 4, 1999.

"'Glass Slipper' Glides to Shimmering Start at B'w'y B.O. despite Bad Weather." *Daily Variety*, March 28, 1955, 3.

"Global Film Production/Distribution: US Makes Fewer Feature Films as World Total Sets New Record." *Screen Digest*, July 2008, 205.

"Global Film Production Falls: Key Territories Hold Firm but World Production Levels Drop." *Screen Digest*, July 2009, 205.

Gomery, Douglas. "The Hollywood Blockbuster: Industrial Analysis and Practice." In *Movie Blockbusters*, edited by Julian Stringer, 72–83. New York: Routledge, 2003.

Goodyear, Dana. "Man of Extremes: The Return of James Cameron." *New Yorker*, October 26, 2009.

Grainge, Paul. *Brand Hollywood: Selling Entertainment in a Global Media Age*. New York: Routledge, 2008.

Grainger, James R. "Can't All Be Blockbusters, but 'A' or 'B' Every Pic Must Be Sold." *Variety*, January 2, 1952, 28.

Gramsci, Antonio. *Selections from the Prison Notebooks*. Edited and translated by Quintin Hoare and Geoffrey Nowell Smith. New York: International Publishers, 1971.

Grayling, A. C. *Among the Dead Cities: The History and Moral Legacy of the WWII Bombing of Civilians in Germany and Japan*. London: Bloomsbury, 2006.

Green, Abel. "Kalmenson's WB Lowdown; Trouble Is an Exec Veep's Biz." *Variety*, July 16, 1958, 3, 10.

Green, Abel. "Pix Pioneering—'56 Style; Goldenson Takes New B.O. Slant." *Variety*, August 22, 1956, 1, 16.

Green, Abel. "Towering B.O. Stature of 'Ben-Hur' Vindicates Joe Vogel's Metro Team." *Variety*, November 18, 1959, 1.

Green, Nat. "The Crossroads." *Billboard*, July 24, 1943, 47.

Grieveson, Lee. *Cinema and the Wealth of Nations: Media, Capital, and the Liberal World System*. Oakland: University of California Press, 2017.

Griffiths, Alison. *Shivers down Your Spine: Cinema, Museums, and the Immersive View*. New York: Columbia University Press, 2008.

Hall, Sheldon. "Pass the Ammunition: A Short Etymology of 'Blockbuster.'" In *The Return of the Epic Film: Genre, Aesthetics and History in the 21st Century*, edited by Andrew B. R. Elliott, 147–166. Edinburgh: Edinburgh University Press, 2014.

Hall, Sheldon. "Tall Revenue Features: The Genealogy of the Modern Blockbuster." In *Genre and Contemporary Hollywood*, edited by Steve Neale, 11–26. London: BFI Publishing, 2002.

Hall, Sheldon, and Steve Neale. *Epics, Spectacles, and Blockbusters: A Hollywood History*. Detroit: Wayne State University Press, 2010.

Handel, Leo A. *Hollywood Looks at Its Audience: A Report of Film Audience Research*. Urbana: University of Illinois Press, 1950.

Hansen, Miriam. "The Mass Production of the Senses: Classical Cinema as Vernacular Modernism." In *Reinventing Film Studies*, edited by Christine Gledhill and Linda Williams, 332–350. London: Arnold, 2000.

"Hardsell—Will It Payoff If Release Is Less Than a B.O. Blockbuster?" *Variety*, June 25, 1958, 18.

Hart, Martin. "Solving the Mysteries of MGM Camera 65 and Ultra Panavision 70." *Widescreen Museum*, 1997/2002. www.widescreenmuseum.com.

Hawkins, Robert F. "19 Nations with 32 Pix in Venice Film Fest; 'Thief,' 'Kentuckian' from U.S." *Variety*, August 24, 1955, 2, 75.

Hayes, Dade. "Titanic Titan Takes Time Out." *Variety*, December 17, 2001, 4.

Hayes, Dade, and Jill Goldsmith. "Glum and Glummer." *Variety*, March 31, 2008, 1, 37.

Hayward, Susan. *Cinema Studies: The Key Concepts*. 2nd ed. New York: Routledge, 2000.

"Hazards in 'Blockbusting.'" *Variety*, November 6, 1957, 3.

"Heavy Bombers." *Life*, September 28, 1942, 45–48.

Heineman, William J. "Merchandise Counts." *Independent Film Journal*, June 26, 1958, 110, 162.

Heller, Joseph. *Catch-22*. New York: Simon and Schuster, 1961.

"Hendricks's Wide World at HDTV: Discovery Chief Focuses In on a New Platform." *Multichannel News*, May 5, 2003.

"He Who Strikes Last." *New York Times*, April 15, 1943.

Hift, Fred. "Music Films' Hard-Sell Abroad; Foreigners Like Plenty o' Plot." *Variety*, November 30, 1955, 1, 15.

Higgins, Bill. "All Eyes on *Avatar*; Fellow Directors Shower Praise on Cameron." *Variety*, December 18, 2009. www.variety.com.

Hirsch, W. R. "Agriculture Goes to War at Louisiana State Fair." *Billboard*, January 2, 1943, 114, 121.

"History Comes to Life with . . . *Ben-Hur*." Advertisement. *New York Daily News*, November 22, 1959.

"Hoarding the Blockbusters; Dictated by Payment Plan." *Variety*, February 13, 1957, 67.

"Holdovers Heftiest among L.A. 1st Runs; 'SAC' 66G in Second Round in 10 Sites." *Daily Variety*, July 12, 1955, 3.

"Holiday Bix Here SRO for 'Okla.,' 'G&D,' Cinerama." *Daily Variety*, November 25, 1955, 1, 3.

Hollinger, Hy. "'Lost Audience': Grass vs. Class—Sticks Now on 'Hick Pix' Kick." *Variety*, December 5, 1956, 1, 86.

Hollinger, Hy. "No Biz Like Pix Biz Was Then as Frantic '50's End an Era." *Daily Variety*, December 30, 1959, 1, 7.

Hollinger, Hy. "Semi-annual Hysterics in Film Trade 'No Way to Run a Business'— Wanger." *Variety*, October 23, 1957, 1, 75.

Hollinger, Hy. "20th-Fox Wallopy 'Giant Trailer' Stimulating Entire Film Trade." *Variety*, May 15, 1957, 15.

Holson, Laura M. "Director of *Titanic* Turns to 3-D Film Ventures." *New York Times*, March 31, 2003.

Holston, Kim R. *Movie Roadshows: A History and Filmography of Reserved-Seat Limited Showings, 1911–1973*. Jefferson, NC: McFarland, 2013.

Hopper, Hedda. "Cagney's Ready to Bust—Junior's a Football Hero." *Washington Post and Times Herald*, November 27, 1955.

Hopper, Hedda. "This Man Zugsmith Is the Talk of the Trade." *Washington Post and Times Herald*, December 20, 1959.

Horkheimer, Max, and Theodor Adorno. *Dialectic of Enlightenment*. 1944/1947. Translated by John Cumming. New York: Herder and Herder, 1972.

Houston, Penelope, and John Gillett. "The Theory and Practice of Blockbusting." *Sight and Sound* 32, no. 2 (Spring 1963): 68–74.

"How Does Trade Top Blockbusters?" *Variety*, May 14, 1958, 4.

"How Wide-Screen Movies Fit the 21-Inch Tube." *Broadcasting*, October 3, 1966, 27.

Hoyt, Eric. *Hollywood Vault: Film Libraries before Home Video*. Berkeley: University of California Press, 2014.

Hoyt, Eric, Kit Hughes, and Charles R. Acland. "A Guide to the Arclight Guidebook." In *The Arclight Guidebook to Media History and the Digital Humanities*, edited by Charles R. Acland and Eric Hoyt, 1–29. Brighton, Sussex: REFRAME Books in association with Project Arclight, 2016.

Hudgins, Morgan. "'Ben-Hur' Rides Again; New Film of the Lew Wallace Classic Generates Wide Interest in Italy." *New York Times*, August 10, 1958.

Huggins, Charlotte. "The Three Dimensions of 3-D." *Produced By*, Spring 2008, 25–26.

Huls, Alexander. "Child's Play: The Degeneration of Blockbusters." Roger Ebert, January 8, 2014. www.rogerebert.com.

Hurwitz, Matt. "Beyond the Sea." *Empire*, March 2005.

Hurwitz, Matt. "Exposure: Vince Pace." *International Cinematographers Guild Magazine*, April 2009, 30, 32, 34.

"H'wood Not Romancing Sex." *Variety*, September 12, 1956, 5.

IBM. "Privilege." Advertisement. *Brooklyn Daily Eagle*, June 3, 1943.

"In Quest of an Alibi." *Variety*, December 7, 1955, 3.

"Int'l Top 100 of 2013." *Variety*, January 15, 2014, 42.

"It May Be Filmdom's Best Year." *Picturegoer*, December 24, 1955, 18.

Izod, John. *Hollywood and the Box Office, 1895–1986*. New York: Columbia University Press, 1988.

Jacobs, Matthew. "Not to Be Melodramatic, but Movies as We Know Them Are Dead." *Huffington Post*, June 9, 2016. www.huffingtonpost.ca.

Jameson, Fredric. "Reification and Utopia in Mass Culture." 1979. In *Signatures of the Visible*, 9–34. New York: Routledge, 1992.

"Japanese Gross on 'War' to Top 'Roman Holiday'; 'Giant' Another Socko." *Variety*, March 20, 1957, 16.

Jefferis, Jeff. "Voice from the Stix." *Variety*, January 2, 1952, 14.

Jensen, Jeff. "Great Expectation." *Entertainment Weekly*, January 15, 2007.

Johnson, Derek. *Media Franchising: Creative License and Collaboration in the Cultural Industries*. New York: New York University Press, 2013.

Johnson, Nunnally. "Oh, Men! Oh, Women! Oh, Slightly Colossal!" *New York Times*, February 17, 1957.

The Joker Is Wild. Advertisement. *Daily Variety*, September 17, 1957, 7–14.

Kaiser Wakes the Doctors. Advertisement. *New York Times*, September 26, 1943.

Katz, Ephraim, and Ronald Dean Nolen. *The Film Encyclopedia: The Complete Guide to Film and the Film Industry*. 7th ed. New York: Harper Collins, 2012.

Katzenberg, Jeffery. "Katzenberg Defends 3-D as Format of the Future." *Variety*, September 29, 2008, 7, 11.

Kaufman, Debra. "A Team Effort Finishes *Ghosts*." *American Cinematographer* 84, no. 7 (2003): 64–65.

Keegan, Rebecca. *The Futurist: The Life and Films of James Cameron*. New York: Crown, 2009.

Keightley, Keir. "*Un Voyage Via Barquinho* . . . Global Circulation, Musical Hybridization, and Adult Modernity, 1961–9." In *Migrating Music*, edited by Jason Toynbee and Byron Dueck, 112–126. New York: Routledge, 2011.

Keller, Alexandra. *James Cameron*. New York: Routledge, 2006.

Kendrick, James. "Marxist Overtones in Three Films by James Cameron." *Journal of Popular Film and Television* 27, no. 3 (1999): 36–44.

Kerr, Walter F. "Review: *No Time for Sergeants*." *New York Herald Tribune*, October 21, 1955.

Kilgallen, Dorothy. "Bid Runs High for Sanders Story." *Washington Post and Times Herald*, November 17, 1958.

Kilgallen, Dorothy. "No Journey's End without a Loan." *Washington Post and Times Herald*, June 28, 1955.

King, Geoff. "Spectacle, Narrative, and the Spectacular Hollywood Blockbuster." In *Movie Blockbusters*, edited by Julian Stringer, 114–127. New York: Routledge, 2003.

Klinger, Barbara. *Beyond the Multiplex: Cinema, New Technologies, and the Home*. Berkeley: University of California Press, 2006.

Koehler, Robert. "*Ghosts of the Abyss*." *Variety*, April 14, 2003, 20.

Kokas, Aynne. *Hollywood Made in China*. Oakland: University of California Press, 2017.

Kracauer, Siegfried. "Cult of Distraction." 1927. In *The Mass Ornament: Weimar Essays*, edited and translated by Thomas Y. Levin, 323–328. Cambridge, MA: Harvard University Press, 1995.

Krämer, Peter. "'Want to Take a Ride?': Reflections on the Blockbuster Experience in *Contact* (1997)." In *Movie Blockbusters*, edited by Julian Stringer, 128–140. New York: Routledge, 2003.

Krämer, Peter. "Women First: *Titanic*, Action-Adventure Films, and Hollywood's Female Audience." In *Titanic: Anatomy of a Blockbuster*, edited by Kevin S. Sandler and Gaylyn Studlar, 108–131. New Brunswick, NJ: Rutgers University Press, 1999.

Kramer, Stanley. "Pix Can't Live by Bigness Alone." *Variety*, January 2, 1952, 53.

Kramer, Stanley. "The Subliminal Blockbuster." *Independent Film Journal*, June 26, 1958, 128, 160.

Krim, Arthur B. "No Fixed Limits." *Independent Film Journal*, June 26, 1958, 62, 216.

Kubasik, Ben. "'Ben-Hur' Is Nine Lively Minutes Wrapped in 3½ Hrs. of Nothing." *Newsday*, November 19, 1959.

Kuhn, Annette. "Introduction: Cultural Theory and Science Fiction Cinema." In *Alien Zone: Cultural Theory and Contemporary Science Fiction Cinema*, edited by Annette Kuhn, 1–12. New York: Verso, 1990.

Lambert, Gavin. "From a Hollywood Notebook." *Sight and Sound* 28, no. 2 (Spring 1959): 68–73.

Lampert, Nicole. "Has James Cameron, Hollywood's Scariest Man, Blown £200 Million on the Biggest Movie Flop Ever?" *Daily Mail*, December 11, 2009.

Landry, Robert J. "Appraising the Judges: Inscrutable Public Has the Last Word in Determining Movie Attendance." *New York Times*, February 24, 1957.

Landry, Robert J. "Fight 'Greater TV' Season." *Variety*, July 2, 1958, 13.

Landry, Robert J. "Films May Be Doing Dandy, Taking into Account Mortgaged Masses in a Dead-Centre Calm." *Variety*, July 2, 1958, 13.

Landry, Robert J. "Statistics Never Very Reliable in Film Biz Anyhow, and Today's Changes Easily Misread." *Variety*, July 2, 1958, 13.

Lang, Brent. "Overseas Top 100 of 2015." *Variety*, January 19, 2016, 28.

Lang, Brent, and James Rainey. "Revenue Record for U.S. Box Office." *Variety*, January 3, 2017, 21–22.

Lange, André, ed. *Focus 1998: World Film Market Trends*. European Audiovisual Observatory. Paris: Marché du film/Festival de Cannes, 1998. www.obs.coe.int.

Lange, André, ed. *Focus 1999: World Film Market Trends*. European Audiovisual Observatory. Paris: Marché du film/Festival de Cannes, 1999. www.obs.coe.int.

Lange, André, ed. *Focus 2000: World Film Market Trends*. European Audiovisual Observatory. Paris: Marché du film/Festival de Cannes, 2000. www.obs.coe.int.

Lange, André, and Susan Newman, eds. *Focus 2001: World Film Market Trends*. European Audiovisual Observatory. Paris: Marché du film/Festival de Cannes, 2001. www.obs.coe.int.

Lange, André, and Susan Newman-Baudais, eds. *Focus 2002: World Film Market Trends*. European Audiovisual Observatory. Paris: Marché du film/Festival de Cannes, 2002. www.obs.coe.int.

Lange, André, and Susan Newman-Baudais, eds. *Focus 2003: World Film Market Trends*. European Audiovisual Observatory. Paris: Marché du Film/Festival de Cannes, 2003. www.obs.coe.int.

Lawrence of Arabia. Advertisement. *Variety*, May 29, 1963, 14.

"Less 'Verbiage' (Translate 'Garbiage') as Columbia Updates Press Books." *Variety*, August 7, 1957, 20.

"Let's Go! It's Movietime, U.S.A. . . ." Advertisement, *New York Times*, October 3, 1951.

Lev, Peter. *The Fifties: Transforming the Screen, 1950–1959*. Berkeley: University of California Press, 2003.

Levadi, Dave. "B&K's Slogan Is: 'No Slogans'—Wallerstein Reaction to Golden Jubilee Fiasco—Consistent, Point-of-Sale Showmanship Pays." *Variety*, November 13, 1957, 5, 18.

Lewis, Jon. "Following the Money in America's Sunniest Company Town: Some Notes on the Political Economy of the Hollywood Blockbuster." In *Movie Blockbusters*, edited by Julian Stringer, 61–71. New York: Routledge, 2003.

Leydon, Joe. "*Terminator 2 3-D*." *Variety*, May 6, 1996, 82.

Lincoln, Freeman. "The Comeback of the Movies." *Fortune*, February 1955, 127–131+.

"Line Up Big Films in the Summer Alleys (with Blockbusters Included)." *Variety*, May 2, 1956, 13.

Lockheed. Advertisement. *Victory* 1, no. 6 (1943): 55.

"Long-Run-Short-Week Woe; 20th's Big List Needs More Time." *Variety*, July 16, 1958, 5.

Lubove, Seth. "Sinking Ship." *Forbes*, November 14, 2005.

MacInnis, Joseph. *James Cameron's "Aliens of the Deep."* Washington, DC: National Geographic, 2004.

Maddaus, Gene. "Dirty Business: How the Country's Biggest Exhibition Chains Exploit the Men and Women Who Clean Their Theaters." *Variety*, March 26, 2019, 45–47.

Malsky, Matthew. "The Grandeur(s) of CinemaScope: Early Experiments in Cinematic Stereophony." In *Living Stereo: Histories and Cultures of Multichannel Sound*, edited by Paul Théberge, Kyle Devine, and Tom Everrett, 207–222. London: Bloomsbury, 2015.

Maltby, Richard. *Hollywood Cinema*. 2nd ed. Malden, MA: Blackwell, 2003.

Mann, Denise. *Hollywood Independents: The Postwar Talent Takeover*. Minneapolis: University of Minnesota Press, 2008.

"Many See Exhibits of War's Horrors; Tableaux in Rockefeller Center Depict Six Phases of 'The Nature of the Enemy'; Maimed Victim Speaks." *New York Times*, May 18, 1943.

Marc, David. *Demographic Vistas: Television in American Culture*. Philadelphia: University of Pennsylvania Press, 1984.

Marchand, Roland. *Advertising the American Dream: Making Way for Modernity, 1920–1940*. Berkeley: University of California Press, 1986.

Marchand, Roland. *Creating the Corporate Soul*. Berkeley: University of California Press, 1998.

Marx, Leo. "Does Improved Technology Mean Progress?" *Technology Review* 90, no. 1 (January 1987): 32–41.

Marx, Leo. *The Machine in the Garden: Technology and the Pastoral Ideal in America*. New York: Oxford University Press, 1964.

Marx, Leo, and Bruce Mazlish, eds. *Progress: Fact or Illusion?* Ann Arbor: University of Michigan Press, 1996.

Maslin, Janet. "Golden Age: Just Before They Invented the Blockbuster." *New York Times*, May 1, 1994.

"'Matinee' Call for 4,000 Actors; NBC-TV's 5-a-Week Using No Producers and No Big Names." *Daily Variety*, July 21, 1955, 23.

Mayer, Vicki. *Almost Hollywood, Nearly New Orleans: The Lure of the Local Film Economy*. Oakland: University of California Press, 2017.

McCall, George. "Sticks Nix Hick Pix: Not Interested in Farm Drama." *Variety*, July 17, 1935, 1, 51.

McCarthy, Anna. *The Citizen Machine: Governing by Television in 1950s America*. New York: New Press, 2010.

McClintock, Pamela. "King of the 3-D World." *Variety*, July 20, 2009, 3, 30.

McKay, Julia. "TV Doc Visits Sunken *Bismarck*." *Kingston Whig-Standard*, December 7, 2002.

McNary, Dave. "'Finding Dory' Swimming for Record $140 Million Opening." *Variety*, June 18, 2016. www.variety.com.

Meehan, Eileen R. "Ancillary Markets—Television: From Challenge to Safe Haven." In *The Contemporary Hollywood Film Industry*, edited by Paul McDonald and Janet Wasko, 106–119. Oxford: Blackwell, 2008.

Melnick, Ross. *American Showman: Samuel "Roxy" Rothafel and the Birth of the Entertainment Industry, 1908–1935*. New York: Columbia University Press, 2012.

Mencken, H. L. "War Words in England." *American Speech* 19, no. 1 (1944): 3–15.
Merritt, Rick. "Popcorn, Soda and Two Aspirin." *Electronic Engineering Times*, August 1, 2005, 13.
Mersereau, Don. "Newsmen See Simultaneous Filming of Three 20th-Fox Blockbusters." *Boxoffice*, June 22, 1964, 6.
Metro-Goldwyn-Mayer. *The Story of the Making of Ben-Hur: A Tale of the Christ*. New York: Random House, 1959.
"Million Strong, City Salutes American Day; Central Park Throng Hears Wallace Urge Freedom for All 'Plain People.'" *New York Herald Tribune*, May 17, 1943.
Mills, C. Wright. "Culture and Politics." 1963. In *The Sixties: Art, Politics, and Media of Our Most Explosive Decade*, edited by Gerald Howard, 74–84. New York: Paragon House, 1991.
"Modesty (in Budgets) Returns; All-Blockbuster Plan Too Risky." *Variety*, June 27, 1956, 3, 7.
Moeller, Robert G. "The Bombing War in Germany, 2005–1940: Back to the Future?" In *Bombing Civilians: A Twentieth-Century History*, edited by Yuki Tanaka and Marilyn B. Young, 46–76. New York: New Press, 2009.
MOMA, Sarah Newmeyer to City Editors. *Road to Victory* exhibit. Press release, May 13, 1942. New York Public Library.
"More Areas of Berlin Wrecked." *Times* (London), December 31, 1943.
Morris, Chris. "A Game Changer? *Avatar* Looks to Alter H'w'd Vidgame Push." *Variety*, June 15, 2009, 4, 12.
Morris, Joe Alex. "Allies Deliver Heavy Blows." *Berkeley Daily Gazette*, August 1, 1942.
Morse, Leon. "CBS-TV Skeds Blockbuster Million-Dollar Features." *Billboard*, August 6, 1955, 2.
Moskowitz, Gene. "Films along the Seine: 'Les Miserables' Ushers Blockbuster Era into France—Other Matters." *New York Times*, April 20, 1958.
Mumford, Lewis. *The Myth of the Machine*. 2 vols. New York: Harcourt Brace Jovanovich, 1967–1970.
Murphy, A. D. "Hard-Sell and Skid Row Blockbuster." *Variety*, December 9, 1959, 19.
Murrow, Edward R. "The Target Was to Be the Big City." 1943. In *Reporting World War II: Part One, American Journalism, 1938–1944*, 713–720. New York: Literary Classics of the United States, 1995.
Naremore, James. *More Than Night: Film Noir in Its Contexts*. Berkeley: University of California Press, 1998.
Nason, Richard. "'Hercules' Starts Flood of Movies: Levine's Success Is First of Many Spectaculars on Way—New Bill at Cameo." *New York Times*, October 24, 1959.
Nason, Richard. "On 'Ben-Hur's' Record." *New York Times*, November 15, 1959.
"'Nature of Enemy' Show Thronged at Opening." *New York Post*, May 17, 1943.
Neale, Steve. "Hollywood Blockbusters: Historical Dimensions." In *Movie Blockbusters*, edited by Julian Stringer, 47–60. New York: Routledge, 2003.
"Need Exhibitors in Production—Fabian: Producers Don't Figure, Theatres Don't Recognize Blockbusters Ahead of Time." *Variety*, March 6, 1957.

Nepales, Ruben V. "Will James Cameron Be 'World's King' Again?" *Philippine Daily Inquirer*, August 8, 2009. services.inquirer.net.

"New *Avatar* Behind-the-Scene Photos." *Coming Soon*, January 12, 2009. www.comingsoon.net.

Newcomb, Horace, and Paul M. Hirsch. "TV as a Cultural Forum." *Quarterly Review of Film Studies* 8, no. 3 (Summer 1983): 45–55.

"New Group of Potential Blockbusters Rising to Hold Hands with 'GWTW.'" *Variety*, August 29, 1956, 1.

New Loew's Capitol. Advertisement. *New York Times*, December 24, 1959.

Newman-Baudais, Susan, ed. *Focus 2004: World Film Market Trends*. European Audiovisual Observatory. Paris: Marché du film/Festival de Cannes, 2004. www.obs.coe.int.

Newman-Baudais, Susan, ed. *Focus 2005: World Film Market Trends*. European Audiovisual Observatory. Paris: Marché du film/Festival de Cannes, 2005. www.obs.coe.int.

Newman-Baudais, Susan, ed. *Focus 2006: World Film Market Trends*. European Audiovisual Observatory. Paris: Marché du film/Festival de Cannes, 2006. www.obs.coe.int.

Newman-Baudais, Susan, ed. *Focus 2007: World Film Market Trends*. European Audiovisual Observatory. Paris: Marché du film/Festival de Cannes, 2007. www.obs.coe.int.

"New Uni-Int Set Up." *Daily Variety*, August 14, 1946, front page.

"Nicholson Scores 'Dollar Snobbery,' 'Provincialism.'" *Independent Film Journal*, October 26, 1957, 22.

"$93 Million Week's Film Jackpot." *Broadcasting*, October 3, 1966, 25–27.

"Nitery Reviews." *Daily Variety*, December 17, 1954, 6.

"No Carny Hokum, Open 'Ben-Hur' on Dignified Plane." *Variety*, November 25, 1959, 17.

"No More a Poor Man's Show; 'Kwai' in Newark as $3 Hard Tic." *Variety*, May 28, 1958, 7.

"Not 'Anti-American'—but 'Pro-Arty.'" *Variety*, May 15, 1957, 5.

"Notes on Science." *New York Times*, December 9, 1945.

No Time for Love. Advertisement. *Daily Variety*, January 18, 1944, 8–9.

No Time for Sergeants. Advertisement. *New York Times*, October 22, 1955.

"N.Y. Critic's 'Bests': 'Ben-Hur,' Audrey Hepburn, Jas. Stewart, Zinnemann." *Variety*, December 30, 1959, 1, 46.

Nye, David. *American Technological Sublime*. Cambridge, MA: MIT Press, 1994.

Ohmer, Susan. *George Gallup in Hollywood*. New York: Columbia University Press, 2006.

"$119 Million for 65 Pix; High Priced Films Lined Up for '49." *Daily Variety*, December 2, 1948, 1, 13.

"Only Blockbusters Get Theatre Bally Attention; In-Betweener's Slapped." *Variety*, April 30, 1958, 3, 20.

Operation Petticoat. Advertisement. *Variety*, December 30, 1959, 17.

Opus 21. Advertisement. *New York Times*, July 17, 1949.

Orpheus Descending. Advertisement. *New York Times*, November 14, 1959.

Ortner, Sherry B. *Not Hollywood: Independent Film at the Twilight of the American Dream*. Durham, NC: Duke University Press, 2013.

"Overseas Top 100 of 2014." *Variety*, January 14, 2015, 40.

"O.W.I. Exhibit of Axis Terror Is Opened Here: 2,500 Throng Rockefeller Center Promenade, Hear Powell, Eve Curie, Swing." *New York Herald Tribune*, May 18, 1943.

Painter, Kim. "Falling TVs Can Kill, but Few Parents Aware of Risks." *USA Today*, December 13, 2012.

"Panasonic and Twentieth Century Fox Team for Global Promotion of James Cameron's *Avatar*." *Asia Corporate News Newswire*, August 21, 2009. en.acnnewswire.com.

"Panasonic Rolls with HD 3-D Home Theater Truck Tour." *Entertainment Close-Up*, September 5, 2009. www.highbeam.com.

"Paramount Considers Acquiring Companies outside Movie Field: Balaban Tells Meeting There May Be Some Announcements 'during 1959–60 Period.'" *Wall Street Journal*, June 3, 1959.

"Paramount Pictures Says Operating Net for 9 Months Tops '57: Cost-Cutting at Movie Studios Cited; 20 'Million Dollar Plus' Films Slated for '59." *Wall Street Journal*, September 30, 1958.

Parks, Lisa. *Rethinking Media Coverage: Vertical Mediation and the War on Terror*. New York: Routledge, 2018.

"Par Nixes '10C' Free Rides; All Must Pay at Drive-Ins." *Variety*, May 14, 1958, 5.

Peck, Seymour. "The $15,000,000 Chariot Race." *New York Times Magazine*, November 8, 1959.

Pedelty, Donovan. "The Shape of Films to Come." *Picturegoer*, February 7, 1959, 6–7.

Pedelty, Donovan. "The Year of the Blockbusters." *Picturegoer*, December 27, 1958, 20–21.

Penley, Constance. "Time Travel, Primal Scene and the Critical Dystopia." *Camera Obscura* 5, no. 3 (15) (1986): 66–85.

Penn, Stanley W. "Blockbuster Movies: Outlays Soar as Firms Gamble for Big Returns from Fewer Pictures." *Wall Street Journal*, April 2, 1962.

"Perspective vs. Hysterics." *Variety*, December 18, 1957, 4.

Pickard, Christopher. "Visionary Award: James Cameron." *Variety*, June 19, 2006, A6.

Pierson, Michelle. *Special Effects: Still in Search of Wonder*. New York: Columbia University Press, 2002.

"'Pix Safe from TV for 4 Years'; Both in Eventual Co-op, Sez Schary." *Variety*, November 7, 1951, 1, 22.

"Popular Items." *Billboard*, March 29, 1943, 51.

Post, Robert P. "12 of Raiders Lost; Night Fighters Met over German City—Large Fires Set; Nazis Gun British Towns." *New York Times*, December 23, 1942.

"Post'48 'Blockbusters' as Panacea for Dwindling Pre-'48 Features." *Variety*, April 29, 1959, 46.

"Precedental Policy Certain to Echo as Others Follow 'Ten Commandments.'" *Variety*, May 14, 1958, 5.

Prince, Stephen. *Digital Visual Effects in Cinema: The Seduction of Reality*. New Brunswick, NJ: Rutgers University Press, 2012.

Prince, Stephen. *A New Pot of Gold: Hollywood under the Electronic Rainbow, 1980–1989*. Berkeley: University of California Press, 2000.

"Production's Fiscal Danger Zone Is between 'Lil' and 'All-Out' Budgets." *Variety*, July 2, 1958, 20.

Proud Rebel. Advertisement. *New York Times*, July 3, 1958.

Proud Rebel. Advertisement. *New York Times*, July 11, 1958.

"'Proud Rebel' Tested." *Variety*, July 2, 1958, 20.

Pryor, Thomas M. "Film Men Report on TV Competition: Studio Chiefs Hear Box Office Didn't Succumb to Sunday's 'Diamond Jubilee' Telecast." *New York Times*, October 29, 1954.

Pryor, Thomas M. "Hollywood Review: Year's Problems Faced by Hopeful Industry." *New York Times*, January 4, 1959.

Pryor, Thomas M. "Hollywood Vista: Three Authoritative 'Reporters' Add Background to Production Picture." *New York Times*, October 26, 1958.

Pryor, Thomas M. "Warners to Back Movie by Monroe." *New York Times*, March 2, 1956.

"Puzzle: 'How' Get 'More' Films; Playdate-Bank Idea Up Anew." *Variety*, December 17, 1958, 7.

Quandt, James. "Everyone I Know Is Stayin' Home: The New Cinephilia." *Framework* 50, nos. 1/2 (Spring–Fall 2009): 206–209.

Quittner, Josh. "The Next Dimension." *Time*, March 30, 2009.

Raby, Mark. "Avatar Blu-ray 3D Tied to Panasonic until 2012." *TG Daily*, December 14, 2010. www.tgdaily.com.

"RAF 'Block Busters' Blast Hamburg." *Reading Eagle*, July 27, 1942.

Rampton, James. "James Cameron: King of All He Surveys." *Independent* (London), December 19, 2006.

Ransom! Advertisement. *Daily Variety*, December 28, 1955, 15.

Ransom! Advertisement. *Lockport Union-Sun and Journal*, May 31, 1956.

Ransom! Advertisement. *Saratogian*, February 4, 1956.

Reade, John Collingwood. "The War Today—German Tactical Lines in Russia More Dangerous." *Globe and Mail*, August 5, 1942.

"Report 300G Payoff by Col for 11 Kramer Pix; Includes 'Caine Mutiny.'" *Daily Variety*, November 24, 1954, 1, 21.

"Review: *No Time For Love*." *Boxoffice*, November 13, 1943, 100.

Review of *Thirty Seconds over Tokyo*. *Farm Journal* 69 (1945): n.p.

"Review: *The Ten Commandments*." *Variety*, October 10, 1956, 6.

"Review: *War and Peace*." *Variety*, August 22, 1956, 6.

"'Roadshow' Keys Metro Thinking." *Variety*, November 18, 1959, 3, 86.

The Road to Serfdom. Advertisement. *New York Times*, April 8, 1945.

Rogers, Ariel. *Cinematic Appeals: The Experience of New Movie Technologies*. New York: Columbia University Press, 2013.

Roxborough, Scott, and Jonathan Landreth. "Private Equity Changing Face of Film Industry." *Hollywood Reporter*, May 23, 2007. www.hollywoodreporter.com.

Sanders, John. *The Film Genre Book*. Leighton Buzzard, UK: Auteur, 2009.

Sandler, Kevin S., and Gaylyn Studlar, eds. *Titanic: Anatomy of a Blockbuster*. New Brunswick, NJ: Rutgers University Press, 1999.

Sanogo, Aboubakar. "Regarding Cinephilia and Africa." *Framework* 50, nos. 1/2 (Spring–Fall 2009): 226–228.

Schaffer, Ronald. "The Bombing Campaigns in World War II: The European Theater." In *Bombing Civilians: A Twentieth-Century History*, edited by Yuki Tanaka and Marilyn B. Young, 30–45. New York: New Press, 2009.

Schatz, Thomas. *Boom and Bust: American Cinema in the 1940s*. Berkeley: University of California Press, 1997.

Schatz, Thomas. "Film Industry Studies and Hollywood History." In *Media Industries: History, Theory, and Method*, edited by Jennifer Holt and Alisa Perren, 45–56. Malden, MA: Wiley-Blackwell, 2009.

Schatz, Thomas. "The New Hollywood." In *Film Theory Goes to the Movies*, edited by Jim Collins, Hilary Radner, and Ava Preacher Collins, 3–36. New York: Routledge, 1993.

Schatz, Thomas. "Seismic Shifts in the American Film Industry." In *The Wiley-Blackwell History of American Film*, edited by Cynthia Lucia, Roy Gundmann, and Art Simon, 1–21. London: Blackwell, 2012.

Schatz, Thomas. "The Studio System and Conglomerate Hollywood." In *The Contemporary Hollywood Film Industry*, edited by Paul McDonald and Janet Wasko, 13–42. Oxford: Blackwell, 2008.

Scheib, Ronnie. "*Aliens of the Deep*." *Variety*, February 7, 2005, 67.

Schoenfeld, Joe. "Film Review—*Oklahoma!*" *Daily Variety*, October 11, 1955, 3.

Schoenfeld, Joe. "Time and Place." *Daily Variety*, August 18, 1955, 2.

Schumach, Murray. "Filmland Jargon Vital, Ambiguous: If a Movie Fails, It's 'Built-In Values' Were Misused, Say Boldly Cautious Aides." *New York Times*, June 22, 1959.

Schumach, Murray. "Hollywood Teams: The Promotional Pairing of Pictures and Products Is Popular Practice." *New York Times*, November 22, 1959.

Schumach, Murray. "Metro Stills Leo for the First Time: Famous Roaring Lion Kept Silent in 'Ben-Hur' to Save Religious Mood of Opening." *New York Times*, November 26, 1959.

Schwartz, Vanessa R. *It's So French! Hollywood, Paris, and the Making of Cosmopolitan Film Culture*. Chicago: University of Chicago Press, 2007.

Sconce, Jeffrey. "Explosive Apathy." In *B Is for Bad Cinema: Aesthetics, Politics, and Cultural Value*, edited by Claire Perkins and Constantine Verenis, 21–41. New York: SUNY Press, 2014.

Sconce, Jeffrey. "Trashing the Academy: Taste, Excess, and an Emerging Politics of Cinematic Style." *Screen* 36, no. 4 (1995): 371–393.

Scorsese, Martin. "I Said Marvel Movies Aren't Cinema. Let Me Explain." *New York Times*, November 5, 2019.

Screen Gems. "Powerhouse" advertisement. *Variety*, December 10, 1958, 24–25.

Scully, Frank. "Scully's Scrapbook." *Variety*, April 25, 1956, 77.

Sebald, W. G. *On the Natural History of Destruction*. 1999. Translated by Anthea Bell. Toronto: Vintage Canada, 2003.

"Secret Explosive Is Demonstrated; Nature of Ingredients Going into 'Blockbusters' Bared with U.S. Approval; Other Processes Shown; Du Pont Plant Experts Reveal New Silver-Plate Method at E Award Fete." *New York Times*, June 4, 1943.

"Sees Blockbusters as Boost to Short Films." *Variety*, December 18, 1957, 12.

"Selznick's Top-Money-Film Crown Threatened by '57 Blockbusters." *Variety*, January 8, 1958, 6.

Shalett, Sidney M. "Air Magic Shown at Wright Field." *New York Times*, December 30, 1942.

Shone, Tom. *Blockbuster: How Hollywood Learned to Stop Worrying and Love the Summer*. New York: Simon and Schuster, 2004.

"Shortage?—Only of Blockbusters." *Variety*, November 9, 1960, 15.

"'Sick' Screen Given Senatorial Advice." *New York Times*, August 5, 1953.

Sidney, George. "An 18-Year-Old Marine Stirs Some Memories." *Variety*, January 2, 1952, 53.

"Signs of Better Times for Films." *Financial Times*, November 10, 1959.

Sindlinger, Albert. "Take Them Straight!" *Independent Film Journal*, June 26, 1958, 180, 208.

Skouras, Charles P. "Chas. Skouras Sees a Big Theatre TV in the Future of the Picture Business." *Variety*, January 2, 1952, 14.

Sloterdijk, Peter. *Bubbles*. Vol. 1 of *Spheres*. 1998. Translated by Wieland Hoban. Los Angeles: Semiotext(e), 2011.

Snyder, Gabriel, and Nicole LaPorte. "Cameron Gets *Avatar* Going." *Variety*, January 8, 2007. www.variety.com.

Snyder, Marjorie B. "Much-Touted 'Story in 3-D' Would Interest Dr. Kinsey." *Washington Post*, September 20, 1953.

Sobchack, Vivian. "What Is Film History?, or, the Riddle of the Sphinxes." In *Reinventing Film Studies*, edited by Christine Gledhill and Linda Williams, 300–315. London: Arnold, 2000.

Solomon, John. *Ben-Hur: The Original Blockbuster*. Edinburgh: Edinburgh University Press, 2016.

Solomon and Sheba. Advertisement. *New York Post*, December 27, 1959.

Solomon and Sheba. Advertisement. *New York Times*, December 24, 1959.

Some Like It Hot. Advertisement. *Washington Post and Times Herald*, March 25, 1959.

Sontag, Susan. "The Decay of Cinema." *New York Times Magazine*, February 25, 1996.

Sontag, Susan. "Fascinating Fascism." *New York Review of Books*, February 15, 1975.

Sontag, Susan. "The Imagination of Disaster." *Commentary* 40, no. 4 (October 1965): 42–48.

Spear, Ivan. "Impressive Production Outlook for 1957." *Boxoffice Barometer*, February 9, 1957, 15, 18.

Staiger, Janet. "Matters of Taste, Subjects of Rank." *Framework* 45, no. 2 (Fall 2004): 76–80.

Staniszewski, Mary Anne. *The Power of Display: A History of Exhibition Installations at the Museum of Modern Art*. Cambridge, MA: MIT Press, 1998.

Steinbeck, John. *Bombs Away: The Story of a Bomber Team*. 1942. New York: Penguin Books, 2009.
Sterne, Jonathan. *MP3: The Meaning of a Format*. Durham, NC: Duke University Press, 2012.
"Steve Broidy Turns the Tables on Exhibs, Pins Blame on Them for Pix Shortage." *Daily Variety*, March 23, 1955, 1, 4.
Stewart, Susan. *On Longing: Narratives of the Miniature, the Gigantic, the Souvenir, the Collection*. Durham, NC: Duke University Press, 1993.
Stole, Inger L. *Advertising at War: Business, Consumers, and Government in the 1940s*. Urbana: University of Illinois Press, 2015.
"'Stranger' Mighty 40G, Pitt; 'Lady' 25." *Daily Variety*, July 27, 1955, 8.
Strauss, Theodore. "Miss Bankhead Back from the Sea." *New York Times*, December 5, 1943.
Stringer, Julian. "Introduction." In *Movie Blockbusters*, edited by Julian Stringer, 1–14. New York: Routledge, 2003.
Stringer, Julian, ed. *Movie Blockbusters*. New York: Routledge, 2003.
"Studios Star-Stud Pix to Bolster Limp Box-Office." *Daily Variety*, April 27, 1948, 3, 8.
"Study of 'Giant': Killer of B.O. Blues—Sindlinger Poses Science of Blockbuster 'Know-About' and 'Talk-About' Factors Unique Case History Startled Showmen." *Variety*, March 6, 1957, 7.
A Summer Place. Advertisement. *New York Times*, October 21, 1959.
"'Sword and Cross' TV Series Themed to Blockbusters." *Variety*, December 16, 1959, 22.
Tanaka, Yuki, and Marilyn B. Young, eds. *Bombing Civilians: A Twentieth-Century History*. New York: New Press, 2009.
Tasker, Yvonne. "Dumb Movies for Dumb People: Masculinity, the Body, and the Voice in Contemporary Action Cinema." In *Screening the Male: Exploring Masculinities in Hollywood Cinema*, edited by Steven Cohan and Ina Rae Hark, 230–244. New York: Routledge, 1993.
Tasker, Yvonne. *Spectacular Bodies: Gender, Genre and the Action Film*. New York: Routledge, 1993.
Taubin, Amy. "Art and Industry." *Village Voice*, July 9, 1991.
Telotte, J. P. *The Mouse Machine: Disney and Technology*. Urbana: University of Illinois Press, 2008.
Ten Seconds to Hell. Advertisement. *Variety*, September 2, 1959, 14.
There's a Waar On. Advertisement. *The Stage*, August 19, 1943, 6.
Thirty Seconds over Tokyo. Advertisement. *New York Times*, July 13, 1943.
Thirty Seconds over Tokyo. Advertisement. *Times-News*, February 9, 1956.
"This Month . . ." *American Gas Journal* 173, no. 4 (1950): 3.
Thom, Michael. "Lights, Camera, but No Action? Tax and Economic Development Lessons from State Motion Picture Incentive Programs." *American Review of Public Administration* 48, no. 1 (2018): 33–51.
Thomas, Kevin. "Robinson Crusoe as a Stranded Astronaut." *Washington Post*, August 23, 1964.

Thompson, Kristin. *The Frodo Franchise: The Lord of the Rings and Modern Hollywood*. Berkeley: University of California Press, 2007.
"Titanic Helmer Docks with CAA." *Variety*, June 8, 2009, 2.
"TOA Pushing Idea of Exhibs' Buy of Post-1948 Video Residuals; Might Then Sell Non-blockbusters." *Variety*, October 22, 1958, 5.
"Top International Grossers 2012." *Variety*, January 14–27, 2013, 10.
"Top 250 of 2013." *Variety*, January 6, 2014, 38–39.
"Top 250 of 2014." *Variety*, January 6, 2015, 30–31.
"Top 250 of 2015." *Variety*, January 13, 2016, 42–43.
"Top 2016 Movies at the Domestic Box Office." Accessed November 24, 2019. www.the-numbers.com.
"Top Worldwide Grossers 2010." *Variety*, January 17–23, 2011, 8.
"Top Worldwide Grossers 2011." *Variety*, January 16–22, 2012, 11.
"'Trapeze' Swings toward $7,000,000 for U.S. and Canada." *Variety*, August 15, 1956, 4.
Trout, Bob. Letter to the editor. *American Speech* 19, no. 4 (1944): 293.
Turner, Fred. *The Democratic Surround: Multimedia and American Liberalism from World War II to the Psychedelic Sixties*. Chicago: University of Chicago Press, 2013.
Turnock, Julie. *Plastic Reality: Special Effects, Technology, and the Emergence of 1970s Blockbuster Aesthetics*. New York: Columbia University Press, 2015.
"'12 O'Clock' Wow $34,000 in Philly." *Variety*, February 1, 1950, 11.
20th Century Fox. Advertisement. *Variety*, October 30, 1957, 11–14.
"20th Century-Fox Plans One Blockbuster Monthly." *Boxoffice*, November 6, 1961, 5.
"Two Views on Filmdom's Future." *Picturegoer*, August 2, 1958, 8.
"UA Boast: Blockbusters in Bunches." *Variety*, February 18, 1959, 5, 14.
"UA List Promises 10 'Blockbusters.'" *Variety*, February 20, 1957, 7.
"UA's Gross for 1952 up by 50 Per Cent." *Boxoffice*, January 17, 1953, 16.
"Ubisoft and Fox Team for *Avatar* Game." *Coming Soon*, July 24, 2007. www.comingsoon.net.
United Artists. Advertisement for 1958 releases. *Daily Variety*, December 3, 1957, 8–9.
United Artists. Advertisement for 1959 releases. *Boxoffice Barometer*, February 16, 1959, 3–6.
United States Strategic Bombing Survey Summary Report (European War). Washington, DC: U.S. Government Printing Office, 1945.
"Universal Cuts Size of Program; Martin Details Present Strategy." *Variety*, July 16, 1958, 3.
"Universal Pictures Says Net Shows Sharp Gains." *Wall Street Journal*, December 22, 1959.
"Universal Pictures to Sell, Lease Back Real Estate, Studios: MCA, Inc., TV Show Producer and Talent Agency, to Buy Them for $11,250,000." *Wall Street Journal*, December 19, 1958.
"Universal's Money-Making Habit vs. Industry Blockbuster Theory." *Variety*, October 24, 1956, 28.
U.S. Congress, Senate Select Committee on Small Business. *Problems of Independent Motion Picture Exhibitions*. Report of the Select Committee on Small Business, 83rd Cong., 1st sess., August 3, 1953.

U.S. Office of War Information. "The Four Freedoms." Pamphlet. Washington, DC, 1942. New York Public Library.

U.S. Office of War Information. "Release." Washington, DC, May 26, 1943. New York Public Library.

Van Dijck, José. *The Culture of Connectivity: A Critical History of Social Media*. New York: Oxford University Press, 2013.

"Viewpoint." Editorial. *Picturegoer*, March 7, 1959, 4.

Villarreal, Yvonne. "MPAA Blasts USC over Film Tax Credit Report." *Los Angeles Times*, September 14, 2016.

Wajcman, Judy. *Feminism Confronts Technology*. Cambridge: Polity, 1991.

Wakelam, Randall T. *The Science of Bombing: Operational Research in R.A.F. Bomber Command*. Toronto: University of Toronto Press, 2009.

Wallis, Hal. "No Fan Has Yet Stopt to Ask a Mgr., 'How Much Did This Film Cost?'; Blockbusters Are OK but the Main Thing Is 'Is It a Good Show?'" *Variety*, January 2, 1952, 7.

"Wall Street and Society Predominate Audience at Dignified 'Ben-Hur' Bow." *Variety*, November 18, 1959, 3, 86.

"Warners Zingy First Quarter, up 70%; but Second Won't Be Comparable; Blockbusters Swell the Total." *Variety*, February 13, 1957, 4.

Wasko, Janet. *How Hollywood Works*. Thousand Oaks, CA: Sage, 2003.

Wasson, Haidee. *Everyday Movies: Portable Projectors and the Transformation of American Culture*. Oakland: University of California Press, forthcoming.

Wasson, Haidee. "Formatting Film Studies." *Film Studies* 12 (Spring 2015): 57–61.

Waxman, Sharon. "Computers Join Actors in Hybrids on Screen." *New York Times*, January 9, 2007.

"WB Blockbusters for TV Series; Brochure Names 'Casablanca,' 'King's Row,' 'Cheyenne,' in TV Plans; Prep Aviation Series." *Daily Variety*, April 8, 1955, 1, 13.

"WB Policy: 12–14 a Year, All Big; Vidpix Uses Up Studio Facilities." *Variety*, November 12, 1958, 4.

Weiler, A. H. "Moving Sentiment." *New York Times*, July 2, 1958.

Weiler, A. H. "Passing Picture Scene." *New York Times*, May 4, 1958.

Weiler, A. H. "View from a Local Vantage Point." *New York Times*, April 13, 1958.

Weldon, Michael. *Psychotronic Encyclopedia of Film*. New York: Ballantine Books, 1983.

We're No Angels. Advertisement. *Variety*, July 6, 1955, 14.

"What's Going On at Du Mont Tele? Retrenchment Blues Evident." *Billboard*, November 24, 1945, 15.

"What the Newspaper Critics Say." *Film Bulletin*, February 5, 1945, 31.

Whissel, Kristen. "The Digital Multitude." *Cinema Journal* 49, no. 4 (2010): 90–110.

Whissel, Kristen. "Tales of Upward Mobility: The New Verticality and Digital Special Effects." *Film Quarterly* 59, no. 4 (2006): 23–34.

Whitney, Simon N. "The Impact of Antitrust Laws: Vertical Disintegration in the Motion Picture Industry." *American Economic Review* 45, no. 2 (May 1955): 491–498.

"Who's Who? Twenty Questions. What's What?" *New York Times*, August 9, 1942.

Williams, Linda. "Film Genres: Gender, Genre, and Excess." *Film Quarterly* 44, no. 4 (Summer 1991): 2–13.

Williams, Raymond. *Marxism and Literature*. New York: Oxford University Press, 1977.

Wilson, Alleis C. "Child's Play Often Doubles as Education." *New York Times*, November 9, 1952.

WOR. Advertisement. *Billboard*, November 1, 1947, 11.

Wyatt, Justin. *High Concept: Movies and Marketing in Hollywood*. Austin: University of Texas Press, 1994.

Wyatt, Justin, and Katherine Vlesmas. "The Drama of Recoupment: On the Mass Media Negotiation of *Titanic*." In *Titanic: Anatomy of a Blockbuster*, edited by Kevin S. Sandler and Gaylyn Studlar, 29–44. New Brunswick, NJ: Rutgers University Press, 1999.

"Your Business Will Continue to Thrive in 'Fifty-Five with More Blockbusters from Paramount." Advertisement. *Variety*, January 5, 1955, 26.

Žižek, Slavoj. "*Avatar*: The Return of the Natives." *New Statesman*, March 8, 2010.

Žižek, Slavoj. *Trouble in Paradise: From the End of History to the End of Capitalism*. Brooklyn, NY: Melville House, 2014.

(INDEX)

Note: Page numbers followed by *f* indicate a figure; page numbers followed by *t* indicate a table.

The Abyss, 236, 241, 248, 251
Academy Awards: *Avatar's* campaign, 279; *Ben-Hur* at, 221; in-betweeners at, 165–166; James Cameron at, 233–234; and revenue expectations, 165; for technological accomplishment, 237
Adorno, Theodor, 109
The Adventures of Pluto Nash, 6
advertising: adjectives used as nouns, 189; blockbuster bombs in, 106–111, 118, 121; blockbuster term, 116–118, 149–150, 199, 200*f*, 215–217, 220, 221*f*; bombing run depictions, 111–112, 113*f*; largeness and giganticism in, 215–217; studio campaigns, 181–183; technology in, 181; television, 222; war imagery, 109–111, 110*f*; war propaganda in, 108–111
aesthetics: of *Aliens of the Deep*, 257–258; and blockbuster criticism, 196; commercial, 82; continuity across blockbusters, 230; of power, 134; technological, 252; universal, 223
The African Queen, 153
The Agony and the Ecstasy, 227
Airport, 225
Aliens, 236, 252
Aliens of the Deep, 236, 249; *The Abyss* references, 257; aesthetics of, 257–258; budget, 236; CGI, 258; Dijanna Figueroa, 257–258; environmental ethic of, 260; reviews, 249; stills from, 249*f*; student scientists, 259; techno-fetishism, 257, 259–260; 3-D shooting, 249; and Vince Pace, 249
Allen, Michael, 10
Allied Artists, 177, 187, 188*t*
All the King's Men (theater), 213
All the President's Men, 292
Altman, Rick, 189
American Broadcasting Corporation (ABC), 222

American Graffiti, 18
American International Pictures (AIP), 162, 179, 228
Angels and Demons, 71
Anobile, Richard J., 269–270
Apocalypse Now, 19
April Love, 181
Arclight, Project, 30
Around the World in 80 Days: advertisements for, 181, 183; cosmopolitanism of, 69, 78, 193; format of, 143, 157; length of, 163; production budget, 196; run of, 185; success of, 193; ticket prices, 179; and United Artists, 219
art: appreciation, 272–273; blockbusters as not, 20, 33, 193–194, 206; Bourdieu on, 19–20, 33–34; film's legitimization as, 224; and the future, 301; in-betweener films, 194, 196, 205; and industry, 301; markets, 70
art/commerce divide, 224
art films, 193, 224, 228
aspect ratios, 136–137. *See also* widescreen formats
The Atomic City, 151, 152f, 153f
audience research, 140, 145–146, 172–175
audiences: of blockbusters, 3–4, 197; as discerning, 197; postwar affluence of, 201; rural versus urban, 171; and smart-aleck figures, 290–291; and technological wonder, 82
auteurist blockbusters, 4–5
auteurs, 20, 156, 237, 240–241, 264
autodidacticism, 270–271
Avatar, 43, 235; advertisements for, 12, 13f, 14f; appropriations of, 38, 279; assimilation theme, 263; budget, 62t, 64, 240; colonialism theme, 262–263; corporate branding, 70; cross-promotions, 243; expectations for, 239–240; as faith in blockbusters, 285; and *Farewell to the King*, 262; financial success of, 62t, 64, 238, 240; game-changer hyperbole, 239–241, 243; ideology of, 16–17, 262, 279; inspirations, 333n68; intellectual property development, 260; international visibility, 71; James Cameron's work on, 234, 250; jokes about, 238; as jungle expedition film, 333n68; Katie Ellis on, 17; media culture in, 261–263; media format promotion, 12, 13f, 14f, 275; *A Message from Pandora* documentary, 276–277, 279; motion capture, 250–251; mutability of, 275–279; the Na'vi, 262–263; Panasonic cross-promotions, 12, 14f, 243, 261; promotion of, 239, 280f; racial politics of, 262–263; release of, 238–239; re-releases of, 275–279, 281; reviews, early, 241–242; Slavoj Žižek on, 16–17; success of, 234, 238; symbolic efficiency of, 53–54; technological aesthetics, 252; technological exhibitionism, 265, 275; technological requirements, 240–241; as technological tentpole, 12, 261; as tentpole film, 44, 238; and 3-D, 241–242, 250, 261, 276; and Ubisoft, 243; video game adaptation, 239, 243
Avengers: Endgame, 298

Balaban, Barney, 203
Balides, Constance, 7
baroque tendencies, 35–36
Barry, Iris, 158
Barthes, Roland, 144, 288, 291
Batman, 43
Baudrillard, Jean, 46, 48
Baumann, Shyon, 224
Ben-Hur, 211; versus art films, 224; awards won, 221; blockbuster strategy, 214, 221; Bosley Crowther on, 211, 215, 217; and Camera 65, 211–212, 214; chariot race, 211–213, 217, 218f; cultural framing of, 214–215, 224; director, 108, 209; financial success, 226; historical contexts, 210–211; human drama, 217; influence of, 212;

and Judaism, 217–218; largeness of, 35–36, 211–212, 215–217; market competition, 227; merchandising, 214–215; politics of, 217; premiere of, 212–215; prerelease buzz, 211; promotion of, 142, 211–213, 215–217, 220; religious reverence of, 215; reviews of, 215, 217–218; roadshow release, 213; running time, 218; and scale, 288; screenplay, 213; souvenir release program, 213–214; ticket sales, 214

Benjamin, Walter, 301

Berman, Marshall, 111

Bernstein, Irving. See *Hollywood at the Crossroads: An Economic Study*

Berryman, Clifford Kennedy, 114

The BFG, 298

The Big Country, 209

Biskind, Peter, 17–18

Blackboard Jungle, 165

Blade Runner, 278

Block Buster, 119

blockbuster bombs (munitions), 94; in advertising, 106–111, 118, 121; in Allied strategy, 94–97, 101, 120; in animated shorts, 112; characteristics of, 94–95; design of, 96–97; in firebombing, 101, 301–302; inaccuracy of, 97–98, 101, 120; meanings of, 96, 104, 112–113, 115, 122; merchandising, 112; misinformation about, 101, 104; name origins, 95; names for, 94–95; obsolescence of, 120–122; in political cartoons, 114–115, 116f; in the press, 95, 103, 105, 302; as progress examples, 96; in propaganda, 114; public displays of, 88, 91, 93, 108; public familiarity with, 105, 112, 114; size of, 94, 97; targets of, 97, 104

blockbuster movies: aesthetic continuity of, 230; Americanness of, 15, 76–78, 83; budget ranges, 60, 61–62t, 64; and capitalism, 7, 80; categorical stabilization, 228; characteristics of, 4, 6, 15, 53, 228; classical Hollywood influences, 53; and commodity circulation, 6; communitarian spirit of, 291; as comparison points, 191, 199–200; criteria for, 22–23, 26, 164, 184, 195; and cross-media properties, 209; cultural-economic power, 303; debates over, 297; and digital media, 45; display value, 81, 83; distinctiveness of, 15; distribution, 64, 68; duration of, 162–163; emotional impacts of, 285; entertainment, promise of, 5; ephemerality of, 80; era of, 234; as events, 225; as exclusionary, 192; expectations for, increasing, 42–43, 185, 192, 298; familiarity of, 36; global commonality of, 64, 68, 70–71; identifying, 198; international visibility of, 71, 72–76, 77t, 81, 223; investment in, 59–60, 69; library value of, 38; moviegoers targeted by, 229; as moving image apex, 297; 1960s, 226–227; 1970s, 18–19; as obligation, 294; origins of, 7–8, 18, 22–23; overproduction of, 227; politics of, 10, 77–78; as prestige productions, 223; presumptions about, 16–17, 34, 206; as product and experience, 38, 54; production of, 68–69, 78, 80–81; revenue emphasis, 39, 58; revenue lags, 178; secondary market, 180–181; skyscraper metaphor, 70, 80–81; versus sleeper hits, 42; summer, 166; symbolic coherence of, 52–53; technological emphasis, 9–11, 273; as technological prototypes, 261; universalism of, 229; vilification of, 15–16; visibility of, 5–6

blockbuster movies, criticisms of: aesthetic, 196; as artless, 20, 33, 193–194, 206; as childish, 15–16; commercialism, 297; as crass, 196; cultural value, 207; economic, 26, 33, 228; as industrial culture, 193, 196; running times, 196–197; as soulless, 193 blockbuster strategy, 8–9, 189; accounting methods, 208–209; adoption of, 185, 189–190, 207; British, 202; budget, making visible, 56–57; conservatism of, 39, 41, 44; cultural-economic relations, 171; distributors, advantaging, 178; durability of, 21, 226; effects of, 33, 194; as entrenched, 223; export of, 201–202; and film shortages, 163–164, 179, 204, 209; films reaffirming, 43; financial emphasis, 58–59; French, 202; and globalism, 223; historical summaries of, 224–225; as industrial strategy, 6–8, 13, 81, 84, 166–167; investment and risk, 33, 41, 44, 177; and investor confidence, 177, 205; launches, 68; media production impact, 237; and 1950s crisis, 8, 141, 161–162, 205; in 1958, 207–210; 1960s collapse, 224; 1970s resurgence, 225; origins of, 159; problems with, 161–162, 202; production size promotion, 56, 159; pushback on, 172; reducing movie totals, 163–164; research supporting, 174–175; skepticism of, 195, 220; success of, early, 189; and technological infrastructures, 299–300; and television, 222

blockbuster strategy economics: break-even point, 39, 218; investment escalation, 161, 229; investment rationales, 41; market domination, 39; problems, 161–162; profitability, 59, 202–203, 223; profit expectations, 161, 177; promotional costs, 218–219; rapid returns, 70; success, defining, 38–39, 41; universal appeal, 202, 229

blockbuster syndrome, 8

blockbuster term: adjective-noun changes, 189; advertising and promotion, 107, 118, 149–150, 199–200, 200f, 215–217, 220, 221f; and bigness, 158; as binary, 191, 199; in book advertising and reviews, 116, 117f, 118, 149; and budget, 150; as command metaphor, 32–33; concepts referenced by, 36; connotations, 116, 118–123, 150; critics, 184; and distributor-exhibitor relations, 167; diversity of uses, early, 149–150; early, 118, 150–151, 153, 155–156; early nonmilitary uses, 116, 118, 123; in film reference books, 22; financial success, signaling, 119, 153; functions of, 29; genre films, 151; historical summary, 167; history of, 21–24, 26; inconsistencies in, 202, 211; international use of, 36; longevity of, 21; meanings of, 7, 28, 33, 189, 223; military references, 220; as nodal point, 32; origins of, film, 21, 23, 26, 71, 107; origins of, military, 93–95; as overused, 228; postwar, 150; promotional uses, 81, 150, 209; and the public, 203; as relational, 166–167; retrospective uses, 165, 195; in reviews, 118–119; stabilization of, 223–224, 228; studio management of, 155; and technological change, 156–158; television uses, 149; theatrical uses, 119, 170–171, 191, 213; thematic impact, 151; and visibility, 164–165

Blockbuster Video, 41

blogs, 49–50

B movies, 139, 162

body genres, 225–226

Bombardier, 99, 101, 106–108

bombing, World War II: in advertising, 111–112, 113f; American-British cooperation, 314n34; atomic, 120–122; civilian casualties, 98–102; ethics of, 97–100, 104–105; *The Fire*, 99, 105, 314n40; firebombing, 100–102, 104; history of, 97–98; inaccuracy of, 97–98, 101, 120; justifications for, 105; in literature, 99; pride in, 102; rationales for, 102, 105; reporting on, 102–105, 109–110; scale of, 313n21; thousand-

bomber raids, 111; verticality, 98, 105.
See also blockbuster bombs
bombing in film: *Bombardier*, 99, 101, 106–108, 118; *The Dam Busters*, 99; depictions of, 98–99; *Fighter Squadron*, 99; *The Memphis Belle: A Story of a Flying Fortress*, 108; *One of Our Aircraft Is Missing*, 106–107, 118; *Thirty Seconds over Tokyo*, 118, 155, 180; *Twelve O'Clock High*, 99, 150; *Victory through Air Power*, 106
Bordwell, David, 53
Bourdieu, Pierre: on art, 19–20, 33–34; autonomous versus heteronomous culture, 20; on cinephile practices, 267, 270; on connoisseurship and class, 267; cultural taste hierarchies, 20, 185, 196, 272, 274
The Bourne Identity, 291
Brazil, 119
Breathless, 278
The Bridge on the River Kwai, 179, 183–184, 209, 222
The Bridges at Toko-Ri, 163, 164f, 195
Broidy, Steve, 164
The Brothers Karamazov, 199–200
The Buccaneer, 184
budgets, production: as aesthetic, 82; *Aliens of the Deep*, 236; *Around the World in 80 Days*, 196; *Avatar*, 62t, 64, 240; averages, 64, 65–67t; as blockbuster criteria, 56; and blockbuster term, 150; in marketing strategies, 57–58; as popular news item, 56; range of, 60, 61–62t, 64; visibility of, 56–57, 82; *War and Peace*, 196
Bukatman, Scott, 11, 53
Butch Cassidy and the Sundance Kid, 289

The Caine Mutiny, 155
Caldwell, John, 264
Cameron, James: *The Abyss*, 236, 241, 248, 251; *Aliens*, 236, 252; and *Avatar* title, 276; awards won, 233–234, 236–237; and Canadian oil sands, 279; career path, 235–237; celebrity activism, 258; on colonialism, 262; deep-sea shooting techniques, 333n65; and Digital Domain, 243–244; and digital projection standards, 245; documentaries, 235–236, 247, 251–253, 258–259; in *Entourage*, 235; *Expedition: Bismarck*, 248–249, 257–259, 261; and expedition film tradition, 259; exploration vehicle investments, 258; female characters, 247, 262; filmmaker ethos, 246–247; and frame rates, 244–245; and Hollywood, 263–264; ideological critique, 251–252; and immersion, 247, 258–259; influences, 235, 259, 333n68; media coverage, 239, 241; oeuvre continuity, 264; reputation, 233, 235, 251; and science, 235–236; Simulcam, 250–251; technofetishism, 257, 259–260; as technological auteur, 237, 240–241, 264; underwater experience, 251, 258, 333n65. See also *Aliens of the Deep*; *Avatar*; *Ghosts of the Abyss*; *The Terminator*; *Titanic*
Cameron, James, and 3-D: *Avatar*, 240–241, 243; camera systems, 248–250; Cameron Pace Group, 250; documentaries, 247; *Expedition: Bismarck*, 248–249; faith in moviegoing, 247; frame rates, 244–245; *Ghosts of the Abyss*, 247–248; motion-capture technologies, 250–251; promotion of, 238; sensory involvement, 246–247; shooting, 244–245, 247; theme park attractions, 243–244
Cameron Pace Group (CPG), 249–251
Campbell, Patrick, 250
Can-Can, 226
Cannes Film Festival, 193
capitalism, 7, 48–51, 111, 135
Captain America: Civil War, 39, 40t
Carousel, 195
Carpenter, Russell, 244

INDEX · 377

Casablanca, 165, 270
Casetti, Francesco, 273
CBS Television, 170
Chase a Crooked Shadow, 185
Cheyenne, 165
China, 37, 69–70, 79
Chinatown, 292
"The Chronicles of Narnia" books, 135–136
Churchill, Winston, 98, 100
Cimarron, 212
cinemagoing. *See* moviegoing
CinemaScope, 137, 223; anniversary event, 168; Barthes on, 144; at festivals, 158; films in, 144, 146–148, 167, 181, 212; problems with, 158, 201; promotions mentioning, 146–148; and screen giganticism, 136, 143; success of, 148
cinephilia, 266–267, 269–273, 294
Cineplex, 282
Cinerama: Audience Research Institute survey, 145–146; and blockbuster term, 156; impact of, 136, 143; market creation, 168; theater run durations, 179; *This Is Cinerama*, 143, 185; ticket fees, 179; and Todd-AO, 156
Cinerama Holiday, 157
Citizen Kane, 247
class reproduction, 267, 270
clearances, 178
Cleopatra, 212, 222, 227–228
Close Encounters of the Third Kind, 19, 278, 288–289
Coe, Richard L., 185, 210
colossal films, 151
Columbia: and Audience Research Institute, 145; blockbuster management, early, 155; blockbusters, switch to, 160, 203; Chinese partnerships, 69; diversification, 187; film-to-television distribution, 180; *Lawrence of Arabia* promotion, 227; press books, 197–198; production declines, 139; profit declines, 187, 188t; revenue distribution, 183; and Stanley Kramer Productions, 155; television production, 177
commodity-service clusters, 38
communicative capitalism, 48–51
Compulsion, 209–210
connectivity, conspicuous, 303
Connor, J. D., 7
consumer research, 175
Contact, 10
contemplation, 9–10
Coppola, Francis Ford, 7, 19
cosmopolitan artlessness, 193, 234, 302
cosmopolitan ease, limited, 38, 68, 78, 83, 225
cosmopolitan films, 69; *Around the World in 80 Days*, 69, 78, 193; versus art films, 193; blockbusters as, 69, 71, 159, 223; examples of, 78; international tour approach, 78; Schwartz on, 69, 78, 159, 193
costuming and wonderment, 127
creative destruction, 299
crises of meaning, 48
crisis of the 1950s: AFL report on, 185–188; Audience Research Institute survey, 145–146; and blockbuster strategy, 8, 141, 161–162, 205; and blockbuster term, 156; and diversification strategies, 186; end of, 160–161, 167, 173; and exhibitors, 141; moviegoer surveys, 140; moviegoing declines, 137, 141; moviegoing promotion, 137, 138f, 141; optimism during, 140; output decline, 139; and prestige films, 141; profit declines, 187, 188t; and risk aversion, 139; roadshowing, 141–143, 150, 159; small productions during, 161–162; television's role in, 136–137, 141, 146, 186; widescreen experiments, 143–145. *See also* Paramount Decree
cross-media activity, 186–187, 209
Crowther, Bosley, 194, 207, 211, 215, 217, 227

Cubitt, Sean, 11–12, 294
Cucco, Marco, 23
cultural literacy, 196
cultural value, 16–17, 34, 225–226, 275; in blockbuster criticisms, 230; blockbusters, dualistic nature of, 225; Bourdieu on, 20, 185, 196, 272, 274; and class divisions, 196; media occasions creating, 274; and perennial films, 196; and platforms, 294; and social action, 20

The Dam Busters, 99
darkness, dream of, 281–283
Deadline (trade publication), 40t
Deadpool, 39, 40t
Dean, Jodi, 48–51
The Defiant Ones, 155, 209
Demetrius and the Gladiators, 147–148, 149f
DeMille, Cecil B., 124, 126–128, 132, 160, 220
de Seversky, Alexander P., 105–106, 112
Desperate Journey, 91
desperation pictures, 205
Deuze, Mark, 251
The Diary of Anne Frank, 209–210
Die Hard, 290
Digital Domain, 243–244, 248
digital exhibition transition, 241–242
disaster films, 299
discoverability, 267, 269
Disney, 187, 188t, 260, 298, 301
display technologies, 302–303
distributors, global business strategies, 37–38
diversification, studio, 186–187, 223, 260
diversity as risk, 41
Doctor Dolittle, 224, 227
double bills, 139
Dower, John, 100, 102, 105
Drucker, Johanna, 29
Dune Entertainment, 59, 240
DVD extras, 278–279
Dyer, Richard, 5

Easy Rider, 292
editing, spatially confused, 53
Elberse, Anita, 43–45
Elsaesser, Thomas, 13, 38, 272–273
The Enemy Below, 181
environments, built, 134
epic films: baroque tendencies of, 35–36; and blockbuster term, 150; religious, 143–144; scale of, 55–56; and waste, 56. See also *Ben-Hur*; *Quo Vadis*; *Samson and Delilah*
Epstein, Edward J., 260
Epstein, Gady, 44–45
exhibitors: and blockbusters, 163, 178–179, 181, 226; distributor relations, 179, 181; and film shortages, 163–164, 179, 204, 226; and the Great Depression, 139; and in-betweener films, 204; and 1950s crisis, 141; nonblockbusters and, 178; and the Paramount Decree, 139–140, 188; technical standards, 158; and tentpole films, 238
expectations, increasing, 42–43, 161, 185, 192, 298
extras, 55–56
eyes of wonder shots, 288–290

Falling Hare, 112
Fanchi, Mariagrazia, 273
Farber, Manny, 144, 185, 207–209
A Farewell to Arms, 181, 184
The F.B.I. Story, 220, 222f
Fighter Squadron, 99
film: the baroque in, 11–12, 35; and economic swings, 140; jargon, 220; legitimization as art, 224; portable technologies, 135; as production and experience, 38; technological advantages, 136–137; versus television, 169–170
film industry, American: advantages, structural, 37; AFL report on, 185–188; boom of 1956, 167–169, 172, 189–190; health of, 160–161;

film industry, American (*continued*)
hit-driven reorientation, 168; international circulation, 36–37; labor, 186; strategies, varying, 189–190. *See also* crisis of the 1950s; Hollywood
Final Destination 3D, 250–251
Finding Dory, 39, 40t
The Five Pennies, 209–210
Forlong, Michael, 202
The Four Horsemen of the Apocalypse, 212
frame rates, 244–245
franchises: business plan, 275; and creative destruction, 299; as cross-media commodities, 54–55; development of, 33; examples of, 4; global visibility, 36; "The Godfather," 18–19, 225, 240; and intellectual property, 260; and merchandising, 275; "Mission: Impossible," 78–80; "Pirates of the Caribbean," 260; special effects inflation, 10; success of, 234; as technological tentpoles, 54; "Terminator," 234, 241, 243–246, 251–252; "Transformers," 70–71; world destroying, 298–299
Frank, Fredric M., 126
Frankenstein, 270
Friedrich, Jörg, 99, 105, 314n40

Gallup, George, 172
Garvin, David A., 39
gender and spectacle, 10
The General, 270
Ghosts of the Abyss, 248; actors, use of, 253, 255; Bill Paxton in, 247–248, 257, 259; CGI, 255, 258; crew, 248, 250; environmental ethic of, 260; postproduction, 253; profitability, 264; reviews, 248; shooting, 248; stills from, 248f, 254f, 255f, 256f; technofetishism, 253, 255, 257; 3-D format, 247–248; wreck uses, 255
Giant, 172–175, 193, 195
giganticism. *See* largeness and giganticism

Gigi, 179
Gillet, John, 206, 228–229
gimmick films, 162, 166, 179, 192, 219, 225
Gitelman, Lisa, 28–29, 224
Gladwell, Malcolm, 41–42
Goldenson, Leonard H., 161, 195
Goldwyn, Samuel, 179, 207
Gomery, Douglas, 225
Gone with the Wind, 157, 184, 195
Google Ngram Viewer, 29–30
Gramsci, Antonio, 35–36, 132
Great Depression, 139
The Greatest Show on Earth, 208
The Greatest Story Ever Told, 212
Griffith, Andy, 170
Guess Who's Coming to Dinner, 155
Guys and Dolls, 157, 159

Hall, Sheldon, 9, 22–23, 107
Handel, Leo A., 140, 172
Hansen, Miriam, 36–37
Harris, Arthur, 98, 100, 105
Harry Potter and the Half-Blood Prince, 71
The Hateful Eight, 212
Hello, Dolly!, 227
Hercules, 214
Heston, Charlton, 209, 288, 335n22
High Noon, 153
historical methods, 28–33
Holiday in Mexico, 119
Hollinger, Hy, 172, 222–223
Hollywood: business surveys, 204; competition in, 264; contemporary business structures, 264; dominance of, 37; film format experiments, 9; global vernacular, 37; and the Great Depression, 139; historiographies of, 17; and independent film, 19–20; and internationalism, 38; postwar changes, 7–8; release reduction, 209; sex, attitudes toward, 16; television, reaction to, 222; wartime, 106, 124
Hollywood at the Crossroads: An Economic Study (Bernstein), 186–189, 223

Houston, Penelope, 228–229
Hoyt, Eric, 180
Huls, Alexander, 15–16
humor of deflation, 288–290, 295

Ice Age: Dawn of the Dinosaurs, 71
identification, 291–292
ideological critiques, 251–252
ideologies: of *Avatar*, 16–17, 262, 279; in blockbusters, 13, 54–55, 76–78, 192; circulation of, 7; entertainment, 5; normalization of, 13; in popular culture, 7, 54; of progress, 83, 133–135; romantic couplings, 16; smart-aleck figures, 293
imagination of disaster, 120–121
in-betweener films, 166, 192; as adult, 197, 228; as artful, 194, 196, 205; awards won by, 221–222; blockbusters, as defined against, 197, 224; blockbusters' impact on, 185, 201; criticism of, 185; dramatic realism of, 224; and exhibitors, 204; potential of, 209; praise of, 205, 210; success of, 189, 193; Universal's focus on, 194–195
Independence Day, 289–290
independent film, 19–20, 205
independent production outfits, 168–169
indigeneity, 262–263
individualism, 76
industrial culture, 20, 60, 193, 224
information overload, 46, 51
Ingenious Media, 240
Inherit the Wind, 155
intellectual property, 260
international circulation, 36–37
international films, 185
internationalism, 38, 68–69, 71, 78–80, 159
internationalist film style, 76
international visibility, 71, 72–76t, 76, 77t, 81
internet, 47–48, 50–52

investment: defining blockbusters, 60; escalation in, 161, 229; international, 69; rationales for, 41; and risk, 33, 41, 44, 177, 227; stars driving, 59
investors, promotional campaigns for, 184
Iron Man 3, 80
It's a Mad, Mad, Mad, Mad World, 155–156
Izod, John, 126, 139, 161, 225

Jaffe, Leo, 203
Jameson, Fredric, 7
Jaws, 234; acting, 290; and blockbuster resurgence, 225–226; first blockbuster claim, 21–22; humor of deflation, 290; influence of, 7, 39; and New Hollywood, 18–19; revenue, 58
The Jazz Singer, 263
Johnson, Nunnally, 196–197
The Joker Is Wild, 181
Journey to the Center of the Earth, 250
Judgment at Nuremberg, 155
Julius Caesar, 288
The Jungle Book, 39, 40t

kaleidoscopic perception, 53
The Karate Kid, 69–70
Katzenberg, Jeffrey, 240, 242
Keightley, Keir, 311n42
Kendrick, James, 252
King, Geoff, 9–10
The King and I, 195
King Kong (1933), 259
King Kong (1976), 57
King's Row, 165
Kiss Them for Me, 181
Kracauer, Siegfried, 289
Krämer, Peter, 9–10
Kramer, Stanley, 155–156, 167, 183, 209
Kuhn, Annette, 252

Ladd, Alan, 184, 198
Lambert, Gavin, 205–206

Landry, Robert J., 197, 201
largeness and giganticism: in advertising, 215–217; of *Ben-Hur*, 35–36, 211–212, 215–217; of blockbusters, 56–58, 60; and capitalism, 135; and cultural value, 202; and entertainment, 196; epic films, 55–56; fascination with, 56; and home theaters, 288; limits of, 135–136; logic of, 156; and masculinity, 133; organization of, 288; and power, 133–134; and progress ideologies, 133–135; as relative, 135; screen formats, 136, 143; and theaters, 287
Lasky, Jesse L., Jr., 126
Lassie Come Home, 180
Lawrence of Arabia, 227, 229
Lean, David, 9, 20
Les Misérables, 202
Lev, Peter, 132, 158
Lewis, Jon, 9, 59, 242
Leydon, Joe, 246
Lifeboat, 118
Light's Diamond Jubilee (television), 169–170
Lightstorm Entertainment, 240, 263
limited cosmopolitan ease, 38, 68, 78, 83, 225
Lincoln, Freeman, 167–168
Little Big Man, 292
Loew's. *See* MGM
Loew's Capitol Theatre, 219
Loew's State Theatre, 212–213
The Longest Day, 222, 227
long tail, 41–45
The Lord of the Rings: The Return of the King, 221
Lucas, George, 19–20, 241, 260, 288

The Magnificent Matador, 150
Maltby, Richard, 82
Mann, Denise, 168–169
Mann, Michael, 240
The Man with the Golden Arm, 189
Marchand, Roland, 2, 7, 109

market research, 175–178. *See also* audience research
markets: art, 70; assessments of, 201; consumer, 175; film, 37–38, 172, 201, 227–228; media, 39, 41–42, 44–45
Martin, Henry H., 202
Marty, 165, 189, 205
Marx, Leo, 134
Maslin, Janet, 18
Matinee (television), 169
McCabe and Mrs. Miller, 292
McCleery, Albert, 169
McKelvey, Fenwick, 30
media: abundance, 45–51; and culture, 28–29; digital, 41–45, 48–51; and the familiar, 48; historical contexts, 29; occasions, 274, 286–287; scarcity, 267
media culture, 41, 46, 52, 282
media environments, 219
media formats: *Avatar* promoting, 12, 13f, 14f, 275; Camera 65, 211–212, 214, 223; content supporting, 261; and extra footage, 278; and film mutability, 274–279; films crossing, 38; format theory, 307n33; new, introductions of, 261; Super 70 Technirama, 219
Media History Digital Library (MHDL), 30
Meehan, Eileen, 6
Melnick, Ross, 83
The Memphis Belle: A Story of a Flying Fortress, 108
merchandising, 198, 275
MGM, 139, 150, 180, 187, 188t, 203. *See also Samson and Delilah*; United Artists
middlebrow, 19, 159, 194, 225, 298–299
middlebrow films, 141, 157, 171
Mills, C. Wright, 304
Miramax, 18–19
Mission: Impossible—Ghost Protocol, 78, 79f
Mission: Impossible—Rogue Nation, 78–80
Mister Roberts, 167
Mnuchin, Steven, 59–60

Moby Dick, 195
Motion Picture Audience Action Index, 173
Motion Picture Production Code, 136
moviegoing: and darkness, 281; declines in, 137, 186, 207; economic resilience, presumed, 140–141; as escape, 282; as event, 189; expectations of, 210; and illumination, 281; industry promotion of, 137, 138f, 141; and media attention, 282–283; reasons for, 284; television's impact on, 136
MovieLens, 42
Mumford, Lewis, 82–83, 98, 134, 300
Murrow, Edward R., 102–103

Naremore, James, 28
Nashville, 18–19
naturalism, 291
Neale, Steve, 9, 22–23
neobaroque cinema, 11–12, 294
Netflix, 42, 52
New Hollywood, 17–19, 292
The News Parade of 1943, 105
nonblockbusters: AIP's strategy, 179; blockbuster strategy effects, 194; B movies, 139, 162; boom of 1956, 168; critics praising, 210; exhibitors and, 178; exploitation films, 192; financing, 204; gimmick films, 162, 166, 179, 192, 219, 225; market room for, 192–193, 204; midrange films, 43, 168, 194, 204–205; as nonindustrial, 224; positioning of, 179–180; promotion of, 198–199, 203; quality films, 146, 180, 192, 209; returns on, 183, 227; risk of, 194, 204; success of, 193; and the tasteful middle, 194; television distribution, 179–180, 207. *See also* in-betweener films
Not as a Stranger, 167
No Time for Love, 118–119
No Time for Sergeants, 170–171
Nye, David, 134

obligatory consumption, 294–295
obsolescence, 121, 303
Office of War Information (OWI), 87, 91–93, 96, 108–109. *See also* World War II propaganda
Oh, Men! Oh, Women!, 196
Oklahoma!, 143, 156–157, 159, 195
One from the Heart, 19
One of Our Aircraft Is Missing, 106–107, 118
On the Beach, 155
On the Waterfront, 165
Operation Burma, 119
Operation Petticoat, 220, 226
Orpheus Descending (theater), 213
Ortner, Sherry B., 19

Pace, Vince, 248–250
Pace company. *See* Cameron Pace Group
Pal Joey, 183
Panasonic, 12, 14f, 243, 261
paracinema, 273
Parallax View, 292
Paramount: *The Atomic City* promotion, 151; blockbuster promotion, 163; blockbuster strategy, 202–203, 220; blockbuster successes, 177; diversification, 187; production declines, 139, 188; profit declines, 187, 188t; promotional experiments, 198. *See also* VistaVision format
Paramount Decree, 139; encroachments on, 178; impact of, 8, 139–140, 161, 186; problems with, 198; significance of, 186; and small films, 168
Paranormal Activity, 6, 240
Parks, Gordon, 88
patents, 260
Paxton, Bill, 247–248, 257, 259
Penley, Constance, 252
perennial films, 195–196
Peyton Place, 181, 209
Pierson, Michele, 11–12
Planet of the Apes, 335n22

platform agnosticism, 286
platform consciousness, 12
platforms, 261, 271, 274, 286, 294
Poole, Jim, 202
popular culture, 5, 7, 15, 20, 32, 54
The Poseidon Adventure, 225
Poverty Row, 139
Powell, John B., 88
power, 133–134
predictability, 172
Prelude to War, 93
press books and kits, 197–198
prestige blockbusters, 225–226
prestige films, 141
The Prince and the Showgirl, 184
profit expectations, 42–43, 161, 185, 192, 298
progress, ideologies of, 83, 133–135
promotion: adjectives as nouns in, 189; blockbuster, use of term, 119, 170–171, 209, 213; of *The Brothers Karamazov*, 199–200; coordination difficulties, 198; criticism of, 207; entities included in, 219; experiment with, 198; of gimmick films, 219; hard-sell tactics, 197; largeness, 56, 159, 183; for *Lawrence of Arabia*, 227; and merchandising, 198; of nonblockbusters, 198–199, 203; Paramount Decree's impact on, 139, 198; press books, 197–198; size emphasis, 211; of *The Sound of Music*, 227; technology emphasis, 181, 183, 211–212, 219
Proud Rebel, 198–199, 200f
Pryor, Thomas, 204–205
Psycho, 226, 270

quality films, 146, 180, 192, 209
Quandt, James, 271
Quo Vadis, 124, 188; aspect ratio, 143; financial success of, 208; lobby card, 24f; multitudes, on-screen, 55; promotional strategy, 151; *Variety* review, 24, 25f

Rackmil, Milton R., 203–204
Raibourn, Paul, 203
Raiders of the Lost Ark, 289
Raintree County, 194, 212
Ransom!, 153, 154f, 155, 199
reading as method, 29–31
recommendation systems, 42, 44–45
RegalScope, 201
relatability, 291–292
release scheduling, 166, 183, 202, 214
Republic Pictures, 187, 188t
revolutionary shift discourses, 239–241, 243, 264–265
risk: aversion to, 139; from competition, 227; diversity as, 41; management, 172–173; and market research, 176; of nonblockbusters, 194, 204; and the Paramount Decree, 139
RKO, 139, 187, 188t
roadshows, 141–143, 150, 159, 185, 201, 213, 228
The Robe: distributor fees, 162; financial success of, 157, 168; promotion of, 146–147; reviews of, 144; sequel to, 147–148; television distribution, 222; widescreen format, 144–146
Rogers, Ariel, 136
Rogue One: A Star Wars Story, 38–39, 40t
rollercoaster set pieces, 9–10
romantic couplings, 16
Room at the Top, 165–166, 221–222, 224
Ross, Steve, 243
running times, 82, 163, 196–197, 212, 229

Samson and Delilah: authoritarianism theme, 127; blockbuster characteristics, 132–133, 226; and blockbuster strategy, 159; camp, 226; color use, 126–127, 129; costuming, 127, 130, 132; DeMille's direction of, 126; epic qualities of, 124–125; freedom theme of, 128–130; grandiosity of, 127, 129; historical authenticity claims of, 127;

and Judaism, 129; location filming for, 126–127, 132; material luxury in, 129–130; opening credits, 125–127; pedigree of, 126; and photographic processes, 126; political contexts, 124, 127, 132; as prestige film, 141; prologue, 127–128; sensationalism in, 130, 132; stills from, 128f, 129f, 130f, 131f, 132f; success of, 124; *The Ten Commandments* connections, 127–128, 132; women in, 129–130, 132
Sanders, John, 22–23
Sanogo, Aboubakar, 272
Schatz, Thomas, 6–8, 124, 260
Schoedsack, Ernest B., 259
Schoenfeld, Joe, 156–157
Schwartz, Vanessa R., 69, 78, 159, 193
science fiction, 57, 120, 252, 299
Sconce, Jeffrey, 273
Scorsese, Martin, 298
Sebald, W. G., 100
second screens, 281–282
The Secret Life of Pets, 39, 40t
Selznick, David O., 168–169, 195
sensory appeals, 219, 225
The Seven Little Foys, 163
Shampoo, 292
Shone, Tom, 10, 22, 290
shortages of films, 163–164, 179, 204, 209
Siegel, Arthur S., 88
Sindlinger, Albert, 172–173, 175
Sindlinger and Company audience research, 172–175
Skyfall, 78
sleeper hits, 42, 151, 190, 225
Sloterdijk, Peter, 97
small films. *See* nonblockbusters
smart-aleck figures, 77, 99, 290–294
smartphones, 303, 334n76
Smith, Roger, 88
social activism, 50
social media, 294
social realism, 7

Soderbergh, Steven, 240
Solomon and Sheba, 219, 226
Some Like It Hot, 210
Sontag, Susan, 120, 134, 272, 293, 299
Sony, 59
sound, 145–146, 158, 212, 223
The Sound of Music, 227
South Pacific, 195
Spartacus, 214, 219–220, 226, 235
special effects, 9–12, 55, 241. *See also* Digital Domain
spectacle: of bigness, 158; blockbusters as, 229–230, 234, 297; and entertainment history, 13, 15; epic films as, 55–56, 143–144, 219; functions of, 5, 9; and gender, 10; and humor of deflation, 289; sensory, 225–226; technological, 136, 143, 148, 220, 234, 301
Spider-Man—Turn Off the Dark (theater), 60
Spielberg, Steven, 19–20, 225, 288–289, 298. *See also Jaws*
Staiger, Janet, 272
Star!, 224, 227
Starlight Runner Entertainment, 260
stars, 43–44, 59, 184, 292–293
Star Wars: Episode I—The Phantom Menace, 241
Star Wars: Episode IV—A New Hope, 19, 57–58, 99, 278
Star Wars: Episode VII—The Force Awakens, 42–43
Steinbeck, John, 99
stereo sound, 145–146, 158
Sterne, Jonathan, 307n33
Stewart, Susan, 135
Stole, Inger L., 109
The Story of Ruth, 212
streaming services, 42, 298
Stringer, Julian, 20, 71, 81–82
success criteria, 38–39
superhero films, 293, 299
Super 70 Technirama, 219, 223

symbolic efficiency: of blockbusters, 52–55; declines in, 48–51; digital media, 48–49; and significatory openness, 53–54

A Tale of Two Cities, 180
Tasker, Yvonne, 10
tasteful middles, 194, 298–299
technocratic society, 82–83, 122, 299–300, 304
technofetishism, 252–253, 257, 259
technological advancement: and the arms race, 120–121; blockbusters exemplifying, 12–13, 223; and cultural value, 225–226; divisive, 302; as entertainment, 148–149; and entertainment industry, 223; expectations of, 279, 281, 300; industrial sector, 303–304; meanings of, 237; milestone moments, 242; and obsolescence, 304; platform changes, 274; and prestige, 146; pursuit of, mindless, 134; and technocratic society, 122; ubiquity of, 273–274; value assessment, 121–122; and wartime, 109–112, 120; and wonder, 304; and working relationships, 251
technological auterism, 237
technological exhibitionism, 82, 134; *Avatar*, 265, 275; blockbusters as, 301–302; and cultural events, 159; dangers of, 302; examples of, 82–83; film as, 300; and progress ideology, 83; and uplift, 159; and widescreen formats, 143, 148
technological sublime, 134
technological systems: consumption of, 294; and cultural value, 275; and intellectual property, 260; normalization of, 299–300; standardization of, 158, 164; theaters as, 283, 285–287
technological tentpoles. *See* tentpoles, technological
technological wonder, 11, 82–83, 284, 304

technology: in advertising, 181; blockbusters highlighting, 10–12; content dependence, 261; in disaster movies, 299; display, 302–303; introduction of new, 12; in science fiction, 120
television: as advanced technology, 169; blockbuster licensing, 180, 222–223; blockbuster programs, 169–170; and blockbuster strategy, 222; cinema, impact on, 136, 222; as civic participation, 294; and crisis of the 1950s, 136–137, 141, 146, 186; films on, 170, 179–180, 207; in-betweener films, 185; moviegoing, impact on, 8; quality of, 298; *The Sword and the Cross*, 219; technological limitations, 136–137; 3-D, 243
television guides, 267–269
televisual realism, 165
Telotte, J. P., 12, 301
The Ten Commandments, 166, 184, 188, 218; as blockbuster, 184; and blockbuster strategy, 159, 177; costuming, 197; exclusive runs, 178; financial success of, 157, 177–178, 203; and Judaism, 129; length of, 162–163; market competition, 227; multitudes, on-screen, 55; as perennial film, 195; *Samson and Delilah* connections, 127–128, 132; and scale, 288; on the secondary market, 181; success of, 193; theatrical run, 203; ticket fees, 178
Ten Seconds to Hell, 220
tent-pegs, technological, 334n76
tentpole films, 43–44, 238
tentpoles, technological, 6, 36, 261; *Avatar* as, 12, 261; blockbusters as, 36, 54, 84; and corporate dominance, 265; early examples of, 157; franchises as, 54; Marvel Cinematic Universe as, 298; uses of, 12
The Terminator, 235, 251–252
Terminator 2: Judgment Day, 241

Terminator 2-3D: Battle across Time, 243–246
theater, African American, 191
theaters, home, 288
theaters, movie: and blockbuster movies, 144–145, 285; and blockbusters, 285–286; contemporary, 284; control of audience technology use, 282; and darkness, 281–283; digital transition, 241–242; employees, 284; features of, 285; first-run chains, 286; and giganticism, 287; megaplex cinemas, 284, 286; movie palaces, 283–284, 289; and platform agnosticism, 286–287; as retreats, 282–283; strata of, 300–301; as technological systems, 283, 285–287
theatrical runs, 58, 192, 201–202
theatrical splendor, 283–284
"The Theory and Practice of Blockbusting," 228–230
Thirty Seconds over Tokyo, 118, 155, 180
This Is Cinerama, 143, 185
Thom, Michael, 81
Those Magnificent Men and Their Flying Machines, 227
3-D: Audience Research Institute survey, 145–146; camera systems, 244; conversion to, 332n34; early, 143; focal length, 244; Pace/Cameron Fusion System, 249–250; Reality Camera System, 248–249; television, 243; transition to, 241–242, 332n34; T2-3D theme park attraction, 243–246. *See also* Cameron, James, and 3-D
Three Days of the Condor, 292
ticket prices, 179, 185–186
Timeplay, 282
Titanic, 236–237; awards won, 221, 233; blockbuster strategy, reaffirming, 234; as classic blockbuster, 234; and Digital Domain, 244; failure expectations, 233–234; opening sequence, 247–248; release, 239; technical achievements, 246; underwater shooting, 251

To Catch a Thief, 167
Todd, Michael, 143, 156, 160, 260
Todd-AO format, 136, 143, 156–158, 185
The Towering Inferno, 225
Trapeze, 166
Treasure Island, 180
Turnock, Julie, 19
Twelve O'Clock High, 99, 150
Twentieth Century Fox: advertising campaigns, 181; and *Avatar*, 240; *The Big Show* promotional campaign, 183–184; blockbusters, early, 150; blockbusters, production increases, 177, 228; diversification, 187; European publicity tour, 227; production declines, 139; profit declines, 187, 188t; venture financing of, 59. *See also* CinemaScope
The Twilight Saga: New Moon, 71

Ultra Panavision, 211–212
United Artists: advertising campaigns, 181–183; blockbuster strategy, 160, 177, 183, 203–204, 219; cost advantages, 158; counter-blockbuster efforts, 43–44; film-to-television distribution, 180; monthly blockbuster strategy, 161; production declines, 139; small film strategy, 179; *Spartacus*, 219–220; and Stanley Kramer Productions, 155; and Tom Cruise, 43; venture financing of, 59; and World War II propaganda, 106
Universal: blockbuster strategy, 160, 177, 225; in-betweener films, 194–195; investors, 59; production declines, 139; profit declines, 187, 188t
Up, 71

Van Dijck, José, 52, 55
Venice Film Festival, 158–159
venture capital firms, 59
Victory through Air Power, 106, 108, 112
video rental stores, 41, 52
The Vikings, 208–209

virtual reality, 282
vistas, 9, 55
VistaVision format, 127, 136, 157–158, 163, 167

Wald, Jerry, 207
WALL-E, 38
Wanger, Walter, 198
War and Peace, 157–158, 163, 174, 195–196
war bond campaigns, 88, 91, 109
warfare, industrial, 104
Warner Brothers: blockbuster profits, 176–177; corporate structure, 6; diversification, 187; and investment firms, 60; production declines, 139; profit declines, 187, 188t
War of the Worlds, 290
Wasson, Haidee, 135, 307n33
Weiler, A. H., 184, 199
We're No Angels, 163
Whissel, Kristen, 11, 55
Whitney, Simon, 139–141
widescreen formats: Barthes on, 144; early, 9, 136, 143–145; Farber on, 144; at festivals, 158; financial returns, 185; Gallup audience survey (1953), 145–146; and giganticism, 143; and prestige, 146–148; problems with, 185; and progress narratives, 143; standardization of, 148; technological emphasis of, 144; on television, 222; and ticket prices, 185; Todd-AO, 136, 143, 156–158, 185; and vistas, use of, 9; VistaVision, 127, 136, 157–158, 163, 167. *See also* CinemaScope; Cinerama
Williams, Linda, 225–226
Williams, Raymond, 32
Winter Kills, 292
wonder, technological, 11, 82–83, 259, 282, 284–85, 300, 304
World War II, 93–94, 104, 109, 111, 139. *See also* blockbuster bombs; bombing, World War II
World War II propaganda: in advertising, 108–111; blockbusters in, 114; and citizen engagement, 105; "The Four Freedoms" pamphlet, 91–92; monumental photography use, 88, 92; *The Nature of the Enemy* exhibit, 87–88, 89f, 90f, 92–93, 312n4; *Road to Victory* exhibit, 92; Rockwell's four freedoms exhibit, 91–92; *United Nations* exhibit, 312n4; weapon displays, 88, 91

Žižek, Slavoj, 16–17, 47–48, 50–51
Zootopia, 39, 40t
Zugsmith, Albert, 220

www.ingramcontent.com/pod-product-compliance
Lightning Source LLC
Chambersburg PA
CBHW072017290525

27270CB00018BA/247